Baseball, Inc.

Baseball, Inc.

The National Pastime as Big Business

FRANK P. JOZSA, JR.

McFarland & Company, Inc., Publishers
Jefferson, North Carolina, and London

Library of Congress Cataloguing-in-Publication Data

Jozsa, Frank P., 1941–
Baseball, Inc. : the national pastime as big business / Frank P. Jozsa, Jr.
p.   cm.
Includes bibliographical references and index.

ISBN 0-7864-2534-2 (softcover : 50# alkaline paper) ∞

1. Baseball — Economic aspects— United States.
2. Baseball — Social aspects— United States.
I. Title.
GV880.J69   2006   331.2'81796357093 — dc22   2006001510

British Library cataloguing data are available

Cover image ©2006 Brand X Pictures

Manufactured in the United States of America

McFarland & Company, Inc., Publishers
Box 611, Jefferson, North Carolina 28640
www.mcfarlandpub.com

To my former baseball
coaches and teammates

Table of Contents

PART IV. Management and Leadership

PART V. Sports Marketing

Preface

This former athlete's inspiration to write this book was established several decades ago. My initial interest in the sport emerged in the late 1940s. It started from my participation in baseball for fun on city streets and dirt fields with friends from my neighborhood. I played official games while on teams at Spencer Field in Terre Haute, Indiana, and during the early 1950s, performing as a catcher on a team in Little League Baseball. At 13 years old I joined a team in Terre Haute's Babe Ruth League. An all-star team from that league won the national championship in 1955 and two years later, another Babe Ruth all-star team from Terre Haute won the Indiana title. Meanwhile, there were four years of baseball games as a pitcher and catcher at Gerstmeyer High School, followed by four years competing for Indiana State University, and during the summers playing on a local American Legion team. After I graduated from the university, no big league clubs seemed interested in signing me to a minor league contract as a right-hand pitcher who threw a good fastball but a mediocre curve. Thus my ambition of a career in professional baseball had ended by the mid–1960s.

Even so, during the late 1960s and early to mid–1970s I found it interesting to read about organized baseball's teams, coaches and players in the sports section of Atlanta newspapers while attending Georgia State University as a graduate student in economics. My experiences at the university concluded in 1977 after I completed my doctoral dissertation, "An Economic Analysis of Franchise Relocation and League Expansion in Professional Team Sports, 1950–1975." Despite the many years I had spent playing baseball and other sports, it was a challenge for me to merge economic theories with empirical data and mathematics.

When a strike by the Major League Baseball Players Association cancelled much of the 1994 regular season and World Series, and then another strike delayed the start of the 2005 season, my academic interest in professional sports was rejuvenated. Newly motivated, I researched the industry and co-authored (with John Guthrie) *Relocating Teams and Expanding Leagues in Professional Sports: How the Major Leagues Respond to Market Conditions* in 1999, and then wrote *American Sports Empire: How the League Breed Success* in 2003 and *Sports Capitalism: The Foreign Business of American Professional Leagues* in 2004. These titles, in part, analyzed the business operations and entertainment aspects of professional baseball during its development and growth, that is, from the late 1800s to early 2000s. In *Relocating Teams and Expanding Leagues in Professional Sports* my co-author and I applied metropolitan area statistics and the game attendances and estimated market values of teams to examine the business decisions made by individual clubs in Major League Baseball; in *American Sports Empire* I analyzed the performances of professional baseball teams and players, strategies of franchise owners, roles of government officials and the sports media, and loyalties of fans. were analyzed; and in *Sports Capitalism*, the focus was on global baseball markets, foreign players, and other topics such as baseball academies in nations of Latin America, an international player draft system, and women's baseball leagues in North America.

Since the mid–1990s I have read numerous sports articles in journals, magazines and newspapers, and studied several reports and books about the operation and business of baseball. I filed the information from this research for reference. After I reviewed these materials in mid–2004, it was apparent that a number of the most important and controversial topics and related activities, events and issues in the literature on baseball had not been discussed in my previous books. This led me to develop a proposal for a book that incorporated the past and present commercial elements of organized baseball. These include topics in the areas of business and finance, human resources and relationships, international relations, management and leadership, and sport marketing. As a result, five chapters about each area of baseball appear as chapters in Parts I–V of *Baseball, Inc.*

Many U.S. and foreign organizations and sports analysts, educators and journalists, and big league officials, team owners and executives have an interest in and demand for information about topics in the business of baseball. These matters, for example, may involve revenue sharing policies and financing of stadiums as contained in Part I, labor relations and teams' community affairs in Part II, baseball in foreign countries and the types of international tournaments in Part III, organized baseball's former commissioners and teams' previous coaches in Part IV, and average ticket prices of games and kinds of sponsorships in Part V. Overall, I have attempted to satisfy the reader seeking a factual account of how baseball has operated in the marketplace and as an entertainment option for consumers in America and elsewhere.

Several organizations and individuals contributed to this book in different ways, and I want to acknowledge their help.

Located at Pfeiffer University's campus library in Charlotte, North Carolina, is Frank C. Chance, who is the university's director of information support services and an assistant professor of library science. As he did with *American Sports Empire* and *Sports Capitalism*, Frank made a special effort to research sport topics and then obtain any publications that I requested. Furthermore, he recommended various concepts for me to consider as I wrote. His knowledge about baseball events and players proved being equal or superior to mine. Frank's assistance was immeasurable, and his contribution to this book will not be forgotten.

Pfeiffer's assistant dean for student services at Charlotte, Michael Utsman, is a topnotch computer expert, sports fan, and a friend. He provided me with technical support. Although he was always extremely busy with assisting students, faculty and staff, Michael never refused to help me with this and three other sports books, and each semester scheduled my regular and online graduate courses in business, economics and finance. It has been a pleasure and a rewarding experience for me to know and work with Michael at Pfeiffer University since the early 1990s.

Other individuals promptly and conscientiously responded to my questions about various topics and institutions in baseball. Janice L. Ogurcak, director of the Little League Museum in South Williamsport, Pennsylvania, and Christopher D. Downs, media relations manager of Little League Baseball and Softball, mailed me information about the foreign teams that have performed in the World Series of Little League Baseball and appeared in the international tournaments of the Senior, Junior, and Big League Baseball divisions. Gerry Foster, who coordinated the Grand Forks International Baseball Tournament, stated in a message that one or more teams from China, Japan, Taiwan, or Russia had participated in the tournaments played during the 1980s, 1990s and 2000s. From the Society for American Baseball Research (SABR), the Business of Baseball section's co-chair, Maury Brown, and the Latin America section's vice-chair, Anthony Salazar, each provided their suggestions on how and where to research baseball topics. SABR's mission is to encourage and promote the study of this sport and to provide an outlet for scholars and other researchers to find information about the game.

Since the mid–1990s, Maureen Fogel has graciously permitted me to use a room in her house as a work area and office, and to use another room for storing my materials. Although this space was normally cluttered with many books and readings on baseball and other sports, these rooms provided a central and convenient location for me to write articles for publication, organize and complete manuscripts, and teach online courses.

In November 2004, a beagle–basset hound mix named Lucy was added to our household. As a puppy, Lucy contributed to my scholarly efforts by gnawing on any documents that were left on the rug in the office, hiding her bones in files that contained sports information, leaving her toys scattered on the rug, and snoring while sleeping by the desk.

If any other individuals, organizations and animals helped me to successfully complete the manuscript of *Baseball, Inc.* but were not mentioned in this Preface, their good deeds are appreciated.

Finally, this book is dedicated to my former baseball teammates and coaches of teams at Spencer Field, and of teams in Little League Baseball, Babe Ruth League, American Legion Baseball, Gerstmeyer High School and Indiana State University. My closest teammate and buddy was John A. Roshel, Jr., now an orthodontist in Terre Haute. Although we frequently played on the same baseball team, since childhood we also fiercely competed against each other, hitting rocks with a broomstick, fielding grounders and catching fly balls, throwing and batting a rubber ball at the side of John's father's grocery store, and choosing different teams for practice. Despite the agony of losing games to each other, we became better baseball players and have remained lifelong friends.

Introduction

Since the mid-to-late 1970s, various interdependent and somewhat affiliated groups such as sports fans, commentators and reporters, and academic professors, government officials and research experts with an interest in sports, have become increasingly aware and concerned about the short- and long-term economic, financial and cultural events, issues and problems that involve organized, professional baseball. In part, these matters began to emerge in the early 1920s after Justice Oliver Wendell Holmes had declared that the Supreme Court construed baseball exhibitions to be purely state affairs and thus not within the federal jurisdiction of interstate commerce. The exhibitions, therefore, were beyond the reach of the United States (U.S.) antitrust laws. As a result, between the 1920s and 1950s Major League Baseball (MLB) and its member clubs in the American League (AL) and National League (NL) had gradually evolved from being recognized as local and regional entities to being considered as national business organizations that provide a type of sport entertainment for profits. Consequently, the AL and NL team owners required increasing amounts of financial capital and economic resources to be invested in their operations in order to successfully compete and win regular season and postseason championships in this elite American professional baseball league, that is, MLB.

Beginning in the 1950s, the economic structure, conduct and performance of professional baseball organizations including MLB, and in the 1960s, the Major League Baseball Players Association (MLBPA), became intriguing institutions to analyze and evaluate from a business perspective. To illustrate, during these decades MLB owners jointly decided to permit the relocation of the Braves from Boston, Massachusetts to Milwaukee, Wisconsin, and the Dodgers and Giants from the New York City area to, respectively, Los Angeles and San Francisco on the west coast of the U.S. Furthermore, during the 1960s the major leagues approved the expansion of franchises in the AL at such cities as Kansas City in Kansas, Los Angeles in California, Seattle in Washington and in Washington, D.C., and in the NL at Houston in Texas, Montreal in Canada, San Diego in California and in New York City. Then, after America had experienced a war in Southeast Asia and economic development and growth, and social unrest, it was in the 1970s that executive director Marvin Miller and the MLBPA became more powerful and the courts awarded players the right to declare themselves as free agents giving them the freedom to negotiate and sign contracts with, and play for MLB teams who had bid the highest dollar amounts for their services.[1]

Following the relocation and expansion of teams between the 1950s and 1970s, MLB was confronted by several strikes and lockouts, absorbed an influx of foreign baseball players, continued to expand the number of franchises, and eventually became identified and marketed as a growing international sport.[2] Consequently, the history and results of these and other aspects of baseball were researched to establish the contents of the present work.

The books described in the literature review below highlight the core business elements of baseball. They provide the foundation and theories on which this book is built.

Literature Review

Most of the books included in this Literature Review focus largely on a selection of controversial and provocative economic, financial and legal issues. These emerged because of (1) how MLB has historically operated as a monopoly; (2) how large-market clubs have comparative and competitive advantages over small-market teams and as a result, are successful at winning division titles, AL and NL pennants and World Series championships; (3) how outstanding teams' high-salaried players have performed during regular season and postseason games, and especially with respect to these players' bonuses and other forms of compensation; (4) how the MLBPA and collective bargaining process have impacted franchise owners' business strategies and coaches decisions; (5) how questions have arisen regarding whether the construction and operating costs of new baseball stadiums should be financed proportionately by governments or franchise owners as investors; and (6) how various factors and the size and wealth of local and regional sport markets have determined teams' home and away attendances, television revenues and fan bases.

Two prominent baseball books authored by historian Harold Seymour and published in 1960 and 1971 were, respectively, *Baseball: The Early Years* and *Baseball: The Golden Age*. The first volume documented the evolution of the sport and its impact on American society from the mid–1800s to 1903, which was two years after the basic organizational structure of MLB had formed with two eight-team leagues, a structure that existed until the early 1950s. Seymour's second volume traced baseball's immense prosperity in America from 1903 to 1930. These titles primarily emphasized the history and sociological aspects of the sport. The books, however, also analyzed business and economic topics in the sport. In *Baseball: The Golden Age*, for example, there were chapters on "The Components of Profit" and "The Magnets at Work"; "The Seeds of Union" and "Federal League Challenge"; "Minors and Farmers" and "Some Other Notables." In other words, Seymour's books depicted how professional baseball had incrementally progressed and became increasingly more popular and embedded in American culture despite depressions, wars and other historic events that had created instability and uncertainty in the United States and the world.[3]

The operations of professional team sports and the effects of government policies on the financial performances of teams were analyzed by economists and other experts in *Government and the Sport Business: Studies in the Regulation of Economic Activity*. This 12-chapter book, which was edited by author and former professor Roger G. Noll and published in 1974, concluded that the following relationships and tendencies existed with respect to professional team sports: first, an important element in the financial success of clubs is uncertainty in the outcome of games; second, franchises are more equal financially when market competition is restricted even though the playing strengths of teams are unequal; and third, to make baseball games more competitive there are government policies, rules and alternative institutional arrangements that would be just as effective as the present system had provided. In Chapter Ten of Noll's book, Lance E. Davis studied the organizational structure and market conduct of MLB as an economic cartel during 1909–1971. Although he viewed MLB as an ineffective cartel because of ongoing disputes between member clubs and the failure to self-regulate its behavior, Davis contended that the general public and players would benefit the most from a total repeal of the sport's antitrust exemption and that, in theory, the estimated social benefits and costs from government regulation of MLB are indeterminate. Besides antitrust, other relevant baseball topics in *Government and the Sport Business* included attendance and price setting, taxation, labor relations, racial discrimination, broadcasting rights, taxpayer subsidies for building and maintaining ballparks, and the extent and effect of competition in the player and product markets.[4]

Subsequent to the publications of Seymour and Noll, in 1989 University of Texas professor of management Gerald W. Scully wrote a book titled *The Business of Major League Baseball*. Essentially, Scully proceeded to rigorously analyze modern baseball from an economic perspective. For example, in three consecutive chapters, he examined "The Fans' Demand for Winning," "Team Revenue and Costs," and "Profitability, Survivability, and League Expansion." Since organized professional baseball experienced several reforms and numerous events from the mid–1970s to the late 1980s, Scully had a wealth of information to report about the economics of the sports industry. He updated some of the findings in Noll's book and contributed to improvements in modeling racial discrimination in baseball and explaining salary arbitration, tax sheltering of team ownership, profitability of teams, significance of television, and disputes between free agents and owners about collusion practices.[5]

During the 1990s, at least four well-researched books analyzed similar topics that involved the business and economics of professional baseball. In *Balls and Strikes: The Money Game in Professional Baseball*, author Kenneth M. Jennings reviewed the major collective bargaining efforts and participants in baseball from the late 1860s to the late 1980s. In other words, from an industrial relations viewpoint he discussed approximately 125 years of interrelationships between baseball's commissioners, team owners, players, agents, managers, the media and unions. He also looked at other sensitive but important contemporary topics such as the drug and alcohol abuses of players, and race and ethics, salary arbitration processes, salary trends and the linkages between players' pay and performance. Based on his research, Jennings determined some new insights about the participants' attitudes and behaviors, and he revealed an appreciation by fans and the public for baseball's off-the-field excitement and controversy.[6]

Then, following Jennings' analysis of baseball, in 1992 Paul M. Sommers edited a book titled *Diamonds Are Forever: The Business of Baseball*; in 1994 Andrew Zimbalist authored *Baseball and Billions: A Probing Look Inside the Big Business of Our National Pastime*; and in 1997 Daniel R. Marburger wrote his book and named it *Stee-Rike Four! What's Wrong with the Business of Baseball?* These three books, in part, covered many of the sports topics included in Noll's *Government and the Sports Business* and Jennings' *Balls and Strikes*. Sommers, Zimbalist and Marburger all focused on such economic issues in baseball as the antitrust exemption, cartels and the players' labor market, arbitration and free agency, the impact of race on players' salaries, league expansion and team relocation, implementation of reforms for broadcasting games, adoption of a luxury tax and salary cap, taxpayers and their subsidies of stadiums, and the revenue and payroll disparities and conflicts that prevailed between MLB teams that were located in small and large markets. Sommers, Zimbalist and Marburger provided testable models to quantitatively assess the business of baseball, and to recommend policies to overcome the inequalities, inefficiencies and misallocations that had plagued the sport for years.[7]

In 2003, two excellent and well-regarded books were published about the commercial activities of organized baseball. The titles were *The Business of Baseball* by Albert Theodore Powers and *May the Best Team Win: Baseball Economics and Public Policy* by Andrew Zimbalist. Interestingly, Powers proposed that the business structure of baseball undoubtedly needed incentives and internal reforms to encourage more cooperation between team owners and players and to promote and increase the growth of the sport. Some notable changes he recommended and justified, for business purposes, were revising the marketing of products, restructuring the equity ownership of teams, realigning divisions and regular season and postseason schedules to accommodate fans, instituting a competitive balance draft for players, and introducing federal legislation to assist a hypothetical corporation named Baseball Inc. in how to govern the sport. According to Powers, the implementation of his reforms would eventually close the economic disparities between rich and poor or have and have-not teams, increase fan loyalties and game attendances during regular seasons and postseasons, reduce hostilities about money that existed between team owners and players, and discourage the movements of experienced and superior players from financially weak to strong teams.[8]

Meanwhile, Zimbalist concluded that the U.S. Congress should intervene and equitably legislate and minimize MLB's monopolistic practices, which had resulted in high financial returns for franchise owners, but also had produced the misallocation of scarce sports resources and abuse of consumers. In total, *May the Best Team Win* analyzed the operations of the professional baseball industry, and then proposed which public policy measures make sense to adopt and initiate with respect to issues such as collective bargaining, taxation and profitability of teams, broadcasting games on cable, and the antitrust exemption.

Besides these books, the present work draws on other sources including various journal, magazine and newspaper articles, companies' and teams' media guides, and readings from such Internet websites as ballparks.com, ballparkwatch.com, cnnsi.com, mlb.com, sportsbusinessdaily.com, sportsbusinessjournal.com, sportsbusinessnews.com and usatoday.com. Some of the periodicals used include *Business Week, Charlotte Observer, Forbes, Fortune, Harvard Business Review, New York Times, Newsweek, Sport, Sports Illustrated* and *Wall Street Journal*.[9]

Book Overview

This book is divided into five parts, each focusing on a specific business topic: Business and Finance, Human Resources and Relationships, International Relations, Management and Leadership, and Sports Marketing. Each baseball topic is specifically related to at least one of these business areas, and perhaps to a lesser extent, to other areas of commerce.

Part I, Business and Finance begins with "Affairs, Issues and Reforms in the Major Leagues," a discussion of the actual and potential outcomes of imposing various rules on the sport. What are the consequences, if any, of the luxury tax and revenue sharing on parity and competitive balance between teams of the AL and NL? Furthermore, should MLB mandate and strictly enforce an annual cap or maximum dollar amount on team payrolls to control escalating player salaries, or simply continue to allow each team owner to compete for players and thereby disproportionately inflate their organization's payroll?

Chapter 2, "Finance and Major League Franchises," examines teams' revenues and relevant cash flows, and evaluates the rank order of franchises based on their estimated valuations. Chapter 3, "Replacing Ballparks: History and Consequences for MLB Teams" lists in a table — and appropriately describes — the current status of some ballparks, and the effects on attendance at games when a new ballpark has been built as a replacement venue for a home team. There is specific information on when the stadiums were constructed, their capacities and costs, and how much attendance changed for the regular seasons before and after the ballpark had existed.

The fourth and fifth chapters are, respectively, "Relocating Teams in Professional Baseball" and "The Organization and Business of Minor League Baseball." The former chapter denotes the business reasons and implications for MLB, other league franchises, fans and communities when one or more teams permanently move from one site to another, while the latter chapter highlights the history of minor league baseball, provides reasons why these teams appeal to local sports fans, and considers their commercial success as baseball organizations. The chapter also describes the clubs' tendency to locate in small-to-medium sized cities and play in ballparks with relatively low seating capacities.

In Part II, the chapters represent important and interesting baseball topics with respect to the business area of Human Resources and Relationships. Chapter 6, "An Overview of Labor Relations," is an analysis of the MLBPA and its structure, role and power as the collective bargaining agent for MLB players. Besides the monetary rewards received by this organization's members, has this union benefited or damaged the sport's image and reputation because of the players' demands and strikes? Certainly, the research suggests that the MLBPA continues to be a vital factor in MLB's decisions and in Major League ball as a whole.

The next chapter, "Does the Drug Culture Corrupt Baseball?" discusses the league's drug testing policy and program. How effective is the application and enforcement of the program? Is MLB's drug policy designed to be proactive or reactive concerning the substance abuse? Finally, are the penalties sufficient and equitable for those players who fail their tests?

Chapter 8, "Major League Players' Salaries and Team Payrolls," considers the financial effects of players' compensation on teams and the franchise owners' abilities and commitments to spend excessive amounts of money to hire or retain rookies who have great potential, free agent superstars, and perhaps mediocre veteran players. Since the early 1990s, the salaries and benefits of MLB players have risen considerably faster than the U.S. economy's rate of inflation. Did this trend continue throughout the early 2000s? Chapter 8 answers this question.

"The Concentration and Status of Minorities in Baseball" and "Social Investment by Sports in Community Affairs" are the ninth and tenth chapters, closing out the section on Human Resources and Relationships. With respect to integration of the sport, the proportion of African American players on MLB teams had dwindled to approximately 10 percent by 2005. Meanwhile, Hispanics and other athletes from foreign nations represent about 29 percent of MLB players, and approximately 50 percent of those on minor league clubs. The reasons why international athletes are recruited, the way they are trained in baseball academies, and the current and future implications for professional baseball are all explained in Chapter 9. Chapter 10 focuses on and identifies the numerous social activities and programs that the league, teams and players, and the MLBPA have sponsored or contributed to in some way. A table lists three community programs of each club. As discussed, these teams have been and continue to be socially responsible business organizations in their local areas.

Because it is a current issue and potentially a lucrative source of revenues and resources for MLB, International Relations is the focus of the Chapters in Part III. Essentially, this section is about the business and dispersion of professional baseball as a global sport. These five chapters provide the most interesting and relevant reasons for why, when and where American professional baseball has become internationalized. Included in Part III are Chapter 11, "Global Business Strategies and Markets"; Chapter 12, "Organized Baseball in Foreign Countries"; Chapter 13 "America's Teams Demand Foreign Players"; Chapter 14 "International Tournaments and Championship Teams"; and Chapter 15, "International Issues and Global Relations." Respectively, they cover the methods and techniques by which MLB sells its brands and products overseas, and the sites and characteristics of those baseball markets; the organizations and operations of a sample of non–American professional baseball leagues that are located in some countries of Asia and other areas of the world; the 14 AL and 16 NL teams' short- and long-term demands for foreign-born athletes and why these clubs need them to play baseball for their organizations; the types of international tournaments and teams that have won those tournaments, and the managerial experiences and difficulties of MLB officials in scheduling the World Baseball Classic in 2006, which is an international baseball tournament championship between a team from the U.S. and 15 teams from selected foreign nations; and the activities and programs of MLB teams that have established business relationships with foreign leagues, teams, companies and other organizations, the existence and quality of baseball training camps or academies abroad, the league's drug policy with respect to international players, and a description of the draft system used by MLB and the flaws of that system.

In Part IV, the chapters focus on Management and Leadership topics. Chapter 16, "How Commissioners Govern Baseball," examines the styles, responsibilities and accomplishments of the leagues' commissioners. Chapter 17, "The Strategy and Prosperity of Franchise Owners," discusses the roles, styles and investments of various owners of MLB franchises. Chapter 18, "The Performances of Managers in Coaching Professional Teams," describes the supervisory skills and leadership qualities of successful teams' managers who have served as coaches. The performances of the superior teams from the early 1900s to 2000s are examined in Chapter 19, "Team Dynasties and Leaders Since 1903." Chapter 20, "Expansion Teams in the Major Leagues," provides the reasons and business decisions compelling MLB to expand the number of franchises and furthermore, to consider folding or actually eliminating some AL and NL teams in the best interests of the sport.

Part V, Sports Marketing, contains information about the marketing strategies and other promotional activities and events that involve MLB and one or more of the AL and NL teams. Its five chapters are Chapter 21, "The Business of Marketing a League"; Chapter 22, "Evaluating Big League Team Brands"; Chapter 23, "Ticket Prices and Fan Costs"; Chapter 24, "Marketing: Partnerships, Sponsorships and Licensing"; and Chapter 25, The Programming and Broadcasting Business." Chapter 21 shows how the league distributes its products and services, and markets the organization through the media; Chapter 22, how teams create and apply the concepts, values and benefits of brands; Chapter 23, what the ticket prices and full costs have been for an individual and four-person family to attend a MLB game at the teams' ballparks each season from 1995 to 2004; Chapter 24, what types of deals and relationships exist between MLB and its numerous business partners, sponsors and licensees; and Chapter 25, why programming and broadcasts agreements are vital to the domestic and international exposure, development and growth of professional baseball for penetrating markets in the U.S. and worldwide. All these elements are important in sustaining MLB's growth and success across the planet.

All the chapters in *Baseball, Inc.* should be of interest to avid baseball fans, to educators who teach students enrolled in sports and pop culture courses with baseball tie-ins, and to professional scholars and experts who have committed to research and perhaps publish articles or books about the business and history of professional sports, and especially about the topics in Major League Baseball.

PART I. BUSINESS AND FINANCE

1. Affairs, Issues and Reforms in the Major Leagues

Prior to 1901, the primary organizations in professional baseball consisted of the National League (1876–2006), American Association (1882–1891) and Union Association (1884). Then, in 1901 the composition of Major League Baseball (MLB) was officially established with eight teams each in the American League (AL) and National League (NL). This 16-team structure remained until the expansions that occurred between the early 1960s and late 1990s. As such, in 2005 there were 13 AL and 16 NL clubs located in the United States (U.S.) and one AL club at a site in Canada.

During its 105 years in existence, MLB has experienced a number of events that have affected the way organized baseball operates as a professional sport in the entertainment business. Besides expansion, the events include the relocation of franchises, formation and development of a player's union and negotiation of collective bargaining agreements, league's adoption of free agency, eight work stoppages, construction of new stadiums and the renovation of existing ballparks, and the increase in foreign players on the rosters of AL, NL and minor league teams. With respect to these and other matters, however, during the history of MLB a collection of avoidable and unavoidable, yet controversial business issues and problems emerged that required decisions to be made and implemented by this sport's various commissioners and team owners, players and their union, and government officials. Even so, there are many baseball officials and sports fans, community leaders, and local and national politicians who are concerned and uncertain about the sport's financial stability, and its short- and long-term economic prospects for further self-development, growth and prosperity.

Baseball Affairs and Issues

After studying a large portion of the academic literature, reviewing the results of surveys of sports fans, and reading numerous articles published in the media on the business and operation of professional baseball, this sport's most frequently cited and reoccurring opportunities, troubles and trends relate to the inflation of ticket prices, food and merchandise affecting individuals and families who attend regular season, playoff and World Series games at the ballparks; big league players' guaranteed multiyear and multimillion-dollar contracts; the growing revenue gap between the small- and large-market teams in each AL and NL division; implementation, enforcement and impact of an effective steroid policy; the enormous expenditures of public monies to pay for the construction of new stadiums and the renovation of current ballparks; and the scheduling of single games and series each season between teams in the AL and NL. For sure, these matters are multifaceted, interconnected and complex since MLB's commissioner, the league's franchise owners and officials of the Major League Baseball Players Association (MLBPA) frequently disagree with each other and this sport's fans about the affect, significance and solution of them.

Before addressing the previous list of issues, it is necessary to establish how well baseball has performed in its industry. Essentially, the game has recovered from a 234-day work stoppage that eliminated much of the 1994 season and cancelled the playoffs and World Series, and delayed the start of the 1995 season. In 2004, a total of 73 million people attended MLB games, which amounted to approximately 31,000 fans per game, and from the 2004 to 2005 season, advanced tickets sold had increased by 8 percent and 90 percent of the big league clubs experienced higher sales. Furthermore, gross revenues of $4.5 billion were projected for MLB teams in 2005 compared to $4.1 billion a year earlier, and the league added such new sponsors as Wheaties, Home Depot and DHL. With the higher merchandise and online sales, and additional corporate spending to advertise products and services at stadiums, initial success of the NL's Washington Nationals, and the leveling off of aggregate players' salaries, professional baseball appears to be popular and thriving from a business perspective.

Two experts have provided their opinions about the current status and welfare of the sport. Regarding the renaissance of baseball since the mid–1990s, Commissioner Bud Selig stated his reasons. "There were a lot of new ballparks. A change in the economic system [revenue sharing and luxury tax] was critical because it created much more competitive balance. The wild card and inter-league play have worked. The game is still the best ever invented." Echoing Selig's comments in an article, the author, columnist and pundit George Will expressed his observations about the late 1900s to early 2000s as being the sport's most recent Golden Age. "Baseball's competitive balance is much improved and compares favorably with the NFL and NBA. The National League has sent seven different teams to the last seven World Series and 22 of baseball's 30 teams have played in the postseason since the wild-card system was adopted. Baseball also is thriving because it is a bargain at $19.82 per ticket [in 2004] and because of the flood of Spanish-speaking talent."[1]

Regarding the future of baseball and MLB, sports writer Rick Harrow is optimistic. He said, "Nevertheless, the baseball core fan base provides a solid fan foundation from which to build. According to a recent Intersearch poll, 66.7 percent of the population has played organized baseball or softball at some point, and the Sporting Goods Manufacturers Association revealed last year [2004] that over 5.9 million kids aged 6–17 participate in baseball and softball." According to Selig, Will and Harrow, the game of baseball is growing in popularity such that the AL and NL teams have benefited financially because of the league's recent innovations and its appeal to fans and young athletes, the sport's relative low cost, and improvements in the competitive balance of divisions.[2]

As stated before, there are disputes and conflicts between Selig, some franchise owners, ballplayers and fans, and the sports media about the implications and effects of baseball's opportunities, troubles and trends. Based on this author's research of the baseball literature, and on the contents of other chapters in this book, a basic understanding of the following topics is crucial to analyzing the affairs, issues and reforms in big league baseball.

Games: Prices and Costs

Despite the moderate inflation of goods and services in the marketplace, and complaints of fans and the criticism of academics, attending big league baseball games at the ballparks located in American cities and the SkyDome in Toronto, Canada are a good bargain for spectators in contrast to watching games at arenas and stadiums in the other major professional sports. To illustrate, from the 2004 to 2005 regular season, the average price of a ticket in MLB increased from approximately $19.91 to $21.17. Meanwhile, during their 2004–2005 seasons the mean ticket prices per game in the National Basketball Association (NBA) were $45.28, and $54.75 in the National Football League (NFL). Because of a lockout that cancelled its 2004–2005 season, a typical ticket in the National Hockey League (NHL) cost $43.57 per game two years ago, which was the 2003–2004 season. Furthermore, for a four-person family to attend a game in each professional sport during these seasons, the Chicago-based Team Marketing Report calculated and reported a Fan Cost Index (FCI) for each league and team. As a result, MLB's FCI totaled $164.43 and the NBA's $263.44, NFL's $321.62 and NHL's $253.65.[3]

Although these prices and costs are relatively expensive for many individuals and groups, the average baseball fan and/or his or her family can still afford to attend a few games each season. Nonetheless, the price and cost amounts vary among the teams. For example, to see the 2004 World Series champion Red Sox play the New York Yankees at 33,871-seat Fenway Park in Boston during 2005, on average the admission price was $44.56 for a single ticket and $276.24 for a four-person family. Alternatively, to root for the AL's Royals against the Minnesota Twins at 40,625-seat Kauffman Stadium in Kansas City, a fan's ticket was priced at $13.71 and the Royal's FCI totaled only $119.85.

To promote sales, some MLB franchises have recently adopted a variable pricing strategy whereby the values of tickets at each game depends on who a team is playing, the day and time of the game that week, and what impact the game's outcome will have on the teams' divisional standings and league's pennant race. Also, in 2005 four clubs had reduced their ticket prices while nine clubs held their price increases below 2 percent. In short, baseball fans and other spectators must evaluate the values of prices and costs before choosing whether to attend one or more MLB games, and to economize at the ballparks, families could share their hot dogs and drinks, and decide not to purchase programs or baseball caps.

Players' Contracts

According to a sum of the salaries contained in their contracts, during 2006–2010 a total of 190 players on the 30 big league teams are guaranteed about $2.97 billion. In fact, these amounts will decrease from $1.4 billion in 2006 to $137.4 million in 2010. The MLB teams with the highest and lowest commitments in guaranteed salaries for the five years are, respectively, the New York Yankees at $425.6 million, Boston Red Sox at $177 million and New York Mets at $171 million, relative to the Pittsburgh Pirates at $6.3 million, Tampa Bay Devil Rays at $13 million and Cleveland Indians at $13.5 million. The five players with the largest dollar amounts are the Yankees' Alex Rodriguez at $115.6 million and Derek Jeter at $108 million, and the Mets' Carlos Beltran at $87.3 million, Rockies' Todd Helton at $83 million and Cardinals' Albert Pujois at $70.8 million. In a statement about the teams' obligations as reported in *USA Today*, Commissioner Bud Selig said, "Debt of this magnitude is a matter of serious concern. We [MLB and MLBPA] do have rules in our labor agreement that deal with that, but it's something that I monitor very closely because certainly it can affect the way we operate in the future."[4]

Because of their market's total population and large fan and revenue bases, the Yankees, Red Sox and Mets have the economic power and net cash flows to provide the payments of compensation to their players. Moreover, beginning in 2007 the marginal amounts owed by each franchise in guaranteed contracts will decline each year. Nevertheless, to control commitments beyond 2010 and set an example, it may be beneficial for some owners of teams in large markets to consider banning or at least limiting the number of multiyear contracts awarded to players. When prominent baseball athletes are injured or have their skills rapidly deplete during the life of their contracts, then it will be a challenge for these teams to win games and more difficult for them to trade those players for others in the league. Therefore, it is a competitive advantage for teams to stop issuing, or reduce the number of years contained in, multiyear contracts to their star players.

For another strategy, the league could modify its 60/40 equity to debt rule, which prohibits the accumulation of debt higher than 40 percent of a franchise's value and counts long-term player contracts as a type of debt. Since Selig's office enforces this rule, it is suggested here that the ratios of teams be applied in a range such as 60/40 to 65/35 or to 70/30. The former ratio would include small-market clubs, and the latter two ratios relate to large-market teams. Although this revision adjusts the upper limit from 40 percent to a smaller proportion, it will gradually reduce the deviation in debt between high and low payroll clubs in the AL and NL.

Revenue Sharing and Luxury Taxes

In the 2002 Collective Bargaining Agreement (CBA) that was negotiated between and approved by the MLB and the MLBPA, there are specific provisions that involve the distributions of local and central fund revenues, and the values of luxury tax thresholds and percentage rates. Indeed, these are ways for MLB to achieve parity or a competitive balance between teams. It is in the league's interest to increasingly redistribute a greater proportion of revenues from large-market teams to a number of small-market clubs with relatively low revenues. That is, the reallocation of funds occurs from such clubs as the Yankees in New York City, Red Sox in Boston and Cubs in Chicago to the Brewers in Milwaukee, Pirates in Pittsburgh and Reds in Cincinnati. To that end, the 2002 CBA increased the 30 teams' proportion of local revenues shared to 34 percent from 20 percent as specified in the 1996 CBA. As a result, the teams' net of amounts paid and received in revenues exceeded $169 million in 2002, $220 million in 2003, $250 million in 2004, an estimated $280 million in 2005 and more than $300 million in 2006 and 2007.[5]

Besides the amounts from revenue sharing, the clubs with high payrolls must pay luxury taxes. According to the CBA of 2002, the tax rates increased from 0 percent in 2002 to 17.5 percent in 2003, and then in 2004 from 22.5 percent for first time and 30 percent for second time violators to 22.5 percent for first time, 30 percent for second time and 40 percent for third time violators in 2005. During 2006, the rates are 0 percent for first time, 30 percent for second time and 40 percent for third and fourth time violators. The teams receiving the luxury taxes must use the money for player benefits and contributions to the industry growth fund, and for player development activities and training in foreign countries that lack organized high school baseball programs.

Relative to the AL and NL teams' performances since 2002, the results have been mixed. During the 2003 and 2004 regular seasons, very few of the small-market teams had qualified for the postseasons. In the AL, these were the Oakland Athletics in 2003 and Minnesota Twins in 2003 and 2004, and in NL, it was the World Series champion Florida Marlins in 2003 and in 2004, the St. Louis Cardinals who had won the pennant. From the 2004 to 2005 season, some small-market teams that had improved in quality and played more competitively included the AL's Baltimore Orioles and Cleveland Indians and the NL's Florida Marlins and San Diego Padres.

Certainly, raising the revenue sharing percentages and imposing higher luxury tax rates have caused the redistribution of hundreds of millions of dollars from the wealthy, high revenue and payroll franchises to the lesser-valued, low revenue and payroll teams. Yet, for various reasons some teams have manipulated these policies. The Yankees, for example, appear to be using the luxury tax as a cost of doing business. Each season, the club's fans, television partners and investors demand great performances from it. Thus, the tax did not deter owner George Steinbrenner from spending $208 million in 2005 for his roster including $97 million for his pitching staff, since his team expected to earn more than $120 million from just the gate receipts.

In retrospect, there may be a portion of small-market team owners who are incompetent, indecisive or simply not interested in spending the redistributed revenues to greatly upgrade their teams' rosters or to develop an infrastructure and staff for improving their minor league operations. In other words, the money received by these owners should be used to sign talented free agents, to scout and draft high school and college players, and to organize baseball academies in the nations of Latin America where there is an abundance of amateur prospects and semi-professional players. It has been reported in articles about baseball that this misallocation of revenues and luxury taxes could apply to such owners as the Tampa Bay Devils' Vince Naimoli, Kansas City Royals' David Glass, Pittsburgh Pirates' Kevin McClatchy and Milwaukee Brewers' Mark Attanasio. In fact, these individuals and perhaps some other owners with clubs in small markets have preferred to maintain tight budgets and preserve their cash balances rather than recruit the league's better players when the athletes are free to negotiate and sign a new contract. This strategy was expressed, in part, by McClatchy in early 2005 when he said, "As we go toward a new [CBA], there's going to have to be some form of constraints because these guys [large-market team owners] can't control themselves. I'm tired of other people affecting the marketplace and making it more challenging for small market teams."[6]

To promote economic parity or a movement to competitive balance between the AL and NL teams, MLB and the MLBPA need to conscientiously discuss various proposals to increase the percentages of local revenues to be shared and/or the luxury tax rates, agree on a set of revised percentages and rates, and then include those amended numbers in the CBA of 2006. If the two groups decide, for example, that these percentages and rates will each be increased to 40–50 percent between 2006 and 2010, this policy would certainly generate additional funds for teams that are located in small and medium sized markets to spend on player development benefits, programs and facilities. If adopted, however, MLB and the MLBPA should perform audits of financial statements and inspections of property to verify that the owners of clubs in small and medium sized markets used this money for the appropriate purposes. Furthermore, the league and players union should determine how the redistribution of revenues had affected these teams' performances during the 2006–2010 regular seasons. With respect to parity as a goal in baseball, during early 2005 Commissioner Selig remarked, "There is work yet to be done, there is no question about that. But I think the changes [in revenue sharing and luxury taxes] are beginning to work better than people are giving us credit for. At least we've got a system that's working. Let's give the last two years of this agreement [2002 CBA] a chance, because things do get tighter. I'm very confident that we will achieve what we set out to achieve."[7]

Steroid Policy

In an Associated Press–AOL poll conducted during April of 2005, the respondents identified the use of steroids by players as baseball's second biggest problem. Of those individuals surveyed, more than 50 percent care "a lot" about the issue, 70 percent believe that any player who used steroids or other performance enhancing drugs should not be elected to the Baseball Hall of Fame, and 40 percent think that Congress should intervene about the problem and do more to eliminate steroids in U.S. amateur and professional baseball organizations.[8]

As of mid-to-late 2005, it appeared from statements in the press that MLB and the MLBPA would eventually reach an agreement and allow the league to implement new policies regarding drug tests and penalizing violators. In a presentation delivered to the U.S. House of Representatives during May of 2005, Commissioner Selig had suggested four changes to the Major League Drug Policy. Generally, these included toughening the penalties for first, second and third time offenders, and banning amphetamines, increasing the frequency of testing players for drugs, and assigning an independent administrator to be responsible for scheduling tests, collecting samples and analyzing results. Before the Commissioner's visit to Congress in May, the league's team owners had unanimously endorsed Selig's proposal, which was also presented to the MLBPA in late April of 2005. Interestingly, the specific penalties of the policy included a 50-game suspension of first time offenders and 100-game suspension of second time violators, and finally a lifetime ban of players for a third positive test. As of mid–June in 2005, approximately three major leaguers and 77 minor league players had tested positive and were suspended based on the penalties contained in the then-current policy and not those listed in Selig's proposal.[9]

Meanwhile, during early 2005 a House Commerce subcommittee and Congress' Committee on Government Reform had each met, held hearings and proposed legislation to eliminate the use of steroids by players in the professional sports leagues. As a result, Representative Cliff Stearns, who was then the Chairman of the Commerce, Trade and Consumer Protection Subcommittee, introduced the Drug Free Sports Act in early May of 2005. According to this piece of legislation, an athlete would be suspended for one-half of a season for the first offense, a full season for the second and a lifetime ban for the third. Based on information from the hearings and his knowledge of the problem, Stearns boasted, "It's clear that the leagues, teams and players don't want to impose strict standards. We need to get their attention and this is the way to do it. There is momentum in favor of my bill."

During the same month that the Drug Free Sports Act was introduced in the House of Representatives, Senator John McCain and Congressmen Tom Davis and Henry Waxman announced the contents of their bill, which was titled the Clean Sports Act of 2005. Basically, this bill strengthened the leagues' testing procedures and provided tougher penalties for players who used performance-enhancing drugs in MLB and the NFL, NBA and NHL. In short, the Clean Sports Act of 2005 established uniform and very strict standards for the prohibition of illegal drugs including the consumption of steroids and amphetamines, since the Act included a two-year ban for a first time violation by a player and a lifetime ban for a second infraction. According to Congressman Davis, "Steroid use is a national public health crisis. This legislation is aimed at not only getting rid of performance-enhancing drugs on the professional level, but also sends a message loud and clear to the young people of America. Steroids are illegal. Steroids are dangerous. They can be deadly. And there is no place for them in our sports leagues or our school grounds." Subsequently, the sports leagues and unions reacted by adamantly objecting to the types of penalties and other mandates contained in the bills as submitted by Congressmen Stearns and Davis. In the end, it is predicted that Congress will pass some form of legislation that sets minimum standards and penalties regarding the use of steroids by players on the rosters of professional sports teams.

Legislation aside, MLB had banned players from using steroids in late 2002. Since that year, the numbers of home runs and home runs per game that were hit during the first two months of each season had first increased and then decreased. These were, respectively, 953 and 2.07 in 2003, 990 and 2.16 in 2004, and 908 and 1.97 in 2005. The last set of numbers are the lowest since 2002's 878 and 1.93, and substantially less than in 1996–2004 when the averages were 962 and 2.16. Furthermore, during April–May of 2004 relative to 2005 the number of runs per game had declined by 5 percent or from 9.72 to 9.23, total hits per game fell by 3.1 percent or from 18.37 to 17.80, and major league batting averages decreased marginally or from .265 to .261. Did the changes in these statistics occur in 2005 because of the tougher steroid test policy that was enacted by MLB in 2004? This question is answered in the next two paragraphs.[10]

A number of MLB players and coaches contend that the average home runs and other results had diminished in 2005 for reasons other than the enforcement of MLB's steroid policy. These factors were the cold and wet Spring training period in Florida and the bad weather during the first few weeks of the regular season, restoring the original and expanded strike zone of batters, improved pitching performances, smaller-sized players, and the absence of the San Francisco Giants slugger Barry Bonds. But, Florida Marlins pitcher Todd Jones and Los Angeles Angels bench coach Joe Maddon think that testing was a factor for the lower productivity of players as hitters and base runners. According to Jones, "I hate it, but there has been a correction made in the [drug testing] system, and the numbers are going to suffer for a couple of years." Maddon said, "I don't know exactly to what extent, but you see people maybe not as big as they had been in the past or don't look as strong as maybe they had been in the past. So, just being a thinking person, and you know what's been going on, you have to tie them together a little bit."

In his *Sports Illustrated* article titled "When Bigger Gets Smaller, Smaller Gets Big," Tom Verducci claimed that the crackdown on steroid use by MLB officials helped to end an era when power hitting had dominated other aspects of play. As a result, the other skills of players have risen in importance such as base running, ability of infielders to catch fast ground balls, and the superb defense performed by outfielders. The vice president of Minor League Baseball's governing panel Stan Brand put it this way, "Whatever the reasons, 'the era of juice' is indeed over — just as the pre–1920s 'dead ball' era marked by soft, hand-made balls and 10-home-run records ended, followed by the 'live ball' era and then a focus on pitching, and so on and so on down through the years." Whether illegal substances were involved or not, Commissioner Selig has declared that no MLB records will be taken away from any of the players who have been suspected of steroid use.[11]

New Ballparks

During the 2005 regular season, 22 MLB teams played their home games in stadiums that were owned by the public sector and managed by various local government units. In other words, teams owned the other two AL and six NL ballparks. These were respectively, the Red Sox' Fenway Park in Boston and Blue Jays' SkyDome in Toronto, and the Cardinals' Busch Stadium in St. Louis, Dodgers' Dodger Stadium in Los Angeles, Marlins' Pro Player Stadium in Miami, Giants' SBC Park in San Francisco, Braves' Turner Field in Atlanta and Cubs' Wrigley Field in Chicago. Although a publicly funded stadium will be built to replace 40-year Busch Stadium in 2006, many baseball officials are concerned that taxpayers who live in metropolitan areas and local politicians will become increasingly reluctant to approve the sale of bonds or other securities to finance the construction of new, or renovation of existing big league stadiums. If that should happen, then baseball's franchise owners must pay these costs or move their clubs to another city.

To illustrate, since the late 1990s to early 2000s there have been plenty of conversations and negotiations about funding new stadiums between teams and public interest groups or municipalities such as in New York City for the Yankees and Mets, and in Kansas City for the Royals, Oakland for the Athletics, Minneapolis for the Twins and Miami for the Marlins. On numerous occasions, the owners of these six franchises have said they could not compete each season against other clubs because of their inferior ballparks. Even 93 year-old Yankee Stadium, which was renovated in 1976, contains only 18 luxury suites and lacks other modern and revenue-producing amenities. As a result, there was a proposal completed that committed New York taxpayers to contribute $135 million for infrastructure improvements, $70 million for new parking garages, $90 million for new and renovated metropolitan transit stations, and perhaps millions of dollars to pay for any potential cost overruns with respect to the construction of a new $1.5 billion baseball facility. If the new ballpark would contain 60 luxury suites, the Yankees will earn an additional $25 million each year plus an estimated one-time payment of $200 million from sponsors who purchase the naming rights. Because of more luxury suites and 6,000 fewer seats in the lower and upper decks, the team's ticket prices could be increased, which would generate more revenues for the wealthiest and most valuable franchise in the history of U.S. professional sports. Meanwhile, in June of 2005 the NL New York Mets announced plans to have a new $600 million ballpark built next to Shea Stadium, which was constructed in 1964.[12]

Between 2010 and 2020, there will probably be a new round of stadium deals to be negotiated between some MLB teams and various government officials. Besides the improvements needed to upgrade Kaufman Stadium in Kansas City, Network Associates Stadium in Oakland, the Metrodome in Minneapolis and Pro Player Stadium in Miami, other aging baseball stadiums to be renovated or replaced include the Angels' Anaheim Stadium in southern California, Blue Jays' SkyDome in Toronto, Cubs' Wrigley Field in Chicago, and Dodgers Stadium in Los Angeles. Consequently, if city and/or county governments are not willing or financially prepared to issue bonds to finance the repair of or replace the teams' stadiums, then the small-market Royals, Athletics, Twins and Marlins are likely to relocate to another urban area in the U.S. or to a foreign city such as Monterrey, Mexico or Mexico City.

Interleague Play

As an innovation of Commissioner Bud Selig, the competition between teams in the AL and NL began in 1997. Selig initiated this type of play so baseball fans could attend regular season games that featured teams, players and coaches from the other league. Furthermore, there were some intriguing geographic rivalries for MLB to exploit such as the Mets and Yankees in New York City, Cubs and White Sox in Chicago, Angels and Dodgers in the Los Angeles area, Athletics and Giants in the Oakland–San Francisco area, and the Astros and Rangers in Texas and Indians and Reds in Ohio. Besides those based on location, other rivalries to highlight were games between two teams from the AL and NL East, and from the AL and NL Central and West Divisions. There is, for example, the Red Sox and Phillies in the East Division, Twins and Cardinals in the Central Division, and Mariners and Padres in the West Division. Nevertheless, during the late 1990s some journalists and former players had criticized Selig for violating the long-standing tradition of keeping AL and NL clubs separated until the World Series, and for implementing a novel experiment whose value would wear off as fans rejected the concept. So, has interleague play been a success for MLB?

During 1997–2004, the attendance at interleague games averaged 32,663 per game, which represents a 13.4 percent increase above the regular season attendances. In 2005, there was difference each game of 11.5 percent or 32,985 as opposed to 29,511 for conventional games. Relative to performances for the eight seasons, the NL teams won 50.7 percent of games played against their AL opponents, and posted a higher batting average by .001 or .268 versus .267, and a lower earned run average by .01 or 4.44 versus 4.45. The most and least productive teams in each league were, respectively, the NL's Atlanta Braves and Pittsburgh Pirates, and the AL's Oakland Athletics and Baltimore Orioles.[13]

Before 2005, sports reporter Mike Bauman had strenuously objected to interleague play. He said, in part, that the idea was flawed, ill conceived and risky. However, because of greater attendances and fan interest at games, and the development of specific rivalries between AL and NL teams, Bauman has changed his mind and currently supports interleague play. "The traditional arguments against interleague baseball have once again taken their annual beating," said Bauman. "In retail the adage is that the customer is always right. The retail business of baseball probably shouldn't be any different. The paying customers like interleague baseball."

Baseball Reforms

For decades, sports economists and other scholars have studied the structure, conduct and performance of big league baseball including the commissioners, franchises and team owners, players and coaches. As a result of their research, they have recommended several proposals to improve the degree of parity or competition that exists between the clubs in MLB. Listed in no specific sequence, these are expanding the number of players in the labor pool, increasing to at least 50 percent the proportion of locally generated revenues shared by teams, raising the luxury tax to 50 percent or more, establishing a minimum and maximum payroll for each team, promoting the sport to international baseball fans, providing low revenue clubs with a disproportionate share of the league's income from national broadcasting and licensing rights, and adjusting the debt-equity rule to give an advantage to the small-market teams. Although these proposals have short- and long-term economic benefits, costs and risks, MLB and the MLBPA should jointly evaluate them to determine their potential financial impact on franchises, players, fans and the sport.

In contrast to the previous proposals, it was in 2004 that the readers of *Baseball Digest* offered six ways to improve the game at the major league level. From their perspective, the ways were to eliminate the designated hitter rule, discontinue inter-league play, ban multiyear contracts, alter the save rule, revise the policy of awarding home-field advantage in the World Series to the team of the winning league in the previous year's All-Star Game, and playing each season's opening games in the U.S. In the end, MLB's decision to accept or reject one or more of the above recommendations and ways should completely depend on whether the policy is or is not "in the best interests of baseball."[14]

Summary

This chapter identified and discussed the primary affairs and issues, and listed some reforms that have involved the organization, operation and business of big league baseball. After highlighting the major events that affected the development and growth of the sport and MLB since the late 1800s to early 1900s, there is a section containing the business practicalities and implications of the prices and costs for individuals and families to attend teams' games, and other topics such as players contracts, revenue sharing and luxury taxes, steroid policy, new ballparks and interleague play. Then, some reforms are presented in the final two paragraphs of a section.

For organized baseball to expand its fan base and prosper in America and foreign countries during and beyond the early 2000s, Commissioner Bud Selig and the teams' owners, and the MLBPA need to communicate with each other and decide which policies are best for the sport and then to its fans. Since total attendance at MLB games established a record in 2004 at 73 million, there is widespread support for baseball, at least in the U.S., Japan and some Latin American countries. If the owners and players can avoid work stoppages, and bargain in good faith ever four years until a CBA is completed, then the average fan will accept the majority of new or amended policies implemented by the league. Despite the elimination of baseball from the 2012 Olympic Games, a successful World Baseball Classic sponsored by MLB and held in 2006 or 2007, and intense competition and rivalries between teams in the AL and NL during the regular seasons, playoffs and World Series, will each increase baseball's popularity and market share in nations across the globe.

2. Finance and Major League Franchises

Based on comments from Major League Baseball (MLB) Commissioner Bud Selig and team owners, and on studies performed by various sports economists and other officials who have researched the business of professional baseball organizations, there are controversial beliefs and conflicting facts about the short- and long-term financial operations, profits and values of the league's franchises. Selig and the owners, for example, stress that during the majority of seasons the annual increases in player compensation and such operating and non-operating costs as marketing and transportation expenses and interest amounts on borrowed capital exceed the teams' revenues obtained from game receipts and broadcasts, ballpark operations, and the sale of merchandise, clothing and other products. Alternatively, some experts who have collected and analyzed data and assorted financial information on the teams argue that professional baseball franchises have an abundance and array of cash flow, income and wealth. As such, these experts claim that teams are normally profitable and generally appreciate in market value each season. Therefore, to provide some facts and insights about the economic returns and risks of MLB franchises in the American League (AL) and National League (NL), this chapter presents selected quantitative evidence for the reader to consider when evaluating public statements and accounting documents about the financial conditions and future business prospects of teams.[1]

For most years and baseball seasons during the 1990s and early 2000s, the operating cash flows and revenues, and valuations of MLB teams were estimated by prominent sports economists and financial analysts, and published in a variety of media. In this chapter, an assortment of financial information —from a series of reputable sources— is organized for each club in the AL and NL, which are listed in alphabetical order in two of the three tables. Then, the tabled data is discussed especially with regard to the differences and relationships between small- and large-market, and among high- and low-payroll teams in each league.

Team Values

Table 2.1 lists the estimated market values of 14 AL and 16 NL teams that — except for the Devil Rays, Diamondbacks, Rockies and Marlins— had performed during three seasons in the 1990s and two seasons in the early 2000s. Interestingly, the table reveals four key financial matters and insights about one or more of the teams.

First, between 1992 and 2004 the five teams in each league with the largest percentage increases in valuations were the AL's Yankees at 420 percent, Mariners at 361 percent, Red Sox at 292 percent, Tigers at 143 percent and White Sox at 102 percent. In the NL, the teams were the Astros at 268 percent, Giants at 258 percent, Cubs at 255 percent, Cardinals at 220 percent and Dodgers at 196 percent. Indeed, because of the population and other demographic characteristics and special factors at their home sites, five of the teams each had played home games in the very large markets of Boston, Chicago, Los Angeles and New York, three in the large to mid-sized markets of Detroit, Houston

TABLE 2.1. ESTIMATED VALUES OF AL AND
NL TEAMS FOR SELECTED YEARS

Team	1992	1995	1998	2001	2004
AL					
Anaheim Angels	105	90	157	198	241
Baltimore Orioles	130	168	323	335	296
Boston Red Sox	136	143	230	339	533
Chicago White Sox	23	144	214	215	248
Cleveland Indians	81	125	322	372	292
Detroit Tigers	97	106	137	290	235
Kansas City Royals	111	80	108	138	171
Minnesota Twins	95	74	94	99	168
New York Yankees	160	209	362	635	832
Oakland Athletics	124	97	118	149	186
Seattle Mariners	86	92	251	332	396
Tampa Bay Devil Rays	NA*	NA	NA	150	152
Texas Rangers	106	138	254	342	306
Toronto Blue Jays	155	152	141	161	169
NL					
Atlanta Braves	88	163	299	407	374
Arizona Diamondbacks	NA	NA	NA	245	276
Chicago Cubs	101	140	204	247	358
Cincinnati Reds	103	99	136	187	245
Colorado Rockies	NA	133	303	334	285
Florida Marlins	NA	98	159	128	172
Houston Astros	87	97	190	318	320
Los Angeles Dodgers	135	147	236	381	399
Montreal Expos	86	68	87	92	145
Milwaukee Brewers	86	71	127	209	174
New York Mets	145	131	193	454	442
Philadelphia Phillies	96	103	131	158	281
Pittsburgh Pirates	95	62	133	211	217
San Diego Padres	103	67	161	176	265
San Francisco Giants	103	122	188	333	368
St. Louis Cardinals	98	112	174	243	314

* NA means that the team did not exist that year. The Milwaukee Brewers' values during 1992, 1995 and 1998 represented the team when it played in the AL.

Sources: "MLB Cash Flows," at http://www.baseballguru.com cited 9 November 2004; Michael K. Ozanian, "Selective Accounting," *Forbes* (14 December 1998), 124–134; "The Boys of Summer," at http://www.forbes.com cited 9 November 2004; "Forbes Financial 2004 Valuation For MLB Franchise," at http://www.sportsbusinessnews.com cited 5 October 2004.

and San Francisco, and two in the small markets of Seattle and St. Louis. These characteristics and factors included the amenities provided by the teams' ballparks, the successful negotiation of cable network and regional broadcasting deals with media companies, and the outstanding debts of the franchises, quality and stability of ownership and management of these baseball organizations, and the beneficial effects of marketing campaigns in increasing attendance at home games and expanding the fan base.[2]

Second, in 2004 the three highest- and lowest-valued teams were, respectively, the AL's Yankees, Red Sox and Mariners, and the Twins, Blue Jays and Royals. In the NL, these teams were the Mets, Dodgers and Braves, and the Expos, Brewers and Pirates.

Relative to the valuations of two teams, the small-market Mariners in Seattle at $396 million had negotiated a lucrative cable contract and played in state-of-the-art Safeco Field, while the Blue Jays in Toronto at $169 million experienced a change in ownership during 2000 and also, the team had ranked mediocre with respect to gate receipts, revenues from local and regional broadcasts of its games, and other operating revenues (see Tables 2.2 and 2.3).

Third, Table 2.1 also denotes the absolute and relative growth in the valuations of four expansion teams. That is, the Devil Rays in Tampa Bay increased by $2 million or approximately 2 percent, the Diamondbacks in Phoenix by $31 million or 13 percent, the Rockies in Denver by $152 million or 214 percent, and the Marlins in Miami by $74 million or 76 percent. To explain these disparities in growth between teams, the Devil Rays play in an oversaturated sports market and the club has been poorly managed. Meanwhile, the Diamondbacks must compete for fans with the National Basketball Association Suns, National Football League Cardinals and National Hockey League Coyotes. Despite the appeal of 50,400-seat Coors Field, the Rockies appear to have peaked in popularity because of poor performances during recent seasons. Finally, the Marlins had changed owners three times since the late 1990s and the team's ballpark needs to be modernized, or replaced with a baseball-only facility that contains more club seats, luxury suites and concessions than 47,700-seat Pro Player Stadium

Fourth, between 1992 and 2004 the valuations for eight AL and seven NL clubs were unstable, that is, the annualized values rose (fell) and then fell (rose). For example, five AL and six NL teams had depreciated in value from 1992 to 1995 while eight AL and seven NL teams appreciated. Likewise, from 2001 to 2004 ten AL and 13 NL clubs had appreciated in value and four AL and NL clubs had each depreciated. As such, proportionately more of the teams prospered during the latter three-year period, or in 2001 to 2004, than in 1992 to 1995. This occurred, in part, because the public's demand for professional baseball had increased in America since the early 1990s, and because the games of sports teams had generated increasing amounts of cash flows, operating revenues and earnings before taxes. As a result of this prosperity, the average value of AL franchises rose by 160 percent or from $116 million in 1992 to $302 million in 2004, and NL franchises increased by 184 percent or from $102 million in 1992 to $290 million in 2004. It appears, therefore, that the gap in average franchise values between the AL and NL had moderately narrowed due to the popularity of such expansion teams as the Diamondbacks and Rockies and the sluggish growth rates in the estimated values of the Devil Rays and Blue Jays.

In Table 4-3 of his book, *May the Best Team Win*, sports economist and Smith College professor Andrew Zimbalist reported the sales prices of 30 MLB teams that were sold between 1970 and 2002. To compare a sample of these prices with the estimated team values for a particular year in Table 2.1, it was useful to construct and interpret Table 2.2.[3]

For the eight business deals in Table 2.2, the average estimated values of the Tigers, Athletics, Rangers and Giants were overstated by $8.5 million, and the average estimated values of the Mariners, Astros, Cardinals and Dodgers were understated by $50 million. Furthermore, for the broadcast rights and fees in America's second largest media market, which is Los Angeles, the table shows that Rupert Murdoch's News Corporation paid more than a $100 million premium for the Dodgers in 1998. Besides these eight transactions, the sales prices of each expansion team was $95 million for the Marlins and Rockies in 1993, and $130 million for the Diamondbacks and Devil Rays in 1998.

In short, the prices of the eight MLB teams in Table 2.2 that were sold during the 1990s tended to be underestimated by approximately $40–45 million. Perhaps the high sales prices may have happened because prospective owners failed to perform a thorough business study or the owners did not accurately measure the teams' net worth. Anyway, they knowingly or unknowingly overbid to acquire the assets of one or more of the franchises in MLB. So, the methods used by sports economists to estimate the values of teams are flawed, unrealistic and apparently do not reflect the true prices that these baseball businesses would be established in the marketplace from a sale.

Excluding the Tampa Bay Devil Rays and Arizona Diamondbacks, which were also expansion teams, the Florida Marlins was the only MLB franchise that declined in value from 1998 to 2001. Indeed, during those years the Marlins' estimated value fell by $31 million or 20 percent. This meant that the team's worth at $128 million in 2001 ranked it as the third lowest franchise in the league.

Table 2.2. Sales Prices and Values of Various AL and NL Teams, 1992–1998

Team	Year*	Sales Price	Value	Difference
AL				
Detroit Tigers	1992	82	97	-15
Seattle Mariners	1992	106	86	20
Oakland Athletics	1995	85	97	-12
Texas Rangers	1998	250	254	-4
NL				
Houston Astros	1992	115	87	28
San Francisco Giants	1992	100	103	-3
St. Louis Cardinals	1995	150	112	38
Los Angeles Dodgers	1998	350	236	114

* Year is when the teams were sold. Value is the estimated value of the teams in millions of dollars based on the Year in Table 2.1. The Difference column is the Sales Price less Value.

Sources: See the *Note* in Table 2.1; Andrew Zimbalist, *May the Best Team Win: Baseball Economics and Public Policy* (Washington, D.C.: Brookings Institution Press, 2003), 73.

Team Financials

To focus on and be more specific about revenues, and to further expose why and how MLB teams rated as businesses in 2001 from a financial perspective, the late chairman of the Society For American Baseball Research's Business of Baseball Committee,

TABLE 2.3. ATTENDANCE AND FINANCIAL
DATA OF MLB TEAMS, 2001

Team	HomeAtt*	GameRec	MediaMon	OperRev
AL				
Anaheim Angels	2.00	30.21	10.92	26.20
Baltimore Orioles	2.98	53.22	20.99	29.69
Boston Red Sox	2.59	89.74	33.35	29.49
Chicago White Sox	1.77	30.90	30.09	26.29
Cleveland Indians	3.18	69.47	21.08	45.30
Detroit Tigers	1.88	42.30	19.07	21.02
Kansas City Royals	1.54	19.52	6.51	13.27
Minnesota Twins	1.78	17.61	7.27	6.99
New York Yankees	3.26	98.00	56.75	47.06
Oakland Athletics	2.13	24.99	9.46	13.93
Seattle Mariners	3.51	76.57	37.86	56.21
Tampa Bay Devil Rays	1.30	18.19	15.51	28.63
Texas Rangers	2.83	50.66	25.28	34.56
Toronto Blue Jays	1.92	25.36	14.46	14.26
NL				
Atlanta Braves	2.74	62.14	19.99	37.69
Arizona Diamondbacks	2.74	46.51	14.17	32.97
Chicago Cubs	2.78	51.19	23.56	30.64
Cincinnati Reds	1.88	32.10	7.86	6.52
Colorado Rockies	3.12	54.02	18.20	35.20
Florida Marlins	1.26	16.76	15.35	4.04
Houston Astros	2.90	49.16	13.72	36.83
Los Angeles Dodgers	3.02	50.76	27.34	41.10
Montreal Expos	.64	6.41	.54	2.83
Milwaukee Brewers	2.81	46.02	5.92	37.01
New York Mets	2.66	73.97	46.25	38.16
Philadelphia Phillies	1.78	30.44	18.94	7.74
Pittsburgh Pirates	2.40	48.61	9.10	26.60
San Diego Padres	2.38	34.38	12.44	8.50
San Francisco Giants	3.31	67.17	17.20	61.52
St. Louis Cardinals	3.11	67.08	11.91	27.58

* HomeAtt is the 2001 regular season home attendance of each team in millions. GameRec is the teams' total game receipts collected at home during the 2001 MLB season in millions of dollars. The amounts include the revenues from ticket sales but not from luxury suite rentals. MediaMon is each club's local media money, which are the revenues from local television, radio and cable contracts in millions of dollars. OperRev is the clubs' other local operating revenue in millions of dollars. This account includes income from concessions, parking, stadium advertising, luxury boxes and club seats.

Sources: Doug Pappas, "The Numbers: Gate Receipts," at http://www.baseballprospectus.com cited 9 November 2004; Idem., "The Numbers: Local Media Revenues," at http://www.baseballprospectus.com cited 9 November 2004; Idem., "The Numbers: More Revenues," at http://www.baseballprospectus.com cited 9 November 2004.

Doug Pappas, analyzed the sport's teams in a series of articles. Consequently, for this chapter Table 2.3 contains some important financial information and facts that were extracted from Pappas's articles. Exactly like the first column in Table 2.1, the AL and NL teams are each listed in alphabetical order in Table 2.3.[4]

Based on Table 2.3, in 2001 the teams with the highest and lowest home attendances were, respectively, the Mariners, Yankees and Indians, and the Devil Rays, Royals and

White Sox in the AL, and the Giants, Rockies and Cardinals, and the Expos, Marlins and Phillies in the NL. In part, the Mariners, Indians, Giants and Rockies had excellent attendances at home because fans enjoyed these teams' relatively modern ballparks while the Royals, Expos and Phillies had poor attendances in their home stadiums that were each built during the 1970s.

Besides the appeal and condition of their ballparks, the baseball team's attendances were also influenced by the size of the local sports market and ticket prices at home games. These, in turn, determined the amount of game receipts as shown in column three of Table 2.3. To be sure, competitive teams that existed in such relatively large markets as the Yankees and Mets in New York, Red Sox in Boston and Braves in Atlanta, in medium-sized markets like the Giants in San Francisco, and in a small market like the Cardinals in St. Louis, had each earned high game receipts. Excluding the Mariners in Seattle and Indians in Cleveland, the clubs in small markets generally received below-average receipts from home games. There are exceptions, however, as depicted in Table 2.3.

In 2001, Doug Pappas calculated another statistic, labeled revenue per ticket, for MLB teams. That statistic related the quality of the home ballpark with local market size, home attendance and game receipts. To illustrate, at 40,000-seat Comerica Park in Detroit the AL's Tigers placed low in attendance and eighteenth in game receipts but ranked fifth in revenue per ticket. Furthermore, although the NL's Braves and Diamondbacks had nearly tied in attendance, the Braves' game receipts and revenue per ticket far exceeded those of the Diamondbacks. Finally, in 2001 the AL's Red Sox attracted 400,000 fewer spectators than the NL's Dodgers, yet realized $39 million more in game receipts. In sum, these statistics suggest that the financial returns to teams are highly dependent on the local market size, optimal pricing of tickets at regular season games, and the amenities from an existing ballpark at the home site.[5]

In Table 2.3's column four are the millions in revenues that teams had earned from local media companies during 2001. These amounts are interesting to interpret and compare with respect to each of the franchises. For example, although the Yankees and Mets in New York are the dominant teams in local media money, the Yankees ranked seventh at $5.35 and the Mets fourteenth at $4.36 in media dollars per person. In fact, it was the Mariners in Seattle at $10.65, Indians in Cleveland at $7.15 and Rockies in Denver at $7.05 that ranked first, second and third in local media money per capita. These three teams are in contrast to the Tigers in Detroit and Brewers in Milwaukee whose media dollars were each $3.50 per person even though their local media money differed by more than $13 million.

Besides those observations about revenues, other factors may have contributed to the distribution of local media dollars among MLB teams in 2001. For example, in Table 2.3 the allocation of local broadcast monies among teams shows that the media deals signed by the Angels, Cubs and Mets were inferior with respect to the contracts negotiated by the Dodgers, White Sox and Yankees. Since the Dodgers and Yankees are superior baseball organizations, their games are demanded on television, radio and cable by fans in the Los Angeles and New York City areas. Regarding the Chicago area, however, the Cubs' media contracts that totaled $23.56 million appear, for some reason, to be undervalued and/or inaccurately estimated. In his article on this topic, Doug Pappas stated, "An MLB spokesman recently told the *Chicago Tribune* that the superstation part of the Cubs' TV deal is valued separately from the local broadcast rights. The Cubs keep about 30 percent of the superstation money, with the rest paid into the common pool, an arrangement that only increases the incentive to undervalue the Cubs' contract." Nevertheless, unless the Angels, Cubs and Mets become more consistent winners and increase market shares in their areas, the differences in media dollars between the teams will persist, respectively, with the Dodgers in Los Angeles, White Sox in Chicago and Yankees in New York City.[6]

Second, perhaps the implementation of MLB reforms such as revenue sharing and the luxury tax, which reallocate revenues from high- to low-payroll teams, has provided additional funds above the amounts of media money earned locally by the Royals, Twins and Athletics in the AL, and Reds, Expos and Pirates in the NL. However, despite their shortfalls in cash from local television, radio and cable networks, the Twins and Athletics are frequently competitive teams that play above .500 and occasionally win their respective divisions. Alternatively, the Royals, Reds, Expos and Pirates rarely compete for their division titles.

As denoted in column five of Table 2.3, in 2001 the local operating revenues from the ballparks of the Mariners, Yankees, Indians, Giants and Dodgers each exceeded $40 million. In contrast, what are the opportunities to earn more than $10–20 million in operating revenues per year for the Twins, Marlins, Expos, Phillies and Padres? If new ballparks are constructed in Minneapolis and Miami, then the Twins and Marlins, respectively, have the potential to increase their cash flows from concessions, parking, stadium advertising, luxury boxes and club seats. This is evident at the 43,000-seat Citizens Bank Park for the Phillies in Philadelphia and at the 46,000-seat Petco Park for the Padres in San Diego. More specifically, these stadiums are likely to produce generous amounts of cash for the franchises because they have more amenities and other attractions for spectators relative to the former ballparks, which were 62,400-seat Veterans Stadium in Philadelphia and 67,500-seat Qualcomm Stadium in San Diego.[7]

Summary

This chapter revealed, for various years, the distribution of estimated values and other financial aspects of teams in the AL and NL. With respect to the data, Table 2.1 showed that the majority of teams had non-constant but positive changes in values from 1992 to 2004. This occurred, in part, because of new or refurbished ballparks, growth in operating and media revenues, and other economic and demographic factors.

In Table 2.2, there were four of the eight teams whose sales prices exceeded their estimated values. That is, the new owners had likely overbid and paid a premium for these teams. Meanwhile, Table 2.3 displayed the home attendances and three revenues sources of fourteen AL and sixteen NL teams. The New York Yankees ranked first or second in each category of revenues while the Montreal Expos placed thirtieth in each category. Besides the Yankees, other teams such as the Seattle Mariners and San Francisco Giants scored above average in home attendances and revenues, and besides the Expos, the Minnesota Twins and Florida Marlins rated below average in game receipts, media monies and other operating revenues. Therefore, as expected the data collected for this chapter confirmed that AL and NL teams sited in large-markets tend to be more highly valued, and generate greater cash flows from local media deals and their ballparks than the teams located in medium-sized and small markets.

3. Replacing Ballparks: History and Consequences for MLB Teams

During the 1990s, the operating losses had accumulated for several American League (AL) and National League (NL) baseball franchises. These losses occurred, in part, because of the substantial disparities that existed between the revenue growth rates and payroll amounts of large- and small-market clubs. As a result, in July 2000 an economic study committee urged Major League Baseball (MLB) officials to increase revenue sharing from high to low payroll clubs and second, to relax restrictions and allow one or more economically inferior teams to move from their home sites to another city located in perhaps, a more populated metropolitan area. Furthermore, as committee member and former Senate Majority Leader George Mitchell remarked, "Clubs that have little likelihood of securing a new ballpark at their current location ... should have the opportunity to relocate."[1]

Indeed, Mitchell's comment infers that the construction of a new ballpark in the city of a professional baseball club will likely boost the home team's attendances and cash flows, provide an opportunity for the respective franchise owner to expand his club's payroll and employ superior players, and thus upgrade his team to become relatively more competitive with other clubs in the division. Accordingly, "Replacing Ballparks" focuses on the frequency, value and impact of a sample of new ballparks that were constructed during years from the early 1900s to the present for various AL and NL teams. To determine and measure the frequency, value and impact of new venues, some historical data will be included in the discussion and tables such as the ballparks' name, construction cost and ownership, and the changes in the capacities and home attendances that resulted when the former ballparks were replaced by new facilities. Finally, there are a few examples that illustrate how new ballparks had affected specific teams' performances for a series of years.

Current Ballparks

To compete during MLB's 2005 season, there were 14 AL and 16 NL teams. The home ballparks of these 30 clubs are listed in the first column of Table 3.1. Generally, the table reflects that one AL and one NL team have played all home games in their original ballparks. In the AL, this team was the Tampa Bay Devil Rays, which has played at 45,000-

seat Tropicana Field in St. Petersburg, Florida since becoming an expansion team in 1998. In the NL, the Florida Marlins have competed at home games in 43,000-seat Pro Player Stadium in Miami since 1993.

In short, at least 28 of the teams that are represented in Table 3.1 has experienced the exposure and challenge of playing their home games in different ballparks when the previous stadiums were declared obsolete and replaced. Finally, the table reveals that the

TABLE **3.1.** NAMES AND CHARACTERISTICS
OF **MLB** BALLPARKS, 2004 SEASON

Ballpark	Capacity*	Cost	Pub%	Owner
AL				
Ameriquest Field at Arlington	49.2	191	71	Sports Facilities Authority
Angel Stadium	45.0	24	100	City of Anaheim
Camden Yards	48.3	100	100	Maryland Stadium Authority
Comerica Park	40.0	300	35	County Stadium Authority
Fenway Park	36.3	1	0	Boston Red Sox
Jacobs Field	43.3	175	48	Cuyahoga County
Kauffman Stadium	40.6	70	100	Jackson County
Metrodome	55.8	68	100	Sports Facilities Commission
Network Associates Coliseum	48.2	26	100	City of Oakland/Alameda Co.
Safeco Field	46.6	517	66	County Stadium Authority
SkyDome	50.5	500	11	Interbrew/Penfund/Can.Bank
Tropicana Field	45.0	138	100	City of St. Petersburg
U.S. Cellular Field	46.0	167	100	Sports Facilities Authority
Yankee Stadium	58.0	3	100	City of New York
NL				
Bank One Ballpark	48.6	349	68	County Stadium District
Busch Stadium	49.7	NA	0	St. Louis Cardinals
Citizens Bank Park	43.0	346	50	City of Philadelphia
Coors Field	50.4	215	78	Metro Stadium District
Dodger Stadium	56.0	23	100	Los Angeles Dodgers
Great American Ballpark	42.1	297	100	City of Cincinnati/County
Miller Park	43.0	400	64	Wisconsin Sports District
Minute Maid Park	41.0	250	72	Houston Sports Authority
Olympic Stadium	43.7	999	100	City of Montreal
Petco Park	46.0	456	50	City of San Diego/ Padres
PNC Park	38.4	262	100	Sports Exhibition Authority
Pro Player Stadium	43.0	115	0	Florida Marlins
SBC Park	41.0	255	4	San Francisco Giants
Shea Stadium	55.6	26	100	City of New York
Turner Field	49.8	235	0	Atlanta Braves
Wrigley Field	38.9	1	100	Chicago Cubs

* Capacity is the total number of ballpark seats in thousands. Cost is the construction outlays in millions of U.S. dollars. The cost of Busch Stadium is NA, or not available. Pub% is the proportion of the construction costs paid by taxpayers. Owner is self-explanatory. After they were built, nine of the original ballparks were renamed. These are Ameriquest Field at Arlington, Angel Stadium, Kauffman Stadium, Net Associates Coliseum, Tropicana Field and U.S. Cellular Field in the AL, and Minute Maid Park, Pro Player Stadium and SBC Park in the NL.

Source: See "Ballparks," at http://www.ballparks.com cited 24 November 2004, and the teams' websites at http://www.mlb.com.

oldest venues in each league included Fenway Park built in 1912 for the Boston Red Sox, Wrigley Field (then named Weegham Park) in 1914 for the Chicago Cubs, and Yankee Stadium in 1923 for the New York Yankees. Alternatively, the newest venues constructed are Citizens Bank Park for the Philadelphia Phillies and Petco Park for the San Diego Padres in 2004, and Miller Park for the Milwaukee Brewers in 2001.[2]

Besides these general facts, Table 3.1 primarily identifies in columns one to five some specific business aspects about the 30 ballparks. That is, the table reports the name, capacity, construction cost, public subsidy as a percent, and the ownership of each venue. To clarify how these facts relate to the business and success of professional baseball teams, the following information is discussed beginning with column one.

Naming rights are a growing source of local revenues that clubs retain and thus do not share with the league. According to Denver-based sports marketing consultant Dean Bonham, "In 1988 there were only three naming-rights deals at major league sports facilities, with a total value of $25 million. Today, there are 67 such deals valued at $3.63 billion." Based on my research of this topic, in Table 3.1 there are four ballparks named for current or former owners. They are Kauffman Stadium in Kansas City for Ewing Kauffman, Jacobs Field in Cleveland for Richard E. Jacobs, Turner Field in Atlanta for Ted Turner, and Busch Stadium in St. Louis for August Busch. The majority of clubs, however, leases the naming rights to corporations in the beverage, financial and communications industries, and secures a long-term commitment of at least ten years. For the values and variety of rights in MLB and other professional sports, see the website leagueoffans.org. This website provides a summary of stadium rights deals for MLB teams as of 2003. The information on the website includes the clubs and stadium names, and brief descriptions about the naming rights deals, who the sponsors are, and profiles of the sponsors.[3]

In Table 3.1's second column are the ballparks' seating capacities that existed during the 2004 season. Based on the distribution, the AL and NL ballparks averaged, respectively, 47,600 and 46,600 seats. Relative to the teams, the New York Yankees, Minneapolis Twins and Toronto Bluejays in the AL, and the Los Angeles Dodgers, New York Mets and Colorado Rockies in the NL played their home games in the largest venues, while the smallest ballparks existed for the AL's Boston Red Sox, Detroit Tigers and Kansas City Royals, and for the NL's Pittsburgh Pirates, Chicago Cubs, and San Francisco Giants and Houston Astros (tied for third). Interestingly, the Royals in Kansas City and Pirates in Pittsburgh play in small markets, the Twins in Minneapolis and Rockies in Denver are located in small to medium-sized metropolitan markets, and the Yankees and Mets in the New York City area and Red Sox in Boston, Tigers in Detroit, Cubs in Chicago, Giants in San Francisco and Astros in Houston compete at home in large metropolitan markets. Given those wide variations in markets and populations, and in their ballparks' capacities, in 2005 the Angels, Brewers, Cardinals, Cubs, Red Sox, Yankees set all-time franchise records for total attendances, while in 2004 the Bluejays, Royals and Giants experienced a decline in attendances. Consequently, the revenues of these and other clubs are contingent, in part, on the size and location of the home site stadiums.

The ballparks construction costs listed in column three are determined by many factors. These include the local and regional populations, inflation and cost-of-living indices, age and capacity of the venue, and the taxpayer subsidy percentages and owners as reported in columns four and five. The three most expensive baseball ballparks to build were Montreal's Olympic Stadium in 1976 at approximately $1 billion, Seattle's Safeco

Field in 1999 at $517 million, and Toronto's SkyDome in 1989 at $500 million. Because the cost valuations in Table 3.1 exclude ballpark renovations, rehabilitations and other projects, the total capital expenditures on the facilities are normally understated especially for the oldest venues such as Fenway Park, Yankee Stadium and Wrigley Field. As such, the cost estimates of the most recent baseball structures more accurately reflect the purchasing power of current dollars and economic conditions.

As reported in column four, 14 or 47 percent of the ballparks were entirely subsidized with public monies and four or 13 percent with private capital. The variation in subsidies per ballpark of the remaining 12 ranged from 4 percent for the Giants at SBC Park in San Francisco to 78 percent for the Rockies at Coors Field in Denver.

Since 2000, on average taxpayers have assumed 55 percent of the construction costs of three stadiums, that is, Miller Park in Milwaukee, Citizens Bank Park in Philadelphia and Petco Park in San Diego. Furthermore, as indicated in column five, two of these are publicly owned and the City of San Diego and the Padres jointly own Petco Park.

To recap, a total of 20 or 66 percent of the ballparks are publicly owned, three or 10 percent have joint ownership, and seven or 24 percent are privately owned. In short, it is a combination of hotel, land use, sales, transportation and other types of local and municipal taxes on businesses and consumers that are collected to pay the interest and principal on the public's debts, and to represent the public's investment in sports venues for which professional baseball teams are the primary tenants.

Former and Replacement Ballparks

Numerous ballparks for professional baseball teams have been built, abandoned and demolished since the early 1900s. For our purposes, a sample of 24 former and 24 replacement venues in the AL and NL were identified and selected for this study. Besides the names and first year in operation of the 24 replacement ballparks, the capacities and attendances of the sample for a series of baseball seasons are reported in Table 3.2. In detail, columns one, two, four and six contain some important statistics about the 24 replacement stadiums, and columns three and five about the former or replaced ballparks.[4]

That is, before or during 2004 new rights were acquired to promote Coca Cola's Minute Maid products in Houston and to showcase U.S. Cellular Inc. in Chicago and SBC Inc. in San Francisco. Also, the publicly owned Anaheim Stadium was re-titled Edison International Field of Anaheim in 1997 and then Angel Stadium in 2003; Royals Stadium changed its name to Municipal Stadium in 1969 and then to Kauffman Stadium in 1973; and the Ballpark at Arlington became Ameriquest Field in Arlington in 2004. Nevertheless, 24 or 80 percent of the ballparks have retained their identities since the first season as a replacement facility.

An examination of columns three and four in Table 3.2 provides three essential differences in capacities between the 24 former and the 24 listed replacement ballparks. First, the average capacity declined by 6 percent, or from 49,100 to 46,600 seats in the AL relative to a decrease of 11 percent, or from 51,800 to 45,800 seats in the NL. Second, the capacities of six, or 50 percent of the replacement ballparks in the AL and five, or 42 percent in the NL exceeded those of the former venues. Third, the most significant capacity increases occurred in 1912 when 36,300-seat Fenway Park replaced 11,500-seat Huntington Avenue Baseball Grounds, and in 1916 when 38,900-seat Weegham

TABLE 3.2. REPLACEMENT BALLPARKS, BY
LEAGUE AND YEAR, 1912–2001

Ballpark	Year*	Capacity Former	Capacity Replacement	Attendance Former	Attendance Replacement
AL					
Fenway Park	1912	11.5	36.3	.60	.50
Yankee Stadium	1923	55.0	58.0	1.18	.92
Anaheim Stadium	1966	56.0	45.0	.72	1.27
Royals Stadium	1973	35.5	40.6	.77	1.22
Metrodome	1982	45.9	55.8	.76	1.13
SkyDome	1989	43.7	50.5	2.60	3.75
New Comiskey Park	1991	52.0	46.0	1.39	2.73
Camden Yards	1992	53.3	48.3	2.53	3.24
Ballpark in Arlington	1994	43.5	49.2	2.24	2.45
Jacobs Field	1994	74.5	43.3	1.48	2.71
Safeco Field	1999	66.0	46.6	2.85	3.18
Comerica Park	2000	52.4	40.0	1.58	1.98
NL					
Wrigley Field	1916	16.0	38.9	.27	.37
Dodger Stadium	1962	94.6	56.0	2.04	2.51
Shea Stadium	1964	55.0	55.6	1.00	1.74
Busch Stadium	1966	30.5	49.7	1.18	1.93
Olympic Stadium	1977	28.5	43.7	.86	1.65
Coors Field	1995	76.1	50.4	3.88	3.64
Turner Field	1997	52.0	49.8	2.66	3.37
Enron Field	2000	59.8	41.0	2.39	2.82
Great American Ballpark	2000	39.0	42.1	1.88	2.11
Pacific Bell Park	2000	58.0	41.0	1.89	3.29
Miller Park	2001	53.1	43.0	1.69	2.16
PNC Park	2001	59.0	38.4	1.65	1.95

* Year is the initial season of the home team in the replacement ballpark. For example, the Boston Red Sox's first season in Fenway Park occurred in 1912. Weegham Park was built in 1914 and the Cubs played there beginning in 1916. Then, Weegham Park was renamed Cubs Park in 1920 and then six years later renamed Wrigley Field. Capacity and Attendance are, respectively, the average three-year ballpark capacities, in thousands, and attendances, in millions, of the home teams in the former and replacement ballparks. That is, during 1909–1911 the Red Sox played in the 11,500-seat Huntington Avenue Grounds before approximately 600,000 spectators per season, while during 1912–1914 the club played in 36,300-seat Fenway Park before 500,000 per season. Table 3.2 excludes the ballparks of the Oakland Athletics and Tampa Bay Devil Rays in the AL, and the Arizona Diamondbacks, Florida Marlins, Philadelphia Phillies and San Diego Padres in the NL. The Athletics, Devil Rays, Diamondbacks and Marlins have each played their home games in one ballpark, while the Phillies opened the 2004 season in 43,000-seat Citizens Bank Park and the Padres in 46,000-seat Petco Park. The table also excludes the ballparks of failed MLB franchises such as the Seattle Pilots and Washington Senators.

Source: See the websites http://www.mlb.com, http://www.ballparks.com, http://www.baseball-almanac.com, and http://www.ballparkwatch.com.

Park (renamed Cubs Park in 1920 and Wrigley Field in 1926) replaced 16,000-seat West Side Grounds.

Meanwhile, in 1962 Dodger Stadium had 38,600 fewer seats than the Memorial Coliseum in Los Angeles, and in 1994 Jacobs Field did not contain 31,200 seats that were available in Cleveland Stadium. These capacity differences can be explained as follows.

Boston and Chicago were relatively large baseball markets even during the 1910s, and the Memorial Coliseum and Cleveland Stadium were primarily built to accommodate professional football games rather than for competition between MLB teams. For sure, these four stadiums account for much of the total variation in seating capacities of the 24 former and replacement ballparks represented in Table 3.2.

Given the measured capacity differences of the facilities at each home site, the next issue to be considered is how much did average attendances change during the initial three-year period at the new ballparks? Based on the numbers in columns five and six of Table 3.2, the AL's average three-year attendance increased by 34 percent at the replacement ballparks from the former venues, and the NL's by 29 percent. However, at Yankee Stadium in New York City and Coors Field in Denver, Colorado, the average three-year attendances declined relative to, respectively, what they were at the Polo Grounds and Mile High Stadium. In part, the Yankees were more popular and competitive at the Polo Grounds during 1920–1922 when Babe Ruth was traded by the Boston Red Sox, joined the team in New York City and excelled as a player. Alternatively, although the Colorado Rockies' average winning percentage increased from .433 in 1993–1994 at Mile High Stadium to .523 in 1995–1996 at Coors Field, the team's average attendance at home marginally decreased from 3.88 million to 3.64 million. This happened because Coors Field had less capacity than Mile High Stadium, and also because the sports fans in the Denver area allocated their disposable income to sports and enjoyed attending football games played at Mile High Stadium, which was the home site of the successful NFL Denver Broncos.

It is apparent from the sample of ballparks that except for Yankee Stadium and Coors Field, the average 20-year-old attendances at 22 replacement ballparks had increased regardless of how capacity had changed. This was evident especially in the AL at Comiskey Park in Chicago for the White Sox and at Jacobs Field in Cleveland for the Indians, and in the NL at Olympic Stadium in Montreal for the (former) Expos and at Pacific Bell Park (now SBC Park) in San Francisco for the Giants.

Given the enthusiasm from, and expenditures by spectators who watch their home team compete at games in a new ballpark, a team's fluctuation in winning percentages should also be a factor in determining changes in attendances and cash flows. Notwithstanding, when the Toronto Bluejays' average winning percentage dropped from .572 in 1986–1988 at Exhibition Stadium to .560 in 1989–1991 at the SkyDome, and the Texas Rangers from .543 in 1991–1993 at Arlington Stadium to .536 in 1994–1996 at The Ballpark in Arlington, the home attendances of the teams rose, respectively, by 44 and 9 percent. Alternatively, when the average winning percentage of the Minneapolis Twins increased from .478 in 1979–1981 at Metropolitan Stadium to .498 in 1982–1984 at the Metrodome, and the Los Angeles Dodgers from .573 in 1959–1961 at the Memorial Coliseum to .591 in 1962–1964 at Dodger Stadium, the home attendance of the Twins grew by 49 percent and the Dodgers by 23 percent.

These affects illustrate that in making decisions about viewing baseball events, the marginal benefits realized by spectators who attend games in a new ballpark generally exceed the marginal costs of tickets, parking and food. Consequently, at least in the short-run a majority of baseball fans in a market will attend and support their team's home games in a new venue despite the team's quality. As a result, the cash inflows from ticket and concession sales will likely inflate the team's revenues if prices at the ballpark remain constant or increase for the regular season.

Summary

This chapter revealed how and why the construction of new ballparks for teams in MLB has important business implications for the AL and NL, and for specific franchise owners and communities, and especially for baseball fans. Because of increasing construction costs and taxpayer resistance to higher taxes, baseball and government policymakers will need to research and study publications such as "Replacing Ballparks" for optimal decisions about stadium capacities, naming rights, and financial and ownership issues.[5]

4. Relocating Teams in Professional Baseball

The National League (NL) was officially organized in 1876 with franchises placed in Boston, Chicago, Cincinnati, Hartford, Louisville, New York, Philadelphia and St. Louis. After several entries, resignations and/or replacements of franchises from 1877 to 1886, the NL consisted of one team in Boston, Chicago, Detroit, Kansas City, New York, Philadelphia, St. Louis and Washington, D.C. Then, in 1901 the American League (AL) was established with franchises located in Baltimore, Boston, Chicago, Cleveland, Detroit, Milwaukee, Philadelphia and Washington, D.C. In short, each league had formed with eight franchises that operated in cities with large, medium and small metropolitan populations.[1]

For business purposes, and because of various demographic, economic and sport-specific reasons, the relocation of teams in the NL began in 1887 and 15 years later in the AL. Indeed, from 1887 to 2005 six NL and eight AL teams had moved from one city to another. From a historical perspective, these 14 relocations are listed by league in Table 4.1.

Relocation Studies

In their book, *Relocating Teams and Expanding Leagues in Professional Sports: How the Major Leagues Respond to Market Conditions*, authors Frank P. Jozsa Jr. and John J. Guthrie Jr. analyzed the movements of Major League Baseball (MLB) franchises from the early 1950s to the mid–1990s. However, since their book, which was published in 1999, focused on the activities of the U.S.–based sports leagues after World War II, Jozsa and Guthrie had decided to exclude the moves by the St. Louis Cardinals to Indianapolis in 1887, Milwaukee Brewers to St. Louis in 1902 and Baltimore Orioles to New York in 1903. Furthermore, since the league's approval to transfer the Montreal Expos to Washington, D.C. and rename the team as the Nationals had occurred in late 2004, the facts of that relocation are also not analyzed in *Relocating Teams and Expanding Leagues in Professional Sports*.[2]

To examine, therefore, ten of the franchise movements in MLB that are listed in Table 4.1, there were tables in Chapters 1, 3 and 5 of *Relocating Teams and Expanding Leagues in Professional Sports* that contained various statistics and other data about team perfor-

Table 4.1. NL and AL Team Relocations, 1887–2005

Year	Team	Pre-Move City	Team	Post-Move City
NL				
1887	Cardinals	St. Louis	Cardinals	Indianapolis
1953	Braves	Boston	Braves	Milwaukee
1958	Dodgers	Brooklyn	Dodgers	Los Angeles
1958	Giants	New York	Giants	San Francisco
1966	Braves	Milwaukee	Braves	Atlanta
2005	Expos*	Montreal	Nationals	Washington, D.C.
AL				
1902	Brewers	Milwaukee	Browns	St. Louis
1903	Orioles	Baltimore	Yankees	New York
1953	Browns	St. Louis	Orioles	Baltimore
1954	Athletics	Philadelphia	Athletics	Kansas City
1961	Senators	Washington, D.C.	Twins	Minneapolis/St. Paul
1967	Athletics	Kansas City	Athletics	Oakland
1970	Pilots	Seattle	Brewers	Milwaukee
1972	Senators	Washington, D.C.	Rangers	Arlington

* In late 2004, the Expos were renamed the Nationals in Washington, D.C. This relocation was unanimously approved by MLB based, in part, on the construction of a new ballpark somewhere in the D.C. area for the Nationals.

Sources: "MLB Franchise Chronology," at http://www.mlb.com cited 9 November 2004; Frank P. Jozsa, Jr. and John J. Guthrie, Jr., *Relocating Teams and Expanding Leagues in Professional Sports: How the Major Leagues Respond to Market Conditions* (Westport, CT: Quorum Books, 1999), 23, 46.

mances, regular season attendances, and the presence of other professional sports teams at the pre- and post-move sites. Furthermore, the tables included relevant information with respect to the pre- and post-move cities' populations, per capita personal incomes and percentage growths in total population.

As a result of their research of MLB, Jozsa and Guthrie concluded that, first, the population and population growth of cities are more important factors than per capita personal income in relocation decisions made by team owners; second, a proportion of baseball teams that moved had fewer competitors, or other professional team sports clubs at the post-move site; third, the attendances of teams improved at the post-move site while their performances remained about the same; fourth, the relocated teams' estimated values tended to increase because of new or renovated ballparks at the post-move site; fifth, after constructing an index that combined and measured the pre- and post-move performances, attendances and values of eight teams, a large majority or six of the teams ranked average or superior in quality at their post-move sites relative to the pre-move sites. The Brewers in Milwaukee and Twins in Minneapolis, however, did worse at their post-move sites because of below-average win-loss percentages, weak attendances and marginal increases in their estimated market values.

Meanwhile, the superior teams at their post-move sites were the Orioles in Baltimore, Braves in Atlanta and Dodgers in Los Angeles, and the average teams that relocated were the Giants in San Francisco, Athletics in Oakland and Rangers in Arlington; and sixth, the small-market teams that relocated will struggle to compete in their respective divisions unless the league adopts more liberal policies and expands the redistribution of operating revenues from the large market franchises to such clubs as the Athletics, Twins and Brewers.

Besides *Relocating Teams and Expanding Leagues in Professional Sports*, other authors have published books and articles that theoretically and empirically analyzed why, when and which team relocations have occurred in MLB. In 1974, for example, sports economist Roger G. Noll edited *Government and the Sports Business*. This book discussed some reforms and the implementation of government policies that would make the allocation of baseball teams more efficient and better for consumers and the sport especially in the long run. As a group, Noll and other economists have tended to criticize MLB because the league has the power and authority to restrict franchise movements from city A to B, and to not permit team owners from making decisions unilaterally or without the group's inputs. That is, MLB prefers that teams remain at one location if feasible because the frequent movements of teams would discourage local fans from becoming attached to their home clubs, would create organizational instability due to frequent relocations, and would exploit cities and communities who demand to watch live professional baseball games during the regular season and post season. As a result of MLB's authority to restrict relocations, no teams in MLB had moved between 1972 and 2003.[3]

Expos Problems

After MLB had agreed to add four new franchises and accept bids offered by prospective owners, in 1969 the AL expanded with teams nicknamed the Royals in Kansas City, Kansas and Mariners in Seattle, Washington. Meanwhile, that year the NL grew with teams being branded as the Padres in San Diego, California and Expos in Montreal, Canada.

As reflected in the tables of Chapter 2 of this book, from a financial perspective the Expos' franchise has floundered, in part, because of its negligent proprietors in Montreal, especially since the early-to-mid–1990s. As a result, the team has been unable to establish and sustain a fan base, and in 2001 the franchise's annual game receipts of about $6–7 million, local media money of $500,00–600,000 and annual operating revenues of $2–3 million were dismal and ranked thirtieth or last when compared with the other clubs in MLB. Even though the Expos had played competitively in its division during a few regular seasons, the club's best players such as pitcher Pedro Martinez and outfielder Vladimir Guerrero eventually became free agents and joined other teams for whom they signed long-term contracts and earned substantially more money. Thus, it was apparent that in order to retain their highly skilled players and compete to win division titles and league championships, the club needed to replace Olympic Stadium with a new ballpark in downtown Montreal. When various proposals to finance a new stadium were rejected by Canadian taxpayers and/or local politicians during the mid-to-late 1990s and early 2000s, the fate of the Expos became newsworthy and a much-discussed topic since the franchise's long-term existence in Montreal was questionable.[4]

In 2001, rumors had circulated that MLB was evaluating whether to fold and/or consolidate some combination of small-market teams including the Montreal Expos and Florida Marlins in the NL, and the Minnesota Twins and Tampa Bay Devil Rays in the AL. However, instead of contracting or consolidating one or more of these teams, in 2002 the league decided to acquire the Expos for $120 million from owner Jeffrey Loria and his minority partners, and then operate the franchise until new owners could be identified and approved to purchase the club as an investment and perhaps revive it. When investors did not offer to bid on, own and reinvigorate the team in Montreal, in 2004 MLB decided to vacate Montreal and find a new home site for the Expos. Besides considering the local and regional population totals and consumer disposable income levels, and other demographic and economic factors, the league's most important criteria in choosing a city to relocate the club to was the availability and quality of a ballpark at the new site.[5]

Before analyzing the managerial decision by MLB to move the Expos from Montreal to Washington, D.C. prior to the 2005 season, Table 4.2 is presented. Essentially, the table reflects the annual performances and attendances of the team from 1990 to 2004, and whether the move from Montreal was justified from a business and organizational perspective.

TABLE 4.2. EXPOS TEAM CHARACTERISTICS, 1990–2004

Year	WL*	GB	POS	ATT
1990	.525	10	3rd	1.373
1991	.441	26	6th	.934
1992	.537	9	2nd	1.669
1993	.580	3	2nd	1.641
1994	.649	NA	NA	1.276
1995	.458	24	5th	1.309
1996	.543	8	2nd	1.616
1997	.481	23	4th	1.497
1998	.401	41	4th	.918
1999	.420	35	4th	.772
2000	.414	28	4th	.926
2001	.420	20	5th	.642
2002	.512	19	2nd	.812
2003	.512	18	4th	1.025
2004	.414	29	5th	.748

* The column WL is the Expos' win-loss percentages for fifteen regular seasons. GB is the number of regular season games that the Expos finished behind the division leader, POS is the team's final position in its division, and ATT is the team's home attendances in hundreds of thousands at Olympic Stadium in Montreal. NA means not applicable because of the player's strike in 1994. When the strike occurred, the Expos were in first place of their division.

Sources: See "Team Sites," at http://www.mlb.com cited 10 December 2004.

As depicted in the respective columns of Table 4.2, on average the Expos won nearly 49 percent of its games, finished approximately 21 games behind the division leader and in third or fourth place in its division, and realized a home attendance of 1.143 million fans per season. Furthermore, since expansion in 1969 the club's only postseason appearance occurred in 1981. That year, the Expos were defeated 3–2 by the Los Angeles Dodgers in the NL Championship Series. In 1994, however, the Expos led the NL East by six games when MLB players struck on August 11. Unfortunately, play never resumed that season so the playoffs and World Series were cancelled.

After studying their histories of performances for regular seasons and postseasons, the Florida Marlins and Minnesota Twins had been more competitive in their respective divisions than the Expos, while the Tampa Bay Devil Rays generally improved and played better against its AL East division rivals, that is, the New York Yankees, Boston Red Sox, Toronto Blue Jays and Baltimore Orioles. In short, the Expos remained inferior relative to the Marlins, Twins and Devil Rays not only with respect to the total amounts of inflows of local media money, game receipts and operating revenues, but also to the Marlins and Twins in regular season and post season performances, and to those clubs and the Devil Rays in home site attendances.

Because the Expos' financial condition extremely deteriorated during the late 1990s and early 2000s, MLB allowed the team to generate more revenues from attendances by playing several regular season home games in Hiram Bithorn Stadium in San Juan, Puerto Rico rather than in Olympic Stadium in Montreal, Canada. Meanwhile, the league's officials had numerous meetings to evaluate other U.S. and Central American cities as future sites to host the team. Indeed, Las Vegas in Nevada, Portland in Oregon, Sacramento in California, Charlotte in North Carolina, Orlando in Florida, Norfolk in Virginia and Washington, D.C., and also Mexico City and Monterrey in Mexico and San Juan in Puerto Rico were each mentioned on one or more occasions in the media as a potential new home city for the Expos. Based on the results, which of these places was deemed the best location by the league?[6]

MLB Selects Site

Finally, after a two-year search, in late September of 2004 MLB announced that the nation's capital was chosen as the preferred city to relocate the team. The deal, which was spearheaded by the District's Mayor Anthony Williams, included the following details: first, the Expos would be renamed, stay in the NL East and likely change the color and style of its logos and team uniforms; second, the team would play the 2005–2007 regular seasons in the oval, two-decked, 43-year-old RFK Stadium, which was a facility that required $13 million in renovations to upgrade it to meet MLB standards; third, a new $400–600 million ballpark would be built at a proposed site in Washington, D.C., that is, along the Anacostia River waterfront near M and South Capital streets; and fourth, MLB would negotiate with, and likely provide monetary compensation to Baltimore Orioles owner Peter Angelos who had opposed the site of the new ballpark because it was located about 35 miles from his club's stadium at Camden Yards.

According to an economic impact study of the relocation as conducted by the Maryland Stadium Authority, and because 25 percent of the Orioles' fans reside in the Washington metropolitan area, the Orioles' regular season home attendance would significantly decline. This means less revenue for the Authority from ticket taxes and other sources but more savings on stadium maintenance, security and other operating bills. In total, the Authority estimated that its net annual loss would be at least $2.6 million while the Orioles forego some revenues but not enough to threaten the viability of the franchise in Baltimore.[7]

According to Mayor Williams, to finance the new ballpark would require lease payments from the new team owners, taxes on big businesses that are located in the D.C. area, and taxes on the revenues generated by the ballpark. Specifically, Williams said, "Not one dime for this ballpark is coming from D.C. revenues. Money that you would expect to fund schools, to fund recreation centers, to fund street repairs will continue to do just that. Look what's happened around new ballparks in Denver, San Francisco and San Diego. The same kind of development is going to happen in Washington, D.C." As such, the project was estimated to generate 3,500 new construction jobs and an additional $15 million in direct revenues per year for the U.S.'s capital city.[8]

A number of interesting and controversial issues had arisen before, during and after the decision to relocate the Expos occurred. These were as follows. One, 14 former Expos minority partners including Fairmont Hotel and Resorts Inc., grocer Loblaw Companies, and Canada's biggest telecommunications company BCE Inc., filed a federal lawsuit to obtain a court injunction to keep the team in Montreal. The group charged that former managing partner Jeffrey Loria had sabotaged their efforts to build a new stadium in Montreal, and that Loria alienated sponsors and undermined efforts to keep the franchise in the city because he planned to move it from the outset. The lawsuit of the minority partners was voided, however, when an arbitration panel concluded that Loria did not commit fraud or breach his fiduciary duty to the minority partners. As an aside, MLB Commissioner Bud Selig and the league were not parties to the arbitration.[9]

Two, during 2003 and 2004 MLB had to assess and determine the economic value and validity of various bids from prospective investors and ownership groups. These consisted, for example, of a nine-member management team called the Washington Baseball Club, which was headed by former Texas Rangers minority partner Fred Malek. This group included various limited partners and such investors as former Washington Redskins great Darrell Green, District power broker Vernon Jordan, the former president of Walt Disney productions Dennis Hightower, and Fannie Mae Chairman Franklin D. Raines. Based on a previous agreement with the District, the Club had the exclusive right to operate a baseball team at RFK Stadium and at the proposed ballpark on the Anacostia waterfront.[10]

Beside the Washington Baseball Club, individuals and other ownership groups who were expected to bid for the Expos consisted of, first, the Virginia Baseball Club that wanted to place the team somewhere in densely populated Northern Virginia. This group spent at least $4 million to attract a MLB team to the area and had allocated funds to the Virginia Stadium Authority to establish a web site titled www.baseballinva.org, and to diligently study and identify a place to construct a 47,000-seat, $300 million baseball stadium; second, an investment syndicate organized by former NL Atlanta Braves, NBA Hawks and NHL Thrashers president Stan Kasten who is a close friend of commissioner Bud Selig. Kasten operated the Ted Turner/Time Warner sports empire in Atlanta and oversaw the construction of Turner Field; third, Long Island real estate builder Mark Broxmeyer, who had political connections in the Washington, D.C. area and raised over $100,000 for President Bush's reelection in 2004; fourth, Cablevision boss and entrepreneur Charles Dolan, who had attempted to purchase the Boston Red Sox in 2001–2002 for $750 million; and fifth, the relatively unknown DSG Baseball organization located in Nashville, Tennessee. This group was led by Memphis investment banker Brian Saulsberry, who is a Howard University graduate and the general partner of the DSG Investment Fund.

Three, to protect his Baltimore Orioles franchise from financial damages, the team's owner Peter Angelos had negotiated with MLB president Bob DuPuy to ensure that the Orioles' locally derived revenue did not fall below a benchmark amount of about $130 million, and that the Orioles' resale value was at least $360 million. Furthermore, the discussions between Angelos and DuPuy reportedly included a regional sports network that would be created by MLB to produce and market the local on-air and cable broadcasts of both clubs into their shared market of nearly eight million people. As an aside, in 2004 the combined Washington-Baltimore area is the fourth largest media market in the U.S.[11]

Four, there were various business incentives and requirements to locate the optimum site for the stadium in the Washington, D.C. area, and to determine the most efficient method to finance its construction. As such, the deal between MLB and the District to relocate the Expos to the area was contingent upon the District's City Council to pass a funding package by December 31, 2004 for building the new stadium and a contribution of $13 million to refurbish RFK Stadium before the regular baseball season began in April of 2005. Nonetheless, to minimize subsidies from D.C. taxpayers and save money on the new ballpark, the Council's chairperson Linda W. Cropp — a 57-year-old former public school teacher — proceeded to recommend a plan that featured $300–350 million of private funds for the project. In mid–November of 2004, she even postponed the date for Council members to vote on Mayor Williams' bill to finance the stadium's construction costs. Then, in early December of 2004 some Council members incurred scheduling conflicts, which delayed the vote.[12]

Meanwhile, Williams and Cropp met and compromised to offer a financing deal to the Council. Ultimately, the Council reached a consensus and agreed that expenditures for the stadium should be capped, that there was an opportunity for private money to be invested in the stadium, and that Mayor Williams sticks to his promise of not imposing a huge burden on local taxpayers. Even though Cropp abstained from the stadium vote, which passed the council by a narrow margin, she positioned herself to be a future mayoral candidate by supporting an alternative financing plan and recommending various cost-cutting proposals. Despite these negotiations and agreement, in mid–December of 2004 Cropp ushered through an amendment by a 10–3 vote at a Council meeting. The amendment mandated that 50 percent of the ballpark's cost must be from private sources. As a result, MLB proceeded with the relocated club's baseball operations but ceased its business and promotional activities until December 31, 2004, that is, when a deal for the stadium must be finalized. However, as of late 2005 the league and D.C. Council were meeting and discussing the requirement to complete a lease stipulating that the city controls the ballpark site and that public funding be available for construction of the stadium.[13]

Future Team Relocations

For various reasons, there are one or more MLB franchise owners who may initiate an economic impact study and then decide that the relocation of their team to a new home site in another city is a profit-maximizing short- and/or long-term business strategy. That is, because of stadium deficiencies and other financial problems at their current sites, the Athletics in Oakland, Marlins in Miami and Twins in Minnesota, for example, may implement a strategy to increase their regular season game receipts, local media money and operating revenues. To prosper, at least in the short-run, these owners visualize huge benefits from the construction of a new taxpayer-funded ballpark in such cities as Las Vegas in Nevada, Nashville in Tennessee, Portland in Oregon, Indianapolis in Indiana, Sacramento and San Jose in California, and perhaps Monterrey or Mexico City in Mexico and San Juan in Puerto Rico.

To illustrate the interest in this baseball topic by a local sports group, in October of 2004 the chairman of Baseball San Jose Mike Fox said, "You had an owner in Peter Angelos in Baltimore who has clearly stated he did not want the Expos to move into his area. From our standpoint, that's a hopeful sign that there might be an ability to get a major-league baseball team in San Jose." Even so, the San Francisco Giants presently claim Santa Clara County as their home territory. As Stanford University economist and authority on sports leagues Roger Noll has said about relocation, "There exists a price. That's always been true. The lesson for this is that if the A's [Oakland Athletics] wanted to move to San Jose or Santa Clara or someplace else in Santa Clara County, all they'd have to do is come up with probably $30 million or $40 million" as a payment to the Giants.[14]

In another case involving a future team movement, such politicians as Miami-Dade Mayor Alex Penelas have commented on the Expos' move to Washington, D.C. According to Penelas, "That makes this more urgent now. It opens that Pandora's box of relocation. Unfortunately, the Marlins are going to be an attractive team. They need a stadium. Hopefully this is a wake-up call." Furthermore, in September of 2004 the Marlins' president David Samson stated that, "The days of baseball not relocating teams are over. Relocation is real and it faces us each day. In the past, relocation was never a possibility. In this day and age, it is a probability, if not a definite, for struggling teams." Do the statements by Penelas and Samson forecast a move by the Marlins from the Miami area?[15]

At baseball's winter meetings in Las Vegas in early December of 2004, Marlins vice chairman Joel Mael and the club's vice president of communications and broadcasting had contacted and met with the city's Mayor, Oscar Goodman. Although the specific topics discussed between the team's officials and Mayor Goodman were not revealed to the public, the 90-minute meeting occurred while the Marlins have been negotiating with the city of Miami and Miami-Dade County to construct a $420 million retractable-roof stadium adjacent to the Orange Bowl. The negotiations reportedly included a proposal for the team, city and county to jointly pay the construction costs of the facility. As a condition to the deal, the Marlins have offered to request $30 million in tax rebates from the Florida legislature.[16]

In any event, it has been reported that the Marlins owner Jeffrey Loria is committed to keeping the team in south Florida, and based on articles printed in Las Vegas newspapers, that Mayor Goodman and other officials are seeking to lure a MLB team to their town. In fact, if the Marlins are denied a new ballpark to replace Pro Player Stadium and Miami's threat to evict the club from the Stadium after 2010 is enforced, then the 36 million tourists visiting Las Vegas each year will have another entertainment option besides minor league baseball, sightseeing, gambling and other casino activities.

Summary

This chapter disclosed some historical facts and discussed relevant topics about relocating professional baseball teams that exist generally in small markets. Furthermore, the chapter provided the strategies, financial reasons for and implications of moving a MLB club such as the Expos from Montreal to Washington, D.C. A table was presented that listed fourteen relocations of teams by year and league, and another table that depicted how the Expos' performances and attendances varied for specific seasons. Then, other professional baseball franchises were identified as potential candidates for relocation after 2004. To that end, several U.S. cities and two in Mexico and one in Puerto Rico were mentioned that might host relocating teams who are struggling from a business perspective at their current sites. Interestingly, these places do not include the metropolitan areas of Chicago, Los Angeles and New York City.

In conclusion, MLB is a cartel and the league's clubs are monopolists whose economic goal is to maximize profits. Based on the research for this chapter, it is the cities constructing a new ballpark, which is entirely funded by local and regional taxpayers, that appeals to franchise owners. Thus, these communities have the best opportunity to attract a MLB team.

5. *The Organization and Business of Minor League Baseball*

Besides the competition and entertainment provided for sports fans by Major League Baseball (MLB) and such amateur organizations as Little League, Junior and Senior Division League Baseball, and the Babe Ruth League and American Legion Baseball, there is an alternative type of baseball other than these sports groups. Renamed as Minor League Baseball (MLBB) in 1999, the National Association of Professional Baseball Leagues (NAPBL) was established in 1901 to be a farm system or player development program for the clubs in MLB. In other words, the teams in the former NAPBL and current MLBB were delegated and assigned the responsibility to prepare and otherwise train their players to eventually become big leaguers. That is, by enabling these athletes to compete and excel in progressively tougher levels of the minor baseball leagues based in cities of North America.

Ranked from most to least competitive, in 2005 the leagues in MLBB were classified as either Triple A (AAA), Double A (AA), Class A Advanced (AADV), Class A (A), Class A Short Season (SS) or Rookie (R). Accordingly, the teams in a minor league are affiliated with various MLB clubs. For the teams that are not affiliated with the big leagues such as the Salt Dogs of Lincoln, Nebraska, they play in an independent league. Besides those in MLBB, whose teams schedule and play their games during the spring/summer seasons, winter leagues with their member clubs exist in nations where baseball is extremely popular such as in the Dominican Republic, Mexico, Panama, Puerto Rico and Venezuela. Indeed, on opening day of the 2005 regular season more than 20 percent of MLB players and 40 percent of minor leaguers were born in Latin American countries.

History of NAPBL/MLBB

The following observations are six facts that highlight the historical structure, development and growth of the NAPBL/MLBB. First, this professional baseball organization expanded from 14 leagues and 96 clubs in 1902 to 17 affiliated leagues with 181 teams that charged admission in 2005, when its total membership consisted of 20 leagues and 242 teams. The peak years of MLBB, however, were in the late 1940s because at least 50 leagues had included more than 400 teams. Second, the NAPBL's all-time total regular season attendance record of 39.6 million in 1949 was broken in 2005 when 41.3 million fans attended MLBB games. Furthermore, as of 2005 the annual attendance of the NAPBL/ MLBB had increased in 20 of the previous 24 regular seasons and surpassed 35 million for seven consecutive seasons. Third, the NAPBL/MLBB's home office was moved from Auburn, New York to Durham, North Carolina in the early 1930s, then from Durham to Columbus, Ohio in the late 1940s, and finally from Columbus to St. Petersburg, Florida in the early 1970s. Generally, these relocations had occurred after a new person was elected as president of minor league baseball.[1]

Fourth, MLB owners passed a Development Plan that guaranteed working agreements for a minimum of 100 minor league teams in 1962, and 29 years later the major leagues' standards for stadiums and other facilities went into affect. As a result, these minimum requirements for minor league ballparks and structures triggered the biggest construction boom in the sport's history. Fifth, in 1992 the NAPBL/MLBB was realigned into a corporate structure whereby the governing authorities of the organization included a president, who is elected to a four-year term in office, a 17-member board of trustees and a council of league presidents. The first president, Patrick Powers of the Eastern League entered the NAPBL office in 1901 while the tenth president, Mike Moore, began his term in 1992. Sixth, in 1998 the number of AAA leagues decreased from three to two, that year an AAA World Series was established and then played in Las Vegas, Nevada from 1998 to 2000, and the Professional Baseball Umpire Corporation began its operation as a subsidiary of the NAPBL/MLBB and as a program administered for games in the minor leagues.

Between the early 1930s and 1980s, some historic events and great performances occurred in the NAPBL. For example, former New York Yankee outfielder and current Hall of Famer Joe DiMaggio hit safely in 61 consecutive games for a San Francisco team of the Pacific Coast League in 1933, and 13 years later African American Jackie Robinson made his debut as a player in Canada with the International League's Montreal franchise. In 1954, slugger Joe Bauman batted .400, hit 72 home runs, scored 188 runs and batted in another 224 while playing just 138 games for a Roswell, New Mexico team in the Longhorn League. Three years before Bauman's achievements, Emmett Ashford became the first African American to umpire in the minor leagues and similarly, in 1972 Bernice Gera became the first female to umpire in professional baseball when she worked in a New York–Penn League game. Although Gera had resigned from umpiring in the minor leagues after that game, it was in 1983 that Pam Postema became the first woman to umpire at all minor league levels including Class AAA.[2]

Team Affiliations

As currently structured, a MLBB team is generally affiliated with one MLB franchise. In this relationship, there is a contractual commitment that requires the minor league club to develop and prepare players for its respective big league affiliate who, in turn, pays these athletes' salaries and benefits. In 2005, these amounts varied from $850 per month for a first year player in a SS league to $2,150 per month on a team in an AAA league, plus $20 per day for meal money while on the road. However, since it is a local and not national business, a MLBB team retains all revenues during a season of play but also is responsible to pay the fixed and variable expenses for the organization to operate.[3]

Table 5.1. Numbers and Types of Affiliations, by Big League and Teams, June 2005.

MLB Team	MLBB Team Classification					
	AAA	AA	AADV	A	SS	R
AL						
Baltimore Orioles	1	1	1	1	1	1
Boston Red Sox	1	1	1	1	1	1
Chicago White Sox	1	1	1	1	0	2
Cleveland Indians	1	1	1	1	1	1
Detroit Tigers	1	1	1	1	1	1
Kansas City Royals	1	1	1	1	0	2
Los Angeles Angels of Anaheim	1	1	1	1	0	2
Minnesota Twins	1	1	1	1	0	2
New York Yankees	1	1	1	1	1	1
Oakland Athletics	1	1	1	1	1	1
Seattle Mariners	1	1	1	1	1	1
Tampa Bay Devil Rays	1	1	1	1	1	1
Texas Rangers	1	1	1	1	1	1
Toronto Blue Jays	1	1	1	1	1	1
NL						
Arizona Diamondbacks	1	1	1	1	1	1
Atlanta Braves	1	1	1	1	0	2
Chicago Cubs	1	1	1	1	1	1
Cincinnati Reds	1	1	1	1	0	2
Colorado Rockies	1	1	1	1	1	1
Florida Marlins	1	1	1	1	1	1
Houston Astros	1	1	1	1	1	1
Los Angeles Dodgers	1	1	1	1	0	2
Milwaukee Brewers	1	1	1	1	0	2
New York Mets	1	1	1	1	1	2
Philadelphia Phillies	1	1	1	1	1	1
Pittsburgh Pirates	1	1	1	1	1	1
San Diego Padres	1	1	1	1	1	1
San Francisco Giants	1	1	1	1	1	1
St. Louis Cardinals	1	1	1	1	1	1
Washington Nationals	1	1	1	1	1	1

Note: Each MLB team has affiliated with a MLBB club that is classified as Class A Advanced (AADV). Although the AADV is listed separately in column four of Table 5.1, it is considered as level A. Some MLB teams' distributions and MLBB classifications may have changed after June of 2005.

Source: "MLB Affiliation," at http://www.minorleaguebaseball.com cited 25 June 2005.

Before discussing the ownership, operation and other business aspects of typical MLBB teams, Table 5.1 was developed to denote the distributions and various types of classifications that existed between the 30 MLB clubs and their respective minor league affiliates in June of 2005. What does the table reveal about MLB teams and the number, classification type and affiliation of their MLBB clubs as of 2005?

Based on the research of MLBB, in 2005 there were 17 independent leagues. These consisted of three in AAA, three in AA, five in A plus AADV, two in SS and four in R. The names of each AAA included the International, Pacific Coast and Mexican League, the AA incorporated the Eastern, Southern and Texas League, the AADV and A encompassed the California, Carolina, Florida State, Midwest and South Atlantic League, the

SS had the New York–Penn and Northwest League, and the R included the Appalachian, Arizona, Gulf Coast and Pioneer League.[4]

According to the distributions in columns two to seven of Table 5.1, there were 181 teams in six minor leagues with 30 each in AAA, AA, AADV and A, 22 in SS and 39 in R. Geographically, 13 of these clubs played their home games in California, 12 played in Florida, 11 played in New York and nine each played in Tennessee and North Carolina. Alternatively, because of poor weather conditions and low temperatures in the Spring season, zero MLBB teams existed in North and South Dakota and Minnesota. Regarding specific farm systems, 21 or 70 percent of the MLB franchises had at least one club in each of the six leagues while eight or 26 percent of them did not place a team in the Class A Short Season. Furthermore, nine or 30 percent of the MLB franchises had two clubs in a Rookie League. Interestingly, the New York Mets was the only MLB franchise affiliated with seven minor league teams. These were the Norfolk Tides in an AAA, Binghamton Mets in an AA, St. Lucie Mets in an AADV, Hagerstown Suns in an A, Brooklyn Cyclones in a SS, and the GCL Mets and Kingsport Mets in an R.

Some MLBB teams were home-based in cities of a regional area and located within 100 to 400 miles of their MLB affiliate such as the Detroit Tigers' Toledo Mud Hens in an AAA, Erie SeaWolves in an AA and West Michigan Whitecaps in an A. However, the average mileage between a typical big league club and a majority of its teams in the minors appeared to be relatively long distances. For example, in the AL and NL there were, respectively, the Los Angeles Angels of Anaheim's Salt Lake Stingers in an AAA, Arkansas Travelers in an AA and Cedar Rapids Kernals in an A, and the Arizona Diamondbacks' Tennessee Smokies in an AA, South Bend Silver Hawks in an A and Yakima Bears in a SS. In short, there does not seem to be a geographical pattern regarding the distances in mileage between the cities of the MLB clubs and the home sites of their affiliated minor league teams.

The next portion of this chapter focuses on the ownership, operation and business of a MLBB team. That is, the section highlights how a typical minor league baseball organization is established, structured and managed, and how it functions and competes from a business perspective. Furthermore, in the analysis there are some comparisons made between the business environments, operations and decisions of clubs that exist in a minor league and those in the AL and/or NL.

MLBB Topics

Similar to most small companies in other industries, there are economic tradeoffs, managerial decisions, and financial risks and rewards from investing in, owning and/or operating a baseball team in the minor league system. Initially, as an owner and entrepreneur a potential investor must evaluate and then decide whether to purchase all or a portion of an independent team or one affiliated with a MLB franchise. This decision depends, in part, on an individual's knowledge and comprehension of baseball economics, willingness to tolerate and deal with risks, management experiences and successes, negotiation skills, number of years residing in a local community, type of education, family wealth, and other sport-related and personal facts.

These elements are each relevant and important in the business of MLBB because the sole proprietor of an independent team is ultimately responsible for all aspects of its operations. These responsibilities include such duties as recruiting and signing amateur and professional baseball players, paying the salaries of the organization's employees, negotiating contracts with others for leasing a stadium and establishing concessions, arranging transportation for away games, and developing budgets and monitoring accounting statements. If an individual is unable or not prepared to allocate the time to efficiently and effectively perform these tasks as a team owner, then he or she should purchase one or more of the 181 clubs listed in Table 5.1 because those are affiliated with MLB franchises.

With respect to this type of investment in a baseball organization, a big league general manager or another senior executive determines who will be the coaches and players on a minor league team. The owner, meanwhile, must hire and organize a staff for the office functions, share the expenses for purchasing baseball equipment and traveling to and from away games, and provide a local stadium and other facilities that meet the standards authorized by MLB. Whether investing in an independent or affiliated minor league baseball team, it is necessary for an owner to measure and anticipate how well a team generates revenues from ticket sales, corporate sponsorships, licensing contracts and concessions, and also how various team-specific and organizational costs are affected by operating a local sports enterprise in a small, medium-sized or large metropolitan area and market.

Regarding the implications and benefits of owning a minor league team, journalist Jerome Cramer stated in his article as published in *Forbes* that, "Successfully operating a minor league team is, basically, an exercise in promoting fun. Business school graduates might call it 'event marketing' or 'targeted entertainment.' But what [MLBB] owners provide is a safe, clean place where children can walk freely, where they can be surprised but not frightened and where they can see young men play a wonderful game on green grass in the height of summer."[5]

As an aside, some high-profile individuals, celebrities and former major leaguers have co-owned minor league baseball teams. These business relationships involved, for example, billionaire investor Warren Buffet and his Kansas City Royals affiliate in Omaha, Nebraska, titled The Spikes; movie director Ron Howard and his Chicago Cubs affiliate in Jackson, Tennessee, nicknamed The West Tenn Diamond Jaxx; and former big league pitcher Nolan Ryan and his Houston Astros affiliate in Round Rock, Texas, named The Express.[6]

Based on this general overview of the ownership expectations and managerial commitments involved in operating a minor league club, the following three sub-titles contain some interesting facts and historical information that highlight why MLBB is an attractive but risky business option, opportunity and venture.

Business Orientation

Since the early 1990s, the prospects and commercial environments for teams in professional baseball improved in various cities across America. Indeed, there are several reasons why minor league baseball has succeeded in many communities and if managed properly during the early 2000s, will likely experience further growth and prosperity. Baseball fans, for example, realize that the sport is a refreshing alternative to other leisure activities and that it has been portrayed as less corrupt, greedy and controversial than MLB and the other major U.S. professional sports leagues. This means, in part, that the minor leagues have not yet been invaded or affected by corporate owners who seek profits as their first priority, by teams whose players are individualistic, selfish and egocentric, and by coaches who place winning games above entertaining and fulfilling the needs of male and female children, teens and adults at the ballparks.[7]

Furthermore, MLBB teams have not tried to gorge fans by charging excessively high prices for tickets, food and merchandise. For a four-person family to attend a minor league game during the 2004 season, the average cost was approximately $80 but nearly double at $155 to watch major leaguers perform in their ballparks. Besides this difference in costs, the majority of spectators have relatively more space and convenient, comfortable and well-maintained seats at a AAA game cheering for the Bulls in Durham, Clippers in Columbus and Riverbats in Louisville, than at a game featuring the White Sox in Chicago, Dodgers in Los Angeles and Mets in New York City.

Another reason for the sport's success is that MLBB has taken advantage of the innovations and trends in sports marketing. Because the minor league teams' ballparks are usually located in small and not medium-sized and large cities as in MLB, the emphasis in marketing the sport has been on community-based, grassroots, cause-oriented and ethnic activities, events and programs. To make that successful, an assortment of advertisements and promotions for the teams' games appear in the columns of local newspapers and are announced on sports talk radio programs. Also, some companies in the local areas lease billboards at the ballparks in Durham, Columbus and Louisville to display their name, location and type of business. In short, the marketing campaigns of clubs in MLBB are personal, direct and targeted to the segments of a local fan base.

Finally, to increase exposure, build relationships and expand their sources of revenue, during recent years many minor leagues and their teams have been creative in implementing Internet strategies. These include, for example, the application of database marketing and programming, and incorporating the concepts of e-commerce. In other words, MLBB organizations are using the latest web-based technologies to attract baseball fans who may live in small urban communities and remote rural areas, which the major sports leagues tend to ignore, overlook and fail to reach.

MLBB Stadiums

Prior to the 1990s, minor league teams played their regular season home and away games in small municipal ballparks, junior college stadiums and if necessary, in renovated sandlots. Then, in 1990 a Professional Baseball Agreement (PBA) was established to govern the relationship between MLB teams and the clubs in their farm systems. As a result, big league baseball teams had decided that their players should perform in modern ballparks with amenities, and on well-maintained ballfields with dimensions like those in the AL and NL. Thus, to retain an affiliation with their parent clubs a large proportion of minor league team owners had to upgrade their stadiums or move to better ballparks. The implementation of the PBA, therefore, had started a multimillion-dollar construction boom that improved the sport for teams and players, and especially for the fans.[8]

From 1990 to 2005, more than 100 new stadiums were built for the games that were played between clubs in MLBB. Several of these 5,000–10,000 seat stadiums contained such revenue-producing features as skyboxes, luxury suites, club seats and picnic areas. Meanwhile, within or connected to other ballparks were one or more engaging activities as a basketball and volleyball court, moon bounce, merry-go-round, videogame room, rock climbing wall, miniature health spa, hot tub, swimming pool, and a pitching and/or batting machine. In part, it was a combination of districts, cities and counties that financed the construction of these ballparks with the proceeds from bonds issued by various municipal governments. Then, to use the stadiums for their home games each season minor league teams paid rents and other fees after signing a short- or long-term lease with the appropriate government office. With new ballparks available to play their regularly scheduled home games, the majority of minor league teams considerably appreciated in value. On average, in 2004 an AAA team was worth an estimated $8 to $20 million, an AA at $6 to $15 million and an A at $2 to $8 million, and a rookie league club at $600,000 to $750,000.

Because they were built as entertainment centers, the new stadiums had motivated the marketing staffs of minor league teams to create, manage and conduct more ballpark activities and thereby generate fun and pleasure for the spectators, especially between innings of the teams' games. A number of these events and programs were held during one season or another and thus, are highlighted as follows. At four minor league ballparks of teams owned by the Goldklang Group, which included Hollywood actor and silent partner Bill Murray, the fans who attended games are referred to as customers and escorted to their seats by "ushertainers." Frequently, these are local actors who moonlight and interact with the kids and lead cheers for the crowds. Located at a site near the City of Dallas, a Texas League club named the Frisco Roughriders plays in a stadium that is the centerpiece of a large real estate development, which consists of shopping malls and office spaces. The Roughriders provide free game sheets to spectators, assign two players to endorse autographs before every game, and hire an 18-member troupe to entertain at its ballpark.

During home games of the Dayton Dragons, a team that performs in a Class A Midwest League, several mascots roam the stands during innings and conduct skits. The most popular mascots have been Heater, a 7-foot-2 dragon and Wink, a Cyclops. Wearing a dress and feather boa, Heater occasionally tries to persuade a reluctant umpire behind home plate or one at a base to break into dance moves, and the home crowd usually roars with delight. Meanwhile, in May of 2005 the River City Rascals of the Frontier League auctioned off a "one-day professional contract" for someone to play on the team at T.R. Hughes Ballpark in O'Fallon, which is a suburb of St. Louis, Missouri. The highest bidder on the eBay listing was awarded 20 tickets to a game, furnished with a uniform, and then allowed to hit with a bat and play an outfield position for one-half inning when the Rascals hosted its rival, the Gateway Grizzlies. To benefit the local community, the United Way received funds from the sale of the contract.

At other ballparks of teams in the minor leagues, fans have raced around the infields and picked up money dropped by a helicopter, or they competed in "dizzy bat races" by running to first, second or third base after being spun around in circles. Furthermore, there have been such activities as automobile giveaways, pony rides and hole-in-one contests. Alan Schwarz, a senior writer of the *Baseball America* magazine made this comment about the rationale of providing entertainment during games at the stadiums of minor league teams. "It makes sense: most of the minor leagues are stocked with players borrowed from major-league clubs that shuttle them back and forth, caring far more about refining a prospect's skills than winning games. This leaves the minor-league clubs having to market everything beyond the on-field competition such as sack races and baby-sitting services."[9]

Licensing and Sponsorships in MLBB

Prior to 1991, only a few MLBB teams had conducted mail order and retail sales operations outside of their stadiums before, during and after a regular baseball season. Therefore, an initiative to increase the revenue streams of minor league clubs occurred in 1991 when MLBB and MLB Properties (MLBP) signed an agreement to establish and operate a national licensing program. According to the contract, MLBP authorizes U.S. and foreign manufacturers to produce and issue officially licensed and genuine minor league merchandise. As a result of this agreement, merchandise that features creative, innovative and exciting logos of minor league clubs is available throughout the year at local, regional and national retailers in the U.S. and elsewhere. As indicated on links of the website titled minorleaguebaseball.com, the resources of the licensing program include player and mascot appearances, ticket giveaways, consumer sweepstakes, sales associate contests, gift with purchases, point-of-purchase material and print advertising. In turn, each of these resources is described in detail at the various links of the website.[10]

To attract media attention and market their businesses to the fans of minor league baseball, any American-based and international company may form a partnership with MLBB and become a sponsor for one or more teams. There are different types of sponsorships, and each of them is customized to fit the marketing needs of a specific company. To illustrate a few of these business opportunities, an outfield fence billboard may be leased for at least five months while an in-between innings contest provides on-the-field exposure for a company to advertise and promote its goods and services. To temporarily claim an area of a ballpark for a season or an afternoon or evening game and entertain its clients, a firm may purchase a "presenting game sponsorship" by acquiring a pre-game picnic admission ticket.

Other types of sponsorships exist in MLBB. For branding their products and services to attract fans in a family oriented and fun atmosphere at a minor league team's ballpark, companies may participate in an entry and exit sampling program. To target the executives who make key decisions in an industry, event sponsorships are held at minor league baseball promotional seminars, and at MLB trade shows and winter meetings. Finally, to take advantage of this sport's local and regional popularity, official sponsorships may be purchased by business allies to use MLBB trademarks in their advertisements and other promotional materials that are mailed to current customers and potential clients. In short, sponsorships have been another revenue-producing activity for MLBB to exploit and expand, especially at the stadiums in cities where the clubs play their home games.

Charlotte Knights

During the majority of years between 1901 and 1989, a minor league baseball team had played at some ballparks located in the Charlotte, North Carolina, metropolitan area. The team was nicknamed as the Charlotte Hornets from 1901 to 1973, Charlotte O's from 1976 to the late 1980s, and then the Charlotte Knights since the late 1980s. It was during the latter period when local entrepreneur George Shinn bought the franchise for $25 million even though it was not operating at a profit. Although $25 million seemed to be an extravagant price for the club, it included the exclusive rights to conduct professional baseball in Mecklenburg County of North Carolina and York County of South Carolina.

Thus, if a MLB team were to relocate anywhere in the region surrounding Charlotte, the Knights' Shinn would be compensated for owning the rights, even if he had acquired the incoming MLB team. In the early-to-mid–1990s, these rights were valued at approximately $15 million.[11]

When negotiations broke down between the Knights and City of Charlotte concerning the construction of a new baseball stadium adjoining the Charlotte Coliseum, in 1989 George Shinn moved his club to 10,000-seat Knights Castle — renamed Knights Stadium — in Fort Mill, South Carolina, which was a small textile town located about 15 miles south of Charlotte. Two years after the team's relocation to Fort Mill, the NAPBL awarded the Knights an AAA franchise, and in 1993 the club withdrew its membership from the Southern League and joined the International League (IL).

Because of the failure of Jim and Tammy Baker's Heritage USA religious resort in the Fort Mill area, and the unlikelihood of attracting a MLB team to Mecklenburg or York County, in December of 1997 Shinn sold the Knights for $10 million to lifelong baseball fan and businessman Don Beaver, who has also owned the Winston-Salem Warthogs of the Carolina League, Hickory Crawdads of the South Atlantic League and New Orleans Zephyrs of the Pacific Coast League. Reportedly, it was Beaver's ambition to purchase the Minnesota Twins and then move the Twins to the Charlotte area.

After home attendance had dropped below 300,000 in the 1998 regular season, the Knights' General Manager Tim Newman implemented a series of financial and marketing initiatives to improve the revenue base of the franchise. For example, efforts were taken to market the club's brand with sales of merchandise at retail shops supported by timely radio broadcasts; an investment of $1.3 million was made to Knights Stadium including $1 million for a new scoreboard and sound system; specific daily promotions were begun such as Sunday All-Faith Days, that is, when local church bulletins provided the parishioners with a $1 discount of a Sunday game ticket; fireworks displays were scheduled after Saturday games; and, an "Ask the General Manager" program was started whereby Newman made himself available to spectators at the Stadium during the sixth inning of every game to address their concerns with the team. That program had provided such results as an improvement in the ballpark's appearance, and more accessibility of the players and entertainment options for fans besides the competitiveness of games. For various reasons, in 1999 Beaver ended the Knights' four-year affiliation with the Sox. After the contract had expired, it was renewed later for a period of years.

To evaluate the Knight's attendances and performances while a member of the IL, Table 5.2 was prepared. It indicates, in part, the history of the club for 12 years while in Fort Mill.

According to the numbers listed in column two of the table, the Knights' attendance at home averaged 334,892 per season or approximately 4,800 each game. Furthermore, the club won about 50 percent of each season's games and generally placed third in its division. Relative to other clubs in the IL, the Knights have been below average in attendance and average in performance. In 2004, the team's Fan Cost Index (FCI) equaled $97.60 per game, which was the highest of all clubs in the IL. Specifically, that amount included two adult and child average ticket prices at $7.65 each, four small soft drinks at $2 per soda, two small beers at $3.50 per drink, four $3 hot dogs and two $3 programs, two $16 adult-size caps and a $2 parking fee. The AAA teams that ranked second, third and fourth in FCIs were, respectively, the Pacific Coast's Edmonton Trappers at $87.78, IL's Scranton/Wilkes-Barre Red Barons at $85.43 and Pacific Coast's Iowa Cubs

TABLE 5.2. CHARLOTTE KNIGHTS ATTENDANCES
AND PERFORMANCES, BY SEASON, 1993–2004

Year	Home Attendance*	Win-Loss %	Rank	Title
1993	429,132	.610	1	Y
1994	404,861	.542	2	N
1995	336,001	.421	5	N
1996	326,761	.440	4	N
1997	322,618	.539	2	N
1998	299,664	.490	3	N
1999	353,303	.569	1	Y
2000	338,928	.545	2	N
2001	370,406	.465	4	N
2002	303,411	.385	4	N
2003	268,374	.514	2	N
2004	265,253	.479	4	N

* Home Attendance is the turnstile count. The Rank column includes 1 for finishing in first place, 2 for second, 3 for third, 4 for fourth and 5 for fifth. In the title column, Y means Yes and N is No. The Knights won the IL Governors' Cup Championship in 1993 and six years later won it again, but finished second in the AAA World Series to a team from Vancouver, Canada.
Source: *2005 Charlotte Knights Media Guide* (Fort Mill, S.C.: Charlotte Knights Media Relations Office, 2005).

at $78.58. Consequently, it appears that Knights Stadium in Fort Mill has been an inferior site to host this AAA team.

For the Knights to retain its AAA classification and ensure a long-term relationship with the Chicago White Sox or another MLB team, the club's home attendances and revenues must improve. Nevertheless, because of taxpayer's commitment to fund a new $256 million downtown arena for the National Basketball Association's Charlotte Hornets and demands from various special interest groups to finance other local projects, Charlotte's government officials have refused to subsidize the purchase of land or the construction of a ballpark for the Knights. Their decision is based, in part, on economic development studies, which denote that Charlotte is a small market and thus not economically capable of hosting a minor league baseball club besides being the current home of professional men and women's basketball franchises and minor league hockey and soccer teams. Therefore, this suggests that the Knights are unlikely to relocate from Fort Mill to Charlotte or another city until at least 2008.

Summary

This chapter discussed some key business elements and specific operations of professional baseball teams to successfully perform in the minor leagues. The first section primarily described the origin, development, structure and history of the NAPBL/MLBB, which are initials that represent the organization of minor league baseball in America. Then, there are some facts about the financial requirements, and managerial commitments and tasks of investing in, operating and owning a minor league team. A table lists the 30 MLB franchises and their number of minor league affiliates, by classification, as of the 2005 season. Indeed, there were a total of 181 MLBB clubs and that number included 30 teams each in Class AAA, Class AA, Class A Advanced and Class A leagues, 22 in Class A Short Season leagues and 39 in the various Rookie leagues.

In another section of this chapter, the commercialization of MLBB is examined. This part contains information about the sport's marketing activities, and an overview of the operational characteristics of the 17 minor leagues and their respective clubs. The economic effects of building new baseball stadiums, and how MLBB's licensing programs and sponsorships at the local level generate more revenues for the individual teams, are other topics of interest.

The ownership, operation and success of the International League's Charlotte Knights are reviewed in this chapter's final section. In a table, there are numbers for the team's attendances and performances for 12 years, that is, from the 1993 through 2004 seasons. The tabled data indicates that the Knights, as an affiliate of the Cleveland Indians and then Florida Marlins and Chicago White Sox, have ranked below average in attendance and average in performance relative to other clubs in the IL.

Despite the area's growth in population since the early-to-mid–1990s, the team is located at an inferior site in Fort Mill, South Carolina. Furthermore, on average the club has experienced annual operating losses since 1993, and in 2004 charged the highest prices of all teams in MLBB for families to attend its games at Knights Stadium. As a result, owner Don Beaver has an incentive to relocate his team to nearby Charlotte or alternatively, to another city before 2010.

PART II. HUMAN RESOURCES AND RELATIONSHIPS

6. *An Overview of Labor Relations*

Since the 1960s, a considerable number of cases, reports and studies published in articles, books, journals, magazines and newspapers have thoroughly documented and analyzed the origin and history of labor relations in Major League Baseball (MLB). These publications include various topics such as the demand for and supply of U.S. and foreign baseball players, determination and distribution of professional baseball players' salaries, trends in the payrolls of teams in MLB's American League (AL) and National League (NL), collusion of club owners, economic power and impact of the Major League Baseball Players Association (MLBPA), collective bargaining agreements (CBAs) that have been established between the league and MLBPA, and the applications of the Labor Management Relations Act (LMRA) and procedures of the National Labor Relations Board (NLRB) to the professional sports industry. As a result of the research performed by academics and practitioners, there is a large amount of data and plenty of information available in the literature regarding these and other topics to review and interpret.

It is interesting, educational and beneficial, therefore, to identify and discuss a few of the human resource elements and business aspects of labor relations issues that involve MLB, AL and NL teams, MLBPA, baseball players, sports fans and/or government policies. Because the issues are complex, controversial and interrelated, those who read this chapter are encouraged to survey and consult other publications for further information and to learn more facts about them.

Players Unions

To challenge the reserve system that was adopted by MLB team owners, between the early 1880s and mid–1940s the big league baseball players made the effort to organize and form five unions. These were the Brotherhood of Professional Baseball Players founded in 1885, Players League in 1889, Players Protective Association in 1900, Fraternity of Professional Baseball Players of America in 1912 and the American Baseball Guild in 1946. With respect to these organizations, after the Brotherhood feuded with the NL and American Association about a fixed salary classification system, professional baseball athletes established the Players League. Because this union was in disarray, under capitalized and lacked effective leadership, it folded in one year. For similar financial and managerial reasons and various legal matters, the other three unions had also failed. As such, these five players' institutions had very limited short- or long-term successes. However, by educating the public and exposing how team owners abused baseball players freedoms and violated their rights in using the reserve clause and monopolistic practices, undoubtedly one or more of these unions justified and paved the way for the initiation of three court cases.[1]

Regarding the first cast, during the early 1920s a Baltimore sports team sued a league in *Federal Baseball Club of Baltimore, Inc. v. National League of Professional Baseball Clubs, et al.* Accordingly, this case resulted in a Supreme Court ruling stipulating that baseball was not interstate commerce and thus, the league was legally exempt from application of the federal antitrust laws. As to the second case, in 1946 big league player Danny Gardella sued MLB because the league's team owners had blacklisted him after he left the New York Giants to play for a club in a newly formed Mexican League. In the end, Gardella decided to accept a settlement that allowed him to play in a professional league and also to receive a financial payment.

Relative to the third case, in 1953 minor leaguer George Toolson challenged baseball's reserve system for players in *Toolson v. New York Yankees.* Even though Toolson claimed that his ability to play for another team besides the Yankees was blocked because of the reserve clause, the Supreme Court again ruled that the baseball business was not interstate commerce. In effect, this outcome meant that the burden to overturn the sport's antitrust legislation had shifted to the U.S. Congress. As a result of these court decisions and other legalities, and despite the increased revenues earned by teams from their radio and television rights and higher ticket prices at games, the average salaries of professional baseball players remained approximately the same, and relative to the general population, from the 1920s to early 1950s. Consequently, in 1954 the MLBPA was formed as a union to increase the dollar amounts in, and develop new ways of, funding the players' pension accounts.

During the late 1950s and early-to-mid–1960s, MLB players grew increasingly frustrated and disillusioned with the progress made by the MLBPA, which was headed then by Wisconsin judge Robert Cannon. According to some baseball historians and players, Cannon had been so friendly with the team owners that they considered him for the position of MLB's Commissioner. This predicament was ultimately resolved in 1966 when a former United Steelworkers chief economic advisor named Marvin Miller became the first full-time executive director of the MLBPA. Because of Miller's talents and experiences as an economist, negotiator and industrial relations expert, the MLBPA gradually became a more stable, unified and formidable organization. The union's solidarity continued to progress so that in 1968, Miller had the power to negotiate with the team owners about the players' terms and conditions of employment, and to persuade them that bargaining in good faith was in the sport's best interests.

Between the mid-to-late 1960s and early 1980s, Miller had successfully negotiated several collective bargaining agreements (CBAs) with MLB's team owners. Indeed, during his tenure as executive director there were significant improvements and gains in players' base salaries, pension funds, licensing and sponsoring rights, and the cash balances from those rights. In the late 1970s, Miller met attorney Donald Fehr and then hired him to be the MLBPA's general counsel. When Miller retired in 1986, the players chose Fehr to be the union's executive director. In retrospect, it was largely because of Miller's leadership, vision and skill as a director, negotiator and administrator that led to the early development and eventual growth and prosperity of the MLBPA.

Prior CBAs

Although it was brief, noncontroversial and elementary, the MLBPA's initial CBA covered the 1968 and 1969 seasons in MLB. This document included an increase of $3,000, or from $7,000 to $10,000 in the player's minimum salary and more money for these athletes to spend from expense allowances. Most importantly, however, it provided a formal structure with which to monitor owner-player relations. Also, it included written procedures for arbitrating players' problems, and especially their grievances with team owners.[2]

The second CBA was a three-year agreement that was finalized in 1970. This contract contained a clause that any players' disputes, which did not involve the integrity of baseball, could be arbitrated before a three-member panel, whose chairman was selected jointly by players and the team owners. While negotiating its third CBA with the MLBPA, in 1973 the owners refused to discuss free agency but agreed with the union that those players with two full seasons in the big leagues may have their salaries determined by an arbitrator. Furthermore, this three-year contract created a rule that a ten-year player, who had spent five years with the same club, had the right to veto his trade to another team. In fact, the Chicago Cubs' Ron Santo became the first player to exercise this option.

When the third CBA expired in 1975, players Andy Messersmith and Dave McNally challenged the league's reserve clause. After much debate, these athletes won their freedom to be free agents. This occurred because arbitrator Peter Seitz ruled that MLB teams had the rights to only one additional year of service from a player and not the perpetual renewal of his contract as the owners had claimed. Seitz's decision meant that every baseball player in the big leagues could become a free agent by not signing a contract and then playing for one season. As discussed in more detail later in this chapter, the owners rebelled by initiating a 17-day lockout during spring training prior to the start of the 1976 regular season.

2002 CBA

Between the late 1960s and early 2000s, the various CBAs in MLB have been renegotiated and renewed, and also revised and updated with new provisions to reflect baseball's environment and the modern era of the sport. For example, the CBA covering the 2002–2006 seasons contains several components that did not appear as sensitive or contentious issues when the earliest agreements were negotiated by Marvin Miller and then Donald Fehr because these labor matters were not significant until the early-to-mid–1990s. That is, during this period of years the emphasis and concern when negotiating a CBA by the team owners and union officials had shifted from free agency, minimum salary and arbitration to other and more current economic, financial and human resource issues. For clarification, a portion of these issues are summarized and described in the next seven paragraphs.[3]

To attain more competitive balance in the abilities of players on the medium-sized, small- and large-market teams within the AL and NL, the proportion of local revenues redistributed by the clubs had significantly increased — net of ballpark expenses—from 20 percent in 1996–2001 to at least 34 percent in 2002–2006. This change in percentages indicates that such high payroll and revenue clubs as the AL's Red Sox and Yankees, and NL's Braves and Giants had to contribute increasingly more dollars to the low payroll and revenue teams in their respective leagues. Besides the local revenue sharing requirements, a central fund amounting to $72.2 million appeared as a separate entity in the 2002 CBA. As stated in the agreement, this money was to be redistributed from teams classified as net payers to those clubs that are net receivers. The designated schedule was 60 percent in 2003, 80 percent in 2004 and 100 percent in 2005–2006.

Another important item contained in the 2002 CBA are the annual thresholds and rates of the luxury taxes imposed by the league on teams. Although there were no thresholds or rates assigned in 2002, based on annual team payrolls during each of the 2003–2006 MLB seasons, the amounts of payrolls included the annual salaries and earned bonuses of all players on each 40-man roster plus a fixed amount per team in benefits and expenses. Specifically, the thresholds and luxury tax rates as listed in this agreement are, respectively, $117 million and 17.5 percent for violations in 2003, $120.5 million and 22.5 percent for first-time and 30 percent for second-time violations in 2004, $128 million and 22.5 percent for first-time, 30 percent for second-time and 40 percent for third-time violations in 2005, and $136.5 million and no tax for first-time, 30 percent for second-time and 40 percent for third- and fourth-time violations in 2006. Furthermore, since these thresholds and rates expire on the final day of the 2006 season, there is no luxury tax on teams in the 2007 season if the clubs decide to compete according to the terms of the 2002 CBA. Finally, the teams that receive any funds each season are expected to spend those amounts on players' benefits, deposit the monies in the industry growth fund, and/or invest the dollars in the development of players in foreign countries that have no organized high school baseball programs.

A worldwide amateur draft is a third item listed in the 2002 CBA. Based on this labor contract, the rules for such a draft are to be established by a committee of owners and players. The group must jointly determine whether teams may or may not trade the athletes they have selected and also, what will be the exact number of rounds in the draft. Moreover, this provision specifies the requirements for teams that do not sign their first-round picks, denotes the draft pick compensation for clubs that lose free agents, and states the owners rights when bargaining with players who are drafted.

With respect to the contraction of baseball franchises, in the 2002 CBA owners agreed to maintain 30 teams through 2006 but are allowed to eliminate one or two teams for the 2007 regular season if they notify the MLBPA no later than July 1, 2006. In turn, when notified the union does not have the right to argue before the NLRB that contraction is a mandatory topic and therefore, subject to collective bargaining. Also, if owners elect to contract the league's size in 2007, it is not necessary for them to inform the players as to which teams' operation will be terminated. However, because of attendance growth, number of clubs that competed for first or second place in their respective divisions, and other business success in the 2004 and 2005 seasons, the contraction of MLB teams will not likely occur in 2007.

According to the 2002 CBA, beginning in 2003 all major league players are to be randomly tested for illegal steroids. If 5 percent of these players test positive, then mandatory tests are to be issued in 2004 and 2005. If less than 2.6 percent of them test positive in consecutive years, then survey tests replace the mandatory, random tests. Regarding penalties, a player is placed in a treatment program for the first violation and then receives suspensions of 30 days up to two years for further violations. In retrospect, these rules are not very effective or strong deterrents to discourage players from using illegal steroids and performance-enhancing drugs. Consequently, during the collective bargaining sessions to be held in 2006, MLB and the MLBPA will likely disagree about most aspects of drug testing, but then compromise to strengthen the program. That is, the 2007 CBA will emphasize educating U.S. and foreign players about the risks of illegal substances, and enrolling first-, second-, third- and fourth-time violators in drug prevention and treatment programs.

Regarding some other items contained in the 2002 agreement, the minimum salaries of players remained at $300,000 during 2003 and 2004, and there is a two-year cost-of-living adjustment in 2005 and a one-year adjustment in 2006. Furthermore, there are increases in the players' expense allowances and the clubs' contributions for supplementary benefits. Finally, a team's total debts may not exceed ten times earnings before interest, depreciation, taxes and amortization, except for the clubs that had moved into new ballparks since 1992. As such, their debts are allowed to accumulate to 15 times that earnings amount.

Owner Lockouts and Player Strikes

Due to various economic, legal and social reasons and relationships, since 1971 there have been more work stoppages in MLB than for the total number that took place in the other major U.S. sports. That is, three occurred in baseball during the 1970s and 1980s, and then two in the 1990s. With respect to the 1970s, the first labor stoppage was a 13-day players strike in early April of 1972. Despite the preparations needed to open the 1972 regular season, members of the MLBPA had voted 663–10 to strike because first, these players resented the Supreme Court's ruling in the *Flood* case and the continuation of the league's reserve clause, and second, the MLBPA demanded improvements in the players' medical benefits and pension plans. After 86 regular season games were cancelled, the dispute ended when the owners accepted the players' demands. However, as a form of punishment and to indicate their dissatisfaction with the outcome of the strike, the owners then traded or released two-thirds of the player representatives.[4]

In February of 1973, a 17-day owners' lockout of players delayed the start of baseball's spring training. Fortunately, this event did not severely interrupt the pre-season since it affected only the players who had voluntarily reported for their training during early-to-mid-February. Nonetheless, the lockout was discontinued on February 25 when the MLBPA and owners agreed to introduce salary arbitration and to postpone discussing the reserve clause until the next round of bargaining. However, in contrast to the dispute in 1973, three years later a 17-day lockout took place during baseball's spring training. When the owners refused to reopen their training camps until the players had accepted major restrictions to their new legal right of free agency, Commissioner Bowie Kuhn ordered the owners to terminate the lockout after March 17 and then prepare the players for the start of the 1976 regular season.

The next work stoppage in this sport happened during the last week of MLB's spring training period, which was April 1–8 in 1980. Basically, this interruption occurred as a result of the owners' free agency policy, and also an increase in the players' average salary, which had rose from $51,500 in 1976 to $143,700 in 1980. After the owners and MLBPA disagreed about how to limit the escalation in salaries, the players initiated a brief strike before the 1980 regular season was scheduled to begin. To temporarily settle their differences, the two groups agreed to study the causes and effects of salary inflation during the final months of 1980 and into 1981. Unfortunately, when the owners demanded that those teams who lost free agents should be allowed to select a replacement from the signing club's major league roster, the union resisted and then implemented a 50-day strike beginning on June 12, 1981. After 712 regular season games were cancelled, the two parties compromised and accepted a new compensation scheme and to extend the then-current 1980 CBA through 1984. Nevertheless, in 1985 team owners decided to change the arbitration eligibility standards, and also demanded that AL and NL clubs with above-average payrolls be prohibited from paying exorbitant salaries to sign players who were free agents. As a result of these proposals, the players proceeded to strike in August of 1985 but returned to their teams in two days when the owners dropped their demands. In the end, the two groups signed a five-year CBA that covered the 1985–1989 MLB seasons.

During early 1990, the league's franchise owners met with and spoke to the MLBPA about the elimination of salary arbitration. Furthermore, they offered the player's union a revenue participation plan that, in fact, operated as a salary cap, and also proposed major restrictions on the use of free agency. When the MLBPA made counterproposals regarding salary arbitration for the players with two or three years of service with teams in the big leagues, the owners rejected that recommendation and locked the players out for 32 days, which was from mid–February to mid–March. The lockout ended when the owners decided to withdraw their proposals to the union. Thereupon, in late March of 1990 the owners and MLBPA approved a new three-year CBA that, with minor changes, essentially continued free agency and the arbitration system.

As such, this agreement specified three primary actions. First, the expansion of arbitration to a portion of the players who had served between two and three years on clubs in MLB; second, the owners' decision to accept triple damages as a penalty for any collusion taking place in the future, and third, the appointment of a commission to study the financial feasibility and operational impact of a revenue sharing plan. After he had forced Commissioner Jay Vincent from office in 1992, the owner of the Chicago White Sox stated his colleagues' new hard-line labor strategy as follows. "You do it by taking a position and telling them [players] we're not going to play unless we make a deal, and being prepared not to play one or two years if you have to."

Subsequently, the 1994 regular season began as scheduled in April even though the 1990 CBA had expired. However, two months after the owners had proposed a salary cap, the MLBPA initiated a strike on August 12 during the mid-season of 1994. Even so, the two groups seemingly continued to negotiate in good faith. Although the union eventually agreed to greater revenue sharing and a small tax on high-payroll clubs, the owners would not change their demands to establish a cap on players' salaries. As a result of this opposition, on September 14 Commissioner Bud Selig proceeded to cancel the remainder of the 1994 regular season and also the playoffs and World Series. After exchanging and discussing numerous proposals and counterproposals while bargaining, in December of 1994 the MLBPA filed an action with the NLRB against the owners who were charged with unfair labor practices.

Despite this action and the walkout of players, the major league teams' training camps opened on March 2, 1995. Twenty-nine days later, the U.S. District Court granted an injunction as requested by the NLRB and ruled that the owner's had not bargained with the union in good faith. In an agreement, the U.S. Court of Appeals confirmed the grant. This decision effectively cancelled the players' strike, which allowed the 1995 regular season to open late on April 26. Consequently, a 144-game schedule was established and played by the teams. This meant that the 232-day players strike had eliminated a total of 938 MLB games and a World Series for the first time since 1904.

Interestingly, even with the effects of an injunction and the absence of a new labor agreement, the 1995 and 1996 regular seasons were played without further interruption. Meanwhile, during these two years the owners and players continued to negotiate until December of 1996, when the parties signed a new five-year CBA. This agreement appeared to be an improvement over the status quo for the owners because it included greater revenue sharing, a luxury tax on the five highest-payroll teams in the 1997–1999 seasons, established an Industry Growth Fund to promote baseball in foreign markets, and authorized limits of interleague games.

In sum, the eight work stoppages and other events that occurred between 1972 and 1995 in baseball had caused a significant shift in the balance of power from team owners to the MLBPA. During the 24-year period, MLB players' average and minimum salaries had dramatically increased and these athletes were no longer required to remain under contract with one team throughout their careers. Furthermore, veteran players gained the right to veto trades, and they and their agents acquired greater bargaining power and freedom to make deals with other clubs. Finally, the shift dictated that MLB's team owners must bargain collectively and in good faith with representatives from the MLBPA.

MLBPA and Drug Policies

As stated before, in 1986 attorney Donald Fehr replaced Marvin Miller and became executive director of the MLBPA. Since his appointment to be the union's chief negotiator and spokesman, Fehr has kept the players united by educating and informing them of the economic, legal and social issues that relate to their professional careers and also about financial matters affecting their families. With respect to a current topic that concerns baseball and interests Fehr, the MLBPA and each player and his family is MLB's drug testing policies and types of prevention and treatment programs, and whether the U.S. government will be involved in solving the sport's problems. Since late September of 2002, organized baseball has banned steroids and other illegal substances. The specific proportions of players to be tested for using drugs, frequency of the tests and penalty system for violations, which were lenient and not strict enough according to many observers, are each contained in the 2002 CBA. However, during the Spring of 2004 it was revealed in a grand jury testimony that a few prominent big league players had allegedly taken, or actually consumed illegal drugs to enhance their performances. Fehr responded to the testimony and said, in part, that he was very concerned about the players' constitutional and privacy rights in tests, and such a matter as implementing a prevention and treatment program is an issue that the MLBPA needs to negotiate with the owners in collective bargaining.

In the May/June 2004 edition of *Scholastic Coach & Athletic Director*, Author Bruce Weber expressed a different view than Fehr about the roles and inputs of the MLBPA's executive director and union in this issue. Weber put it this way. "But where we part ways with Fehr is his apparent anti-drug stance. The use of steroids and other performance-enhancing drugs simply shouldn't be the subject of a collective bargaining agreement. An anti-drug/anti-steroid policy in baseball will simply make the stadium a safer place to work. It will reduce or, hopefully, eliminate cheating. And it will substantially lessen the chances of illegal activity and public doubt about the sport's integrity."[5]

Later in 2004, longtime MLBPA leader and New York Mets pitcher Tom Glavine provided his response to the extent of drug use by professional baseball players. Glavine said, "People have been talking about the steroid issue for several years now. What's coming out of the grand jury testimony, I don't think there's anything surprising. Yes, it's a big story. It needs to be addressed. But it shouldn't be surprising or earth-shattering to anybody."[6]

Because of the testimony of the major league players and criticism from sports journalists, in 2005 Commissioner Bud Selig announced some reforms and a new steroid testing policy for players. That is, Selig proposed a ten-day suspension for a first positive test; a 30-day ban for a second and 60-day ban for a third positive test; and a one-year suspension for a fourth, and discipline determined by the Commissioner for a fifth positive test. Interestingly, these penalties seemed relatively mild after former home run slugger Mark McGwire and current players Sammy Sosa and Rafael Palmeiro had testified before a U.S. Congress committee about the use and abuse of drugs in baseball. Because these players were evasive, unaware and/or indecisive as to whether a serious drug problem existed in the sport, senior politicians such as Arizona Senator John McCain were convinced that a uniform, consistent and tough drug policy needed to be developed and then applied to players in the various U.S. professional sports leagues. Accordingly, McCain and other Senators and House representatives in Congress proposed one or more pieces of legislation to prevent the use of illegal drugs by professional players in the sports industry.

In his remarks to the U.S. House of Representatives' Committee on Energy and Commerce about HR 1862, which is titled the Drug Free Sports Act of 2005, Donald Fehr condemned the unlawful use of steroids and other illegal substances by MLB and minor league players, and dispelled the notion that these drugs enhance players' performances. Furthermore, he outlined the current testing program in MLB and confirmed that it is effective, and stated that collective bargaining is the appropriate forum to consider and resolve drug issues, and concluded that HR 1862 in its present form should not be enacted. To that end, Fehr mentioned the following six reasons for his objection to adopting the proposed legislation.[7]

First, a single federally mandated and operated program, in which an international body selects the substances to be covered and regulated is not an effective way to eliminate the use of illegal drugs in the U.S. professional sports leagues. According to Fehr, it is unclear from reading the proposed legislation whether the final authority and czar of drug policies would be the World Anti-Doping Agency, U.S. Secretary of Commerce or both organizations. While the former group has no obligation or commitment to consider the views or concerns of the AL, NL and teams' owners and players, the latter group is ill prepared and unsure as to which substances are legal or illegal, and why drugs may or may not induce better athletic performances and what are the short- and long-term physical and emotional effects on an athlete's body.

Second, HR 1862 contains no provisions for baseball players' use of substances that the U.S. Congress have determined to be safe and for sale to all adult Americans and readily available for purchase without a doctor's prescription. Therefore, professional athletes should not be restricted, penalized or unfairly treated for the appropriate use of legal substances. That is, there is no justification or precedent in public policy to identify and isolate professional athletes for using such drugs.

Third, the types of punishment being proposed in HR 1862 are discriminatory and too harsh. The goal of a penalty should be to deter the use of illegal substances rather than end a player's career, which would happen with a two-year suspension for the first violation. Because MLB players are diverse and recruited by the league's teams from other nations whose operative medical rules are not uniform or sophisticated, there is the possibility of frequent errors and mistakes given these circumstances. Thus, terminating a player's career as a result of an unintentional error, poor decision or single mistake is unfair and no guarantee that positive drugs tests will be eliminated or even minimal in the future.

Fourth, this legislation's appeal process and system are disorganized, confusing and problematic. It is ambiguous, for example, as to who will determine the final fate of an athlete. That is, the legislation does not specify whether an arbitrator, judge or jury will make that decision, nor whether traditional due process standards will apply, or whether a player has a right to counsel. Moreover, to require that a player's entire appeal process must be completed within 30 days is unreasonable and flawed since controversies may occur when scientific issues, unconfirmed data and biased information are involved in the case and presented as facts. Consequently, the U.S. Congress needs to think more about how the appeal process functions before depriving an athlete of the right to engage in his chosen profession.

Fifth, the Act is very specific in some sections but vague in other parts. This argument primarily applies to the mandate regarding the timing and frequency of random testing where the approach is "one size fits all" rather than a different methodology for each of the professional sports. Furthermore, there is no credible evidence that "drug tests to be administered by an independent party not affiliated" with a professional league is a superior system to the current testing procedures adopted and performed by MLB. Indeed, the major league uses reputable, independent and experienced contractors to select, collect and analyze samples.

Sixth, the bill raises a number of disturbing constitutional questions. For instance, any drug testing of professional baseball players that is suspicionless but mandated by the federal government may, in fact, violate a Fourth Amendment requirement whereby searches must be based on the suspicion of an individual's wrongdoing. To illustrate, in a 1997 case, a court declared it was unconstitutional to require candidates who sought a state office in Georgia to be tested merely for the reason of setting a good example. In other words, any government mandates in HR 1862 may conflict with and violate a player's constitutional rights.

Based on the aforementioned arguments, Donald Fehr adamantly opposes this federal legislation and prefers that the league and MLBPA jointly administer, control and enforce the process of testing major and minor league players for illegal drugs and other substances. Therefore, because HR 1862 applies to all U.S. professional sports leagues, and assuming MLB and the baseball player's union toughen their standards by severely penalizing violators for first, second and third offenses, it is unlikely that Congress will approve HR 1862 or any other laws in 2005 or 2006 to regulate the use of illegal drugs in the U.S. professional baseball leagues.

Besides its role as a labor union, in recent years the MLBPA has become increasingly civic-minded and active in establishing, funding and participating in many community and nationwide programs. To illustrate, on Father's Day in 2005 the union joined with MLB and the Prostate Cancer Foundation to create awareness and raise funds to conquer the disease. That day all players on teams wore blue wristbands and also displayed ribbons on their uniforms to symbolize cancer awareness. Furthermore, for several years the MLBPA has made significant contributions of money and/or resources to the league's Baseball Tomorrow Fund and Breaking Barriers campaign, and also has pledged large donations to victims of the tsunami that struck some countries in Asia.[8]

Along with those and other community affairs and activities, the union and its members have become more involved with the league in marketing baseball and promoting the sport to fans and families in the U.S. and foreign nations. These business actions include participating in commercials and advertisements with MLB Advanced Media, MLB.com and MLB Properties, and engaging in various partnerships and licensing agreements with companies that sell video games and other types of programming software and hardware. In the end, the MLBPA is an experienced and multifaceted organization, and a powerful representative for the players who pursue a career on one or more teams in a professional baseball league that is based in the U.S.

Summary

As highlighted and discussed in this chapter, the history of labor relations in America's professional baseball leagues began in the late 1800s. Although players and their associates had formed five different unions between 1885 and 1946, they were unable to establish a collective bargaining agreement with MLB's team owners. Therefore, each of them had failed to survive in the short- and/or long-term as labor organizations. However, during the mid-to-late 1960s economist Marvin Miller united the members of the MLBPA and then succeeded to negotiate the first CBA in professional sports. In 1986, attorney Donald Fehr replaced Miller as the baseball union's executive director. With Fehr as its leader, the MLBPA has prospered.

Besides implementation of salary arbitrations and free agency, from the early 1970s to the mid–1990s there were eight work stoppages in organized baseball. As these lockouts and strikes occurred, the MLBPA became more unified and powerful while negotiating with team owners. This result led to more favorable CBAs for the players and an expansion of their rights, freedoms and incomes throughout the MLB seasons. This chapter describes the key sections for portions of these CBAs and especially those provisions in the 2002 CBA.

Baseball has experienced years of growth and established fan bases in the U.S. and some foreign countries. Meanwhile, MLB teams' games are the popular event at the big league ballparks and during the summer, on the sports channels of American and international television and radio networks. Even though big league players have become global celebrities and wealthy individuals because of their performances in games, they have continued to seek the protection and security of the MLBPA. Thus, executive director Fehr must negotiate and bargain in good faith with the league's owners about such issues as a salary cap, revenue sharing, luxury taxes, abuse of illegal drugs and other substances by players, the potential contraction of teams and an international draft system.

In sum, the improvements in labor relations between owners and players have contributed to the economic prosperity and international growth of MLB and the broadcast of teams' games to fans in the U.S. and abroad. As such, the MLBPA will continue to be a vital institution that will influence the future development, progress and history of baseball during the early-to-middle years of the twenty-first century.

7. Does the Drug Culture
Corrupt Baseball?

Prior to 2004, the most publicized cases of illegal drugs in Major League Baseball (MLB) involved various players who generally used amphetamine-barbiturates, marijuana and tranquilizers during the 1950s to 1970s, cocaine in the 1980s and 1990s, and steroids, pills, creams and hormone injections since the early 2000s. To illustrate, and as discussed in Chapter 6 of *Balls and Strikes: The Money Game in Professional Baseball*, some of those players included former Los Angeles Dodgers pitcher Steve Howe, San Diego Padres pitcher LaMarr Hoyt, Chicago Cubs pitcher Ferguson Jenkins, New York Mets athletes Keith Hernandez and Dwight Gooden, and such Pittsburgh Pirates power hitters as Bill Madlock, Dave Parker and Willie Stargell. With respect to the 1985 drug trials in Pittsburgh, seven drug dealers went to prison and depending on their testimonies, 11 players were suspended for 60 days-one year, allowed to play if they donated 5–10 percent of their base salaries and contributed 50–100 hours to drug-related community service programs, and submitted to random tests.[1]

In part, these and/or other infractions had occurred despite the implementation of a Drug Education and Prevention Program in 1971 by former MLB commissioner Bowie Kuhn, and a thoughtful but unsuccessful effort to force a voluntary drug program on the Major League Baseball Players Association (MLBPA) in the mid-to-late 1980s by previous commissioner Peter Ueberroth. Thus, from the 1970s to the early 2000s MLB and the MLBPA were unable to agree to incorporate a strict, enforceable and comprehensive testing policy in their collective bargaining agreements that would effectively have prohibited the use of illegal drugs and other substances by the league's players. Even so, Kuhn's and Ueberroth's programs are discussed later in this chapter.

Recent Issues

When the 2004 season concluded, it was reported by the media that some superstar baseball players had admitted to using performance-enhancing drugs sometime in 2001–2004. These athletes included the San Francisco Giants home run record holder Barry Bonds, New York Yankees slugger Jason Giambi, and the former Atlanta Braves and current New York Yankees outfielder Gary Sheffield. Moreover, it was revealed to federal prosecutors that the Bay Area Laboratory Co-Operative (BALCO) in San Francisco had distributed undetectable steroids to certain elite athletes in MLB. As a result, BALCO's founder Victor Conte and three other defendants were indicted and scheduled to appear in a 2005 trial in the U.S. District Court of Northern California.[2]

Before discussing specific information involving the players, reactions from MLB Commissioner Bud Selig and solutions to prevent future drug consumption, Table 7.1 lists three players' statistics for seasons they had allegedly used drugs, including steroids, to enhance their on-the-field performances.

According to Table 7.1, the numbers for Bonds in 2003 and 2004 significantly exceeded his career averages for the four performance characteristics, which were per season, respectively, .300, 37, .611 and .442. Meanwhile, Jason Giambi's statistics in the 2001 and 2002 seasons were above his long-term averages of .297, 23, .540 and .342. His annual totals for the 2003 and 2004 seasons, however, were below average. That occurred because Giambi experienced a slump as a batter and also injured himself, thus, his performances in hitting had declined in 2003 and 2004. Gary Sheffield's 2002 batting average and on base percentage were each marginally above his career average, while his slugging percentage scored moderately below average. As such, it appears that Bonds had overperformed as a batter in 2003 and 2004, as did Giambi in 2001 and 2002. In short, did these players knowingly use drugs to influence their on-field performances during one or more years of the early 2000s?

In his testimony to a grand jury investigating BALCO, Bonds claimed he applied a clear substance and cream supplied by his friend and former weight trainer Greg Anderson during the 2003 season after Anderson said that the substances were nutritional supplement flaxseed oil and a rubbing balm for arthritis. During a recorded telephone conversation to the *San Francisco Chronicle* in 2003, Anderson, who was indicted by the Internal Revenue Service in early 2004 for tax evasion, said he expected advanced warning before Bonds had to submit to a test for steroids. According to the Associated Press, Bonds denied using steroids yet paid Anderson $15,000 in 2003 plus a $20,000 bonus for his productive season. Regarding the relationship between Bonds and Anderson, attorney Michael Rains declared, "Greg knew what Barry's demands were. Nothing illegal. This is Barry's best friend in the world. Barry trusted him. He trusts him today [December 2004]." About illegal drugs, in 2002 Bonds stated that, "Doctors ought to quit worrying about what ballplayers are taking. What they take doesn't matter. It's nobody's

---

TABLE 7.1. SELECTED PERFORMANCE
DATA, BY PLAYER AND SEASON

Player	Season	Batting Average	Home Runs	%Slugging*	%OB
Barry Bonds	2003	.341	45	.749	.529
	2004	.362	45	.812	.609
Jason Giambi	2001	.342	38	.660	.477
	2002	.314	41	.598	.435
	2003	.250	41	.527	.412
	2004	.208	12	.379	.342
Gary Sheffield	2002	.307	25	.512	.404

* Player, Season, Batting Average and Home Runs are self-explanatory. The %Slugging is the player's slugging percentage and %OB is his on-base percentage that season.
Source: "Team Sites," at http://www.mlb.com cited 27 December 2004.

business. The doctors should spend time looking for cures for cancer. It takes more than muscles to hit homers. If all those guys were using stuff, how come they're not all hitting homers?"[3]

Before a grand jury, Jason Giambi testified that he had injected a human growth hormone — received at Gold's Gym in Las Vegas— in his stomach and testosterone in his buttocks, rubbed an undetectable steroid in the form of cream on this body and placed drops of another steroid under his tongue. According to Giambi, Greg Anderson provided him with the latter drugs. Interestingly, even before meeting Anderson on an All-Star tour in Japan in November of 2002, Giambi had admittedly used a steroid named Deca Durabolin since 2001. About Bonds and Anderson's relationship, Giambi mentioned to the grand jury that "… but he [Anderson] never said one time, 'this is what Barry's taking, this is what Barry's doing.' He never gave up another name that he was dealing with or doing anything with." As an aside, Jason's brother Jeremy, who spent 2004 in the minor leagues and played for the Boston Red Sox in 2003, also testified that he used drugs supplied by Anderson.[4]

Subpoenaed in the company's investigation, Gary Sheffield said he used a steroid known as "the cream" that was furnished by BALCO before and during the 2002 season. It appears that Bonds had told Sheffield, after working out together in the post–2001 season, about "a vitamin specifically for your blood type and what your body needs." That vitamin was an illegal steroid unbeknown to Sheffield. As a result, these players ended their friendship and after a poor performance in 2002, Sheffield commented, "I had my worst year ever. I gave [Bonds] too much credit. When you listen to another person on an everyday basis drill into you numbers, numbers, numbers, and you've never been that way, it doesn't work. I don't play for numbers. When I played to try to get numbers, I didn't get them." Given those scenarios and statements of the three players, baseball fans will ultimately determine whether Bonds, Giambi and Sheffield were victims or at fault in their quest to excel by using steroids and/or other illegal drugs.[5]

For how survey testing is performed in baseball, during 2003 all players on the 40-man rosters of each MLB team were tested anonymously in two parts over five-to-seven days primarily during Spring Training or early in the season. Then, 240 of those players were randomly retested later that season. As a result, 5-to-7 percent of the players tested positive, which triggered the punitive testing in 2004 when each player was tested only once unless the initial test came back positive.

Commissioner Selig's Response

MLB adopted penalties for steroid use in 2003 and one year later, the league began testing with samples that were identified by player. It was expected, therefore, that Commissioner Selig would eventually respond to the BALCO investigation and public statements made by Bonds, Giambi and Sheffield about using steroids. That is, he instructed MLB's executive vice president of labor relations and human resources Rob Manfred to consult with the MLBPA, and then together, implement a tougher and more effective drug test program for major leaguers. According to Selig, "This is just another manifestation of why we need that policy right away. My only reaction is, I'm going to leave no stone unturned until we have that policy in place by Spring Training of next year [2005]." Regarding Giambi's future in baseball, he stated "I don't know any more than you do.

I've only read and heard what happened. We'll have a comment on it in a day." And about six-time most valuable player Bonds, the commissioner said, "The only thing I want to say about that, until there's proof there's something wrong, again, I'm not going to comment on it." Furthermore, "I don't think that would be fair. All you have now is a series of allegations."[6]

Selig, in 2001, had instituted moderately strict controls on steroids for the players assigned to minor league teams. These athletes became subject to four year-around unannounced tests and a 15-game suspension for the first violation. The other violations, without pay, are a 30-game suspension for the second, 60-day suspension for the third, one-year suspension for the fourth, and suspension from minor league baseball for the fifth. In contrast to those penalties, in MLB all players are subject to two unannounced tests during the regular season and counseling for the first violation. The second through fifth penalties are, respectively and each without pay, a 15-day suspension and up to a $10,000 fine, 25-day suspension and up to a $25,000 fine, 50-day suspension and up to a $50,000 fine, and a one-year suspension and up to a $100,000 fine.[7]

In other words, the commissioner would implement a more stringent drug policy on MLB players if the MLBPA cooperates and compromises to amend the collective bargaining agreement to reflect the new penalty structure. Recently, at least one sports journalist suggested that if Selig had the freedom and power to govern, as does the National Basketball Association (NBA) Commissioner David Stern, the current scandal would not have dominated the sports pages because of Selig's prior decision to adopt and enforce a zero tolerance drug policy for the sport's players. In short, based on encouraging and forthright statements spoken by Commissioner Selig, by MLB senior vice president Rich Levin and president and chief operating officer Bob DuPuy, and by the union's Don Fehr and chief operating office Gene Orza, the negotiations between the league and MLBPA about reforming the drug policy will focus less on privacy concerns and more on the integrity of baseball and health issues.

Besides those officials, and self-interested politicians and the media, do baseball fans really care about the steroid scandal? For one writer's viewpoint, sports columnist Mark Hyman believes that the scandal has disturbed fans. He cites the results of a Gallup Poll in which 533 professional baseball fans were surveyed in early December of 2004. The Poll's results indicated that, because of the allegations, 61 percent of fans were less enthusiastic about the sport; 86 percent supported an agreement by the MLB and MLBPA to implement new and tougher steroid standards before the 2005 season began; and assuming the league and union do not agree on stricter standards, 59 percent favored Congress passing a law that required more extensive tests for MLB players. According to Hyman, however, there is little evidence that fans will hesitate to purchase tickets in 2005 since MLB set an attendance record in 2004, and the Giants placed second among teams in attracting spectators to Pacific Bell Park in San Francisco and ranked first in attendance at away games. So, although fans are concerned enough to overwhelmingly support a tougher steroid policy for players, they will likely continue to attend games and buy baseball's products, especially those endorsed by Bonds.[8]

Given the fans' attitudes, beliefs and reactions, how will sponsors respond to the scandal? In an article that appeared in *USA Today*, Edward Iwata stated why some sports marketing experts may or may not sign or resign troubled athletes to lucrative deals. For example, Coca-Cola dropped the NBA Los Angeles Lakers star Koby Bryant and LA Gear reviewed its deal with the NBA Indiana Pacers' Ron Artest. With respect to the baseball players who used steroids, Bonds signed a new contract with Topps, a trading card company, and retained his deals with such sports apparel firms as Wilson, Fila and Franklin. For some reason, however, Bonds ended his discussions with MasterCard to establish a promotion program and alternatively, SBC Communications, Anheuser-Busch and Coca-Cola continued to maintain their business relationships with the San Francisco Giants. Finally, as of mid–December 2004 the marketing deals between Jason Giambi and Nike, Pepsi and Arm & Hammer deodorant had not been affected. To highlight the observations of two experts, it was Jonathan Wexler, an executive at Playing Field Promotions in Denver, Colorado who remarked, "The public's patience with athletes now is fairly low, and companies are weary dealing with athletes who have problems. Athletes have to act like good citizens, or they're not going to get these deals." Another marketing executive, Bob Dorfman of Pickett Advertising in San Francisco said "For corporations, the trick now is to keep linking their products to popular sports while avoiding troublesome players." As such, "More corporations are striking deals with entertainers and rap stars, such as the multimillion-dollar sports shoe deal with Reebok and music mogul Jan-Z. They're exploring marketing deals with small groups of athletes, such as the World Series champion Boston Red Sox, rather than the individual stars."[9]

The next section of this chapter describes various solutions that have been put forth about the drug problems in MLB. After that section concludes, there is a Summary.

Drug Policy Proposals

As mentioned earlier in this reading, there have been various MLB policies that attempted to deter the consumption of illegal drugs by players. In 1971, Commissioner Bowie Kuhn initiated the Drug Education and Prevention Program, which included regional seminars organized to educate management officials about how to identify the dangers of drug abuse. Kuhn also developed some Employee Assistance Programs in 1980 and one year later, he and the league's owners established a policy that mandated severe discipline for players that were involved with consuming or trafficking illegal drugs. Because of unintended flaws and legal loopholes in the provisions, professional labor arbitrators proceeded to argue for and defend drug-using players in order to reduce or eliminate their penalties as stated in the league's policy. As a result, Kuhn was only partially successful at eliminating illegal drug usage in baseball. Then, in 1984 the MLBPA, team owners and players jointly created a plan about detecting cocaine use. Unfortunately, the plan did not cover alcohol or drugs besides cocaine and it also failed to include random and mandatory drug tests for players.[10]

In contrast to Kuhn's policies, Commissioner Peter Ueberroth announced a mandatory drug-testing program not for players, but for such personnel as his office staff, and franchise owners, teams' managers and coaches, and union officials. Then, in 1986 he urged players to voluntarily submit to drug tests. Because of poor communications with the MLBPA and unclear disciplinary procedures, Ueberroth had to eventually deemphasize his proposal for a voluntary drug program. Finally, in 1986 the Baltimore Orioles enacted the first voluntary drug-testing program, which was not designated to be a condition of employment or subject to collective bargaining. Again, it was various controversies about grievances, provisions, disciplinary actions and arbitration procedures that had limited the enforceability and effects of the Orioles program.

During the early 2000s, several opinions, recommendations and proposals to eliminate illegal drugs in MLB had been introduced by and debated between various baseball officials and analysts, academics, politicians, and journalists in the sports media. Listed in no specific order or priority, the following are highlights of a few of those opinions, recommendations and/or proposals. First, Commissioner Bud Selig favored a stricter policy that is equivalent to the program mandated for players in minor league baseball. That program features unannounced and more frequent tests at anytime during the year, and greater monetary fines, longer game suspensions, and a permanent suspension from the sport after the fourth positive violation. Because the commissioner's penalties will be viewed by many players as inequitable and punitive, in my judgment the MLBPA will likely resist Selig's proposal and recommend a program that is more tolerant and lenient in that it will emphasize the healthcare, education and counseling of big league players.

Second, Arizona Senator John McCain threatened to propose federal legislation that would override the drug-testing provisions in baseball's Collective Bargaining Agreement. Although McCain had not provided details of or outlined his proposal when this chapter was written, he said, "It [the drug testing agreement between MLB and the MLBPA] would have to be credible, frankly, with the media. It would have to be, at a minimum, the same standards they propose for the minor leagues—things like off-season testing, frequent testing, and testing for substances that are not known. The important aspect of this issue is that high school kids all over America believe that this is the only way to make it. Ask any high school coach." Consequently, whether MLB's reforms and new drug-testing policy wins approval in the court of public opinion, and also satisfies McCain and meets his concept of standards is yet to be determined.[11]

Third, to preserve baseball's integrity, such sports writers as Hal Bodley and Mike Bauman have adamantly supported a forward-looking and more comprehensive drug program that includes year-round testing and much tougher penalties as necessary steps. They want MLB Commissioner Bud Selig and the MLBPA's Don Fehr and Gene Orza to provide the leadership and foresight to enact a policy that eliminates the use of steroids and all other illegal drugs from the game, as well as the suspicion that certain players are using them. According to Bodley, "His [Selig's] innovative moves have made the game stronger, more popular and generated enormous revenue, but that might not be this commissioner's legacy unless he's successful in eliminating the word steroids from baseball's vocabulary." Meanwhile, Bauman revealed his thoughts about the matter this way, "For the sake of the game's future, steroids need to be nowhere near that future. The issue of steroids in baseball requires a determination, a resolution, [and] an end. The identify of the people resolving this issue is not as important as getting this thing fixed, for once and for all."[12]

Fourth, in a December 2004 article in *Newsweek*, reporter Mark Starr offered seven specific items as serious changes for MLB to rid the sport of illegal drugs. These were mandatory year-around and random testing of players; ban and test all performance-enhancing drugs including human-growth hormone; implement harsher penalties for players who use illegal drugs; adopt other penalties such as teams losing their top draft choices; incorporate disincentive clauses for illegal drug use in players' contracts; adopt a "Caminiti tax" on team revenues and player salaries [1996 NL Most Valuable Player Ken Caminiti admitted to using steroids in the 1990s and died in 2004 from cocaine]; and invest league monies and resources in a massive, national public-service campaign that is targeted to the youth who model their behavior after professional athletes. With respect to these items as components of a comprehensive MLB program, Starr applied economic marginal analysis and wrote, "There has always been more investment in cheating than in detection. Baseball doesn't require a foolproof system. When the threat of penalties outweighs the rewards of cheating, the tide will turn."[13]

To conclude this chapter, there have been numerous articles published in the nation's sports pages that focused on whether Barry Bonds' drug use will affect his election into baseball's Hall of Fame when he becomes eligible five years after retirement. After reviewing several publications, here are three quotes from sports writers about that issue. One, "This guy was a Hall of Famer well before he hit 73 home runs. If we start discrediting hitters who took steroids, what about pitchers?" Two, "He's certainly a Hall of Fame talent, even if he's not a Hall of Fame character. I think there is so much more on this case to be played out, but ultimately he's either banned from the Hall of Fame consideration or a first-ballot Hall of Famer." Three, "You can't just say that drug use should keep a player out of the Hall of Fame. Hasn't [former Milwaukee Brewers slugger] Paul Molitor admitted using cocaine during his career?"[14]

Summary

The recognition and report that professional baseball players are covertly using such drugs as steroids, human-growth hormone and cocaine is a critical problem that MLB and the MLBPA must evaluate and resolve to maintain the integrity of the sport. As such, this chapter discusses the culture and environment of the illegal consumption of drugs by players in the big leagues, examines the beliefs and roles of three baseball players who have been taking drugs to boost their performances, and lists some opinions, policies and proposals that have been recommended by prominent baseball officials and sports writers. From the statements and news reported in the media, MLB will reform its drug testing policy in ways that severely penalize players and possibly teams and owners who are directly or indirectly involved with the use of illegal drugs.

8. *Major League Players' Salaries and Team Payrolls*

Despite several expansions in the American League (AL) and National League (NL) of Major League Baseball (MLB), sustained growth in team attendances and incremental amounts of revenue from television and radio contracts for selected franchises, prior to the mid–1970s the reserve clause had caused the salaries of professional baseball players to remain relatively stagnant for many years. Even so, by the late 1960s the players had benefited from a minimum salary of $10,000, from the opportunity to join the Major League Baseball Players Association (MLBPA), which was originally led by labor organizer Marvin Miller, and from a collective bargaining agreement that provided them some leverage with the league and team owners. Then, in a suit filed against MLB Commissioner Bowie Kuhn in 1969, St. Louis Cardinals centerfielder Curt Flood argued that the reserve clause was illegal and therefore, he and various players should be free to negotiate for employment with other teams. Although the U.S. Supreme Court ruled against Flood, free agency was established in 1976 when arbitrator Peter Seitz upheld the grievance case of Montreal Expos pitcher David McNally and Los Angeles Dodger pitcher Andy Messersmith who had each refused to sign their contracts to play the regular season.[1]

As such, free agency in baseball was adopted after a 14-day strike in 1972, 12-day lockout in 1973, 17-day lockout in 1976, and even though the players' average salary had increased nearly 80 percent or from approximately $24,909 in 1969 to $44,676 in 1975. However, because of higher salaries from free agency and team owners' frequent disputes with the MLBPA, there was an 8-day strike in 1980, 50-day strike in 1981, 2-day strike in 1985, 32-day lockout in 1990, and a 232-day strike in 1994–1995. In short, after the mid–1970s the economic benefits in MLB had partially shifted from the league and franchise owners to players and indirectly to the MLBPA. Meanwhile, local taxpayers in MLB cities decided to increasingly subsidize the construction costs of new ballparks in their communities, baseball fans had to spend proportionately more of their disposable incomes at regular season games for tickets, concessions and teams' products, and many players received substantial improvements in their salaries and the employment terms of their contracts.[2]

After the series of strikes and lockouts between the early 1970s and mid–1990s, and because of other factors such as the absence of a hard salary cap, player compensation

gradually became the most significant expense for general managers to successfully operate a MLB team and a primary reason that a franchise had or had not succeeded as a business organization in its market. Furthermore, during the 1990s and early 2000s the
disparities in average salaries and payrolls among and between small- and large-market
clubs in the AL and NL became a controversial and serious issue in the sport. That is,
one or more of the baseball franchises in the Chicago, Los Angeles and New York City
metropolitan areas had the potential to earn more revenues, accumulate wealth, employ
the league's most productive players, remain competitive by winning games during the
regular season, and then qualifying for the playoffs and perhaps winning the World Series.
Alternatively, the small-market teams that played in Cincinnati, Miami, Milwaukee, Minneapolis, Montreal, Kansas City, Pittsburgh and Tampa Bay generally struggled to sign
outstanding free agents or retain their highest skilled hitters and fielders, and to win
enough games and compete for a championship. As a result, during the majority of regular seasons these clubs had likely experienced below average and unstable game attendances, collected insufficient operating revenues, and established limited fan bases with
respect to the markets in their home cities and metropolitan areas. Therefore based on
the literature available, this chapter will provide some historical data to analyze the amounts
and distributions of players' salaries and teams' payrolls in MLB, especially since the early
1990s. The analysis will also include specific information about the highest paid and most
productive athletes in MLB, and about team efficiencies and performances, baseball agents
and other interesting issues relative to sports resources and their allocations.

Evaluation of Players' Salaries

Table 8.1 lists, in five-year increments, the amounts and percentage growths in the
minimum and average salaries of MLB players for the period 1965 to 2005. The tabled
data poses two questions. First, what is the significance of the dollar values and second,
why did they grow at various unequal percentages during that 40-year period?

According to the table, the largest increases in the minimum and average salary
amounts were, respectively, $116,000 in 2000–2005 and $97,000 in 1995–2000, and in
percentages, 100 percent in 1965–1970 and 1980–1985 for the minimum and 222 percent
in 1975–1980 for the average. Generally, the players' strikes in 1972, 1980, 1981, 1985 and
1994–1995 tended to boost the salaries in future years and seemed to have more of an
impact on salaries than the owners' lockouts in 1973, 1976 and 1990 since no regular season games were lost during the three lockouts. Furthermore, after 1965–1970 the average percentage usually increased more the minimum percentage because of the substantial
salaries paid to such superstars as the Houston Astros' Nolan Ryan in the late 1970s, Minnesota Twins' Kirby Puckett in the late 1980s, Los Angeles Dodgers' Kevin Brown in the
late 1990s, and the Texas Rangers' Alex Rodriguez in the early 2000s. As an aside, Ryan
and Puckett have retired from baseball after successful careers, while Brown of the
Dodgers and Rodriguez of the Rangers were traded by their clubs to the New York Yankees before their lucrative contracts had expired. Indeed, the Dodgers and Rangers ownership had considered the multiyear contracts of Brown and Rodriguez as too extravagant
for their franchises to afford and thus, the general managers traded these players while
they were still productive athletes and popular among baseball fans across America.[3]

To be sure, the level of and change in national inflation rates, economic growth and

TABLE 8.1. MLB PLAYERS' SALARIES, IN
DOLLARS AND PERCENTAGES, BY YEAR

Year	Minimum*	PCTCH	Average	PCTCH
1965	6	—	19.0	-
1970	12	100	29.3	54
1975	16	33	44.6	52
1980	30	87	143.7	222
1985	60	100	371.5	158
1990	100	66	578.9	55
1995	109	9	1071.0	85
2000	200	83	1988.0	85
2005	316	58	2589.6	30

* Minimum and Average are, respectively, the players' minimum and average salaries per year in thousands of dollars. The columns labeled PCTCH are the five-year percentage changes of the minimum and average salaries. The — indicates that the percentage changes in 1965 are not applicable while the Average and its PCTCH in 2005 were estimates.

Source: "Who Wants to be a Millionaire?" at http://www.cnnsi.com cited 5 April 2001; "The Baseball Archive," at http://www.baseball1.com cited 30 December 2004.

general trends of the U.S. economy, and the expansion and relocation of MLB teams were other factors that had affected the minimum and average salary amounts presented in Table 8.1. In contrast to those values of 40 years, Table 8.2 was developed to show how the salaries of MLB players appeared in nominal dollars each year during the 1990s and early 2000s. Specifically, this table reveals the annual minimum and average amounts of and percentage changes in the players' salaries for a recent 15-year period of regular seasons.

Besides such labor market factors as competition, free agency, owners' lockouts, strikes and the threat of strikes, and the increase in power of the MLBPA, there are business, economic, demographic and social conditions, events and trends that explain, in part, the amounts of and percentage changes in MLB players' salaries as reflected in Table 8.2. Listed in no particular sequence, the following are six reasons that explain, in part, the variations in minimum and average salaries of players since 1990.

First, teams have increased their operating revenues in different amounts and proportions from business deals with television networks, cable channels, satellite radio and other types of broadcasting companies. This, in turn, had provided most owners with additional cash inflows to competitively bid for free agents and to reward their most valuable players with long-term, multimillion-dollar contracts. Each franchise, for example, received nearly $4 million from MLB's recent agreement with XM Satellite Radio. In fact, this amount exceeds what some small- and mid-market teams collect from their local radio rights. To illustrate, the radio deal may have contributed to the Arizona Diamondbacks signing outfielder Troy Glaus to a four-year, $45 million contract. As one general manager put it, "Here's a guy [Glaus] who was injured for most of the last two seasons [2003 and 2004] and a team that everyone thought has enormous debt problems, and yet, somehow the Diamondbacks give him $45 million over four years. How does that happen?"[4]

Second, the construction of new baseball stadiums in such cities as Cincinnati, Chicago, Cleveland, Detroit, Philadelphia, Pittsburgh, San Diego and San Francisco have probably boosted the current asset balances of, respectively, the Reds, White Sox, Indi-

TABLE 8.2. MLB PLAYERS' SALARIES, IN DOLLARS
AND PERCENTAGES, 1990–2005

Year	Minimum	PCTCH*	Average	PCTCH
1990	100	—	578.9	-
1991	100	0	891.1	53
1992	109	9	1084.4	21
1993	109	0	1120.2	3
1994	109	0	1188.6	6
1995	109	0	1071.0	(9)
1996	109	0	1176.9	9
1997	150	37	1383.5	17
1998	170	13	1441.4	4
1999	200	17	1720.0	19
2000	200	0	1988.0	15
2001	200	0	2264.4	13
2002	200	0	2383.2	5
2003	300	150	2555.4	7
2004	300	0	2490.0	(3)
2005	316	5	2589.6	4

* PCTCH is the annual percentage changes in the minimum and average salaries of MLB players. The — indicates that the percentage changes are not applicable in this table. The percentage changes in parenthesis means a decline in the Average that year.

Source: See the sources in Table 8.1 and "Decline is First Since 1965," at http://www.sports.espn.go.com cited 5 January 2005.

ans, Tigers, Phillies, Pirates, Padres and Giants. With the additional revenues from their ballparks, these teams have the potential to compete more effectively for moderately skilled and experienced players who are not superstars, but who may have been released by large-market teams like the Atlanta Braves, Boston Red Sox, Chicago Cubs, Los Angeles Dodgers, New York Mets and New York Yankees.

Third, after consecutive low-performance seasons some high-revenue teams may be pressured by their fans to become competitive again within two to three years. This occurred, for instance, in Seattle when the Mariners were compelled to offer $112 million to acquire free agents Carlos Beltran and Richie Sexson for the 2005 season. According to a rival baseball executive of the Mariners, "What's ironic is that when they [Mariners] had a legitimate chance to win in 2002 and 2003, they wouldn't spend to improve at the trading deadline. Now they're spending like crazy. Do they really think those two guys [Beltran and Sexson] are going to turn it around for them?"[5]

Fourth, because of their sports agents many MLB players have financially prospered when they signed contracts and earned tens of million of dollars in salaries and other benefits. Some prominent baseball agents include David Falk, Alan and Randy Hendricks, Jim Bronner and Bob Gilhooley, and Scott Boras, who has been a very successful agent since the early 2000s.

Regarded as one of the most accomplished, articulate, powerful and hated agents in sports, Boras is an experienced, conscientious and tough negotiator who convincingly touts the past performances and future potential of his clients at meetings with baseball teams' general managers. His business firm titled The Scott Boras Corporation, which is located in Newport Beach, California employs approximately sixty employees who research baseball economics and prepare detailed player resumes that rely on key data and background information to put their sixty-five client's achievements into historical perspective. To illustrate, in late 2004 Boras had focused on and represented fourteen highly skilled, experienced players including center fielder Carlos Beltran, third baseman Adrian Beltre, outfielders Magglio Ordonez and J.D. Drew, catcher Jason Varitek and pitchers Derek Lowe and Kevin Millwood. As a result of Boras' organization, all but one of the players signed a lucrative, long-term contract with a team. These were Beltran at $119 for seven years with the Mets in New York City, Beltre at $64 million for five years with the Mariners in Seattle, Ordonez at $75 million for five years with the Tigers in Detroit, Drew at $55 million for five years with the Dodgers in Los Angeles, Varitek at $40 million for four years with the Red Sox in Boston, and Lowe at $36 million for four years with the Dodgers in Los Angeles. Rather than a multiyear deal as agreed to by Boras' other clients, Millwood decided to sign a one-year, $7 million contract with the Cleveland Indians. Because of previous elbow injuries, however, his contract provides for bonuses based on the number of starts and innings pitched in the 2005 season.[6]

As an aside, personal observations about the behavior and knowledge of Boras were expressed by two baseball officials and are cited here. Former Dodgers managing partner Bob Daly said, "Personally, I like Scott. I love to talk to him about baseball, and I like to talk to smart people. But I didn't like dealing with him. If you told me there was a player we wanted to sign and you told me to pick the agent I'd like to negotiate with, he'd be the last person I'd pick. That's a compliment to him because he's hard to deal with. He never stops pushing, and that's why his clients like him." Another team official made this statement regarding Boras, "He's very opinionated and very passionate, not only about his players about the game in general. He has definitive opinions on things, and for some people that might rub them the wrong way, and for others they view him as a very educated observer."[7]

Fifth, it is simply the supply of and demand for athletes in the labor market combined with the local, regional, national and international popularity of baseball that have determined why baseball player salaries are extremely high and far above average. Relative to the market's supply, there are only a limited number of individuals who have the ability to throw or hit a 95-mile-per-hour fast ball, which are talents that are not easily taught or replicated. With respect to the market's demand, millions of consumers are willing and able to attend baseball games and tournaments, pay the assigned seat prices in ballparks at those events, and are enthusiastic about watching games on television or listening to them on the radio, and interested in purchasing such baseball products as hats, shirts, gloves, bats and other clothing, equipment and merchandise. Since the supply of skilled baseball players is relatively scarce, while the demand for players has generally increased throughout the twentieth and twenty-first centuries because of population growth, higher consumer incomes and other demand-related factors, MLB teams' revenues have risen and so have the minimum and average salaries of their players. According to a baseball theory of Michael Walden, who is the William Neal Reynolds distinguished professor at North Carolina State University in Raleigh, "The best solution to the modern problems of baseball is to loosen restrictions on team movements and guaranteed markets by allowing unprofitable small-market teams to move to large markets. With the bigger markets split more ways, they will no longer have an advantage over smaller markets, and the big market escalation of player salaries will end."[8]

Sixth, to improve their current and future performances and salary capacities, many professional athletes including baseball players are now training harder and smarter, eat-ing healthier foods and recovering from injuries more rapidly than in previous years. Furthermore, to be prepared and competitive in their divisions, teams are investing increasing amounts of funds and resources in strength facilities and coordination programs for their players because the franchise owners realize that local fans will attend home and away games in which the players are well conditioned and able to run faster around the bases, hit pitched baseballs for higher averages and longer distances, and accurately field ground balls and catch those batted in the air. As a result of players gradually improving their physical skills and abilities, teams are likely to win more regular season and postseason games, realize higher attendances at their ballparks, and earn more revenues from their operations. Consequently, this is another reason why players in MLB have earned higher compensation, especially since the mid–1970s when free agency was approved and implemented.[9]

In retrospect, some MLB franchise owners will regret signing relatively mediocre and inferior players to long-term, multimillion-dollar contracts during the early 2000s. Because a portion of these players are overpaid relative to their performances, the risks of financial losses will continue to emerge as a growing threat to the survival of small-to-medium market teams. If the revenue growth of one or more teams, or of professional baseball levels out or peaks after 2004, it may be necessary for the league and MLBPA to compromise and seriously negotiate in good faith a cap to control the salaries of all or some players by team. To further explore that issue, the next topic of this chapter exposes how AL and NL teams are vulnerable and at risk from a human resource and business operation perspective.

Analysis of Team Payrolls

For historical comparisons and other purposes, the annual payrolls of MLB teams have been reported for various baseball seasons in several publications. As they appear on the *Sports Illustrated* web site at www.cnnsi.com, the payroll totals of teams are compiled by Commissioner Bud Selig's office and include termination pay, prorated shares of signing bonuses and earned incentive bonuses, and buyouts of options and cash transactions. Furthermore, any income deferred without interest is discounted. Besides that web site, there is frequently payroll data on teams available at such online sources as The Baseball Archive at www.baseball1.com, FansInAction at www.sportsfansofamerica.com, and MLB at www.mlb.com. Consequently, since there is more than one source of payroll information for MLB franchises, the researcher must be accurate and consistent when collecting, organizing and interpreting these statistics.[10]

To analyze the payrolls of MLB teams that existed in the AL and NL during the 2000 to 2004 regular seasons, Tables 8.3 and 8.4 were prepared. Since the payrolls were reported on and obtained from the *Sports Illustrated* web site, the values include termination pay, bonuses and other types of player incomes.

Specifically, Table 8.3 displays the total estimated amounts that each franchise owner spent for the players on their rosters in each of five seasons. The significance of these values is that they show the absolute and relative expenditures on human resources as determined by the owners of MLB's small-, mid- and large-market AL and NL teams. As expected, during the five-year period the four teams that consistently had one of the highest payrolls were the AL's New York Yankees and Boston Red Sox, and the NL's Los Angeles Dodgers and New York Mets.

TABLE 8.3. TEAM PAYROLLS, BY LEAGUE, 2000–2004*

Team	2000	2001	2002	2003	2004
AL					
Anaheim Angels	54.3	49.4	62.4	79.9	115.6
Baltimore Orioles	69.3	77.1	62.9	72.1	56.8
Boston Red Sox	75.5	114.3	116.6	108.4	130.3
Chicago White Sox	35.6	62.8	57.2	63.2	64.6
Cleveland Indians	78.3	95.3	77.8	53.4	42.6
Detroit Tigers	54.8	51.1	56.5	55.3	58.8
Kansas City Royals	25.9	36.1	52.2	45.4	44.7
Minnesota Twins	16.7	27.4	41.8	56.9	54.7
New York Yankees	95.2	114.4	138.4	169.5	187.9
Oakland Athletics	30.3	39.7	40.9	51.3	60.2
Seattle Mariners	59.8	79.9	88.3	95.7	81.8
Tampa Bay Devil Rays	61.2	50.9	35.8	27.4	24.4
Texas Rangers	57.8	86.8	108.8	103.3	79.2
Toronto Blue Jays	54.5	74.2	69.2	58.8	50.6
NL					
Atlanta Braves	87.5	94.8	94.7	97.9	79.4
Arizona Diamondbacks	77.2	85.1	109.5	83.7	68.4
Chicago Cubs	59.4	72.8	74.9	84.1	100.6
Cincinnati Reds	42.3	43.9	44.5	50.6	46.2
Colorado Rockies	63.9	68.6	52.0	66.8	69.4
Florida Marlins	22.1	38.0	43.6	55.8	50.3
Houston Astros	50.1	66.4	66.6	72.8	81.9
Los Angeles Dodgers	88.8	115.4	103.1	113.2	101.6
Milwaukee Brewers	36.9	46.6	49.8	43.3	29.5
Montreal Expos	27.2	34.6	36.6	47.2	39.3
New York Mets	82.2	93.1	102.8	112.8	103.1
Philadelphia Phillies	45.7	46.9	61.4	71.5	97.3
Pittsburgh Pirates	33.6	46.6	47.1	53.2	32.5
San Diego Padres	54.2	38.6	40.5	50.8	65.9
San Francisco Giants	50.4	67.5	82.5	89.1	82.4
St. Louis Cardinals	69.1	76.1	73.8	93.1	92.8

* The payroll amounts are expressed in millions of dollars.
Source: "Payroll Comparison," at http://si.printthis.clickability.com cited 2 January 2005.

Other teams such as the Cleveland Indians and Atlanta Braves in 2000 and 2001, Texas Rangers and Arizona Diamondbacks in 2002, Texas Rangers and Atlanta Braves in 2003, and Anaheim Angels and Chicago Cubs in 2004 also ranked high in payroll expenditures. Except for the Indians, Diamondbacks and Angels, these clubs play in ballparks located in medium or large markets.

Alternatively, the teams with the lowest payrolls in 2000–2004 included a combination of the AL's Kansas City Royals, Minnesota Twins, Oakland Athletics and Tampa Bay Devil Rays, and the NL's Cincinnati Reds, Florida Marlins, Milwaukee Brewers, Montreal Expos and Pittsburgh Pirates. Since these clubs are each based in small markets, their owners have relatively limited salaries for free agents and veteran players. Interestingly, even with inferior payrolls and amounts of revenues to spend on marginal athletes, the Twins and Athletics have been successful teams in their respective divisions because in many regular seasons they employ excellent coaches who train their players to compete for or win titles and qualify for the playoffs.

According to Table 8.3, from 2000 the payrolls of the Yankees, Cubs, Astros and Phillies had increased, and the Devil Rays decreased each season. In part, the higher payrolls occurred because of lucrative contracts awarded to the Yankees' Alex Rodriguez, Cubs' Sammy Sosa, Astros' Roger Clemens, and Phillies' Jim Thome. Beside the four clubs mentioned before, the other teams with generous payroll hikes per year were the White Sox and Mariners in 2001, Royals and Giants in 2002, Rockies and Cardinals in 2003, and the Angels and Red Sox in 2004. Alternatively, the Devil Rays was the only club that downsized its payrolls annually from 2000 to 2004 because of disappointing team performances and poor attendances at home games. Meanwhile, because of operating problems, the Orioles, Indians, Blue Jays, Braves, Diamondbacks, Brewers and Pirates had experienced payroll cuts in 2004 relative to 2000. In short, the payrolls of most franchises increased from 2000 to 2004 when the economy improved and baseball fans became spectators at games and consumers of more sports products.[11]

Besides the amounts in Table 8.3, which indicate how much payrolls varied for AL and NL teams during five consecutive seasons, there are also team payrolls per win to compare. This statistic denotes efficiency, that is, it measures how productive a team has been on the field in a season given its total payroll. Ceteris paribus, clubs with high (low) payrolls are expected to win (lose) more games than those with low (high) payrolls. Thus, the lower (higher) are payrolls per win during a season, the higher (lower) is the team's efficiency with respect to utilizing its roster of players to achieve victories.

According to Table 8.4, in the majority of years the most efficient teams were the AL's Minnesota Twins and Oakland Athletics, and the NL's Florida Marlins and Montreal Expos. The least efficient teams, meanwhile, were the AL's Boston Red Sox and New York Yankees, and NL's Los Angeles Dodgers and New York Mets. In general, during 2000–2004 the franchises located in small markets tended to conserve their expenditures on players and spent less per victory than did clubs in large markets. Table 8.4 also denotes that from 2000 to 2004 the AL's Oakland Athletics and Seattle Mariners, and NL's Houston Astros and San Francisco Giants each increased their payroll costs per victory. As such, these four teams became less efficient and none were consistently more efficient throughout the five seasons. The typical club, therefore, experienced variations in payrolls per win in 2000–2004.

The previous paragraphs were an analysis of how player salaries and team payrolls fluctuated during various years in MLB. To conclude the discussion of these topics, the Summary appears next and then Chapter 9.

Summary

An analysis of the minimum and average salaries of baseball players, and of team payrolls and payrolls per win were the primary focus of this chapter. To explain the quantitative data contained in four tables, various business, demographic, economic and sport-specific reasons were discussed to justify the level and growth of salaries and payrolls since free agency was implemented in the mid–1970s. Because of the increases in players salaries and team payrolls, especially since the early 1990s, most of the small-market teams in the AL and NL lack the operating revenues to successfully hire high-priced free agents and to resign their most valuable veteran players.

TABLE 8.4. TEAM PAYROLLS PER WIN,
BY LEAGUE, 2000–2004*

Team	2000	2001	2002	2003	2004
AL					
Anaheim Angels	.66	.65	.63	1.03	1.25
Baltimore Orioles	.93	1.22	.93	1.01	.72
Boston Red Sox	.88	1.39	1.25	1.14	1.32
Chicago White Sox	.37	.75	.70	.73	.77
Cleveland Indians	.87	1.04	1.05	.78	.53
Detroit Tigers	.69	.77	1.02	1.28	.81
Kansas City Royals	.34	.55	.84	.54	.77
Minnesota Twins	.24	.32	.44	.63	.59
New York Yankees	1.09	1.20	1.34	1.67	1.86
Oakland Athletics	.33	.38	.39	.53	.66
Seattle Mariners	.65	.68	.94	1.02	1.29
Tampa Bay Devil Rays	.88	.82	.65	.43	.34
Texas Rangers	.81	1.18	1.51	1.45	.88
Toronto Blue Jays	.65	.92	.88	.68	.75
NL					
Atlanta Braves	.92	1.07	.93	.96	.82
Arizona Diamondbacks	.90	.92	1.11	.99	1.34
Chicago Cubs	.91	.82	1.10	.95	1.13
Cincinnati Reds	.49	.66	.57	.73	.61
Colorado Rockies	.77	.93	.71	.90	1.02
Florida Marlins	.27	.50	.55	.61	.60
Houston Astros	.69	.71	.79	.83	.89
Los Angeles Dodgers	1.03	1.34	1.12	1.33	1.09
Milwaukee Brewers	.50	.68	.88	.63	.44
Montreal Expos	.40	.51	.44	.56	.58
New York Mets	.87	1.13	1.37	1.70	1.45
Philadelphia Phillies	.70	.54	.76	.83	1.13
Pittsburgh Pirates	.48	.75	.65	.70	.45
San Diego Padres	.71	.48	.61	.79	.75
San Francisco Giants	.51	.75	.86	.89	.90
St. Louis Cardinals	.72	.81	.76	1.09	.88

* The tabled values are each team's total payroll in dollars divided by the number of wins during each of five regular seasons. In 2000, for example, the Anaheim Angels spent approximately $660,000 for each win. To interpret, the teams with lower values are more efficient, in dollars per victory, than those with higher values.
Source: See Table 8.3.

Consequently, in 2006 the league will bargain with the MLBPA about a salary cap, greater revenue sharing amounts from high- to low-payroll franchises, and/or an increase in the luxury tax rate. Otherwise, after 2006 the operating revenues and payrolls between the large- and small-market teams will become even more inequitable and concentrated. That is, MLB's business model and system for allocating money and resources between franchises, and the teams' determination of payroll amounts will need to include some of the policies and programs that have been successful in the National Football League and National Basketball Association.

9. The Concentration and Status of Minorities in Baseball

During April of 1947, the color barrier in Major League Baseball (MLB) was demolished when African American Jackie Robinson joined the Brooklyn Dodgers of the National League (NL). Three months after Robinson's appearance with the Dodgers, Larry Doby pinch-hit for the Cleveland Indians in the American League (AL). Indeed, since the late 1940s the racial composition of big league baseball teams has gradually become more diversified with the inflow of black, Latino and foreign players. Furthermore, there have been other advancements for minorities in professional baseball. That is, they have been increasingly hired as team coaches and as staff personnel in MLB offices. For various reasons, however, their opportunities to be approved as a majority owner or employed as a general manager of a professional baseball franchise have been almost non-existent. According to one study, which measured the progress of minorities in non-player positions of professional sports leagues during the late 1990s and early 2000s, their participation in MLB ranked below average when compared to the men and women of color in the National Basketball Association (NBA) and Major League Soccer (MLS), about the same to slightly less than the participation of minorities in the National Football League (NFL), and above the rate that existed for non-white males and females in the National Hockey League (NHL).[1]

To be more specific about the sport of professional baseball, there has been a decrease in the proportion of American black and white players on MLB teams since the late 1970s to the early 2000s. Inversely, the athletes from nations in Central and Latin America, and from countries in Asia have generally increased in number and percentage as players who perform on the baseball clubs in divisions of the AL and NL, and in the minor leagues. Besides the status of professional players, other statistics denote that African American men are more likely to be coaches and instructors in MLB than hired as executives and general managers in the front offices of the league and franchises. Furthermore, in recent years the percentage of black women employed in staff and administrative positions of MLB teams has declined. Regarding Latinos, in 1998 Omar Minaya from the Dominican Republic became the New York Mets' assistant general manager and then the general manager of the Montreal Expos in 2002. Two years later, he was selected to be the Mets' general manager. Moreover, in 2004 Mexican Arturo Moreno became the first Hispanic to be a majority owner of an elite team when he purchased the Anaheim Angels from the

Walt Disney Corporation. In fact, that year Moreno was ranked as the most influential minority in professional sports as discussed later in this chapter. In short, these are examples that illustrate how various minorities have reshaped the racial composition and managerial offices of numerous baseball organizations in the big leagues.

Consequently, this chapter primarily focuses on the progress, and secondarily on the current and future status of minorities in MLB. To adequately analyze that topic, it is necessary to expose the changing relationships and roles of blacks, Latinos and other racial groups in sports, and more significantly, as baseball players and then as professional team coaches, general managers and franchise owners in MLB. After a discussion of these matters, the chapter identifies the investments and interactive programs that MLB has initiated to encourage kids, teenagers and young adults who are African Americans and individuals from foreign countries to learn, play and enjoy the game of baseball. With this knowledge, baseball academics, analysts, practitioners and fans will better comprehend the opportunities, problems and other issues that affect the sport and how it may develop and perhaps prosper during the twenty-first century.

African American Players

Fourteen years after Jackie Robinson had first performed for the Dodgers in Brooklyn, New York, approximately 17 percent of the players on MLB teams consisted of black athletes. The majority of these players had migrated to Organized Baseball from, or was assigned to one or more clubs in the Negro League such as the Indianapolis Clowns, Kansas City Monarchs and Memphis Red Sox. This movement of African American players occurred, in part, because of the higher pay and benefits, and prestige and stability provided by the teams in MLB. Thus, by the early 1960s the best black, and also white and Hispanic baseball players in the U.S. had little choice but to sign contracts with clubs in America's minor or major leagues. According to some historians of the sport, that time period was when African American's interest in baseball, at least from a fan's perspective and then 25 years later from a player's viewpoint, peaked and then began to trend downward, which continued throughout the 1990s and early 2000s. Besides the facts mentioned before, what other factors may help to explain why African Americans have generally become less interested in baseball than they were relative to the late 1940s to mid–1970s? To analyze that event, the following are several reasons why the black community in the U.S. has practically abandoned MLB games as a choice for sports entertainment and baseball as an opportunity for a career.[2]

First, the rise in popularity of the NBA and NFL since the 1960s has enticed many inner city kids who live in large metropolitan areas to play and excel in basketball and football rather than baseball. That is, the greatness and success of Michael Jordan and the Dream Team in the 1992 Olympics, Jordan's ability to produce championships when he was a Chicago Bull, and the hip-hop lifestyle of minorities in urban communities have each attracted more kids, teenagers and young adults to shoot basketballs on asphalt courts in their neighborhoods, to play on elementary, high school and college basketball teams, and to watch NBA games on television and at the local arenas. Football and the NFL, meanwhile, became more appealing to athletes in large to medium-sized cities after the league merged with the American Football League in 1970 and their games appeared each week on national television networks. Since football is the largest revenue sport at many Division I colleges and universities in America, talented high school athletes gravitated to the sport in order to earn a scholarship to play at high-profile schools such as Florida State University, Ohio State University and the University of Oklahoma, and then accept an offer to tryout and be drafted by an NFL team. As a result, secondary school and university baseball programs have received fewer resources and the economic interests of skilled athletes motivated them to become a linemen or running back in football and not a pitcher or infielder on the baseball team in their high schools and colleges.

Second, an official baseball game requires at least 18 players to field two complete teams, and such equipment as baseballs, mitts, bats and uniforms are expensive to purchase especially for poor kids whose parents are underemployed. Furthermore, it is difficult to organize teams and schedule even an unofficial or sandlot baseball game with fewer than ten to 12 players. Alternatively, a basketball and football, respectively, are the only necessities for kids to play a pick up game or to scrimmage in those sports, and numbered uniforms may be ignored particularly in basketball. Consequently, due to the lack of recreational facilities and land area in urban communities, young black athletes discovered that it was more convenient and less costly to forego baseball and play games in other sports.

Third, to be successful in professional baseball, all of the players must invest their time by spending one or more full seasons on teams in a minor league system. Even such superstars as Barry Bonds and Gary Sheffield had to play on clubs in Class A, AA and/or AAA before they were prepared for and promoted to a big league team. All-American and other very good basketball and football players, meanwhile, are generally drafted after their senior year in college, or earlier if a hardship case, and if successful may immediately perform for a team in the NBA or NFL. However, a small proportion of college basketball and football players who were drafted may spend a few seasons in either the National Basketball Development League or NFL Europe before joining, respectively, the parent club in the NBA or NFL. Therefore, super athletes in America's high schools and colleges realize that the most expeditious way to become wealthy and a celebrity, and appear on television and sign endorsements, is to play and excel in basketball or football as a sport, and not baseball.

Fourth, for business, economic and social reasons, MLB has not been able to successfully market its sport to children of color and other minorities who attend elementary and secondary schools of this nation. But then, in the late 1980s to early 1990s big league baseball invested in and implemented several grass roots programs and activities in North America and abroad that involved the participation and commitment of kids, teenagers and young adults, and particularly those who live in densely populated urban areas. A sample of these programs is highlighted later in this chapter and mentioned in other chapters of this book.

Fifth, during the 1980s and 1990s there were some American sports officials, former baseball players and university professors who publicly stated that MLB had discriminated against minority athletes by paying them less than whites with comparable performances. These accusations, in turn, contributed to a decline in the number of African American baseball fans, and a decrease in the participation of black players on teams in elementary and secondary schools, and in colleges. According to other critics, it is because of segregated housing, under funded school systems and high-crime neighborhoods in America for why the races do not interact economically, politically and socially, which means that an invisible wall has always existed between white and black people and their children. Although these problems have not disappeared in society, since the early-to-mid-1990s the races have become more integrated such that several minorities hold positions of power in MLB. For example, in 2004 African American Jimmie Lee Solomon was the senior vice president of baseball operations and Jonathan Mariner performed as the chief financial officer of the league. These and other minority baseball officials are discussed later in this chapter.

Sixth, generally families of color who live in large urban areas have moderate to high poverty and unemployment rates. This misfortune suggests that these groups lack a sufficient amount of disposable income to frequently attend professional sports events, whose costs have dramatically risen throughout the 1990s and early 2000s. In fact, between 1995 and 2004 the average cost for admission to a MLB game during the regular season increased by 84 percent or from $10.73 to $19.82. Indeed, the highest ticket prices for individuals to attend regular season baseball games at ballparks are in such large cities as Boston, Chicago, Los Angeles and New York City. Even more significant than the ticket prices, however, are the full costs for a four-person family to attend a MLB game. Referred to as a Fan Cost Index, this dollar amount increased on average by 60 percent or from $97 in 1995 to $155 in 2004. That is, in 2004 it costs a family of four approximately $263 to watch the Red Sox play a game at Fenway Park in Boston, $194 to see the Cubs at Wrigley Field in Chicago, $153 to cheer the Dodgers at Dodger Stadium in Los Angeles and $183 to root for the Yankees at Yankee Stadium in New York City. As a result, it is expensive for adults with children to attend the MLB games played at ballparks in large cities. Because of these exorbitant costs, since the early 1990s the African American population in America has decreased its demand and passion as a group for professional baseball.[3]

Seventh, since the 1970s there has been a significant increase in the number of Latinos and to a lesser extent, other athletes from foreign countries to participate in American amateur and professional baseball games. Such interest from the Latino population has likely discouraged the parents of African American children and coaches of high school players of devoting their time and energy to develop the skills of blacks in the sport. Since athletes in the Dominican Republic, Mexico, Puerto Rico and Venezuela play baseball games with great passion from an early age, and view the sport as a way to escape a lifetime of deprivation, these Latinos have surpassed African American players in number, and during the 1990s, became the dominant minority on the rosters of MLB teams. In turn, such Spanish-speaking players as the Baltimore Orioles' Sammy Sosa, New York Mets' Pedro Martinez and Red Sox' Manny Ramirez have emerged as the role models for kids to emulate rather than black players named Barry Bonds of the San Francisco Giants, Gary Sheffield of the New York Yankees and Ken Griffey Jr. of the Cincinnati Reds.[4]

Minorities: Productive Resources in Baseball

Despite the smaller proportion of African American athletes on teams in MLB, and the decline of black baseball fans that attend big league games, some minority individuals and groups have been, are and will be valuable resources in the development of the sport. Indeed, of those individuals who have established all-time career records for regular seasons in MLB, there are several black and a few Hispanic players listed in the top 20 of various game-related categories. These outstanding performers include, for example, ten minority players each in home runs and stolen bases, eight in runs batted in, seven each in games and slugging percentages, six in hits, five each in singles and runs scored, four each in doubles and games played, and one in highest batting percentage. Meanwhile, such great athletes as Bob Gibson in lowest earned run average, Rube Foster in consecutive scoreless innings, Pedro Martinez in winning percentage, and Juan Marichal in shutouts are a sample of four minority players who are listed among MLB's regular season career leaders as pitchers.

Historically, most black baseball players experienced discrimination because they were not considered to be team leaders or strategists by various sports officials and fans. As a result, only a few of them have succeeded to win 20 games in a season by pitching for one or more MLB teams. To recognize and promote their achievements, the best minority pitchers are profiled in a book titled *The 12 Black Aces*. In the book, the authors discuss the 12 players who have won 20 games as pitchers and another 12 who, despite their talents, were only able to pitch in the segregated Negro Leagues. The first group of players includes two pitchers that excelled in the 1950s, four in the 1960s and three each in the 1970s and 1980s. Besides Bob Gibson, who won 20 games during five seasons for the St. Louis Cardinals, there is, for example, the Oakland Athletics' Vida Blue, Mike Norris and Dave Stewart, and the Los Angeles Dodgers' Don Newcombe. As the first African American pitcher to ever win 20 games, Newcombe was honored as the NL's Rookie of the Year in 1949 and seven years later, he won the Cy Young and Most Valuable Player awards. Since there were only four African American pitchers among the 30 starting rotations of MLB teams in the 2004 season, it appears that baseball coaches continue to be skeptical and not trust the abilities of black players on the mound. Perhaps the facts in and publication of *The 12 Black Aces* will change these negative perceptions and viewpoints.[5]

As of mid–2004, there were several men and a few women who were prominent minorities in professional and collegiate sports. For the name, rank, age, race and position of the individuals who were affiliated with MLB, Table 9.1 was prepared. As organized, the table contains the 18 individuals in baseball who were listed among a group of minorities that totaled 101 people in the various sports.[6]

Interestingly, a total of nine or 50 percent of the individuals listed in column one of the table are MLB officials and players. With respect to the most significant responsibilities of the officials, Jimmy Lee Solomon oversees the scouting system and minor leagues, and he implements and enforces the league's rules. Jonathan Mariner manages baseball's finances and operates the credit program that was established to provide loans to the member teams. Shawn Cummings directs MLB's international licensing and sponsorship business and Bob Watson makes decisions for the league about discipline issues. Finally, Wendy Lewis controls the league's recruitment and diversity programs including minority-owned enterprises.

Regarding the influences of the four players, Barry Bonds is baseball's biggest star, an all-star who receives the most votes, and the reason for why the Giants appeal to fans in San Francisco and in other MLB cities. Alex Rodriguez has the highest salary in the sport and is the league's best player to market professional baseball to Hispanic fans in the U.S., and in Central and Latin America. Ichiro Suzuki left Japan to play for a team in MLB, and he is an awesome leadoff hitter and the Mariner's most popular player. Hideki Matsui is a power hitter for the Yankees, and a factor for why a $275 million television deal was concluded to broadcast games in Japan.

TABLE 9.1. INFLUENTIAL MINORITIES
IN BASEBALL, BY RANK, 2004

Name*	Rank	Age	Race	Position
Arturo Moreno	1	57	L	Owner, Anaheim Angels
Jimmy Lee Solomon	7	47	B	Senior VP, MLB Operations
Jonathan Mariner	10	49	B	Chief Financial Officer, MLB
Barry Bonds	14	39	B	Outfielder, San Francisco Giants
Alex Rodriguez	17	28	L	Infielder, New York Yankees
Shawn Cummings	26	40	B	International Division, MLB
Kenny Williams	30	40	B	GM, Chicago White Sox
Omar Minaya	32	45	L	GM, Montreal Expos
Dusty Baker	33	55	B	Manager, Chicago Cubs
Kim Ng	37	35	A	Assistant GM, LA Dodgers
Fernando Cuza	54	47	L	Players Agent, Baseball
Bob Watson	61	58	B	Vice President, MLB
Ichiro Suzuki	67	30	A	Outfielder, Seattle Mariners
Felipe Alou	69	69	L	Manager, San Francisco Giants
Don Nomura	76	46	A	Players Agent, Baseball
Hideki Matsui	77	30	A	Outfielder, New York Yankees
Ozzie Guillen	85	40	L	Manager, Chicago White Sox
Wendy Lewis	100	49	B	VP, Strategic Planning, MLB

* To qualify and be listed, the individuals had the power to hire and fire, or substantially influence those who do. Furthermore, they each held a significant senior-level position with a team, league or major sports enterprise, or had a profound impact on the sports economy. The rankings are based on such factors as the size of the person's organization, division or budget, and his or her breadth of influence. The Race variable is labeled L for Latino, B for Black and A for Asian.

Source: Richard Deitsch, et al., "The 101 Most Influential Minorities in Sports," Sports Illustrated (28 June 2004), 80.

Besides these MLB officials and players, Table 9.1 also includes three field managers, two general managers, two players' agents, and an assistant general manager and a franchise owner. These nine minorities had influenced the sport of professional baseball because of their power and positions. That is, Dusty Baker had won three awards for being Manager of the Year, and he coached the Cubs to within five outs of playing in the 2004 World Series. While leading the Giants in San Francisco for ten years, his teams appeared in three NL postseasons. Felipe Alou has been a role model and mentor for Latin American players since the 1970s. As the manager of the Giants in 2003 and 2004, each season his clubs won at least 100 games before three million fans that attended SBC Park. Venezuelan Ozzie Guillen, who played superbly as a shortstop for the White Sox for 13 years, is a charismatic, energetic and inspirational manager. Similar to Alou, Guillen has established friendships and trustworthy relationships with the Latino players in the league.

Regarding the importance of the general managers, assistant general manager and player agents, Kenny Williams hired manager Ozzie Guillen, and he has attracted a number of talented athletes to perform for the White Sox. As a result of Williams' leadership, White Sox teams competed in their division to almost qualify for postseason appearances in 2003, 2004 and 2005. Omar Minaya worked to keep the Expos competitive despite the club's relatively low payroll and frugal owner. Because of that performance, Minaya became the first general manager of the Washington Nationals. Kim Ng, who is perhaps baseball's most powerful woman, oversees the roster changes, trades and contract negotiations for the Los Angeles Dodgers. If successful, she may become the first female general manager in MLB history. Fernando Cuza, who is employed by the prestigious SFX agency, is the agent who has represented the top Latin players including the Mets' Pedro Martinez, Yankees' Mariano Rivera, Orioles' Miguel Tejada and Angels' Vladimir Guerrero. Don Nomura, in part, is responsible for the inflow of baseball players from Japan. That is, he discovered a loophole in Japanese players' contracts that allowed these athletes the freedom to resign and migrate to teams in MLB. As an agent, he has negotiated salaries for some of the top Japanese players such as Hideo Nomo and Akinori Otsuka.

In 2004, the Los Angeles Angels of Anaheim' owner Arturo Moreno was ranked as the most influential minority in baseball. As the first Latino proprietor of a major American sports franchise, he is expected to effectively market the team in predominately Spanish language markets located in the border States of the U.S.' southwest, and especially in southern California and portions of northern Mexico. Because Moreno has succeeded in business and understands the passion and respect that Latinos have for baseball, the Angels will likely set regular season attendance records at 45,000-seat Edison International Field in Anaheim. Furthermore, Moreno's multimillion-dollar investment in the Angels is an incentive and opportunity for wealthy Mexicans and Mexican Americans to own an expansion or relocated MLB franchise, and place it in Monterrey or another prosperous city in Mexico.

MLB Programs for Minorities

Predicated on the leadership of and commitment from Commissioner Bud Selig, one of baseball's short- and long-term strategies is to expand in diversity by encouraging more minorities and foreigners to participate in various aspects of the sport. To attract an increasing number of males and females of color as investors, general managers, coaches, players and vendors during the early 2000s, the league allocated additional resources and expended surplus capital to achieve its economic and social goals. Selig's staff, for instance, investigated whether the Florida Marlins' employment of manager Jack McKeon had followed the league's hiring practices, which specify that teams must provide the commissioner with a list of minority managerial candidates. After the list is reviewed and approved by the commissioner's office, then the teams are allowed to recruit, interview and select the most qualified person for the available position. If there are any infractions of the league's policy, teams may be fined up to $2 million. In short, this is an internal rule that MLB has voluntarily implemented that will raise its mediocre score of C on the University of Central Florida's Racial and Gender Report Card.

Before identifying some of MLB's programs and other activities that have primarily focused on diversity, and are intended to improve race and gender relations, the league recently made two important decisions. First, in late 2004 this baseball organization agreed to distribute more than $1 million in contributions to 29 African American players who were excluded from the big leagues during the late 1940s and 1950s. Specifically, these athletes, who had played in the Negro Leagues for at least four full seasons between 1947 and 1957, were given the option to receive from MLB $833 per month for four years, or $375 per month for life. Furthermore, these players must not otherwise be eligible for a vested benefit under the MLB Benefit Plan or any previous plan. To determine the order for mailing the funds to each individual, baseball established the economic needs of players to be the top criteria.[7]

Second, in February of 2005 MLB made a special effort to celebrate Black History Month by making additional donations to the Jackie Robinson Foundation and by supporting the Negro Leagues Baseball Museum. Besides the league's money contribution and its sponsorship, several teams agreed to conduct fundraisers and blood drives, and to schedule parades that honored the accomplishments of Robinson and recognized the importance of social policies, civil rights and sports in America. Consequently, the $1 million payment to 29 former Negro League players, and the amounts of money and support allocated during Black History Month each represented MLB's interest in promoting the sport among minorities and rewarding the moral strengths and performances of the great African American baseball players.[8]

Since the late 1980s to early 1990s, MLB has implemented a number of programs to increase, by various ways, the diversity of the sport. To illustrate, in 1991 the league began operating a program that was started in 1989 by former major league player John Young, who had grown up in south-central Los Angeles. After naming it Reviving Baseball in Inner Cities (RBI), Young's task was to lure minority kids and teenagers, who live in poor neighborhoods of urban areas, away from gangs by getting them interested in baseball events. Besides the competition from playing on an organized baseball team in a structured league, RBI includes other activities such as an education component whereby teenagers in the program receive tutoring in their academic courses and assistance in preparing for standardized tests completed in high school. Furthermore, the program provides instructions so that the participants learn about the healthcare risks and other consequences of alcohol, illegal drugs and promiscuous sex.[9]

Most of the RBI programs are conducted in large to medium-sized metropolitan areas and the types of minorities vary by city. For example, in New York City there are baseball teams with many players who are Puerto Rican, in Boston who are Dominican, in Miami who are Cuban, and in Houston and Los Angeles who are Mexican. Meanwhile, the proportion of African Americans in RBI programs has decreased from about 61 percent in 2000 to approximately 50 percent in 2004. Even so, MLB has committed to allocating a generous portion of its resources and money capital to promote and operate RBI so that the teenagers of all races are encouraged to change their behaviors and lifestyles, and learn how to have fun by devoting their energy and free time to playing baseball as a member of a group. In the end, the program's existence will help to reestablish baseball's fan base among young African American teenagers, and to expand the sport's popularity within the Latino communities in America.

By sponsoring youth leagues and baseball clinics in the minority neighborhoods of Chicago, Philadelphia, Phoenix, San Diego and other cities, MLB teams have also provided the financial support and an opportunity to involve kids in baseball. Fortunately, the executives of these clubs realize the special need for baseball equipment and the lack of space to locate ball fields in these places. As a result, some facilities have been built for players because of such donations as $1 million from the Cubs to construct a modern baseball field in Chicago. In short, to read about other programs that were implemented by MLB and various teams, which were targeted at minorities and teenagers in inner cities, see the news releases on the clubs' web sites at mlb.com or obtain a copy of their media guides from the public relations departments.

As an incentive to attract female, minority entrepreneurs, MLB began the Diverse Business Partners Program in 1998. Basically, the league awards contracts to businesswomen who operate firms that are able to supply various types of clothing, equipment, products and services to big league teams. Indeed, these vendors have provided clubs with advertising and transportation services, floor covering, janitorial necessities, maintenance, uniforms, printing, stationary, picture framing and office furniture. In recent years, MLB has expanded the program beyond existing partnerships. That is, the league requests that its primary or first-tier suppliers do business with and purchase items and services from second-tier minority-owned firms. To ensure that the Partners Program is promoting and attaining vendor diversity, MLB periodically reviews each team's financial statements, which report the small business contracts that were issued to suppliers. Based on these documents, if there are any significant discrepancies between the gender and race of the vendors who were awarded contracts and the diversity in the marketplace, then the league consults with the teams until an equitable balance is achieved.[10]

For proof about the effectiveness of the program, the observations of two minority vendors are cited. First, there is Towanda Scott. She was the president of ASAP Career Apparel in Atlanta, Georgia. Her firm supplied different uniforms for those employees in the Atlanta Braves organization that were employed as security personnel, ushers and ticket takers for games at Turner Field in Atlanta. After the Braves had submitted a commitment letter enabling Scott to obtain a bank loan and purchase ASAP Career Apparel from the previous owner, Towanda remarked that, "Baseball has been a saving grace for me. If it had not been for baseball's commitment, we wouldn't be here." Second, as a participant in baseball's diversity program for six years in Chicago, the president of RGMA Company Ralph Moore states, "I think the fact that baseball has become a leader in minority diversity is really raising the bar for all of the other sports. There's a need to go beyond employment diversity and beyond philanthropy into the whole issue of vendor diversity, which I thing is the foundation for economic empowerment for minority communities."[11]

In a nutshell, MLB and most of the league's teams have financed, organized and implemented national, regional and/or local community programs, baseball activities and events that, for the most part, are targeted at and involve African Americans, Latinos and other minority kids, teenagers and young adults who live in urban areas. Although thoroughly discussed in another chapter of this book, these are social investments that reflect to what extent the league and various team owners have committed their scarce resources and capital to expand diversity and upgrade the role of minorities within the sport.

Summary

Since the mid-to-late 1970s, the numbers of African Americans who play baseball and those on MLB clubs, and the proportion of the sport's fan base that consists of blacks, have gradually decreased. Meanwhile, there has been a steady upward trend in the quantity and quality of Latinos who play on amateur and professional baseball organizations in America, and also an increase in Latino fans that attend the regular season and post-season games of MLB teams. Although male Caucasians from the U.S. have always been in the majority with respect to baseball's franchise owners, general managers, coaches, players and fans, the sport's diversity has changed among the nation's minorities. This transition, in turn, has likely impacted the growth and business of the league and the competitiveness and fan base of each member team.

To focus on the status and role of minority groups in a popular sport, this chapter provided several reasons for why the interest in and commitment to play and watch U.S. amateur and professional baseball games has shifted from American-born blacks to Latinos and even to foreigners from countries in Asia. Consequently, there is a discussion about the significance of the former Negro Leagues and the contributions of African American and Latino players who have established all-time regular season records in MLB as hitters and pitchers.

Other aspects about the impact of minorities in professional baseball are also explored in this chapter. A table, for example, reveals the age, race and occupation of 18 individuals, who are listed by rank because they were rated as among the most influential minorities in the sport during 2004. The primary role of each individual, and his or her responsibility and authority for being a prominent person in baseball are then briefly examined in several paragraphs following the table.

After that topic is explored, there is a discussion of some U.S.–based diversity programs and activities that are funded and operated by MLB. These are designed and scheduled to encourage minorities from all races to become more involved with and develop a passion for the sport, especially the African American children, teenagers and young adults who have little opportunity to organize and participate in baseball games and other events because they live in poor segregated neighborhoods of large and medium-sized cities. Then, the final portion of this chapter reveals other investments made by MLB and specific teams to increase the sport's diversity from a business perspective. In sum, professional baseball will return to its status as America's pastime if more minorities become passionate about the sport, and learn and enjoy how to be involved as investors, coaches, players and fans, and earn profits as business partners of MLB teams.

10. Social Investment by Sports in Community Affairs

The 14 American League (AL) and 16 National League (NL) franchises in Major League Baseball (MLB) are organized as business enterprises. That is, each of them is granted the right to operate a professional baseball team and provide sports entertainment in the competitive marketplace. The difference between a team's total revenues and costs determines whether it earns a profit, loss or breaks even. Generally, a profit results when the franchise owner, and the team's general manager, field coach and players are very efficient and successful in their respective roles. Otherwise, the club either incurs a loss from its operations or the total revenues and costs are approximately equal. Thus, profit is the primary business incentive for a professional baseball enterprise to win enough of its regular season games to qualify for the postseason and compete for the AL or NL pennant and then a championship title in the World Series.

Nonetheless, to exist and prosper in the short- and long-term as independent businesses and sports organizations in MLB, each AL and NL team relies on the support of people, and especially on the demands of baseball fans who may live within the local community and perhaps metropolitan area. Indeed, any good fellowship and interaction with the population in the community and area is important for clubs that play their home games at ballparks in large cities such as the Cubs and White Sox in Chicago and the Mets and Yankees in New York City, and also significant for teams that entertain fans in small cities like the Brewers in Milwaukee, Pirates in Pittsburgh and Reds in Cincinnati. In short, it is in the best interests of the league commissioner and particularly the individual franchise owners to communicate, interact and maintain friendly relationships with all sports consumers who reside in their respective local and regional market areas.

Consequently, it is rational, prudent and essential for the business of professional baseball, and for earning goodwill, respect and a reputable image, that the commissioner's staff and each of the league teams to proactively and voluntarily invest time, resources and money capital in order to establish an array of social programs, projects, events and other activities, which are targeted to various individuals, organizations and demographic groups in their local and regional communities. This commitment and effort by baseball to improve the well-being of people and condition of non-profit institutions was recently confirmed by MLB's vice president of community affairs Tom Brasuell. In late 2004, he stated, "We support the Commissioner's [Bud Selig's] vision of making the community a better place for our fans, and we look forward to working with our teams who do so much in the community year-around. We want to continue in the Central Office to do our part as well. There is so much all of us can do."[1]

To that end, this chapter identifies and praises a number of the social programs, projects, events and other activities that the league office, AL and NL franchises, and the teams' players have been associated with, operate and/or sponsor in some manner. Unfortunately, these well-intentioned and productive efforts and investments by baseball are not usually reported in the media. Instead, the prominent sports editors, reporters and journalists prefer to arouse their readers interests by publishing information about and critiquing such inflammatory issues as the commissioner's disagreements with the Major League Baseball Players Association (MLBPA), as when team owners threaten to relocate their clubs to another city if a new ballpark is not constructed at home with taxpayer money, and as the consumption of steroids by players is investigated. Likewise, it is reasonable to assume that the academic community will rarely research and write articles about such topics, that is, those which analyze the widespread economic, social and public benefits of baseball's investment in local projects and the participation by teams and players in community affairs. In fact, other than the league's web site at mlb.com and a few articles that had been printed in city newspapers and sports magazines, there are only a few sources used as references to develop the contents of this chapter.

Therefore, based on that literature, the following three sections will initially discuss the league's investments in a variety of programs, projects, events and activities that have been implemented to improve the quality of communities, and then those that have been adopted, sponsored and/or operated by selected professional teams and players.[2]

MLB in the Community

There are several methods that determine how the league has become involved with and contributes to the welfare of various communities. These include the requests that were forwarded to MLB's central administration from individuals, families and local, regional, national and international organizations; second, the requests from the teams' coaches, players and the MLBPA; and third, the requests from municipal, state and federal governments. Nevertheless, the commissioner's staff and the league's community affairs or relations division are likely to propose a portion of the programs, projects, events and activities. Although the step-by-step or decision-making process is an internal and private matter within baseball, the potential social benefits and resource costs of each proposal are probably estimated. As a result, proposals are then approved or disapproved by the commissioner and/or community affairs or relations division. If approved, a plan is developed to implement the proposed investment as a program, project, event and/or activity and a news release is prepared to promote it to the public.

In 2005, MLB's official web site listed and briefly described 12 of the league's community programs. The first one on the list was a 501 c(3) organization titled Baseball Assistance Team (BAT), which is a lasting legacy of former Commissioner Peter Ueberroth. Implemented in 1986, the BAT is an annual event that raises funds to help previous MLB and/or minor league players who are struggling with financial, mental and physical hardships, and need assistance. Between 1986 and 2004, the program had provided 1,700 former players with more than $12 million in health care benefits, financial grants, rehabilitative counseling and other forms of support. To illustrate a typical BAT event, in January of 2004 1,250 individuals attended a $500-a-plate function at the Marriott Marquis in New York City to honor Boston Red Sox pitcher Curt Schilling, sports broadcaster Bob Costas and the retired player and New York Mets manager Jeff Torborg. Commenting on the event, BAT's executive director Jim Martin said, "We have an application process, and we've never turned anyone down for financial reasons. And we never will. We'll always find a way to raise more money." Meanwhile, the Seattle Mariners' outfielder Randy Winn expressed his admiration for the BAT by stating, "This is a way to pay tribute to the people who came before in the game. It's a way to give back."[3]

The next community program listed at mlb.com was the Baseball Tomorrow Fund (BTF), which is a current MLB-MLBPA activity that provides organizations across the globe with money grants to support the youth who play baseball and softball. The funds may be used for such projects as the purchase of equipment and uniforms for players, and for the construction and renovation of baseball fields. Since it was formed in 1999, the BTF has benefited a total of nearly 88,000 American and foreign kids and teenagers in more than 150 sports activities. During the Fourth Quarter of 2004, the program awarded an estimated $550,000 to 11 organizations including a YMCA and Boys & Girls Club, to several Little Leagues, cities and school districts, and to an Creek Indian tribe that used the money to acquire batting cages and pitching machines for at least 100 teenagers to hit baseballs ejected by the machine. For sure, the BTF has generated an interest among youngsters in many nations to become active in sports and learn the values of discipline, teamwork and sportsmanship.

In a partnership that was concluded by Commissioner Bud Selig in 1997, the Boys & Girls Clubs of America (B&GCA) became MLB's official charity. This national network of more than 3,000 neighborhood-based facilities is a hospitable organization for millions of young people who exist in disadvantaged circumstances. B&GCA's programs focus on educational improvements and career opportunities, and on how to avoid alcohol and drugs, receive the benefits of fitness and health, prevention of crime and violence, cultural enrichment, leadership development and community service. Since the late 1990s, this nation-wide partnership has established more than 100 new baseball leagues in America's inner cities and 100 machine-pitch instructional programs throughout the country. With MLB's donations in excess of $16 million, the B&GCA encourages character development and gives children and teenagers a chance to improve their lives. In Selig's view, this partnership is a very good program to fortify the league's relationship with young people during the twenty-first century.

Using baseball-themed activities, features and lessons, Breaking Barriers (BB) consists of an assortment of events and actions that teach children the specific traits and values they need to overcome serious threats, challenges and obstacles, and to fulfill their lives. As devised by the league, the MLB Players' Trust for Children and Scholastic Inc. is one BB program that was established in 2004. This event is an international chapter contest in which students enrolled in grades K–12 had to identify a personal problem or hardship and then deal with that difficulty by applying the values as exhibited by former Los Angeles Dodger Jackie Robinson. Robinson's daughter Sharon toured numerous elementary and secondary schools in the U.S., Canada and Puerto Rico to congratulate the contest winners. They received prizes including an IBM ThinkPad laptop computer, a baseball jacket and signed copy of Sharon's book titled *Promises to Keep*, and two sets of 100-volume Hero Libraries. Two of BB's other activities involve physical fitness contests and the distribution of a teaching guide to help young students learn how to frequently exercise and eat smart.

Before MLB's annual all-star game played each July at a big league ballpark, a Fan-Fest is typically scheduled. Generally, this event provides an opportunity for baseball fans of all ages to experience excitement and fun prior to the game. For example, at the 2004 FanFest as organized in Houston, Texas there was first, a home run derby, second, an online chat with Commissioner Bud Selig who responded to questions from sports fans about the game of baseball, third, a softball game played by legends and celebrities, fourth, stories told by former Negro Leagues star J.C. Hartman who recalled several wonderful memories that resulted from his professional baseball career, and fifth, the presentation of a video about Houston's rich baseball heritage that began in the 1920s. Other activities at FanFest were visits to the area's hospitals by MLB team mascots to entertain kids with illnesses, big league players hosting clinics to improve the skills of young athletes, and town hall meetings that presented highlights of the all-star games played in 2002 and 2003. As an aside, the John Hancock Mutual Life Insurance Company funded the 2004 FanFest. This business firm titled the event "Baseball Heaven on Earth" and placed it at the George R. Brown Convention Center in Houston.

Another worthwhile program of MLB is named Join the Major Leagues @ Your Library. This community affair, which the league developed with the American Library Association in 2001, is designed to help males and females build their literacy skills in order for them to be knowledgeable about the information age. Besides lessons to improve their reading skills, the individuals learn how to use computers and other technology, how to find, evaluate and use information in the library, and how to effectively communicate with that information. To participate in the program, a playbook and game board must be downloaded from a computer and then printed. With these files, the participant answers four categories of increasingly difficult questions—one for each of the four bases on a baseball diamond. After the playbook is taken to the library, one question from each base is selected and the four are solved for the correct answers. A librarian may be consulted for assistance about how to research the questions. Finally, along with an official entry, the completed playbook is mailed to and graded at the program's headquarters located in Chicago, Illinois. If the playbook was accurately completed, the individual was entered into a national drawing for the opportunity to win two tickets to a designated game at the next World Series.

The seventh community-based program of MLB emphasizes three of baseball's most fundamental aspects, that is, the ability of a player to pitch, hit and run. This is a contest, which has no registration fee. Specifically, it provides girls and boys aged 7–14 with an opportunity to display their skills in hurling and hitting a baseball and running the bases. The first requirement for the player is to throw strikes into a batters zone as performed by a big league pitcher. To accomplish the second skill, the hitter must swing a bat and hit a baseball for distance and accuracy. The third opportunity is for the athlete to run from second base to home plate in the minimum amount of time. If contest's winners successfully advance through four levels of competition, they will participate in the program's National Finals, which was scheduled in 2005 at the all-star game held in Detroit, Michigan at Comerica Park. To determine the rules of pitch, hit and run, a handbook must be downloaded from computer software. For how to host a competition or for general information, it is necessary to mail any questions and comments to the pitchhitrun@mlb.com.

Sponsored by MLB since 1991, the Reviving Baseball in Inner Cities (RBI) program was initially organized by former big league player John Young in 1989. He established it as a way promoting baseball to teenage boys and girls who live in poor neighborhoods of metropolitan areas. After being successful in south central Los Angeles, RBI was adopted by sponsors in New York City and in St. Louis and Kansas City, Missouri during the early 1990s. Later, the program spread to the other cities that host a MLB team. As organized, RBI consists of leagues with divisions for junior and senior boys in baseball, and girls in softball. The program is very popular in many underdeveloped communities of large cities because it keeps kids from joining gangs, and also teaches them how to overcome any academic weaknesses and social disadvantages. For example, the Academy of Excellence Program, which is centered at Santa Monica College in California provides the RBI participants with tutors and an opportunity to enroll in college and SAT preparation courses, and in classes that focus on goal setting and time management. The New York Yankees pitcher Kevin Brown, who previously had played for the Dodgers in Los Angeles, contributed money to operate the Academy. Regarding the RBI's benefits, a sports broadcaster remarked, "It keeps kids out of trouble and off the streets, while at the same time teaching them to stay in school. They earn self-esteem and self-respect. The educational components help them realize their potential and work toward achieving college scholarships based not only on athletics, but academics."

MLB's ninth and tenth community-based programs listed on mlb.com are, respectively, Initiative for Kids and the Rookie League Pitching Machine Program. The league implemented Initiative for Kids to support charitable causes for young people and to give kids an opportunity to attend professional baseball games. To that end, the league placed a tax of $1 on stadium tickets sold for the MLB games that are scheduled from mid–August to early September. The proceeds from the tax are then distributed by baseball to the B&GCA and CureSearch National Childhood Cancer Foundation. Furthermore, during 2002 the league began an activity whereby children, who are 5–12 years-old, were given an option to hit a baseball from a machine that ensures all pitches are delivered at the same speed and into the batter's strike zone. As a result of this experience, the boys and girls who bat will gain confidence since they successfully develop their hitting skills. Also, using the machine prevents kids from injuring their arms because they threw hard pitches at a young age. Relative to the program's increasing popularity among young baseball players in America and abroad, the number of Rookie Leagues expanded by 96 in 2002 and 2003, and by 36 in 2004. Moreover, the concept currently exists in several Asian and European nations for kids there to enjoy and learn the techniques to becoming successful hitters of baseballs.

Finally, there are two special programs that honor former big league minority players, that is, the Roberto Clemente Award and Jackie Robinson Foundation. Originally titled as The Commissioner's Award in 1972, one year later it was renamed when Clemente unexpectedly died because his plane crashed while delivering relief supplies to earthquake-stricken people in Nicaragua. As it is sponsored by funds from John Hancock Financial Services, the Award recognizes those ballplayers who truly understand and appreciate the value of helping others. Some recipients of the Award include such former but great baseball athletes as the New York Giants' Willie Mays, St. Louis Cardinals' Ozzie Smith and San Diego Padres' Tony Gwynn.

Meanwhile, the Jackie Robinson Foundation is a public, not-for-profit national organization that was created in 1973 by Jackie's wife Rachel Robinson. Essentially, the

Foundation awards scholarships to academically-gifted minority students who need financial assistance. As a result, the scholarships enabled these and other students to enroll in a college or university of his or her choice. For example, during the 2004–2005 academic year a total of 57 individuals received scholarships and they enrolled in 89 different colleges and universities. With respect to how funds are obtained, there are more than 90 corporations and other entities that contribute to and subsidize the Foundation's education and leadership development activities.

Besides the 12 community programs previously described, since 2004 MLB has sponsored and participated in the New York Cares Spring Clean-up Day, contributed money to the Make-a-Wish campaign, teamed with the MLBPA and donated $1 million to assist the victims of the tsunami that had struck Asia, and introduced a youth baseball edition of a catalogue that was modeled after The Catalogue for Giving of New York City. Indeed, the league's edition raised more than $3 million to operate local sports organizations. These included Little League, American Legion and USA Baseball. As a compliment to MLB's community efforts, each team is socially responsible at its site as follows.[4]

Teams in the Community

Throughout 2004, the majority of MLB teams had aggressively established a number of community campaigns within their host cities and metropolitan areas to reduce illness, poverty and other hardships of people. That is, the baseball clubs participated in numerous projects, events and activities through such sources as charities, community affairs departments, foundations and other methods. To identify a few of the specific programs that were adopted by each franchise during 2004, Table 10.1 was prepared. It lists, in alphabetical order, the 14 AL and 16 NL teams and a sample of three programs that each of these clubs had sponsored, funded and/or operated to improve the social conditions of individuals, families, groups and/or non- profit organizations that existed somewhere in the teams' metropolitan areas.

Based on Table 10.1 and the information that is available on the teams' web sites at mlb.com, there is a community relations, affairs or development department, or another organizational unit that is responsible for planning, managing and completing each franchise's new and existing social investments. Generally, a senior vice president or junior executive leads the department or unit, and this person performs a variety of tasks. These duties may include, for example, coordinating all of the baseball youth programs, and evaluating donation requests, arranging player and staff visits, hosting groups and organizing special awareness days at the local ballpark, and scheduling appearances by the team's mascot. Furthermore, the majority of the clubs' community affairs, functions, relationships and responsibilities are internally centralized and controlled under one title and uniquely identified. To illustrate, in the AL there is the [Los Angeles] Angels [of Anaheim] Baseball Foundation, [Oakland] Athletics Community Fund, [Toronto] Blue Jays Care Initiative, [Cleveland] Indians Charities, [Seattle] Mariners Care and [Chicago] White Sox Charities. Meanwhile, in the NL some are identified as the [Houston] Astros in Action Foundation, [Milwaukee] Brewers Charities, [St. Louis] Cardinals Care, [Los Angeles] Dodgers Dream Foundation, [San Francisco] Giants Community Fund and [Cincinnati] Reds Community Fund. In short, the 30 MLB teams have each committed a portion of their resources and money capital to participate and invest in programs that benefit a specific segment of society.

TABLE 10.1. MLB TEAMS AND COMMUNITY
PROGRAMS, BY LEAGUE, 2004

Team	Types of Community Programs
AL	
Angels	Prostate Cancer Foundation; School Readiness; Home Run Challenge
Athletics	Breast Cancer Awareness Day; Oakland Children's Hospital; 5-K Run
Blue Jays	Student Rally Days; Salvation Army; Field of Dreams Program
Devil Rays	Baseball Clinic; Play Ball Scholarship Fund; United Way
Indians	American Indian Cultural Center; First Pitch Luncheon; Hardball Classic
Mariners	Children's Hospital; Cystic Fibrosis Foundation; Boeing Field Grant
Orioles	Maryland Food Bank; Summer Reading Program; Red Cross Blood Drive
Rangers	American Cancer Society; Shoes for Orphans; Habitat for Humanity
Red Sox	The Jimmy Fund; Red Sox Scholars; Greater Boston Food Bank
Royals	Cleveland Street Project; Operation Breakthrough; Children's Place
Tigers	ProLiteracy Detroit; Ronald McDonald House; Don Bosco Hall
Twins	Minnesota ALS Association; Play Ball Minnesota; Our Fields for Kids
White Sox	Family Field Day; Sox Split Raffle; Picnic in the Park
Yankees	Youth Leadership; MVP Scholarship Program; Community Council
NL	
Astros	Northeast Family YMCA; Foundation Blood Drive; Sunshine Kids Party
Braves	Power Lunch Series; Foundation 50/50 Raffle; Silent Auction
Brewers	Selig Scholarship Fund; Student Achievers Program; Brewers on Deck
Cardinals	Redbird Rookies; Winter Warm-Up; Jerseys Off Our Backs
Cubs	Children's Memorial Hospital; CubsCare; Starlight Children Foundation
Diamondbacks	Golf Classic; Play Ball Scholarship Fund; Field Building Program
Dodgers	Reading Dugout; Japanese Community Week; Sutton Recreation Center
Giants	Traffic Safety Day; Fund's Health Fair; Organ Donor Awareness Day
Marlins	Toys for Tots; Daily Bread Food Bank; Shop-With-A-Cop Program
Mets	Welcome Home Dinner; Run to Home Plate; Jump Rope for Heart
Nationals*	Golf Classic and Auction; Scholastic Achievement; Non-Profit Donations
Padres	Cindy Matters Fund; Little Padres Parks Program; Padres Scholars
Phillies	Police Athletic League; Children's Miracle Network; Phillies Phestival
Pirates	Project Bundle Up; Field of Dreams Program; Presents for Patients
Reds	Special Reds; Shriner's Hospital; Straight-A Ticket Program
Rockies	Denver Rescue Mission; Wives Grab Bags for Charity; Reading Program

* As of late 2005, the Washington Nationals had not yet officially established any community programs with specific titles. However, according to a news release on the website mlb.com the club will participate in some kids activities such as Pepsi Pitch, Hit & Run and Rookie League, and help rebuild baseball fields in the Washington, D.C. area, raise funds to benefit children, sponsor blood drives and conduct autograph sessions to benefit local charities.

Source: "Community," at http://www.mlb.com cited 14 March 2005.

As indicated in Table 10.1, there are several different types of community interests and they vary by team. Nevertheless, for one reason or another it appears the most common programs represented in the table are those that involve raising money to support local charities, healthcare organizations, student activities, baseball clinics and welfare agencies. Although they are not listed in Table 10.1, the local B&CGA, BAT, BB, RBI and Rookie League Program are also sponsored by a majority of the teams. To focus on some specific results from one or more programs, the funds collected and redistributed by most teams were generous and impressive. For a sample of six AL clubs, in 2004 the Angels Baseball Foundation raised $150,000 from an auction at its annual Alumni Golf

Classic in Anaheim; the Athletics Community Fund donated $475,000 to subsidize social programs in Oakland, California; the [Tampa Bay Devil] Rays of Hope Foundation provided $60,000 to thousands of hurricane victims in Florida; the Indians Charities raised at least $45,000 from 12,000 people who had toured Jacobs Field in Cleveland; the Red Sox Foundation Board authorized the distribution of $215,000 to charitable organizations that serve children and adults throughout New England; and through its Community Council, the Yankees Foundation donated $200,000 to various non-profit agencies in New York City.

Likewise, in the NL the Astros in Action Foundation presented a check for $111,000 to the Uterine Cancer Research Program in Houston; the Braves Foundation allocated more than $1 million in monetary donations, grants, food and tickets for programs in the Atlanta area; the Brewers Charities pumped $350,000 to $400,000 into various community groups and events throughout the State of Wisconsin; the Diamondbacks Charities awarded approximately $295,000 in grants to support non-profit entities in the State of Arizona; the Giants Community Fund contributed more than $2 million in cash and in-kind donations for programs operating in the San Francisco area; and the Mets' Welcome Home Dinner raised a sum of $475,000 for the Cystic Fibrosis Foundation. Interestingly, as a complement to the money and donations raised by the 14 AL and 16 NL clubs, in 2004 the MLB players also contributed millions of dollars to support local charities and other non-profit organizations. As such, these activities are discussed in the next section of this chapter.

Players in the Community

Besides the community programs of baseball's central office and those of the 30 franchises, an enormous number of baseball players on the previous and current rosters of teams have devoted significant amounts of time and energy, and contributed relatively large but unreported sums of money, to promote and subsidize social causes in their communities. Consequently, each team has one or more players who have used their influence as celebrities to raise cash for special programs, projects, events and activities at the local level. To highlight a sample of these all-stars in citizenship, the following players on MLB teams were selected because of their outstanding efforts and performances as individuals who care about the development and welfare of other human beings.

Between 1996 and 2003, the New York Yankees' manager Joe Torre, infielder Derek Jeter, catcher Jorge Posada and pitcher Mike Mussina had started their own foundations. Through their respective organizations, these four individuals raised funds by involving themselves in several campaigns and events. Because of his unfortunate experiences as a child, Torre focused on educating people about domestic violence issues. For example, he raised more than $500,000 by organizing a golf outing and an auction, and by persuading the Circuit City Company to donate $1,000 for each of the 242 home runs hit by the Yankees' players in the 2004 regular season. Jeter, meanwhile, concentrated on promoting a healthy, drug- and alcohol-free lifestyle for young people. To acquire funds, his Turn 2 Foundation hosted a fundraising dinner, charity golf tournament and auction, and Jeter held baseball clinics for young players in the States of New York and Michigan. Posada's Foundation decided to arrange a charity dinner and also teamed with the

Wise Foods Corporation to support research on and provide family assistance for craniosynostosis, which is a congenital birth defect that causes an abnormally shaped skull. Indeed, Posada's son Jorge IV had to undergo five major surgeries to correct the condition. To award thousands of dollars in scholarships to students who graduated from high schools in Pennsylvania, Mussina successfully cooperated with the Wolfgang Candy Company to produce and market a candy bar labeled Moose Bar. If they remain in good academic standing while in college, the students may receive the proceeds from the sale of candy bars for up four years.[5]

Accordingly, there are other teams with prominent players who were socially responsible individuals during 2004. To provide examples of their efforts, the Astros' outfielder Larry Berkman helped hundreds of underprivileged children in the Houston area to attend the club's home games while outfielder Craig Biggio and his wife Patty hosted a party at the Minute Maid Park for children diagnosed with cancer. The Rockies' sluggers Charles Johnson and Preston Wilson paid the transportation costs, meal expenses and ticket prices of 30 poor boys and girls who had attended the team's games each Saturday at Coors Field in Denver, Colorado. Furthermore, for making appearances in Philadelphia at the Police Athletic League, Boys and Girls Club, and at a Spanish-speaking council meeting, outfielder Bobby Abreu won the Phillies' Community Service Award in 2004, and that year, Abreu's teammate Jim Thome earned the Marvin Miller Man of the Year Award for inspiring others to attain higher levels of achievement. On the U.S.' west coast, *Sporting News* recognized the Dodgers' Shawn Green as a Good Guy for donating $250,000 each year to the team's Dream Foundation, which had allocated the money to refurbish six youth baseball fields in the Los Angeles area and purchase thousands of books for local students.

For his good deeds, another notable community activist was the Tigers' Mike Maroth. He received the Dick Berardino Alumni and Good Samaritan Awards for starting and managing several local and national programs such as Rock and Wrap It Up, ProLiteracy Detroit and Unity in the Community Festival. Moreover, the Mariners' Jamie Moyer and Edgar Martinez won the prestigious Clemente Award for their sportsmanship and community efforts in Seattle, Washington hospitals, B&GCAs and charitable organizations. Finally, in Oakland, California several of the Athletics' players donated cash to a Community Food Bank that provides meals to the poor during the holidays. They also attended a Muscle Team Dinner that benefited the Muscular Dystrophy Association, participated in a Pitching Pals program for young athletes, and raised funds for the Juvenile Diabetes Research Foundation, American Cancer Society and Special Olympics. In short, these and many other players on teams not mentioned before had made a concerted effort to be productive citizens by initiating community projects and coordinating with local for-profit businesses and non-profit organizations to raise awareness, money and in-kind donations that would support, in part, disadvantaged and sick children, the homeless people in shelters, and elementary and secondary schools and academies.

In any event, to be humane and achieve their objectives in communities, the league, majority of teams and numerous players partnered with and received the support of businesses in the local areas. These included such companies as Coca-Cola in Houston, Texas, Maggiano's Little Italy Restaurant in Atlanta, Georgia, Pepsi in Milwaukee, Wisconsin, The Men's Warehouse in Oakland, California, Staples in Toronto, Canada, Bank of America and The Tribune Company in Chicago, Illinois, Mentor's Great Lakes Mall in Cleveland, Ohio, and the Ameriquest Mortgage Company in Arlington, Texas. In fact, the

Ameriquest Company launched an outreach program in the Dallas/Fort Worth Metroplex. That is, 2,000 vouchers were distributed to local school districts and community centers for students to attend the Texas Rangers' games played in the 2005 regular season. Besides the investments of small and medium-sized businesses and large corporations, it is also important to recognize the efforts and contribution of various players' wives, many city and county governments, and thousands of volunteers from local communities across America.[6]

Consequently, the previous paragraph concludes to what extent Organized Baseball, MLB teams and professional athletes have invested their time and assets in projects and initiated programs within local communities and metropolitan areas. For an overview of this topic, a summary appears next.

Summary

Since the late 1990s, MLB has consisted of 30 baseball franchises that are business organizations. As a result, the teams have made a commitment to serve their communities and provide sports entertainment to the fans that reside in local, regional, national and international markets. To fulfill that mission from a humanistic perspective, the league's commissioner and his community affairs or development staff, and the teams' owners, field managers and players have enthusiastically and voluntarily participated in various programs to promote and support social causes within their respective metropolitan areas. As such, this chapter identified and discussed the primary community programs that baseball has sponsored, and described the types of events, activities and projects that the teams and various players have become with in recent years.

Table 10.1 lists three of the community programs for each team. Thus, the table indicates the kinds of programs that clubs have funded to improve their communications, images and relationships with people and institutions located in the respective communities. As highlighted in that section of the chapter, because of those and other programs there are large amounts of money donated to charities and non-profit organizations. After the teams' endeavors are discussed, there is information about specific players and how they have used their influence and power as athletes to contribute time and raise money especially for the benefit of poor, sick and disadvantaged children. To illustrate, the humane activities of a few players are highlighted and described.

Based on the research and study of this topic, it is apparent that Commissioner Bud Selig, each of the 30 franchise owners, and the teams' field managers and players realize their social responsibilities with respect to helping others in the local communities. If the proceeds from community affairs total $1 million or more per year, then these teams are concerned about the welfare of people and committed to the economic development of their host cities and regions. Consequently, the clubs will likely establish a stronger fan base and in the end, evolve into being a well-respected sports organization and a business to be admired.

PART III. INTERNATIONAL RELATIONS

11. Global Business Strategies and Markets

According to the literature about business operations, there are several different modes that decision makers in companies may implement to enter and penetrate foreign markets. In no specific order, these consist of acquisition, merger, exporting, creating a turnkey project, licensing, franchising, establishing a joint venture and setting up a wholly owned subsidiary. Each entry mode has business advantages and disadvantages that are based, in part, on the actual and potential amounts and types of economic costs, returns and risks. Because professional baseball owners operate their franchises as members of the American League (AL) or National League (NL), they generally have relied on Major League Baseball (MLB) officials to evaluate, initiate and apply league-wide policies to promote and expand the sport and grow its fan base in global markets. This occurred, for example, in Canada when the league approved the Expos to exist in Montreal and the Blue Jays in Toronto. Furthermore, some MLB teams have been encouraged and then allowed to play exhibition, preseason and regular season games in other nations such as Japan, Mexico and Puerto Rico. Thus, since the 1960s organized baseball has adopted various short-, mid- and long-term strategies, methods and campaigns to internationalize and promote the sport, and to establish markets in communities, countries and regions across the globe.

As its primary theme, this chapter discusses MLB's visions, initiatives and actions to globalize the sport of baseball. The specific topics that relate to this theme include the league's decisions to evaluate, approve and implement business policies that are designed to expand the sport abroad, and MLB's restructuring of its internal organization, which is responsible for adopting, managing and monitoring the global strategies, activities and programs that especially appeal to sports fans who reside in places where baseball is popular such as in nations of Asia and Central and South America, and in countries like Australia, Canada and Mexico.

Strategy I: Major League Baseball International

In order to focus exclusively on ways to penetrate new and mature markets, and therefore exploit how popular baseball is in particular foreign countries, that is, beyond the U.S. and Canadian borders, during the late 1980s the league formed a new managerial operation and named it Major League Baseball International (MLBI). With its headquarters in or near the league's central office in New York City, MLBI is composed of four units and three regional offices. Respectively, these are Market Development, Television and Sponsorship Sales, Licensing and Sponsorship and Broadcast Operations. The regional offices, meanwhile, are established for Australia, Europe, the Middle East and Africa, and for Japan.[1]

MLBI's four units are each headed by a vice president or executive producer, and they may contain individual sub-units that represent administration, business and market development, events, client services, licensing, retail services, corporate marketing, game development and broadcast sales. As organized, each regional office consists of a director and support staff, which consists of managers who supervise such areas as game development, sponsorship sales, marketing and customer accounts. To reveal more about MLBI and its role to promote the league and expand the game throughout the world, next is an overview about the business of international broadcasting, and then of licensing, market development, and sponsorships and events.

Broadcasting

From a broadcasting perspective, MLBI provides its foreign affiliates with special productions and technical and operational assistance for its regular season and all-star games, AL and NL championships and World Series. These events are broadcasted on television and radio networks in at least 13 languages into a total of more than 200 countries and territories, and to approximately one million U.S. military personnel including those on duty aboard navy ships. The effort to broadcast globally is accomplished by MLBI because of its profitable and reliable partnerships, agreements and marketing services with various foreign business organizations. For example, with the assistance of rights holder Dentsu, Inc. of Japan, in 2004 three regular season games of MLB teams were transmitted per week on television through the Fuji, NHK and TBS networks, and other games appeared to Japanese households via satellite television on NHK BS and Sky Perfect TV. Furthermore, Dentsu Inc. had sublicensed a nightly baseball news program and footage. Besides these broadcasts, the league's games were also communicated on radio to Japanese baseball fans.

Meanwhile, because of MLB's affiliation with FOX Sports and the ESPN and SBS networks, and due to its partnership with Fox Sports Australia, 2.7 million viewers in that nation had an opportunity to watch more than 650 hours of baseball games, which were televised live each week and then forwarded to the continent throughout the regular season. As a result of that coverage, in 2004 a major shift in television ratings occurred for MLB programming in Australia. Similarly, in Canada cable network Rogers Sportsnet provided coverage of MLB teams' regular season games, the postseason and a special program titled the Extra Innings Package. Interestingly, in late 2004 the AL championship series between the Boston Red Sox and New York Yankees drew 1.1 million viewers, which had established a record audience for Rogers Sportsnet.

In Europe, significant increases in ratings were posted by local and regional broadcast networks with respect to the number of countries and households that received coverage of MLB games played during the regular season, and of the postseason playoffs and World Series. For example, since 2002 terrestrial Channel Five in the United Kingdom has experienced more than a 20 percent boost in the number of viewers who decided to watch weekday games and the World Series. For baseball fans who have residences in Latin American markets, MLB reaffirmed its broadcast deals in 2004 with such networks as

Deportes in Puerto Rico, Televisora Nacional in Panama, RCN in Columbia and CDN in the Dominican Republic. Consequenlty, the audiences that viewed MLB events rose in those countries, as did the number of listeners who had access to radios in Cuba and Mexico.

Licensing

Between 2000 and 2004, MLBI's licensing sales overseas had doubled, or increased in value from $125 to $250 million. This total had occurred for the three regions because of the foreign athletes who had joined MLB teams as players, and owing to the expansion of international games and events. Indeed, such companies as Doublepark in Hong Kong and Mother, Toyo Nuts, Uniqlo, Corinthian and Citizen in Japan each realized higher sales of specialized and branded MLB clothing, food, equipment and other products and items. These included expensive accessories and apparel at Doublepark, popular uniform-style shirts and pink and army-colored tank tops at Mother, artistic designs of the AL, NL and a silhouetted batter logo at Toyo Nuts, tee shirts and other properties at Uniqlo, player figurines and children toys at Corinthian, and at Citizen, a commemorative wristwatch that celebrated the Seattle Mariners' Ichiro Suzuki's for his record-setting season as a batter in 2004. Besides the demands for these products in Hong Kong and Japan, the sales of the league's brands also expanded in South Korea and Taiwan. To illustrate, apparel licensee F&F Company in South Korea remodeled or built new MLB Stores in downtown Busan, Daegu, Gwangju and Seoul, while in Taiwan, retailer Pegasus introduced a new and fashionable MLB girl's line and the Hannspree store produced and sold MLB-themed and branded high-end LCD television sets.

There were also licensed retailers and wholesalers in some nations that had to expand their line of baseball apparel, equipment and other items. To illustrate, the following are a sample of the companies and products in a few of these countries. Rebel Sports Stores in Australia and New Zealand sold baseball and softball hardware goods that included players' gloves; the New Era Cap Company in Canada promoted and sold MLB branded cap walls; in the Dominican Republic, the J&M Alvarez company manufactured for distribution non-replica graphics in adult and youth sizes; the Majestic Athletic and New Era Company hosted a Watch Party and fashion show for clients in Mexico City to showcase and advertise MLB licensees' product lines; and July Sports offered an assortment of MLB officially licensed products to customers at its store openings in Panama. In short, these are examples of recent licensing deals that have triggered an increase in retail sales from consumers for MLB products in various nations.

Market Development

Besides the broadcasting and licensing businesses, this MLBI unit is responsible for developing programs that are targeted at players, coaches and baseball organizations, and for organizing grassroots initiatives that introduce the game to kids, teenagers and young adults. These include a variety of baseball activities and events such as Pitch, Hit & Run, Play Ball!, Training With the Pros, Envoy Program, Coach in Residence, International Equipment Foundation, and the Europe Elite Camp. In turn, each of them is a popular, fun and unique learning experience for those individuals who are participants.

To highlight a portion of them, the Pitch, Hit & Run is a series of classes and skills competition. Essentially, this program provides elementary schools with baseball equipment and instructional resources such as an introductory video, study guides for kids, and training lessons for teachers. Since 1994, more than three million children who live in Italy, South Korea, South Africa and other nations have participated in the program. Meanwhile, the Training With the Pros is a series of baseball clinics that have been held in Brisbane, Sydney and Adelaide, Australia. Professional athletes from that nation taught kids, in part, how to play pitcher, catcher and various infield and outfield positions on a baseball diamond. After the training period concluded, the participants each received a MLB tee shirt, cap and backpack, and a Gatorade squeeze bottle.

During 2004, MLBI's Envoy Program sent a total of 39 experienced and professional college and high school baseball coaches to 27 different foreign countries. While there, these coaches supervised the development of players, managers and umpires, and introduced new fans to the game of baseball. Besides the performances in schools, the free clinics and coaching sessions were also presented to baseball teams in open fields under the direction of the National Baseball Federation in each country. Since 1991, the Envoy Program has completed nearly 600 assignments in 72 nations for coaches, and involved a sum of 500,000 participants. About this activity, the senior vice president of MLBI Paul Archey commented, "The Envoy Program is an integral part of our mission to internationalize baseball and is vital to the long-term growth of the game. The Envoy coaches are a tremendous asset to Major League Baseball as they provide the knowledge and experience necessary to spread the game at the grassroots level in non-traditional countries." With respect to the International Equipment Foundation, MLB has donated thousands of bats, balls and helmets, and other types of supplies and equipment to baseball players and leagues in such nations as Ireland, Mozambique, Saipan and Uganda.[2]

In August of 2004, MLBI organized the fifth Europe Elite Baseball Camp at the Sportpark in Amsterdam, Holland. At the Camp, 50 of the top 15-to-17-year-old baseball players from 15 different European baseball federations learned how to develop some high-level baseball skills and training techniques, which included hitting, pitching, fielding, catching and base running. These skills were effectively taught by a former MLB manager and some professional teams' players, and by a college baseball coach, scouting supervisor and two coordinators from the league's Envoy program. Furthermore, the participants attended seminars and received instructions about such life skills as proper nutrition, career goal planning, strength conditioning and injury prevention and cure. According to MLB's vice president of international market development Jim Small, "The goal of the Elite Camps is to give specialized training and instruction to players who are already gifted with the ability to play baseball at a high level. It is Major League Baseball International's hope that this instruction will help make the difference in these players someday having long careers playing baseball." In short, as a unit of MLBI the Market Development division has implemented a number and variety of programs that have further promoted and contributed to the growth of baseball and expanded MLB's international fan base.[3]

Sponsorships

Sponsors are predominately medium-sized to large U.S.- and foreign-based businesses that generate revenues for themselves and MLB teams as a result of their advertising, promotion, service and different types of sales campaigns before, during and after games. MLBI's sponsorship business exists across the world, and especially in countries of Asia, Europe and Latin America. Several companies that are located in Japan and South Korea, for example, have established marketing relationships with the league and its specific teams. In Japan, a few well-known sponsors of professional baseball events are Aeon, which is a retail supermarket and general merchandise store, Meiji Yasuda and Mass Mutual, which are insurance corporations, and Magnum Dry, which is a beer manufacturer and distributor. Meanwhile, in South Korea the Oriental Brewery collaborated with Anheuser-Busch and launched a MLB promotion in 2004 for Korean consumers, who had to enter a contest to win a trip to New York and attend the World Series.

In Europe, the fast food restaurant Burger King sponsored baseball grassroots initiatives in Germany while Fox Kids ran 30-second television spots and focused on promoting participation by kids in MLBI's Play Ball! youth development program. Besides the sponsorship ventures performed in Germany and other European nations, in the Latin American countries MLBI signed agreements and formed partnerships, and established marketing campaigns. These deals occurred with Gillette in Puerto Rico, MasterCard in Panama, Pepsi in Nicaragua, Presidente in the Dominican Republic, Martin Polar in Venezuela and UTS in Curacao. The types and payoffs of the promotions varied with each of the sponsors. With respect to the first three Latin American countries, at 300 stores in Puerto Rico baseball fans had to spin a prize wheel to receive free Gillette products as they entered a raffle to win an all-expense-paid trip to an AL or NL championship series and the World Series; in Panama, MasterCard ran promotions so that contestants could qualify to win hotel accommodations, transportation tickets, a credit of $1,000 and two round-trip tickets to the 2004 World Series that was played between the St. Louis Cardinals and Boston Red Sox; and at participating venues in Nicaragua, Pepsi had sponsored a sweepstake ballot that included two grand prizes, autographed baseballs and replica team jerseys. Besides the countries in Latin America, there were promotions for MLB from sponsors in Australia such as Mizuno, Radisson Hotels, Rebel Sports and the U.S. Embassy in Canberra.

Events

To reenergize the sport's fan base in foreign countries, and enhance MLBI's relationship with its worldwide, regional and local broadcasters, licensees, retailers and sponsors, during the early-to-mid–1990s MLB collaborated with the Major League Baseball Players Association (MLBPA) and decided that the league's teams would play a combination of exhibition, preseason and regular season games in major cities of the world besides those in the U.S. and Canada. For example, in 1996 three regular season games were played in Monterrey, Mexico. Then, in 1999 MLB teams competed in one game in Monterrey, in 2000 and 2004 two each in Tokyo, Japan, and in San Juan, Puerto Rico, one in 2001, 23 in 2003 and 22 in 2004. Given these games in the three cities, the next five paragraphs highlight a few of the special international baseball events that were operated and managed by MLBI during 2004 and 2005.

First, at the Estadio Foro Sol in Mexico City, Mexico, the defending World Series champion Florida Marlins challenged the Houston Astros in a two-game weekend exhibition series that was titled the Serie de Primavera. As a result, on March 13–14 of 2004 at least 26,000 fans attended the game between the Marlins and Astros. Before the series had concluded, MLB conducted a Youth Baseball Clinic at the stadium. At that event, various players from the Marlins and Astros taught some baseball fundamentals to more than 100 Mexican youngsters.

Second, in late March of 2004 MLB opened its regular season in a foreign country for the fourth year of the last six. That is, the New York Yankees met the Tampa Bay Devil Rays in a two-game opening series at the Tokyo Dome before sellout crowds of 55,000 spectators. MLB's Japanese partner Yomiuri hosted this event, and Ricoh and Master-Card also supported it. Prior to these games, however, the Yankees and Devil Rays had each played back-to-back exhibition games against the Yomiuri Giants and Hanshin Tigers from Nippon Professional Baseball (NPB). The total attendance at the six games was 309,000, and the broadcast of them in Japan on terrestrial by Nippon Television had earned an impressive 12.06 average household rating.

Third, during 2004 a team of MLB all-stars and one from the NPB played eight games in a Japan All-Star Series. This was the league's ninth Series held in Japan since 1986. More than 300,000 baseball fans attended the games, which were played at ballparks in the cities of Fukuoka, Nagoya, Osaka, Sapporo and Tokyo. Furthermore, the games were televised on NTV, TBS and TV-Asahi to audiences in Japan. Aeon and MasterCard sponsored the event and Mainichi Shimbun promoted it. To continue a great tradition of competition between MLB and the NPB, all-star baseball teams from the two organizations have scheduled to play a series against each other in 2006.

Fourth, in 2003 MLBI signed an agreement with the China Baseball Association (CBA) to establish and implement baseball activities and programs for the nation's 1.3 billion people. Because of the agreement with the CBA, MLBI organized events that have involved team, coach and umpire developments, and scheduled youth initiatives to help China's school-age children learn, play and enjoy the game of baseball. Regarding two specific events, during 2004 MLBI and the CBA and sports goods manufacturer Mizuno jointly staged and managed the first national schools baseball tournament in China. This event featured more than 160 teams from schools in four Chinese cities, and the players that competed were grouped and assigned to an elementary, junior high, high school or university division. Interestingly, for the first time the championship games in the tournament appeared on Chinese television.

Fifth, during the Spring of 2005 MLBI and the six-team China Baseball League (CBL) and its coaches and players combined their efforts and took the MLB Road Show on a tour of five Chinese cities. These were Beijing, Chengdu, Guangzhou, Shanghai and Tianjin. Basically, the Road Show, as sponsored by Canon, Hitatchi, Ita Ham, Mizuno and Suntory, is an interactive fan experience that teaches the participants about baseball. Specifically, it allows individuals to swing a baseball bat in a cage, to test their throwing skills in a pitching tunnel, and to become more informed about baseball while visiting an interactive media pavilion. With respect to this event, the CBL's vice chairman Tom McCarthy remarked, "The CBL is very excited to have the opportunity to join with MLB to bring to China this fan oriented activity that is sure to draw great interest and allow fans the opportunity to experience the great game of baseball in a festive atmosphere."[4]

Strategy II: MLB Advanced Media

Besides the activities, programs and other events pertaining to MLBI, the sport of baseball and the league and its players are also promoted and marketed to fans in various international countries in another way, that is, via MLB Advanced Media (MLBAM). This is the interactive media and Internet unit of MLB. Currently, there are six specific modes or methods that MLBAM uses to reach the sports audiences in foreign markets. One, after clicking on the word International at the league's web site, which is MLB.com, many of the baseball topics and publications are reported and interpreted in English, Japanese, Korean and Spanish. With respect to these languages, the articles are not only listed for the reader, but also were authored by baseball experts who are very knowledgeable about the sport and familiar with the operations of MLB. Furthermore, during early 2005 the Spanish version provided detailed news and press releases about such teams as the Chicago White Sox, Florida Marlins, Houston Astros, Los Angeles Angels, Los Angeles Dodgers, San Diego Padres and Texas Rangers.[5]

Two, since the 2003 MLB season international fans are authorized to vote on MLB.com for their favorite players to be selected as members of the AL and NL all-star teams. The fans' ballots may be recorded and tallied in English, Japanese and Spanish, and eventually in the world's other languages. Three, currently the majority of MLB regular season games are broadcast overseas on MLB.TV.com. To participate online, viewers must subscribe to use the service and have access to a high-speed computer connection. In fact, the 2003–2005 World Series games could be seen on MLB.TV.com. Since the Series contests have been archived, any person who subscribes may view the previous games. Four, there are English-speaking and live radio broadcasts of all regular season home and away games available to those households that subscribe to MLB.com. Indeed, nine of the league's teams provide a live audio feed in Spanish.

Five, since 2004 MLBAM has signed various agreements for wireless communication services, including broadband rights, with officials from China, Great Britain, Japan, South Korea and Taiwan, and from seven Latin American territories. Basically, these deals permit the customers of content providers to download MLB logos as wallpaper to their mobile cell phones. In turn, this is a major innovation to deliver and transmit MLB data, and audio and video programs to wireless and broadband users in these nations. With respect to MLBAM's agreement in Taiwan, chief executive officer Sally Chen of mobile content provider ELTA had this to say, "Taiwan is the only country in the world with over a 100% mobile adoption rate. New mobile services are booming every day, and branded content such as MLB will do well in establishing a strong relationship with subscribers." To support Chen's statement, the MLBAM senior vice president of business development George Kliavkoff put it this way, "We are very excited about MLBAM's first-ever wireless distribution initiative in this part of the world. An important part of out charter is to expand and promote the game around the globe and this partnership will help provide exposure for Major League Baseball to millions of fans."[6]

Six, relative to the baseball game that is played between teams from the U.S. and the World on the Sunday of all-star week, international fans are able to email questions directly to their favorite players on these teams. Then, the athletes answer the fans' questions from their respective dugout during the game so that the responses can be viewed at MLB.com. Therefore, for a primary reason why MLBAM exists, the unit's director of international business Alex Pigeon commented as follows. "With converging commonalities and the advent of the global marketplace, the diversity and global reach of Major League Baseball represents on a small scale, the increasingly borderless frontier where we live, work and play."[7]

Strategy III: Global Expansion

Despite the failure of the Expos to efficiently operate in the long-run as a baseball franchise in Montreal, Canada, undoubtedly MLB has considered other medium-sized to large foreign cities to be future relocation or expansion sites for one or more of its teams. Although this is a risky strategy, there are demographic, economic and business opportunities and advantages for MLB to disperse the sites of its member teams beyond the geographical borders of the U.S. and Canada.

For example, because of passionate sports fans and the existence of baseball training academies in some Latin American nations, the league has a strong incentive to eventually locate a team in a relatively large city of the Dominican Republic, Mexico, Puerto Rico and/or Venezuela. Even so, while living in those countries the baseball club's staff and players may encounter such issues as currency devaluations, high poverty rates in the communities, and political and social hostilities at the given sites. As a result of these problems and the capital expenditures necessary for team owners to invest in, renovate and upgrade a local sports stadium for professional baseball, a MLB team in Santo Domingo, Monterrey and/or Mexico City, San Juan and Caracas would struggle financially, and certainly need considerable support from baseball fans in the community and the local media for a few regular seasons. After the early years, however, the club may improve enough to win a majority of its games, receive more media coverage and exposure in the area, expand its attendances at home, grow the franchise's revenues and thus, survive at least in the short-run.

Anyway, to identify a few of the international markets that MLB may evaluate to be potential sites to locate one or more teams during the early-to-mid–2000s, Table 11.1 lists a sample of 13 foreign cities and the total populations of their metropolitan areas. Each city was selected and listed primarily based on its sports culture, local fan base and business area as a home for a professional baseball franchise, and on its location, climate and population density.[8]

Given the distribution of cities and populations as depicted in the table, Mexico is the most attractive foreign country to locate a MLB team in the future. For Mexico's cities, the best site there is in Monterrey, and then in Mexico City and Tijuana. To justify these places, Monterrey is Mexico's wealthiest city. It is located approximately 100 miles southwest of the nearest Texas border. Within Monterrey, there is modern architecture everywhere, and dispersed throughout the urban area are plenty of American and international restaurants, stores and entertainment facilities. Besides Monterrey's prominent sports reputation as the host of the Mexican Baseball Hall of Fame, the Mexican League's Monterrey Sultans play there in a 27,000-seat stadium that could, if necessary, be renovated and expanded to accommodate a capacity crowd of at least 30,000 fans. The Sultans' ballpark, which was built in 1990, is considered the best and most attractive baseball facility in Latin America. As reported in a recent article of the *Wall Street Journal*, "It's hard not to see the appeal of trading Canada for Latin America. The Monterrey market is convenient to a number of Texas cities and is home to 1,500 Dallas Cowboy season ticket holders. Manifestly, Latin America has plenty of budding A-Rods and millions more baseball fans. Isn't it time to give them a real chance to root for the home team?"

Following Monterrey, the second to sixth ranked cities for MLB to locate a relocating or expansion franchise are, respectively, a close choice for second place between Mexico City and Tijuana, and then in San Juan, Santo Domingo and Havana. Mexico City

TABLE 11.1. INTERNATIONAL BASEBALL CITIES,
RANKED BY AREA POPULATION, APRIL 2005

Country	City	MAPOP*
Japan	Tokyo	31.7
Mexico	Mexico City	22.1
South Korea	Seoul	22.0
England	London	13.9
Taiwan	Taipei	8.0
Mexico	Tijuana	4.7
Venezuela	Caracas	4.5
Australia	Sydney	4.2
Mexico	Monterrey	3.7
Dominica Republic	Santo Domingo	3.0
Cuba	Havana	2.6
Puerto Rico	San Juan	2.0
Panama	Panama City	1.1

* Country and City are self-explanatory. MAPOP is the metropolitan area population in millions with respect to a City.

Source: "List of Metropolitan Areas by Population," at http://www.en.wikipedia.org cited 28 April 2005, and "City and Area Population," at http://www.world-gazetteer.com cited 28 April 2005.

and its surrounding metropolitan area each contain a huge population that support local amateur and professional Mexican baseball teams, while San Juan and Santo Domingo are cities where thousands of diehard baseball fans root for their favorite clubs and players. However, because of Fidel Castro's regime and the U.S. trade embargo of Cuba, Havana is not a currently viable location for a big league team although it is the most convenient of the listed cities to stadiums of MLB's Eastern, Midwestern and Southeastern teams.

The remaining cities in Table 11.1 are less attractive as future sites for MLB franchises. Although they are situated in wealthy consumer markets of large metropolitan areas, the cities of Tokyo, Seoul and Taipei are very distant from the coasts of North America, and their populations have distinct cultures and languages relative to those in America. Meanwhile, the London area supports some great and competitive athletic teams and soccer leagues, but the sports fans there are not enthusiastic or passionate about professional baseball. In Sydney, or alternatively Melbourne, baseball is a popular activity and kids, teenagers and young adults play the game for teams in schools and organized leagues. As with sites in Asia, however, there would be high transportation costs and excessive amounts of time needed for U.S.-based teams that travel to and from games in Australia, and furthermore, the stadiums in Australian cities are extremely inferior in capacities and amenities with respect to the ballparks in America.

There are thousands of athletes in Venezuela who love to play baseball on amateur teams, and the games there are well attended by fans across the nation. Nonetheless, Venezuelan president Hugo Chavez's government is controversial and he frequently condemns U.S. economic and political policies in his speeches and reports to the media. Since Chavez is a friend of Fidel Castro and other revolutionaries in Central and South America, it is unlikely that a MLB team could exist in that nation for more than one or two regular seasons. Finally, locating a professional baseball team in Panama City does not appear to be an option since that country is poor, and its teams no longer participate in the Caribbean Series because of inferior players and the lack of resources and money capital that were allocated to the sport.

As an alternative but less risky short-run strategy, MLB may decide before 2010 to organize and operate one or more AAA, AA, A or Rookie baseball groups in selected Latin American countries. These organizations would, in part, consist of privately owned and/or league-subsidized clubs based in relatively large cities or populated metropolitan areas of Monterrey, Mexico City, Tijuana, San Juan and Santo Domingo. While playing games in each area, the minor league teams would be encouraged and assisted by Commissioner Bud Selig's office to establish academies to train these nations' athletes and teach them the skills necessary to be elite baseball players. Although this strategy is a costly investment for MLB franchises in the short-run, it should ultimately increase the demand for baseball in these countries, and expand the international fan base of the league and broadcast markets for the sport across numerous regions.

Summary

For a few decades, MLB has made an effort to promote the game of baseball in various countries, and also to penetrate foreign markets and attract more fans to the sport. The strategies to accomplish these goals include the formation and development of organizational units such as MLB International and MLB Advanced Media, and the decision to evaluate and place expansion teams at sites in international cities. To that end, this chapter provides some specific details about the types of tasks, activities and programs that involve these strategies and what resources are required and have been used by MLB to implement them.

Although MLB had gained some momentum and promoted itself as an international sports organization between the 1970s and early 2000s, the league's teams are not the foreign consumer's first or second choice for sports entertainment. Generally, these are the local outdoor soccer clubs and then the teams in the National Basketball Association or National Football League. This means that MLB International and MLB Advanced Media must continue to implement their most effective strategies, but experiment with new ways to reach sports fans especially in the large European markets, and in China and Russia. Consequently, it is expected that MLB will be prepared to locate one or more franchises in Latin American cities by 2010.

12. Organized Baseball in Foreign Countries

Besides being a traditional, well publicized and prominent sport in America, baseball is also an extremely popular activity and event in many nations across the globe. Indeed, for one reason or another the game of baseball in several countries of Asia and Latin America is more popular than those in basketball, football and ice hockey, but regarded somewhat less or the same as matches in outdoor soccer. For example, in Asia these places are Japan, South Korea and Taiwan, and in Latin America they are Cuba, Dominican Republic, Mexico, Puerto Rico and Venezuela. Meanwhile, since the late 1990s the sport has expanded in Australia, China and Russia, and also throughout such European countries as France, Germany, Greece, Italy, and the Netherlands and United Kingdom. Consequently, there has been a disproportionate worldwide increase in the numbers of athletes who excel in playing the sport and spectators who enjoy attending games, and an expansion in the types of amateur and professional leagues and teams, and in the development of more baseball fields and construction of new stadiums.[1]

As baseball has emerged and then evolved in these and other demographic areas, the sport's business, economic and social aspects have been problematic in some of the countries. There has been a decline in attendances at games among various age groups, for instance, and many professional teams tend to operate at a deficit during specific seasons while some team owners have incurred excessive debts because of higher salaries for managers and players, and due to increases in such expenses as equipment, training and healthcare costs, and insurance and pension payments. Furthermore, for several years the best foreign athletes have left their home countries to play for teams in the American League (AL) and National League (NL) of Major League Baseball (MLB), and for those clubs that exist in the U.S. minor league system. In fact, for the 2005 season approximately 28 percent of the baseball players who made the rosters of big league teams are international, as is 47 percent who are on the rosters of affiliated minor league clubs.

Besides these particular issues, some sports officials have criticized MLB and recommended various reforms for how the major league teams should recruit and draft foreign players, for why the league should compel teams to upgrade their baseball academies located in Latin America, and for when international standards should be designed, adopted and enforced regarding players' contracts, compensation and free agency. For some insights about such matters, there are readings in this and other sections of the book that measure and evaluate these and related problems.

For the reader to realize how baseball has become an international sport, this chapter provides some interesting dates, events and other historical information regarding the sport's presence in nations besides the U.S. To be more specific, the following contents are an analysis about the extent and role of amateur and/or professional baseball and baseball organizations in different countries of Asia, Latin America and Europe. In short, this topic identifies the important factors that indicate why the sport is a component of the culture of these nations.

Baseball in Asia

Japan

Baseball is important to the sports populations that reside in Japan, South Korea and Taiwan, but is relatively unimportant to the people who live in China. Ever since baseball emerged during the 1870s, it has expanded and prospered in Japan. That is, several of the country's most competitive baseball teams have succeeded to win international tournaments and championships by defeating the best clubs from other nations in the Far East, while several Japanese athletes became national heroes when they hit and scored runs against MLB and amateur teams who played exhibition games in Tokyo and other cities. After the nation's first professional baseball team was established in 1934, two years later the Japanese Professional League began its initial season and continued to exist with from six up to eight teams until 1950. After that year, the organization's structure permanently changed to model the AL and NL in MLB, that is, by including six teams each in the Central and Pacific Leagues.[2]

Because they excelled and won a number of titles in their respective leagues, the Yomiuri Giants, Hiroshima Carps and Seibu Lions have been the three most successful professional baseball teams in Japan. These teams had several competitive players such that in 1964, the Giants' Masanori Murakami joined the NL's San Francisco Giants for one season. Gradually, it became apparent to many American baseball managers that Japanese players were talented enough to play in the major or minor leagues of America. Although the Central and Pacific Leagues adopted free agency in 1994, Japanese athletes must play on teams at least nine years before they can leave and perform in MLB. In short, baseball in Japan has an impressive history that is highlighted by competitive teams and experienced, dedicated and well-disciplined players.

Since the early-to-mid–1990s, the quality of teams in Japan's Central and Pacific Leagues has tended to decline because many superior players such as Hideo Nomo, Kenchiro Kawabata, Kazuhiro Sasaki, Ichiro Suzuki, Hideki Matsui and Kazuo Matsui have signed contracts to perform for teams in MLB. In turn, this has caused some Japanese companies to reduce all or a portion of their subsidies to teams in the two leagues. If this continues into the future, the attendances at games will decrease, business of baseball will deteriorate, and perhaps some clubs will fold their operations and withdraw from the Central and/or Pacific League. Indeed, a player's strike occurred in late 2004 because of the owners' strategy to consolidate two of the teams, that is, to merge the Orix Blue Wave and Kintetsu Buffaloes. In any event, it is likely that the baseball officials in Japan will need to reform, revamp or downsize the system, and that MLB teams will be forced to negotiate some type of constraint about signing the best Japanese players who are available when their nine-year contracts have expired.

South Korea

After Missionary Philip L. Gillett introduced baseball in Korea during the early 1900s, athletes participated on teams and the game became increasingly popular in that nation. Thus, by the mid–1960s South Korea had defeated Japan to win the Asia Amateur Baseball Championship. As a result, the sport continued to develop throughout the 1970s and in 1982, the six-team Korean Baseball Organization League (KBOL) formed and completed its first season. After the KBOL established a postseason playoff competition in 1986, during the early 1990s the league decided to expand by two teams and also agreed to compete every four years in a Super Game against a team from Japan's professional leagues.[3]

Interestingly, during and after the 1990s a few significant events occurred that forever changed the structure of baseball in South Korea. First, for various reasons some of the current and prospective Korean pitchers negotiated and endorsed contracts with teams in MLB. These athletes included Park Chan Ho who was signed by the Los Angeles Dodgers in 1994, Sang Hoon Lee by the Boston Red Sox in 1997, and Byung-hyun Kim by the Arizona Diamondbacks in 1999. Second, the majority of Korea's professional baseball players were permitted to play in the Summer Olympics that took place in Atlanta, Georgia in 1996, and one year later 36 non–Korean players were drafted by teams in the KBOL. Third, in 1999 the KBOL was decentralized to establish the Dream and Magix Leagues. Fourth, a free agent system became implemented in 1999 whereby baseball players with 11 or more years of seniority could negotiate with any of the professional clubs in the leagues. Fifth, Korea won a bronze medal in baseball at the 2000 Sydney Olympics by beating a Japanese team. Sixth, in 2001 the Korean athletes who wished to play professional baseball in the U.S. could be posted or assigned to the 30 MLB teams. Consequently, this enabled the big league clubs with the highest bids to negotiate a contract with one or more of these players from Korea.

As an aside, in the KBOL each of the eight teams is appropriately named after the corporation that sponsors it. Two of these, for example, are the Hyundai Unicorns and Samsung Lions. In South Korea, a team's typical baseball season consists of 133 games. Furthermore, after the regular season concludes each club has a right to commit and enter the playoffs to win a Korean Series Championship. Through the 2005 season, the two most successful teams have been the Kia Tigers and Doosan Bears. Since Korea is a relatively small country, it is not unusual for families and individual baseball fans to travel by automobile in order to attend the away games of their hometown team. At these games, there are cheerleaders who normally dance to entertain spectators in the ballpark, and each home team has a mascot who rallies the crowd by making gestures and completing stunts. Because of fans' passion for the game, and the competitiveness and skills of players on the KBOL teams, baseball is a moderately successful sport in Korea and comparable in quality to an AA minor league team in the U.S.

Taiwan

About 100 years after the Japanese had exported baseball to this nation of 23 million people, the Republic of China Professional Baseball League (RPBL) was founded in

1990. Then, after gamblers became connected with the sport during the mid–1990s, the attendances at RPBL games dramatically declined because of a price-fixing scandal that involved some of the league's elite players. As a result, in 1997 the four-team Taiwan Major League (TML) emerged and gradually signed many of the best players from its rival's teams. Inevitably, this competition for players led to the establishment of the six-team Chinese Professional Baseball League (CPBL), which was a merger of the RPBL and TML in 2003.[4]

Relative to the structure of this new Taiwanese league, each team must complete its 50 games per season by rotating among twelve stadiums whose individual capacity varies between 5,000 and 10,000 seats. Generally, the regular season extends for eight or more months since only two to four games are scheduled each week. The average ticket price is approximately six to ten American dollars and attendance per game is nearly 1,000 to 3,000 spectators. Each game is intense and as determined by the Taiwanese, to be a contest between a tiger and dragon. Such CPBL teams as the First Securities Agan, Makota Gida and Sinon Bulls compensate their players who are from Taiwan about $58,000 on average and foreigners about $96,000 per year. Because they have won more titles and placed second, the Brother Elephants and China Trust Whales have been the most successful professional baseball clubs since 2000.

Despite the scandal that occurred from gamblers betting on games, Taiwan has a relatively large and talented supply of baseball players. Many of these athletes, who are usually in their late teens, play a power and speed game. Indeed, they may have performed on a world championship Little League club and/or on a competitive high school and college team in Taiwan. Consequently, a number of MLB teams have invested money and resources in that nation in order to scout players, host baseball clinics in small and large cities, and establish business partnerships with various CPBL clubs. In short, baseball in Taiwan is a popular sport that has the potential of producing more players for the professional teams in America and elsewhere.

China

The Shanghai Baseball Club began to play games in 1863. Thirty years later, the Huiwen College and Tongzhou College in Beijing, and the St. John's College of Shanghai established baseball programs for their students. By 1915, the enthusiasm generated from intercollegiate games held on the mainland coupled with the approval of Sun Yat-sen's revolutionary party led to the formation of the Chinese Overseas Baseball Club. After a series of social upheavals during the mid–1900s, in 1975 baseball was officially rehabilitated and declared as a legal enterprise in China. Then, a national baseball team was formed. From the late 1970s, the team played games in various tournaments, which were frequently scheduled in Beijing, Tianjin, Shanghai and Guangdong. Interestingly, for the first time in history a professional baseball team from Japan competed against China's national team in 1996.[5]

Currently, the China Baseball League (CBL) is one of the country's growing professional sports organizations. It consists of four teams that have the athletes who, in part, will represent China in baseball at the 2008 Olympic Games in Beijing. To sponsor and assist with the identification, recruitment and development of these players to complete China's national baseball team, in 2003 MLB signed a contract with the nation's Baseball Association. One aspect of the agreement is that it allows U.S. collegiate coaches to train

Chinese baseball players and for China's coaches to visit with and learn the fundamentals of the sport from various managers of MLB clubs. Furthermore, the contract stipulates that resources be used to conduct baseball clinics for kids in China. To further increase interest in the sport and appeal to people who live in metropolitan areas, the CBL and MLB International agreed to consolidate their efforts and tour a few large Chinese cities during 2005. The highlight of the tour was the MLB Road Show. This event is an interactive fan experience that teaches participants how to swing at a baseball in a batting cage, how to throw baseballs in a pitching tunnel, and how to learn the sport at a media pavilion. About MLB's Road Show, the CBL's co-sponsor and vice chairman Tom McCarthy said, "The CBL is very excited to have the opportunity to join with MLB to bring to China this fan oriented activity that is sure to draw great interest and allow fans the opportunity to experience the great game of baseball in a festive atmosphere."

To conclude this section of the reading, there are formal baseball organizations that exist in these four Asian nations. Accordingly, Japan is very advanced in the development of the sport and quality of its teams. Unfortunately, the migration of players from Japanese clubs to teams in MLB has created a crisis for the corporate owners of franchises in the Central and Pacific Leagues. Alternatively, in Korea and Taiwan baseball is well played by the athletes and popular, especially among sports fans. However, these two countries produce only a few players each season who are eligible and talented enough to join the roster of a team in MLB or in the U.S. minor leagues. Finally, the athletes in China will gradually be taught the hitting, fielding and pitching techniques to improve their baseball skills. With the assistance of MLB International, hopefully the Chinese national baseball team will become more competitive and win some games at the 2008 Olympics in Beijing.

Baseball in Latin America

Since 1970, the Caribbean Federation has consisted of baseball organizations located in the Dominican Republic, Mexico, Puerto Rico and Venezuela. After the winter baseball season is over in each country, there are playoffs between teams to determine a champion. The four teams that win their respective playoffs become champions and earn the right to compete in a tournament named The Caribbean Series. Historically, in that tournament are four clubs with several foreign players who have great raw abilities and the potential to play for the New York Yankees and others in MLB or in America's minor league system. In fact, many of the Latinos in the AL and NL have played for teams that are in organized leagues of the Caribbean Federation. Based on that brief introduction, this section of the chapter will contrast how the amateur and/or professional baseball activities differ in these four nations that are south of the U.S. border. As such, the countries are listed and discussed in alphabetical sequence.

Dominican Republic

During the mid–1860s, refugees migrated from Cuba and introduced the game of baseball to this small country of nine million people. As a result, Dominican athletes quickly learned the sport and gradually teams, leagues and tournaments were organized in that country. Between 1907 and 1921, such teams as The Tigers, Eastern Stars, The Eagles and Lions of the Chosen One were formed and they have continued to play in the nation's most prestigious league. Thus, these four and two other clubs are members of the Dominican League, whose season ranges from October to December. Because these are months when production in the sugar mills has slowed down, a baseball game becomes a popular event for the people.[6]

During each winter the league's teams play their regular season games at stadiums in Santo Domingo, Santiago, San Pedro de Macoris and La Romana. Based on the specifications of MLB facilities, these are very small ballparks. But, the fans that decide to attend games played in them are enthusiastic, energetic and loud. That is, to antagonize the opponents they blow whistles, wave flags and scream for their favorite teams. While music is played on loudspeakers in the stadiums, local cheerleaders frequently dance on the dugouts between innings. In short, the games held in the Dominican Republic are festive and special events for spectators because the baseball season provides an opportunity for families to forget about poverty, and for people to smile and rejoice as they celebrate in the streets and at the ballparks.

Despite the population's high unemployment rates, low per capita income and shabby living conditions, some of the country's best athletes have excelled as competitive players on MLB teams. For example, there is the Baltimore Orioles' Sammy Sosa, St. Louis Cardinals' Albert Pujols, Boston Red Sox' Manny Ramirez and the Los Angeles Angels of Anaheim's Vladimir Guerrero. To discover and establish relationships with these veteran players before they became adults, MLB teams have operated academies and similar baseball facilities to recruit, train and develop athletes in the Dominican Republic. Moreover, when they were children and teenagers, Sosa and the others probably played sports games in grassy fields and on parking lots, and used broomsticks for bats and tennis balls for baseballs. Besides the athletes from the Dominican Republic, there are also American and foreign MLB players who need to upgrade their fielding, hitting, running and pitching skills, and those in the minor leagues who will later join a big league team. To improve their talents, they play games there on teams in a season during October to December.

The Dominican people are obsessed with and passionate about baseball, especially those who are fans, players and families and friends of players. It is likely, therefore, that MLB teams will continue to search for, recruit, train and sign to contracts the best baseball athletes from the island. Furthermore, even though the chance to become a big league player is remote, there are tremendous economic incentives for kids from sugar mill towns of the nation to learn the game of baseball and dream of a future as a player in the sport.

Mexico

Some historians declare that the game of baseball originated in the cities and rural areas of Mexico between 1840 and 1850. During the late 1800s and early 1900s, Mexican laborers and workers from other places proceeded to play the sport across the country as they laid tracks for the railroads. Then, in the 1920s organizers formed the nation's most eminent baseball league. However, the Mexican people did not become extremely fascinated with baseball until 1957, that is, when a team from Monterrey defeated one from La Mesa, California by a score of four to zero to win the Little League World Series in Williamsport, Pennsylvania. To clinch that championship, Angel Macias excelled by pitching a perfect game. After a Mexican team won the Series again in 1958, baseball surged in popularity and prospered as a sport in the country.[7]

Established in 1925, the Mexican League consists of 16 elite teams that are home-based in such cities as Cancun, Puebla, Tijuana, Veracruz and of course, Mexico City and Monterrey. The league features a 116-game regular season schedule that begins in mid–March and ends in late June. Each season, 12 of the 16 teams are expected to qualify for the playoffs and compete until eliminated in the long postseason, which takes place during July and August. In contrast to the Mexican League, there is also a Pacific League that plays a 58-game season during October to December.

With respect to some features of a game, at the ballparks ticket prices are low and frequently teams score several runs per game because at high altitudes any batted balls will travel further in distance. Furthermore, there are unique food and beverage items, and souvenirs sold at particular stadiums in cities. For the games played in Oaxaca, vendors sell fried grasshoppers besides the typical menu of tamales, tortas and empanadas. In fact, it is such benefits as the competition between teams, on-the-field action, ambience at the ballparks, low prices for admission and delicious food that make Mexican League games fun and exciting events for the spectators.

During several months of 2003 and 2004, Mexican billionaire Carlos Bremer made a sincere effort presenting his bid to persuade MLB to relocate the Expos from Montreal, Canada to Monterrey, Mexico. However, the league selected Washington, D.C. instead because of the following concerns with a big league team located in that Mexican city. First, the team's home games would be scheduled at 26,000-seat Estadio Monterry, which is an undersized and obsolete facility relative to the big league stadiums in America. Second, the terms of Bremer's bid were likely inferior regarding the total dollar amount to be offered for the Expos and the timing of payments on debts owed to the league and any creditors. Third, in Monterrey the franchise would not be financially protected from a devaluation of the peso, which means that the revenues earned by the club would be valued in pesos while the team's players are compensated in dollars that have appreciated. Fourth, some interruptions with scheduling evening games and traveling by teams could occur since Monterrey is in the central time zone and located approximately 2,000 miles from New York City. Fifth, the team's above average to high ticket prices for premium seats at the ballpark would likely discourage many poor and perhaps middle-class Mexicans from attending more than one or two home games during a season. Consequently, these and other potential problems suggest that it will be at least a decade before MLB considers approving the relocation of an existing team or location of an expansion franchise to a major city in Mexico.

As an aside, the North American Free Trade Agreement (NAFTA) guarantees the eventual elimination of trade and direct investment barriers that exist between Canada, Mexico and the U.S. According to integration effects and international economic theories, because of NAFTA the wage levels of Mexican workers will gradually rise to create a larger middle class with higher disposable incomes per capita and more wealth. If the political leaders of these three countries determine how to control the export of drugs and illegal entry of people from Mexico into the U.S. and Canada, the nations' economic and social relationships will improve. If that occurs, an opportunity may develop to place a MLB franchise or minor league team in one or more cities located in the northern or central regions of Mexico.

Puerto Rico

Baseball was introduced there in 1898, that is, when the U.S. had occupied the island. During the early 1900s, the sport flourished because kids, teenagers and young adults formed teams and had fun while competing in baseball games. Then, in 1940 the Puerto Rican Winter League was established and scheduled its 54-game regular season from November to January. Each season, the best team from that league has qualified to play in the Caribbean Series. As a result, Puerto Rico dominated the Series during the 1950s, and won ten more championships between 1970 and 2004 inclusive.[8]

However, since the mid–1990s the nation's Winter League has lagged in attendances at games and in revenues from sales. Indeed, the growth of other sports on the island such as basketball, volleyball, horse racing and even professional wrestling have reduced the number of athletes and fans who are passionate about the game of baseball. Furthermore, in recent years many teens and young adults in Puerto Rico have realized more enjoyment and pleasure from watching movies, playing video games and tuning in cable television networks that broadcast games of many MLB teams. Thus, to revive the Winter League, a few sports officials in Puerto Rico have implemented marketing programs that have been successfully applied by numerous teams in the U.S. minor league system. To thrill the baseball fans attending games at renovated Hiram Bithorn Stadium, for example, there are family-friendly activities. These include live music from a band, team mascots that focus on entertaining children, between-inning events that involve kids, and interaction of the players with the crowd before and after games.

A number of famous athletes were born in Puerto Rico. Besides such great baseball legends as Roberto Clemente, Orlando Cepeda and Roberto Alomar, four active players who claim Puerto Rico as their home are the New York Yankees outfielder Bernie Williams, Detroit Tigers catcher Ivan Rodriguez, Florida Marlins outfielder Carlos Delgado and Baltimore Orioles catcher Javy Lopez. Despite these former and current stars in MLB, it was extremely disappointing and a letdown to baseball fans in Puerto Rico after the 2004 season when the franchise in Montreal relocated to Washington, D.C. instead of to San Juan. Apparently, MLB officials were reluctant to transfer the Expos to the island's largest city even though the Texas Rangers and Toronto Blue Jays played against each other there in 2001 and the Expos scheduled 44 games on the island in the 2003 and 2004 seasons. In short, the league's final decision most likely depended on the demographic factors of the cities, quality of the stadiums, and the prices that were offered for the Expos franchise by the ownership groups representing Washington, D.C. and San Juan.

Venezuela

In the 1920s, U.S. oil workers introduced baseball to this nation whose current population is about 27 million people. The sport became so popular during the 1930s that in 1942 the Venezuelan Baseball League (VBL) was organized. Despite the cancellation of regular season games caused by player strikes in 1959 and 1974, and by a nationwide work stoppage to oust President Hugo Chavez in 2003, the VBL has continued to operate as the premier baseball organization in the country.[9]

With respect to a typical season, which begins in October and ends in December, the VBL generally consists of four teams each that play in the Eastern and Western Divisions. After a regular season concludes, six of the eight teams compete to become the VBL champion. In order to win that title, the process requires team victories during the qualifier round, and then in a round robin and the final series. The team that succeeds earns the right to play in the Caribbean Series against championship clubs from the

Dominican Republic, Mexico and Puerto Rico. Since 1970, Venezuela has been champion in five of the Caribbean Series tournaments.

In 1997, baseball officials established a Venezuelan Summer League (VSL). This is a minor league consisting of teams whose rosters primarily contain rookie players from the Latin American, Spanish-speaking countries, except for athletes from the Dominican Republic and Puerto Rico. For various seasons, such MLB clubs as the Baltimore Orioles, Boston Red Sox, Cincinnati Reds, Florida Marlins, Houston Astros, New York Mets, Philadelphia Phillies, Pittsburgh Pirates, San Diego Padres and Seattle Mariners have sponsored one or more teams in the VSL. A 64-game regular season schedule, which starts in May and finishes in August, is played on the baseball fields located in seven cities. When the regular season concludes, there is a playoff series to determine the league champion.

To improve the skills and welfare of athletes from the country, and prepare them for playing professional baseball in America, several MLB teams have established academies in Venezuela. Despite criticism from the media and some professors, it is a net social benefit to communities for major league clubs to operate these academies in cities of Venezuela and other nations. According to a Minnesota Twins' pitching coach who lives in the Dominican Republic, "Scouting is tough here. It's tough to get to the places where baseball is played on this island, and in Venezuela. Having an academy gives you a chance to see a player more than once. A lot of kids down here [in Latin American countries] wouldn't have a chance [to play professional baseball] without the academies."

Baseball in Europe

Since the early 1990s, the amateur and professional baseball leagues, tournaments and other activities are popular for the sports fans in the Netherlands and Italy. Meanwhile, the sport has experienced low to moderate growth in France, Germany and the United Kingdom. To monitor the baseball leagues of countries and enforce international policies, regulations and rules, there is a European Baseball Confederation. In turn, each nation has established a federation, which is the central organization that guides and controls the various baseball leagues that exist within each nation. When MLB teams decide to teach the fundamentals of baseball to European kids, teenagers and young adults, the league will sponsor youth programs and clinics, and then coordinate these activities and events with the federations of the specific nations. Besides the Confederation, more than 40 European countries are affiliated with the International Baseball Association. This organization also promotes the development of the sport in Europe and elsewhere.[10]

According to observers of games and reporters in the media, European baseball teams are primarily focused on outscoring their opponents rather than training pitchers to throw fastballs, curves and changeups into the strike zone and positioning infielders and outfielders to catch pop ups and ground balls. Furthermore, during baseball games played in European nations many of the fans at the ballparks seem confused or unaware about such team strategies as bunting to move a player to the next base, attempting a hit-and-run play, stealing second and third base by a runner, and relaying signals to the hitters by coaches on the field and in the dugout. Unless the fans and other spectators in attendance at games are informed and knowledgeable about a team's strategies to beat their rivals by scoring more and/or preventing less runs, baseball will lag behind the growth of basketball, ice hockey and outdoor soccer in one or several of these European nations.

During the late 1990s and early 2000s, MLB officials have tried various marketing schemes about how to advertise and further promote the sport to fans in Europe. Besides sponsoring baseball youth programs, tournaments and clinics at the grassroots levels, these activities also include the scheduling of exhibition, preseason and regular season games in such large cities as Amsterdam, London, Munich, Paris and Rome. Moreover, it would be good publicity for foreign teams from Greece, Spain and the Czech Republic and Ukraine to play one or more games, for example, against AAA, AA, A and Rookie minor league teams of the Boston Red Sox, Florida Marlins, Los Angeles Dodgers and New York Yankees.

Finally, it seems inevitable that a World Cup–type tournament would be held in 2006 since some foreign nations have organized national baseball teams to compete at the 2008 Olympic Games in Beijing, China. If superstars Barry Bonds, Derek Jeter and Curt Schilling played on an American team, this tournament would be broadcast on television networks and transmitted across the world into the small and large cities of Africa, Asia, Latin America, New Zealand, and Eastern and Western Europe. In short, the World Baseball Classic is an excellent forum for national clubs from Europe and elsewhere to measure their progress in the sport, that is, by playing an experienced team from the U.S., Japan and Venezuela, and perhaps from China, Cuba and Russia.

Besides the presence of baseball in selected nations of Asia, Latin America and Europe, the game is also played in Canada, Germany and the Philippines, and regarded with great affection by fans in Australia and Cuba. In fact, if Cuba's form of government ever becomes a representative democracy and the nation's economy is reformed to operate as a free market, the City of Havana would be an attractive home site for one or more affiliated clubs in the minor league system of MLB.[11]

Summary

To explore how the sport became a global industry based on when it began to the early 2000s, this chapter discussed the origin, development and organization of amateur and/or professional baseball in several countries of Asia, Latin America and Europe. The research revealed that the sport is moderately to very popular in Japan and South Korea, and in the Dominican Republic, Mexico, Puerto Rico and Venezuela, and in Italy and the Netherlands. In some of these places, there are leagues and specific teams that have existed since the late 1800s to early 1900s. Consequently, for many diehard fans and others who are enthusiastic about the sport, baseball is more than a game of nine or less innings to be played between two teams starting a total of 18 players. That is, baseball reflects the history and traditions of a country and represents the interests, spirit and values of its people.

For the sport to continue expanding internationally, MLB must aggressively market and constantly promote the game abroad, in part, by hosting and sponsoring a World Cup tournament, broadcasting games to viewers across the world, and eventually placing teams in one or more foreign nations. Since approximately 28 percent of the players on MLB teams, and 48 percent of those on clubs in the U.S. minor leagues are not from

America, the major leagues have strong business and social incentives to further globalize the game and brands of its teams. If big league officials in the U.S. and aforementioned nations are willing to establish uniform standards, loosen the restrictions on the emigration and importation of players, and compromise on the implementation of an equitable free agent system, then baseball has an opportunity to expand into new markets and become the sports consumer's first choice of entertainment.

13. America's Teams Demand Foreign Players

For many of the baseball seasons since the late 1950s, a growing number of international players have gradually appeared on the active rosters of American League (AL) and National League (NL) teams in Major League Baseball (MLB). In fact, the proportions were reported as 3.6 percent in 1958, 6.9 percent in 1968, 8.8 percent in 1978 and 19.8 percent in 1998. Then, during the early 2000s the percentages continued to increase except for 2004. That is, they were 25.3 percent in 2001, 26.1 percent in 2002, 27.8 percent in 2003, 27.3 percent in 2004 and 29.2 percent in 2005. Furthermore, since 2000 the fraction of foreign players on minor league teams, when affiliated with those in the AL and NL, has varied between 45 and 50 percent. It is likely, therefore, that these trends in percentages have been tracked, updated and analyzed by baseball officials because they reflect historical changes in the nationalities of athletes on MLB teams and also, because the inflows of international players into MLB has impacted the cultural, social and commercial aspects of the business of baseball in cities and regions of North America and in numerous sports markets across the globe.[1]

Foreign Players in MLB History

As a result of the effects on communities, fans, league rules and teams' attendances and profits, this chapter will provide a portion of the history, and some interesting and specific baseball statistics, activities and information about the foreign baseball players who have migrated from their home countries to join various teams in MLB. Several of these athletes had great careers on AL and NL teams as pitchers, catchers, infielders and outfielders. As such, their contributions to the sport are outlined and discussed in the following sections. However, the first task is to list the numbers of players from each nation that had performed as major and minor leaguers in organized baseball between the early 1870s and 2000s. This data has been condensed and incorporated in Table 13.1. Then, in Table 13.2 a list of players and their home countries is presented for the opening games of the 2004 and 2005 regular seasons. In turn, the information in each table is highlighted and analyzed.

Based on the demographic statistics from 47 countries, Table 13.1 denotes that 1,088 or 72 percent of the 1,506 big league players on teams in MLB were natives of five nations.

That is, they had been born in Canada and Cuba beginning in 1871, Venezuela in 1939, Puerto Rico in 1942 and the Dominican Republic in 1956. Although Canada's first three professional baseball players were members of teams in the National Association or American Association, in 1879 Canadian infielder Bill Phillips joined the NL's Cleveland Blues. Historically, the most prominent athlete from Canada was the Chicago Cubs and Texas Rangers right hand pitcher Ferguson Jenkins. Because of his 19 years in the big leagues, Cy Young award, 3,000 plus strikeouts and 20 victories in seven different seasons, Jenkins was elected into the Canadian Baseball Hall of Fame in 1987 and also into MLB's Hall of Fame in Cooperstown, New York.[2] There were several great Cuban athletes who had excelled on various clubs in the major leagues. These included first, pitcher Adolfo Luque, who played for 20 seasons on a total of four teams for which he recorded 194 victories and 179 losses, second, the Cincinnati Reds infielder Tony Perez, who had appeared in 2,777 games and hit 379 home runs with a career batting average of .279, and third, infielder Rafael Palmeriro, who is an elite slugger that will eventually enter MLB's Hall

---

TABLE 13.1. FOREIGN PLAYERS IN THE BIG LEAGUES,
BY COUNTRY OF ORIGIN, 1871–2003

Country	Players	Country	Players
Afghanistan	1	Japan	25
American Samoa	1	Mexico	97
Aruba	9	Netherlands	8
Australia	15	Nicaragua	8
Austria	2	Norway	3
Bahamas	5	Okinawa	2
Belgium	1	Panama	44
Belize	1	Philippines	1
Canada	210	Poland	4
China	1	Puerto Rico	210
Columbia	7	Russia	7
Cuba	148	Scotland	8
Czechoslovakia	4	Singapore	1
Denmark	1	South Korea	9
Dominican Republic	361	Spain	4
England	30	Sweden	4
Finland	1	Switzerland	1
France	7	Taiwan (Chinese Taipei)	2
Germany	37	Territory of Hawaii	3
Greece	1	Venezuela	159
Honduras	1	Vietnam	1
Ireland	38	Virgin Islands	12
Italy	6	Wales	2
Jamaica	3		

* Although a few players had performed on teams in the American Association, National Association and minor leagues, the majority of them played on clubs in the AL and NL of MLB. The nation of Aruba includes Curacao and the Netherlands Antilles, and Russia contains players from the Ukraine. The Territory of Hawaii had existed until 1959, when Hawaii became a U.S. state. Between 1960 and 2003, there were 25 players from Hawaii that played on teams in MLB.

Source: Peter C. Bjarkman, *Diamonds Around the Globe: The Encyclopedia of International Baseball* (Westport, CT: Greenwood Press, 2005).

of Fame after he retires from professional baseball in the U.S. Besides these three exceptional players, baseball historians also respect the former achievements of other Cubans such as the Cleveland Indians' Minnie Minoso and Luis Tiant, Minnesota Twins' Tony Oliva, Oakland Athletics' Jose Canseco, and the Kansas City Athletics' Bert Campaneris.

Similarly, Venezuela's Manny Trillo, Luis Aparicio and Dave Concepcion each played at least 17 seasons for teams in MLB and then retired with batting averages that exceeded .260. Between 1973 and 1990, Trillo had 1,562 hits in 1,780 games. Furthermore, in 2004 Aparicio deserved his admission into the Professional Hall of Fame in Venezuela and also in Cooperstown, New York because of his adept fielding talents, spray hitting and swift base running. Meanwhile, as the Reds' shortstop during the 1970s, Concepcion earned five NL Gold Glove awards for his abilities to catch ground and fly balls, and then for his leadership skills that propelled his Reds' teams to win back-to-back World Series in 1975 and 1976.

As Puerto Rico's greatest baseball star and the island's national hero, Hall of Famer Roberto Clemente played 2,433 games in 18 seasons for the Pittsburgh Pirates. Besides his .317 lifetime batting average and 3,000 hits, Clemente reached double figures by hitting ten or more triples for six consecutive years. Some sports historians consider Clemente to be one of the finest all-around athletes to ever play the game. Other former big leaguers from Puerto Rico with outstanding batting statistics during their careers are infielder Orlando Cepeda, outfielder Jose Cruz and second baseman Roberto Alomar.

Finally, from the Dominican Republic it was outfielder Manny Mota, pitcher Juan Marichal and outfielders Felipe and Matty Alou who became some of the most memorable Latin American players of their eras. Mota played 1,536 games in 20 seasons and batted .304, while Marichal pitched over 300 innings during four years and won 20 or more games in six of seven seasons. Felipe Alou hit .286 during his 17-year career and Matty collected 1,777 hits in 1,667 games through 15 seasons, and batted .307. Big leaguers Vladimir Guerrero, Pedro Martinez, Sammy Sosa and Albert Pujols are current superstar players from that nation. In short, these are a few of the superior and popular players, from each of the five aforementioned countries, who have or had performed for teams in the AL and/or NL during various baseball seasons between 1871 and 2005.

Team Rosters: 2004 and 2005 Seasons

During the Spring of 2004 and 2005, the web site mlb.com provided by country, the names and numerical counts of international players who had appeared on the opening day rosters of the 30 teams in MLB. According to the league, the teams' rosters each consisted of 25 players plus those disabled because of various injuries. For 2004, the listing included 227 players who represented 13 foreign nations and Puerto Rico, and for 2005, there were a total of 242 players identified from 15 non–U.S. countries, Puerto Rico and the Virgin Islands. This information is interesting, insightful and significant to study and analyze since the data indicates to what extent MLB teams have successfully scouted, recruited and signed players who were born in countries other than the U.S. Consequently, Table 13.2 was prepared for these purposes, and also for an evaluation in another section about the distribution of foreign players by teams and regions of the world.[3]

With respect to Table 13.2, at least some facts can be stated about a player or the players from one or a few of the nations. Listed in no specific order, 11 of these observations are highlighted as follows. First, Sidney Ponson was the only remaining MLB player from Aruba who appeared on opening day rosters in 2004 and 2005. Although his career statistics as a right hand pitcher for the Baltimore Orioles has been mediocre, he has performed for the team since 1998. Second, after being released or sent to the minors by their clubs during 2004, Australians Trent Durrington, Damian Moss and Brad Thomas were not listed on any of the teams' opening rosters in 2005. Besides the Minnesota Twins' Grant Balfour, the other Australian in 2005 was the Seattle Mariners' Travis Blackley. Third, the two best ball players from Canada are Eric Gagne and Larry Walker. Gagne has been an outstanding relief pitcher for the Los Angeles Dodgers since 1999, and Walker had played 15 seasons and hit 315 home runs in total for the Montreal Expos and Colorado Rockies. Then, he joined the St. Louis Cardinals and helped the team win the NL pennant in 2004.

Fourth, in 2005 the Columbian players were two shortstops, that is, the Boston Red Sox' Edgar Renteria and Los Angeles Angels' Orlando Cabrera. They each became big leaguers in the mid–1990s for, respectively, the Florida Marlins and Montreal Expos. Fifth, according to mlb.com the number of Cuban players decreased from nine in 2004 to six in 2005 because Vladimir Nunez, Alex Sanchez and Adrian Hernandez failed to

TABLE 13.2. FOREIGN PLAYERS ON OPENING DAY
ROSTERS, BY COUNTRY, 2004 AND 2005

Number of Players

Country	2004	2005	Percentage Growth
Aruba*	1	1	0
Australia	4	2	-50
Canada	11	15	36
Columbia	3	2	-33
Cuba	9	6	-33
Curacao	2	1	-50
Dominican Republic	79	91	15
Japan	10	12	20
Korea	4	1	-75
Mexico	16	18	12
Nicaragua	1	1	0
Panama	6	6	0
Puerto Rico	36	34	-5
South Korea	0	4	400
Taiwan	0	1	100
Venezuela	45	46	2
Virgin Islands	0	1	100

* The players on team rosters from Aruba and Curacao are listed separately by MLB. In 2004, four players represented Korea while South Korea did not appear on mlb.com's list. Then in 2005, mlb.com listed Korea and South Korea as different countries. Except for the rookies, the players who entered the major leagues before the 2004 season are included in Table 13.1. Many players appeared in the columns for 2004 and 2005 such as the Baltimore Orioles' right hand pitcher Sidney Ponson, who is from Noord, Aruba.

Source: "27.3 Percent of Major League Baseball Players Born Outside the United States," at http://www.mlb.com cited 29 March 2005, and "29.2 Percent of Major League Baseball Players Born Outside the U.S.," at http://www.mlb.com cited 12 April 2005.

qualify for the opening day rosters of any MLB team. Each player is a pitcher that apparently has underperformed while in the major leagues. Sixth, Curacao's Andruw Jones has been with the Atlanta Braves since 1996. He plays center field on defense, bats fourth in the line-up on offense, and hits with power. Seventh, in 2005 the players from the Dominican Republic had, in total, expanded their presence in MLB from the previous season. To retain these special athletes, MLB has finally updated its policy, that is, to randomly test for drugs and to provide better treatment and programs for the Dominican players who are active in the major and minor leagues.

Eighth, Dae-Sung Koo of South Korea did not perform in the major leagues during 2004. One year later, however, Koo became a rookie relief pitcher for the New York Mets. Ninth, Nicaragua's Vicente Padilla signed his first professional baseball contract with the Arizona Diamondbacks in 1999. Then, in 2005 he joined the starting rotation of the Philadelphia Phillies as a right hand pitcher. Tenth, in 2003 pitcher Chin-hui Tsao of Taiwan signed with the Colorado Rockies. Because of his sub par performances, he did not appear on the Rockies' opening day roster in 2004. But, he was assigned to the club's bullpen for the 2005 season. Eleventh, in 2005 the Virgin Islands' Calvin Pickering appeared on the Kansas City Royals' lineup as a designated hitter. Although the Baltimore Orioles had signed Pickering to a MLB contract in 1998, his career batting average remains below .250. Unless he improves his hitting productivity during the 2005 season, the Athletics may decide to release or trade Pickering. In short, these are 11 observations that revealed some characteristics about players from various countries in 2004 and/or 2005.

MLB Teams' Foreign Players in 2005

Based on the research, the third aspect of this chapter is to measure and evaluate how diverse the rosters of each MLB team were in early 2005. To accomplish that objective, the numbers and nationalities of the foreign-born players on the 25-man rosters and disabled lists of all clubs are listed in columns three, four and five of Table 13.3. Given the data in the table, what can be inferred about the allocation of international players relative to the 30 teams in organized baseball?[4]

According to the final three columns of the table, in April of 2005 there were a total of 243 foreign players on the opening day rosters of the 14 AL and 16 NL teams. As to each of the international groups, 208 or approximately 85 percent of the players had migrated from nations in Latin America, 17 or 7 percent from countries in the Asia Pacific and 18 or 8 percent from countries in the Other column. These include Australia, Canada and the Virgin Islands.

The totals of each league are also relevant to the distribution. That is, counting the numbers of AL and then NL players in columns three, four and five amounted to, respectively, 97, 7 and 11, and 111, 10 and 7. This distribution indicates that relative to the group of teams in the AL, the NL clubs employed more athletes from Latin America and the Asia Pacific region, but fewer from the Other category. This occurred, in part, because of the 15 Latino players on the 2005 roster of the Washington Nationals, the three Asian Pacific players of the New York Mets, and the three players from other nations who were listed on the roster of the Minnesota Twins and the two representing the Kansas City Royals. For sure, these teams played their foreign athletes in positions

TABLE 13.3. DISTRIBUTION OF FOREIGN PLAYERS,
BY LEAGUES AND TEAMS, APRIL 2005

Team	U.S.	Latin American	Asian Pacific	Other
AL				
Baltimore Orioles	15	12	0	1
Boston Red Sox	22	4	0	1
Chicago White Sox	16	9	2	0
Cleveland Indians	23	6	0	0
Detroit Tigers	22	9	0	0
Kansas City Royals	19	7	0	2
Los Angeles Angels	20	10	0	0
Minnesota Twins	20	6	0	3
New York Yankees	18	6	1	1
Oakland Athletics	19	6	1	1
Seattle Mariners	22	6	2	1
Tampa Bay Devil Rays	23	5	1	0
Texas Rangers	21	9	0	0
Toronto Blue Jays	22	2	0	1
NL				
Arizona Diamondbacks	22	7	0	0
Atlanta Braves	16	8	0	1
Chicago Cubs	22	5	0	1
Cincinnati Reds	22	7	1	0
Colorado Rockies	22	4	2	1
Florida Marlins	19	8	0	0
Houston Astros	23	3	0	0
Los Angeles Dodgers	18	11	1	1
Milwaukee Brewers	22	3	0	0
New York Mets	17	10	3	0
Philadelphia Phillies	20	6	0	1
Pittsburgh Pirates	22	6	0	1
San Diego Padres	20	5	1	0
San Francisco Giants	20	6	0	0
St. Louis Cardinals	17	7	1	1
Washington Nationals	15	15	1	0

Note: Each team's total number of players consisted of the 25-man roster and those on the disabled list. This conforms to how mlb.com reported the foreign players, by country, on each team. The nations in Latin America and Asia Pacific can be easily identified. Other includes the professional baseball players from Australia, Canada and the Virgin Islands.

Source: "29.2 Percent of Major League Baseball Players Born Outside the U.S.," at http://www.mlb.com cited 12 April 2005, and "Team Sites," at http://www.mlb.com cited 14 April 2005.

on the field and at bat as a strategy to win more games and compete for a division title or a wild card.

To be more specific about the distributions across the two leagues, the teams with the largest number of players from the Latin American nations were the Washington Nationals at 15, Baltimore Orioles at 12, Los Angeles Dodgers at 11, and the Los Angeles Angels and New York Mets each at ten. Interestingly, a few of the key Latino players who have started in the lineup for these clubs include the Nationals' Endy Chavez, Jose Vidro and Vinny Castilla, Orioles' Melvin Mora, Miguel Tejada and Javy Lopez, Dodgers' Cesar

Izturis, Wilson Alverez and Odalis Perez, Angels' Orlando Cabrera, Bartolo Colon and Bengie Molina, and the Mets' Carlos Beltran, Victor Zambrano and Felix Heredia.

Based on their productivities thus far, it appears that especially Castilla, Tejada and Beltran, and also other Latino players such as the Tigers' Ivan Rodriguez and Carlos Guillen, and the Giants' Edgardo Alfonzo and Marlins' Miguel Cabrera will each be very effective hitters for their respective teams in 2005 and future seasons. Alternatively, for one reason or another the Toronto Blue Jays, Houston Astros and Milwaukee Brewers each employed the fewest ballplayers from the countries in Latin America. As an aside, the Blue Jays and Astros are teams that are contenders. That is, they have the potential to compete and qualify for the playoffs. Meanwhile, the Brewers continue to place below .500 and struggle in the NL's Central Division.

The Mets and then the Chicago White Sox, Seattle Mariners and Colorado Rockies each have the most athletes, in total, from Japan, South Korea and Taiwan. The Asians who play regularly for these teams are the Mets' Dae-Sung Koo, Kazuhisa Ishii and Kazuo Matsui, White Sox' Tadahito Iguchi and Shingo Takatsu, Mariners' Ichiro Suzuki and S. Hasegawa, and the Rockies' Chin-hui Tsao and Byung-Hyun Kim. During games in the early 2005 season, Suzuki led the AL in hitting with a batting average above .400, and the Mets' Kaz Matsui from Japan had accumulated an impressive number of runs batted in as a national leaguer.

Meanwhile, the Minnesota Twins' roster included one player from Australia and two from Canada, and the Kansas City Royals had one from Canada and another from the Virgin Islands. These athletes played various positions in the field. For the Twins, Australian Grant Balfour and Canadian Jesse Crain are pitchers, and Canadian Justin Morneau excels at first base. For the Royals, Canadian Matt Stairs is a right fielder and the Virgin Islands' Calvin Pickering catches baseballs at first base. Besides Crain, Morneau and Stairs, other competitive players from Canada are the Orioles' pitcher Erik Bedard, Blue Jays' infielder Corey Koskie, Athletics' pitcher Rich Harden, Pirates' outfielder Jason Bay and Cubs' pitcher Ryan Dempster.

A more in-depth study of Table 13.3 reveals the AL and NL teams that each had the most players from particular foreign nations on their rosters. If the numbers of players on two or more teams from one nation are equal such as three each from nations A, B and C, that country is excluded in the groups for the AL and NL. As a result, the teams with the most international players are as follows. In the AL, it was the Orioles with one player from Aruba, Twins with two from Canada, White Sox with two from Cuba, Orioles and Athletics with two each from Mexico, the Indians and Yankees with three each from Puerto Rico, White Sox and Rangers with six each from the Dominican Republic, Tigers with five from Venezuela, White Sox and Mariners with two each from Japan, and the Royals with one from the Virgin Islands. In the NL, it was the Nationals with four players from Mexico, Phillies with one from Nicaragua, Diamondbacks with three from Puerto Rico, the Cubs, Mets and Nationals with six each from the Dominican Republic, Dodgers and Giants with three each from Venezuela, and the Mets with two from Japan. Given this distribution of athletes by teams, only the Blue Jays in the AL and Brewers and Giants in the NL had an equal proportion of foreign players from two or more individual nations.

MLB's Greatest Foreign Players

A portion of the *Official Major League Baseball Fact Book 2005 Edition* lists the names and performances of the U.S. and foreign players who had established a high rank during their careers in service, batting, pitching and fielding for regular MLB seasons. For this section, Table 13.4 denotes a sample of the international players who had appeared in one, two, three, four and/or five of the career statistics of the *Fact Book*. In column one of the table, there are 31 career statistics beginning with Years Played and ending with Outfield. In turn, for each of the statistics there is the name of the foreign player, his country and numerical rank. Organized by category, this information is highlighted next.[5]

TABLE 13.4. ALL-TIME CAREER STATISTICS OF FOREIGN PLAYERS IN MLB, 2005

Career Statistic	Player	Country	Rank
Service			
Years Played	Tony Perez	Cuba	9th-t
Years Pitched	Dennis Martinez	Nicaragua	8th-t
Batting			
Consecutive Games Played	Miguel Tejada	Dominican Republic	11th
Years Leading League in Average	Rod Carew	Panama	4th-t
Years Topping .300	Rod Carew	Panama	10th-t
Consecutive .300 Seasons	Rod Carew	Panama	4th-t
At-Bats	Luis Aparacio	Venezuela	17th
Years Leading League in Runs	Sammy Sosa	Dominican Republic	13th-t
Years Leading League in Hits	Tony Oliva	Cuba	5th
Pinch Hits	Manny Mota	Dominican Republic	2nd
Singles	Rod Carew	Panama	6th
Doubles	Rafael Palmeiro	Cuba	16th
Home Runs	Sammy Sosa	Dominican Republic	7th
Home Runs-AL	Rafael Palmeiro	Cuba	5th
Home Runs-NL	Sammy Sosa	Dominican Republic	5th-t
Pinch-Hit Home Runs	Jose Morales	Virgin Islands	10th-t
Grand Slams	Manny Ramirez	Dominican Republic	4th-t
Total Bases	Rafael Palmeiro	Cuba	11th
Slugging Percentage	Manny Ramirez	Dominican Republic	8th
Runs Batted In	Rafael Palmeiro	Cuba	17th
Pitching			
Opening Day Starts	Ferguson Jenkins	Canada	11th-t
Winning Percentage	Pedro Martinez	Dominican Republic	2nd
Saves	Mariano Rivera	Panama	8th
20 Victories, Righthander	Ferguson Jenkins	Canada	16th-t
Shutouts	Juan Marichal	Dominican Republic	18th
No-Hit Games	Hideo Nomo	Japan	6th-t
Fielding			
Catcher	Ivan Rodriguez	Puerto Rico	1st-t
First Base	Rafael Palmeiro	Cuba	10th-t
Second Base	Roberto Alomar	Puerto Rico	1st
Shortstop	Luis Aparicio	Venezuela	2nd-t
Outfield	Roberto Clemente	Puerto Rico	1st-t

* These were the first foreign players listed in the *Fact Book* for each of the career statistics. The t means a tie in rank between two or more players for that career statistic. In Fielding, the players won Gold Gloves at these positions. Because they were too specific or detailed, a few of the career statistics presented in the *Fact Book* were omitted.

Source: *Official Major League Baseball Fact Book 2005 Edition* (St. Louis, MO: The Sporting News, 2005).

In the category of Service, the ballplayers listed were Tony Perez, who had played 23 seasons in MLB and Dennis Martinez, who pitched for a total of 23 years. During his seasons with the Cincinnati Reds, Perez played in 2,777 games, maintained a lifetime batting average of .279 and clouted 379 home runs. Martinez, who had signed with the Baltimore Orioles, pitched in 692 games, struck out 2,149 batters and finished with a 245–193 win-loss record. Interestingly, there were no foreign players that appeared in the rankings of the other two regular season, career statistics of the *Fact Book*, which was Years One Club and Years Pitched One Club.

Relative to their career records as batters for franchises in MLB, Table 13.4 denotes that the most productive foreign players have been Rod Carew, Sammy Sosa and Rafael Palmeiro. Carew led the league with the highest batting average in seven seasons, hit at least .300 for 15 consecutive seasons, and stroked 2,404 singles. Before the 2005 season had begun, Sosa previously led the league three years in runs, smacked a total of 574 home runs, and hit 545 of these while he played in the NL. The leaders for each of these statistics are, respectively, Babe Ruth with eight years, and Hank Aaron with 755 total home runs, with 733 of those when he played in the NL. Because he is an active player, Palmeiro's career statistics as a hitter will likely increase during the 2005 season while he is with the Baltimore Orioles as an infielder. That is, his 572 doubles, 526 home runs in the AL, 5,223 total bases and 1,775 runs batted are certain to be surpassed, which will rank him even higher in these all-time career statistics when the season concludes. If Palmeiro wins his fourth Gold Glove in 2005 as an Orioles first baseman, he will tie former stars Steve Garvey and Mark Grace for eighth place in fielding.

Besides the all-time great sluggers, whose last names are Carew, Sosa and Palmeiro, other foreign players have established some impressive batting performances. These include Miguel Tejada's 756 consecutive games played, Luis Aparicio's 10,230 at bats, Tony Oliva's five years as the league's leading hitter, Manny Mota's 150 pinch hits, Jose Morales's 12 pinch hit home runs, and Manny Ramirez's 17 grand slams and .599 slugging percentage. If they can avoid serious injuries and lengthy hitting slumps, Tejada and Ramirez may break one or more batting records during the current or a future regular season, league championship, all-star game or World Series for their respective clubs. Lastly, six international baseball players who have achieved very good batting records include Sandy Alomar Sr.'s 648 consecutive games played, Jose Canseco's 462 home runs in the AL and Juan Gonzalez's 429, Andres Galarraga's 380 home runs in the NL and Orlando Cepeda's 358, and Vladimir Guerrero's .588 slugging percentage.

As pitchers for clubs in MLB, foreign athletes have been inferior to and less effective than those individuals born in the U.S. This means that the names and performances of international players rarely appeared in the *Fact Book's* data that represented pitchers. However, in Table 13.4 are the statistics for five of the best foreign players to pitch for MLB teams. There is Hall of Famer Ferguson Jenkins, who started a total of 11 opening day games for the Chicago Cubs and Texas Rangers, and also finished seven seasons with at least 20 victories; Pedro Martinez, who has won seven of ten games as a pitcher during his career and struck out more than 2,623 batters; Mariano Rivera, who saved 336 games as a relief pitcher; Juan Marichal, who shutout the opposing team in 52 games; and Hideo Nomo, who hurled two no-hit games. In addition to these players, other foreign athletes that were listed in the *Fact Book* but ranked lower than the previous five as pitchers included Puerto Rico's Roberto Hernandez and the Dominican Republic's Jose Mesa in saves, Cuba's Luis Tiant in shutouts as a right hander and Mike Cuellar in shutouts as a lefthander, and Mexico's Fernando Valenzuela in strikeouts as a lefthander. Since they were active players in 2005, it appears that Martinez, Rivera and Nomo have an opportunity to improve their career performances and rankings as pitchers for MLB teams.

To be listed in the fielding category of Table 13.4, the players must have earned a sufficient number of gold glove awards at their respective field positions for several regular seasons. Before 2005, Ivan Rodriguez had won 11 awards at catcher, Rafael Palmeiro three at first base, Roberto Alomar ten at second base, Luis Aparicio nine at shortstop and Roberto Clemente 12 at left, center and right in the outfield. Other international players were listed for their fielding performances in the *Fact Book*, but not entered in Table 13.4 because of their lower ranks. These included the Dominican Republic's Tony Pena and Puerto Rico's Benito Santiago at catcher, Puerto Rico's Vic Power at first base, Venezuela's Manny Trillo at second base, Venezuela's Omar Vizquel and Dave Concepcion, Dominican Republic's Tony Fernandez, and Cuba's Rey Ordonez and Zoilo Versalles at shortstop, and Curacao's Andruw Jones in the outfield. Finally, the Dominican Republic's Rafael Fucal recorded an unassisted triple play during the 2003 season while he played shortstop for the Atlanta Braves. Besides Furcal, only 11 other players in MLB history had completed this very difficult play.

As denoted in the *Fact Book,* a number of foreign players are also listed for their career performances, and for their single season and single game records in various League Championship Series, All-Star games and World Series tournaments. Several of these players have not been mentioned in this section of the chapter because they first appeared on the rosters of teams in the big leagues during the mid-to-late 1990s and early 2000s. As of 2005, for example, such athletes as the Mariners' Ichiro Suzuki from Japan, Mets' Carlos Beltran from Puerto Rico, and the Cardinals' Albert Pujols from the Dominican Republic are each ranked in the top 20 for the number of hits as a rookie during a single season. In pitching, some international players had excellent performances for a regular season and deserve recognition. These include three from the Dominican Republic, that is, the Cardinals' Julian Tavarez for total games, and for saves, the Giants' Armondo Benitez and Pirates' Jose Mesa.[6]

The starting lineups, rotations and bullpens of MLB teams for the 2005 season may contain one or more players who will be superstars of the future in professional baseball. In fact, these athletes could excel to establish a mixture of career, regular season, postseason and single game records. To identify a few of the skilled players, in the AL there is the Orioles' Javey Lopez from Puerto Rico, Red Sox' David Ortiz from the Dominican Republic, Rangers' Richard Hidalgo from Venezuela, Athletics' Ricardo Rincon from Mexico and the White Sox' Jose Contreras from Cuba. Meanwhile, the NL's promising foreign players include the Marlins' Miguel Cabrera from Venezuela, Padres' Akinori Otsuka from Japan, and the Diamondbacks' Joe Valverde from the Dominican Republic and Brewers' Carlos Lee from Panama.

As explained before, in 2005 16 foreign athletes were listed on the 25-man roster and disabled list of the Nationals in Washington, D.C. For years, the team had experienced weak support and apathy from local fans, businesses and other organizations while the franchise was located in Montreal, Canada. Because of the new environment, however, the team's athletes from abroad may perform above average in batting, pitching and fielding as they play home games in front of enthusiastic crowds at RFK Stadium in the nation's capital. Indeed, there are high expectations in the community for all-out efforts

from such starters as the Dominican Republic's Cristian Guzman in center field and Jose
Guillen in right field, Puerto Rico's Jose Vidro at second base and Mexico's Vinny Castilla
at third base, and from pitchers like Mexico's Luis Ayala and Esteban Loaiza, Venezuela's
Tony Armas, Japan's Tomo Ohka and Puerto Rico's Chad Cordero. During the preseason, some prominent sports journalists had predicted that the Nationals would finish
fifth, which is last place in the NL's East Division. It appeared after a few games, however, that Vidro, Guillen and Castilla would influence and motivate the club to win games
because of their power as hitters and their leadership abilities on the field.

Meanwhile, the Astros, Blue Jays and Brewers began the 2005 season with less diversity than any of the 27 other teams. That is, each club had three foreign players on its
roster. As such, the Astros' starting lineup, rotation and bullpen did not include any
international foreign athletes. For the Blue Jays, Canada's Corey Koskie started at third
base, Venezuela's Gustavo Chacin pitched in the rotation, and the Dominican Republic's
Miguel Batista received a bullpen assignment. For the Brewers, Panama's Carlos Lee
started in left field, Dominican Republic's Victor Santos pitched in the rotation, and
Mexico's Jorge De La Rosa substituted for a starter. In short, the numbers of foreign
ballplayers on MLB teams varied from 3 to 16 on opening day of the 2005 season.[7]

Summary

In four sections, this chapter essentially analyzed the AL and NL teams' short- and
long-term demands for foreign-born athletes to play baseball for their organizations.
Based on the research conducted, since 1871 the five primary nations from which international ballplayers have been scouted, trained and signed to contracts are the Dominican Republic, Canada, Puerto Rico, Venezuela and Cuba. These five and 42 other
countries, and the total numbers of minor and major league players from each of them,
are listed in a table of section one and then discussed.

For the opening games of MLB's 2004 and 2005 regular seasons, a table in section
two reveals the distribution of foreign players according to their country of origin. In the
table, 16 nations are represented for the league's seasons, which consisted of 227 foreign
players in 2004 and 242 in 2005. The growth in the percentages of players for each of the
16 countries, from 2004 to 2005, is listed in a column of the table. With respect to the
data, 11 observations are stated about some interesting characteristics of various foreign
players who had performed while on the rosters of teams in the regular seasons of 2004
and/or 2005.

After these two sections are completed, in this chapter's third section there is a table
that denotes for each of the 30 teams, the total number of international players who are
natives of nations in Latin America and the Asia Pacific region, and of other foreign countries. This table reflects the distribution of players as of the opening game of baseball's
2005 regular season. Following the table, some of the athletes are identified on several of
the teams, and then there is an overview of how these players have successfully contributed their talents to respective clubs.

In the final section, there is a table that lists 31 career statistics of the outstanding
foreign players who have performed for various MLB teams. The four categories of performances include Service, Batting, Pitching and Fielding. The players who had great
achievements in each category are ranked and their performances evaluated based on

information provided in the *Official Major League Baseball Fact Book 2005 Edition*, and in other publications.

Because of their commitments, skills, and previous, current and potential accomplishments in the sport, it is anticipated that the proportion of foreign players on rosters of clubs in MLB will increase from 29.2 percent in 2005 to at least 30 or 31 percent in 2006. Indeed, if this growth rate continues to occur during the early 2000s, then the professional teams in America's minor and major baseball leagues will become even more diverse and perhaps competitive from business and global perspectives.

14. International Tournaments and Championship Teams

Except for 1903 and 1994, each year since 1902 the teams that won the pennant in the American League (AL) and National League (NL) of Major League Baseball (MLB) have played each other in a World Series. This is not a well diversified international tournament in which teams from three or more foreign nations have participated in the competition given that the AL and NL baseball franchises have always been located in cities of Canada and/or the U.S. Besides MLB's World Series, in various metropolitan areas and regions of the world there are amateur and professional baseball tournaments that include only the clubs and players from a specific nation. In the U.S., for example, the Babe Ruth World Series and American Legion Baseball Championship have involved only American-based teams. As such, these are not the types of baseball events to be explored in this chapter. Alternatively, the focus here is to identify, highlight and discuss some of the primary international baseball tournaments that have occurred between teams from nations before and during the early 2000s, and to indicate which of the nations' teams have succeeded to win a championship or series. This topic, of course, directly affects the business operations, relationships and values of the worldwide baseball industry and the industry's future growth and prosperity.[1]

Besides these global sports competitions, which include various teams in Little League youth programs and those in the International Baseball Federation (IBAF), Caribbean Series and other tournaments, MLB's proposal to arrange, sponsor and host a World Baseball Classic is examined in detail. As of late 2005, the scheduling and implementation of this event depended on such factors as the expiration of the collective bargaining agreement between MLB and the Major League Baseball Players Association (MLBPA) in 2006, changing the preseason training days and games of big league teams during the Spring months and perhaps the dates of the World Series in the Fall, and cooperation of the IBAF and officials who are members of national baseball federations that exist in countries of Asia, Europe and Latin America. However, despite these and other issues, MLB has organized and will host and participate in an international World Baseball Classic during the Spring of 2006, that is, an event that includes baseball teams from the most competitive sports nations in the world.

International Baseball Tournaments for Youth Leagues

The most popular global baseball tournament for pre-teenagers began in the 1940s and then 20 years or more later, some international competitions were established for leagues whose teams consisted of teenagers. From the youngest to oldest age groups of players, these events include the World Series of baseball for the Little League in 1947 and also for other Little League programs such as Junior League Baseball in 1981, Senior League Baseball in 1961 and Big League Baseball in 1968.[2]

With respect to the Little League, Americans' Carl E. Stotz and Bert and George Bebble founded this worldwide baseball organization in 1939 in the City of Williamsport, Pennsylvania. It was formed by Stotz and the Bebble's to provide a healthy activity and sport training, based on good leadership, for children and teenagers who may range in age from 10 to 12, and later to 13 years old. Other purposes of organizing the league includes helping young people to become responsible and decent citizens, inspiring them to achieve goals and enriching their lives until they reach maturity as adults. In short, the league tries hard to emphasize the values of teamwork, sportsmanship and fair play, and teaches the participants how to have fun and enjoy the benefits of playing the game of baseball.

Since 1947, there has been a Little League World Series held during late August of each year. Normally, there are eight all-star teams from the U.S. and eight from foreign countries that have enthusiastically competed at 10,000-seat Howard J. Lamade Stadium in Williamsport. To qualify for and play in a World Series, each domestic and non–U.S. all-star team must have won a local and regional baseball tournament. After the inferior teams are eliminated, the U.S. champion challenges its foreign counterpart in the Series' championship game to determine who will be recognized as the world champion for that year. The attendances at the final game in the tournament have increased from 2,000 spectators in 1947 to an estimated 25,000-30,000 in 2005.

The Junior League Baseball Division, which is composed of clubs whose players are boys and girls aged 13 years old, has assigned its leagues' teams to play their 7-inning games on a conventional 90-foot baseball diamond. When the regular season ends, there are international competitions that consist of teams with all-star players who were selected from other teams in their local leagues. After the international tournaments are over, there is a Junior League Baseball World Series that, since 1981, has featured teams from across the world. To ensure these Series are competitive each year for the teams, coaches and players, and entertaining for the fans, Little League Baseball has paid the travel, meal and housing costs of those teams that qualify for and advance to the Junior League's World Series.

The Senior League Baseball Division was structured for boys and girls who are 13 to 15 years old and the Big League Baseball Division for athletes aged 16 to 18 years old. In each Division, the players are members of clubs in their local leagues. Similar to Little League and Junior League programs, each of these leagues has an option to choose an all-star team consisting of the best players and then enter an international tournament. When that competition concludes, there are Senior League and Big League Baseball World Series tournaments that since 1961 and 1968, respectively, have attracted talented domestic and foreign all-star teams. Again, Little League Baseball provides funds for the teams to attend and players to compete in the Senior and Big League World Series.

During the early 2000s, approximately three million boys and girls of various ages had played on 200,000 Little League teams in at least 80 countries. For each of the age groups, there is a set of rules that are specifically designed to make the game fair and equitable for all participants. Nonetheless, when a player reaches 12 to 13 years old the same rules and procedures apply to games as those designed for major leaguers. To denote the foreign nations that have won one or more World Series in these four international baseball tournaments, Table 14.1 was constructed.

According to the table, the baseball teams from foreign countries had won 83 or 52 percent of the total tournaments completed. Besides the 77 clubs that excelled from the U.S., the most successful teams were from Chinese Taipei (hereinafter Taiwan), which had earned 51 or 32 percent of the total championships. Regarding the leading international champions in the Little League World Series as listed in column one of the table, Mexico won two titles in the 1950s, Japan two in the 1960s, Taiwan seven in the 1970s, five in the 1980s and four in the 1990s, and Japan two from 2000 to 2004. Therefore, for the foreign countries that have been represented in the tournament that is held each year in Williamsport, Pennsylvania, the teams from Taiwan, Japan and Mexico had the most success while the all-star clubs from Canada, Dominican Republic, Panama and Puerto Rico played the worst between 1947 and 2004.

With respect to the other three leagues listed in the table, the most dominant foreign teams were from Puerto Rico in the Junior League World Series and Taiwan in the Senior and Big League World Series. Alternatively, the all-star teams from Japan, and the Philippines and South Korea failed to win a championship when they had participated in any of these respective Series. Meanwhile, one title was earned by Canada, Curacao and the Dominican Republic and Panama. Apparently, it was competitive teams from the U.S. and then Taiwan that had achieved the greatest number of championships in the four tournaments represented in Table 14.1.

TABLE 14.1. INTERNATIONAL BASEBALL CHAMPIONS,
BY COUNTRY AND LEAGUE, SELECTED YEARS

Country	Little League	Junior League	Senior League	Big League
Canada	0	0	0	1
Chinese Taipei (Taiwan)	17	0	17	17
Curacao	1	0	1	0
Dominican Republic	0	0	1	0
Japan	6	0	0	0
Mexico	3	1	2	0
Panama	0	0	1	0
Philippines	1	0	0	0
Puerto Rico	0	5	0	2
South Korea	2	0	0	0
USA	26	17	19	15
Venezuela	2	0	2	1

* The World Series championship years include the 1947–2004 Little Leagues, 1981–2003 Junior Leagues, 1961–2003 Senior Leagues and 1968–2003 Big Leagues. In 1992, the Philippines won the Little League World Series because the Dominican Republic was disqualified for using ineligible players.
Source: "Little League Organization," at http://www.littleleague.org cited 4 April 2005.

International Baseball Federation Tournaments

Besides managing the Women's Baseball World Cup and co-sponsoring the World University Baseball Championship, each of which are excluded in this section because of their very short histories, the IBAF is the administrative organization that supervises the operations of five international baseball tournaments including the Summer Olympic Games. The next three paragraphs are an overview of how the IBAF has evolved as a sports organization.[3]

To consolidate and promote global sports competition between nations, the IBAF was formed in 1938. That year in London, a British team won the first Baseball World Cup in five games by defeating a club from the U.S. As a result, during the early 1940s an increasing number of teams from various countries continued to meet each year in World Cup tournaments to determine a world champion of baseball. While these events were occurring, the IBF changed its name to the Federacion Internacional de Beisbol Amateur (FIBA) in 1944 and nine years later, the Asian and European Baseball Federations— ABF and EBF — each organized and emerged because the game of baseball was spreading as a sport among many nations in Asia and Europe.

During the 1960s and early 1970s, there were frequent contacts between officials from FIBA and the ABF and EBF, and also between administrators who represented baseball federations in other countries. Meanwhile, teams from Chinese Taipei, Cuba, Italy, Japan, Holland, the U.S. and several smaller nations competed in World Cup tournaments. However, there were conflicts within the IBF. So, in 1973 a new organization named the Federacion Mundial de Beisbol Amateur (FEMBA), or World Federation of Amateur Baseball assembled and met in Bologna, Italy. Ironically, the meeting coincided with the first Intercontinental Cup tournament that was played in Parma and Rimini, Italy. As a result, in 1973 there were two Baseball World Cups and each winning team claimed to be the world champion of baseball.

After a series of negotiations to resolve their differences, in January of 1976 the FIBA and FEMBA merged and became known as the International Baseball Association (AINBA). Then, in 1984 the delegates at a Congress in Havana, Cuba decided to identify this baseball organization simply as the IBA. Subsequent to demonstration tournaments played at the 1984 and 1988 Olympic Games, and a series of continental qualifying tournaments during the late 1980s and early 1990s, baseball became an official Olympic sport in 1992 at the Games in Barcelona, Spain. Finally, when a federation Congress met in Sydney, Australia in 2000, the IBA returned to its roots and officially renamed itself the International Baseball Federation, which was referred to as the IBAF.

Based on the distribution of IBAF tournaments in Table 14.2, the baseball teams from Cuba and the U.S. won 63 or 75 percent of the total championships. As a group, the Cuban teams' performances were significant, overwhelming and impressive. That is, for the 65 total tournaments that the Cuban baseball teams had entered into since the country had joined the IBAF in 1938, they placed first in 51 or nearly 79 percent of them. The U.S., meanwhile, played in 59 IBAF tournaments and won 12 or 20 percent of them. Furthermore, although their clubs have excelled in the Little League World Series as indicated in column two of Table 14.1, the combined teams from Taiwan and Japan had succeeded to win only six IBAF titles in 92 total appearances. These results suggest that Cuban teams tend to dominate the international tournaments in which the players must be at least 13 years old. As to their teams' performances in four Olympic Games, Cuban

TABLE 14.2. INTERNATIONAL BASEBALL FEDERATION CHAMPIONS,
BY COUNTRY AND TOURNAMENT SELECTED YEARS

Country*	World Cup	Intercontinental Cup	AAA	AA	Olympic Games
Australia	0	1	0	0	0
Brazil	0	0	0	1	0
Canada	0	0	1	0	0
Columbia	2	0	0	0	0
Cuba	24	9	11	4	3
Dominican Republic	1	0	0	0	0
Great Britain	1	0	0	0	0
Japan	0	2	0	2	0
Korea	0	1	3	0	0
Puerto Rico	1	0	0	0	0
Taiwan	0	0	1	1	0
USA	2	2	5	2	1
Venezuela	3	0	0	0	0

* Column one of the table denotes that, in total, the championship teams from 13 countries won 34 World Cups, 15 Intercontinental Cups, 21 World Junior AAA, ten World Youth AA and four Olympic Games. These international tournaments began in different years, that is, the World Cup started in 1938, Intercontinental Cup in 1973, World Junior AAA in 1981 and World Youth AA in 1989. Also, teams earned a gold, silver or bronze medal for baseball in the Olympic Games that were held in 1992 in Barcelona, Spain, in 1996 in Atlanta, Georgia, in 2000 in Sydney, Australia, and in 2004 in Athens, Greece.
Source: "International Baseball Federation," at http://www.baseball.ch cited 4 April 2005.

players won gold medals in 1992, 1996 and 2004, but finished runner-up to a U.S. team in 2000 and earned silver medals. Besides Cuba and the U.S., the other successful nations at winning medals in baseball at the Olympic Games have been Japan with one silver and two bronze medals, Australia and Chinese Taipei each with a silver medal, and South Korea with a bronze medal.

Given the results of IBAF tournaments listed in Table 14.2, the baseball teams with one championship have included those from Australia, Brazil, Canada, Dominican Republic, Great Britain and Puerto Rico. If ranked by the number of tournament championships won per appearance, these six nations' winning percentages are, respectively, 3 percent, 5 percent, 2 percent, 4 percent, 100 percent and 3 percent. Because the British Federation of Baseball has not updated the number of IBAF tournament appearances on the web site www.baseball.ch since a team from Great Britain won the World Cup in 1938, the worst performing teams on a percentage basis have been from Canada, Australia and Puerto Rico, and then from the Dominican Republic and Brazil. Nevertheless, it is interesting that clubs from Australia, Puerto Rico and the Dominican Republic have not won more IBAF tournaments even though the game of baseball is very popular in these countries, especially among kids and teenagers.

If the Olympic Games are excluded, the four IBAF tournaments have occurred in several nations. Cuba has hosted 16 of them, Canada 14, the U.S seven, Nicaragua six, and Mexico and Italy each five. Also, 13 other nations have welcomed one or more of the remaining 27 tournaments. Relative to their teams that participated in the tournaments, Cuba has made the most appearances at 65 followed by the U.S.' 59, Taiwan's 51, South Korea's 46 and Japan's 41. Between 20 and 37 appearances were teams from Brazil, Columbia, Dominican Republic, Australia, Puerto Rico, Venezuela and Canada. As explained in the previous paragraph, Great Britain appeared in and won the Baseball World Cup in 1938. In short, these are the nations that have been moderate to very successful at winning championships, and at hosting and competing in the four IBAF tournaments.

Caribbean Series

To attract and retain talented players, and also establish their organization's identity, independence and performance from clubs in MLB, the owners of baseball teams in the Winter Leagues of Cuba, Panama, Puerto Rico and Venezuela formed the Caribbean Confederation in 1948. One year later, the first Caribbean World Series was played in Havana, Cuba. This annual event thrived until 1960, when a revolution led by Fidel Castro and political reforms in Cuba caused the tournament to be cancelled, although the Winter Leagues continued to operate. Then, the Series was revived in 1970 but teams from Cuba and Panama were not invited to play in the tournament. However, in order to maintain competition and a balance of power, these two nations were replaced by the Dominican Republic in 1970, and in 1971 Mexico joined the Series.[4]

From the mid–1970s to the early 2000s, the Series experienced instability during some years for various reasons. These were as follows. First, Mexico provided two teams to the tournament in 1974 when Venezuela did not enter a team due to the nation's political problems. Second, the Series was cancelled in 1981 because of money disputes between officials of the four nations. Third, the MLBPA strike that cancelled a portion of the regular season and the 1994 World Series in the U.S. created a greater demand for baseball from people in the Caribbean during the mid-to-late 1990s and thus, the sport surged in popularity throughout Central and Latin America. Fourth, in 2003 Venezuela did not participate in the tournament since there was political turmoil in that country. Fifth, since the 1970s the teams in the Confederation have increasingly lost some of their productive players when those athletes signed lucrative contracts with MLB teams.

Despite these circumstances and events, however, the Series has gradually earned a well-deserved reputation among sports authorities for being the tournament that showcases the most competitive baseball games and best baseball teams in the Caribbean region. To entertain fans that have decided to watch the four teams play at the ballparks, the games generate great excitement and the players perform with intensity, passion and a sense of patriotism since they represent their countries and respect longstanding traditions. Indeed, the level of baseball in each tournament is superior because each country usually enters a team that contains a number of superstar athletes who probably played for a MLB franchise or a minor league team in the U.S. or Canada.

During past tournaments, a sample of the individual batting and/or home run leaders and their respective home countries included Roberto Alomar and Carlos Delgado of Puerto Rico, Miguel Tejada and Raul Mondesi of the Dominican Republic, Tony Armas and Andres Galarraga of Venezuela, and Erubiel Durazo and Cornelio Garcia of Mexico. Four former professional players who had pitched one or more games in the Caribbean Series were Puerto Rico's Juan Pizaro, Dominican Republic's Pedro Borbon, Venezuela's Orlando Pena and Mexico's Jaime Orozco. If they had participated in a winter league regular season, then non–Latino players would also be allowed to participate in the Series. For example, three American athletes from MLB teams were sluggers Monte Irvin, Willie Mays, and Wally Joyner.

As stated before, the first version of the Caribbean Series championships lasted from 1949 to 1960. During these 12 years, the Series consisted of baseball teams from various cities in Cuba, Panama, Puerto Rico and Venezuela, and the players on these teams had performed in the regular winter league season. The sites of the tournament sites rotated each year, that is, from Havana in Cuba to San Juan in Puerto Rico, and then to Caracas in Venezuela and finally to Panama City in Panama. Because of such great baseball coaches as Fermin Guerra, Napoleon Reyes and Antonio Castanos, and a winning percentage of .718, Cuba won seven of the championships and in the other five Series finished second in three and third in two of them. With regard to teams from the other three countries, their winning percentages and first, second, third and fourth place finishes in the 12 Series were, respectively, Puerto Rico at .528 and winning four championships and one team placing second, five in third and two in fourth; Panama at .397 and winning one championship and four teams placing second, four in third and three in fourth; and Venezuela at .361 and winning zero championships and four teams placing second, one in third and seven in fourth. Consequently, Cuban teams earned the most, and Venezuelan clubs the least number of victories and titles during the first dozen Series.

After a ten-year absence, the Caribbean Series championships resumed in 1970 without Cuba and Panama but with the Dominican Republic, and then with Mexico in 1971. During this period of the Series, players from other teams in their leagues and from leagues in other countries were permitted to join the rosters of the clubs that won their winter league postseason tournaments. To depict how teams from the four nations had performed in 35 of the Series, Table 14.3 was developed.

Based on the distribution of the number of games, average winning percentages and total championships as presented in the table, the baseball teams from the Dominican Republic had performed the best followed by the clubs from Puerto Rico, Venezuela and Mexico. Nevertheless, after placing second at 4–2 in the 2004 Series, Mexico won the six-day, round robin tournament in 2005. Mexico's team, which was nicknamed the Venados finished at 5–1 even though the 25-member Dominican club titled Aguilas contained 18 veteran players with major league baseball affiliations such as the Washington Nationals' Luis Polonia and Jose Guillen, and the San Diego Padres' Bernie Castro.

TABLE 14.3. CARIBBEAN SERIES BASEBALL
CHAMPIONS, 1970–1980, 1982–2005

Country	Games	Winning Percentages	Championships
Dominican Republic*	214	.605	15
Puerto Rico	220	.529	10
Venezuela	201	.477	5
Mexico	203	.343	5

* The Dominican Republic entered the Series in 1970 and Mexico in 1971. Mexico had provided two teams to the tournament in 1974 when Venezuela failed to participate. The tournament was cancelled in 1981. Puerto Rico entered two, and Venezuela zero teams in 2003.

Source: Peter C. Bjarkman, Diamonds Around the Globe: The Encyclopedia of International Baseball (Westport, CT: Greenwood Press, 2005).

For the first time in history, the 2005 Series was held in Mazatlan, Mexico at the Estadio Teodoro Mariscal, and current big league players Vinny Castilla of the Washington Nationals, Erubiel Durazo of the Oakland Athletics and Miguel Ojeda of the San Diego Padres had agreed to join the Venados. But, the tournament's star athlete was pitcher Francisco Campos. He struck out 13 Dominican batters, which clinched the championship for Mexico. After that victory Durazo said, "It was an honor to be a part of the Caribbean Series and win it here. They invited us to come and we did. We did the job." Durazo's teammate Ojeda made similar remarks about the Series when he stated, "This is an emotional win for us. We put together a great team to win and we beat several great teams. This is a great win for our country. We deserve it."

During one or more of the Caribbean Series performed since 1970, the championship teams were coached by productive managers and had successfully scored runs because of their talented players. That is, four different clubs from Puerto Rico had each won a championship in the 1970s and so did two separate teams from Venezuela in the 1980s. Then, between 1990 and 2003 the Escogido Leones, Licey Tigres and Aguilas Cibaenas of the Dominican Republic collectively won eight titles in the Series.

For Puerto Rico, in 1974 American Bobby Wine from MLB's Philadelphia Phillies of the NL coached such Hall of Fame players as infielder Mike Schmidt and catcher Gary Carter, and in 1975 slugger Ken Griffey led the Series with a batting average of .500. Meanwhile, former Kansas City and Oakland Athletics' player, Rene Lachemann managed the Mayaguez Indios and that team won five of six games to ensure a championship in 1978 for Puerto Rico. His best player was batting champion Jose Morales who led the tournament with a .421 average. Other great players excelled in the Series for that nation during the 1970s. They included former major leaguers Sandy Alomar, Don Baylor, Pat Corrales and Bernie Carbo.

Venezuela's clubs won the Series in 1982, 1984 and 1989. One outstanding Venezuelan team nicknamed Zulia Aguilas featured the tournament's Most Valuable Player Phil Stevenson of MLB's Chicago Cubs, and former pitchers Dale Polley of the Atlanta Braves and Leonard Damian of the Chicago Cubs, and manager Pete McKannin. Besides the three victories during the 1980s, Venezuelan teams also achieved championships in 1970 and 1979.

For the Dominican Republic, several star players emerged on tournament teams in the 1990s and early 2000s. They were Raul Mondesi, Nefei Perez and Miguel Tejada, who each led the Series in hitting, and Guillermo Garcia and the Los Angles Angels' Vladimir Guerrero, who each had the most home runs in one of the Series, and Anthony Chavez and Hipolito Pichardo, who were each undefeated at two wins and zero losses as pitchers. As an aside, *Baseball America* selected Aguilas Cibaenas' pitchers Bartolo Colon in 1996–1997 and Arnie Munoz in 2002–2003, who were natives of the Dominican Republic, as the Winter League Players of the Year.

Given the tournament's 47 total championships since 1949, there was a greater disparity between the performances of teams from the four countries during the first phase of the Series than in the second phase, which began in 1970. These differences occurred because clubs from the Dominican Republic have been less dominate relative to those from Cuba, and also, the teams from Venezuela have improved in the second phase compared to Panama's teams in phase one. As a result, the Caribbean Series will continue to be one of the most competitive events in international baseball during the early 2000s.

Other International Baseball Championships

Besides the aforementioned tournaments, there are other popular international and world baseball championships that have been played between nations for various periods of time. Generally, these competitions are scheduled annually, biennially or quadrennially. Because of their history and tradition, and significance to the sport, Table 14.4 provides some interesting facts about seven of these events. That is, the table indicates each tournament's title and the number of times it was played during a specific range of years, and the number of championships won by teams from the respective countries.[5]

Given the information published about these events, Cuban teams won 34 or 33 percent of the 102 tournaments listed in the table while those from the Netherlands had succeeded in 18 or 17 percent of them and those from Japan in 14 or 13 percent. Specifically, for the 42 tournaments they entered between 1926 and 2005, Cuban teams earned gold medals by finishing in first place in 34, silver medals for second place in five, and a bronze medal for third place in one. In total, the 42 teams achieved a remarkable record of 299–38, which is a winning percentage of .88. For obvious reasons, Cuban teams did not participate in the 53 total events of the Asia Baseball Federation (ABF), European Championship (EC) and Oceania Baseball Confederation (OBC).

Between 1954 and 2001, Japanese clubs dominated the ABF championships. As a group, they won 12 gold medals, eight silver medals and one bronze medal. The countries that have not medaled in the ABF tournaments include Australia, China, Guam, India, Indonesia, North Korea and Thailand.

Besides the achievements of clubs from Cuba and Japan, very impressive performances have been accomplished by baseball teams from the Netherlands in EC competitions and Guam in the OBC tournaments. That is, from 1956 to 2003 the clubs from the Netherlands won 18 gold and six silver medals in 24 of them. Alternatively, the weakest baseball teams in the EC have been France, Spain and Sweden, and since the mid–1990s, Croatia, the Czech Republic, Russia, Slovenia and the Ukraine. Meanwhile, baseball teams

---

TABLE 14.4. FOREIGN BASEBALL CHAMPIONS,
BY TOURNAMENT, SELECTED YEARS

Tournament	Number	Champions
Intercontinental Cup	15	Cuba(9), Japan(2), US*(2), Korea(1), Australia(1)
Pan American Games	14	Cuba(11), Ven(1), DR(1), US(1)
Central American Games	19	Cuba(13), DR(2), PR(2),Ven(1), Columbia(1)
Asia Baseball Federation	21	Japan(12), Korea(6), Taiwan(2), Philippines(1)
European Championship	28	Netherlands(18), Italy(8), Spain(1), Belgium(1)
Oceania Baseball Confederation	4	Guam(3), Australia(1)
World University Championships	1	Cuba(1)

* US is the abbreviation for United States, Korea for South Korea, Ven for Venezuela, DR for Dominican Rep, PR for Puerto Rico and Taipei for Chinese Taipei. The International Cup includes those competitions played during various years in 1973–2002, Pan American Games in 1951–2003, Central American Games in 1926–2002, Asia Baseball Federation in 1954–2001, European Championship in 1954–2003, Oceania Baseball Confederation in 1999–2003 and World University Championships in 2002.

Source: Peter C. Bjarkman, *Diamonds Around the Globe: The Encyclopedia of International Baseball* (Westport, CT: Greenwood Press, 2005).

from Guam won OBC titles in 1999, 2000 and 2003, and finished with a silver medal as a World Cup Qualifier in 2003 when an Australian team won that event in four games. Other countries that have played in the OBC include American Samoa, Commonwealth of the Northern Mariana Islands, Fiji Islands, Micronesia, New Caledonia, Palau and the Solomon Islands.

With respect to the U.S. performances in global baseball tournaments, between 1951 and 2003 the clubs from America won one gold, eight silver and three bonze medals in 14 Pan American Games. Unfortunately, American teams failed to earn medals in the 1979 and 1995 Games because of mediocre hitters and pitchers. Respectively, a U.S. club finished fourth in 1979 with five wins and three losses, and in 1995, the nation's team ended its appearance with zero wins and four losses in the Group A Preliminary Round of the Games.

MLB's World Baseball Classic

Since the early-to-mid–1990s, MLB Commissioner Bud Selig and the league's franchise owners have made a sincere effort to host and sponsor some type of international baseball tournament. That event would feature a U.S. team composed of players from baseball's major and/or minor leagues, and clubs from the professional and/or amateur leagues of a few or several foreign nations. According to Selig and the AL and NL team owners, this two-week event was to be scheduled two to four weeks before the MLB regular season starts in early April. Because of relatively warm temperatures during the spring months of the year, there are plenty of baseball stadiums for professional and college teams that are located in the U.S. southeast, southwest and west. Indeed, these facilities are more than adequate in area and capacity to be sites for playing games in such a tournament.[6]

As a business investment, MLB's international tournament has a number of advantages and economic benefits. First, it is expected to increase the demand for the sport in various ways and perhaps cause the game to expand globally, especially in some countries of Asia and in many nations of Central and Latin America. Second, the event would generate an amount of cash flows from the fans that decide to attend the teams' games at the ballparks. Third, there are incremental revenues to be earned for the participating leagues and team owners from broadcasting games on television, radio and satellite networks, and on the Internet. Fourth, the competition will expose the unique skills and abilities of the U.S. and foreign baseball players on teams. This, in turn, improves these athletes' prestige, image and value relative to basketball, football, hockey and outdoor soccer players.

In February of 2004, officials from Commissioner Selig's office, MLBPA and the IBAF agreed to implement a drug-testing program for the tournament that was consistent with the requirements of the World Anti-Doping Agency and the Olympic movement. Then, for the next few months MLB and the MLBPA began the process of meeting with the various international federations and leagues to determine the eligibility of players, and to evaluate which nations would compete in the tournament. The discussions appeared to be making progress until July of 2004, when the owners of Japanese baseball teams in the Central and Pacific Leagues rejected the plan because of how it was structured. That is, these businessmen preferred that the IBAF, and not MLB should schedule, control and manage the event. Furthermore, they disagreed with the method of how the tournament's profits would be allocated between Selig's office and the MLBPA. Finally, they opposed playing a World Baseball Classic in the early Spring since the professional baseball season in Japan starts during the final week in March or in the first week of April. That means Japanese players on teams entered in the tournament would have only one to two weeks of exhibition games to prepare for their regular baseball season. Besides the conflicts with Japan, South Korean baseball officials also balked at MLB's proposal to devise a tournament.

After MLB's chief operating officer Bob DuPuy met and negotiated with individuals from the Japanese and Korean baseball leagues during the Fall of 2004 and again in 2005, the group compromised and approved the tournament's structure. This agreement included the following provisions. First, the tournament will start before the professional baseball training period occurs in late March of 2006 and then in 2009 and every four years thereafter; second, 16 nations are to compete in the tournament whose games during the early rounds will be contested in ballparks of Asia, Latin America and the U.S.; third, players are eligible to play for a national team based on citizenship; fourth, each national team will select a roster with a minimum of 27 players; fifth, the medal rounds will be played in stadiums located in such cities as Los Angeles and San Diego in southern California, Houston in southeastern Texas, Miami in south Florida and Phoenix in southern Arizona. Financially, 47 percent of the net proceeds are prize money and if available, the remaining 53 percent will be distributed between MLB, MLBPA, the IBAF and the participating professional organizations. After the deal was verified and concluded, Commissioner Selig said, "The concept was approved. The important thing is, it's another step in the internationalization of the game."

Summary

This reading introduced, outlined and described the world's primary international baseball tournaments, that is, those established during the twentieth century and in the early 2000s. The various nations and a number of their teams, which had succeeded to win championships and medals in these events are also identified and highlighted. Specifically, the chapter is organized into five distinct sections. In sequence, these are a discussion of the international baseball tournaments that involve leagues for young baseball players, tournaments that are supervised by the International Baseball Federation or IBAF, games played and champions in the Caribbean Series, other global baseball championships, and MLB's plan to host, sponsor and manage a World Baseball Classic in March of 2006.

Based on the research of this topic, the best and most competitive foreign baseball teams are frequently from such nations as Cuba, Japan, Taiwan and the Netherlands, and then occasionally from South Korea and some countries in Latin America. Because of experienced coaches and motivated players, and the support of their sports fans and government officials, one or more of these nations have dominated the international baseball tournaments, except for the World Series in the Little League and Junior, Senior and Big Leagues.

Since the majority of tournaments have existed for decades, during the early-to-mid–2000s various teams from these nations will participate in and win a disproportionate share of international baseball events, including gold, silver and bronze medals in the Olympics. It is not likely, therefore, that baseball teams from the U.S. will always place first, second or third in many of the international tournaments.

15. *International Issues and Global Relations*

The franchises in the American League (AL) and National League (NL) of Major League Baseball (MLB) are each international sports businesses. In part, their teams scout, interview, recruit, train and sign to contracts baseball players from foreign countries. Furthermore, these enterprises earn revenues by establishing broadcast linkages and forming partnerships, sponsorships and licensing agreements with various types of commercial organizations that exist abroad. Therefore, because of these relationships the 29 MLB clubs that are based in the U.S. and the Toronto Blue Jays located in Canada are influenced by and sensitive to the differences in other nations' cultural environments and to these countries' economic, legal, political and social systems. In other words, the business of operating a professional baseball enterprise for profit is a risky and problematic venture when foreign athletes and entities participate in the process of producing and distributing a product such as sports entertainment to consumers in the global marketplace.

In this and other sections of the book, there have been topics previously discussed that involved the internationalization of the sport of baseball. Besides the effects on fans, communities and the media industry in nations across the world, these topics also relate to the decisions, policies and actions of MLB's commissioner and the league's executive staff, and of the teams' owners, executives, general managers and coaches. Indeed, since the 1960s organized baseball has gradually increased its communications, and business interests and interactions with affiliated organizations and participants beyond the borders of North America. As a result of these and other worldwide activities, there are at least three interesting issues about current and prospective players that need further clarification and analysis from a global perspective. Listed in no specific order, these topics are the big league teams' baseball training facilities or academies that operate in Latin American countries, the league's proposals to design, adopt and implement an international draft system that involves all eligible baseball players, and MLB's drug tests and prevention and treatment programs for foreign players and especially for those athletes from nations in Central and South America. Consequently, the contents that follow are primarily focused on these specific issues since they affect the sport and the league's future outlook as a worldwide business and entertainment organization.

Baseball Academies in Latin America

To help, educate, train and otherwise prepare Latino athletes for a career in American professional baseball, the 30 MLB teams have established and operated facilities, which are identified as academies, in one or more countries, that is, in the Dominican Republic, Venezuela, Puerto Rico and/or Mexico. In early 2005, for example, the St. Louis Cardinals announced its plan to open an academy near the airport in Santo Domingo, which is the capital city of the Dominican Republic. As scheduled for completion in late 2005 or early 2006, the complex is expected to include two baseball fields, living quarters for the players and staff, a deluxe clubhouse, modern exercise and training facilities, a dining room and administrative offices and recreation areas. Jose Mella, a renowned architect who became famous for designing other buildings in the Dominican Republic, will lease the fields and structures to the Cardinals. With respect to the team's foreign investment, the Cardinals' vice president of player procurement Jeff Luhnow said, "We are committed to scouting and player development in Latin America. The Cardinals have had operations in Latin America before, but never to this extent. The academy provides these young players the best chance of being ready when they come to the U.S."[1]

When 16 years old, Latino baseball prospects are normally allowed to enter an academy. If admitted, a MLB team subsidizes their expenses for room and board. While living in an academy the athlete generally receives three well-balanced meals per day, participates in weight training to develop his muscle mass, strength and flexibility, attempts to become reasonably fluent in the English language, and is taught lessons about life in order to avoid culture shock when he arrives in the U.S. After a tryout of about 30 days, the player either commits to a team or if the signing bonus is unsatisfactory, he can seek a 30-day tryout with another club. However, once a contract is signed and the player is living in an academy, he receives training while playing fulltime through the year. It is evident, therefore, that baseball academies in Latin America provide their residents with an advantage of two years on 16-year-old athletes from the U.S. That is, American ballplayers are usually sophomores in high school at 16 and have performed for about four to five months on the school's baseball team and perhaps on another one in a summer league.

There are large numbers and different types of sports academies in Latin American countries. Some are owned and operated by unique individuals and groups. The free or street baseball agents called *buscones* or bird dogs, for example, conduct camps for elite young players who are expected to develop their skills and then be signed to agreements when they are eligible to become professionals. Although these athletes continue to receive instructions at the camps and are permitted to play in baseball games, their agents try to negotiate a more lucrative contract for them with a MLB team. In exchange, an agent will earn a portion of the player's signing bonus that was prepaid by the team. Unfortunately, there are many unscrupulous and greedy agents. That is, these *buscones* falsify their players' birth certificates and lie about the individuals' abilities and experiences, and also about their athletes' names, ages and places of birth. In turn, some big league teams fail to verify these records and discover in later years that the records of the players had been revised. To illustrate, in the Fall of 2001 immigration officials discovered that approximately 50 percent of the Dominican players in organized baseball had erroneous baseball records and questionable personal documents.

During 2003, the co-authors of *Stealing Lives: The Globalization of Baseball and the*

Tragic Story of Alexis Quiroz severely criticized a document that was published by Commissioner Bud Selig's office. The document's contents, which listed some key provisions and guidelines to regulate the baseball academies located in the Dominican Republic and Venezuela, were vague and inconclusive with respect to standards, rules and enforcement procedures. Consequently, Arturo J. Marcano and David P. Fidler recommended in a memorandum that the principles of democratization, centralization, harmonization, specialization and implementation be incorporated into the document. In other words, Selig's office must make the standards and rules binding, uniform, enforceable and directly applicable to all of the academies in Latin America. In an Annex attached to their analysis, the authors also listed a number of specific requirements that MLB should enact relative to the academies in the two nations. These included specific sections about the playing field, team facilities, field equipment, maintenance, public comfort stations, and security and first aid supplies. In short, it was recommended that the league office must adopt, impose and enforce standards and rules which improve the treatment and housing conditions of Latin children, families and young men living in the baseball academies.[2]

Two foreign schools are especially unique since they have combined baseball and education experiences for the students-athletes. Angel Macias, who pitched a perfect game in the championship game of the Little League World Series in 1957, is the director of La Academia de la Liga Mexicana. When this baseball academy existed in 2004, the 16 teams in the Mexican League had to fund it. Located near Monterrey, Mexico, the facility consisted then of 56 dormitory rooms and a computer room, classroom and study area. The complex included four each baseball fields and batting cages, a weight room, an infirmary and a plaza where the 100 athletes met for social purposes. Interestingly, at the academy the players had to enroll in education programs that motivated them to improve their reading, writing and speaking skills. The programs' instructors had to meet high standards of performance as teachers while the scouts, who recruited players for the academy, had to be professional and conform to Macias' expectations. As Patricia Rodriguez, the cultural director and in charge of continuing the education of the players in and outside of the academy declared, "We can't force them to continue their studies, but it is our obligation to give them the opportunity if they choose to. They have the option, and they must realize there is life outside of baseball."[3]

Besides Macias' facility in Mexico, since the early 2000s the Baseball Academy and High School has been located in Gurabo, Puerto Rico. Former MLB pitcher Edwin Correa established it there because no baseball programs existed in the nation's public secondary schools. Thus, Correa had contributed $200,000 to organize and partially fund the fully accredited private boys school whose students are also excellent baseball prospects. Typically, the students in the academy practice baseball for up to three hours in the morning. Then, they attend classes in such disciplines as history, mathematics and science for four hours in the afternoon wearing their school uniforms of dark pants and white polo shirts, which bear the academy's logo. To pay a $5,500 tuition fee, approximately 50 percent of the 100 plus students are awarded full scholarships. When an academic year ends, generally MLB teams proceed to draft a significant proportion of the students. For this nation of four million people, Correa's academy is a special place because it pays tribute to and honors the legacy of the most revered ballplayer from Puerto Rico, that is, Roberto Clemente.[4]

In the Dominican Republic and Venezuela, there are a relatively large number of athletes in baseball academies. As such, these countries produce a portion of the world's best ballplayers. Indeed, nearly 50 percent of the foreign players on MLB teams are natives of these two nations. It is no surprise and very prudent, therefore, that the St. Louis Cardinals have joined the majority of other clubs in MLB to scout, recruit and sign to contracts the talented players from teams in the summer baseball leagues that exist in such cities as Higuey, La Romana, Santo Domingo and San Cristobal of the Dominican Republic.[5]

International Player Draft

In response to escalating bonuses and the bidding wars that occurred during the 1950s and early 1960s, MLB's team owners decided to install the first amateur draft in 1965. One year later, the league changed the rules and dropped American Legion players from the draft. Then, when the Milwaukee Brewers signed a Connecticut high school player born in Puerto Rico for $150,000 in the open market during 1985, all foreign athletes who had attended U.S. high schools or colleges were required to enter the draft.[6]

It was in 1989 that the players from Puerto Rico and other U.S. territories, who were previously allowed to sign as free agents at the age of 17, became eligible for the draft after their high school class had graduated. Then, during 1991 and 1993, respectively, Canadian athletes were restricted from the open market and added to the draft followed by the Cuban defectors who were living in America. However, because teams' salaries continued to escalate, in the mid–1990s the league supported a pro-rated bonus cap for draftees and for those international players who had signed contracts. As expected, the Major League Baseball Players Association (MLBPA) unanimously voted against that proposal. Finally, in 1998 a 50-round limit was introduced whereby 30 players would be chosen each round until every team had passed to make a selection.

For more than ten years, MLB has evaluated whether to officially commit to and then recommend a worldwide or global draft system to the MLBPA as a component of the league's collective bargaining agreement. There are a number of compelling reasons for the two groups to adopt such a system. In the following discussion are five of them. First, since approximately 30 percent of major leaguers and nearly 50 percent of minor league players were from foreign nations on opening day of the 2005 regular season, the draft would minimize the signing of underage players by unscrupulous sports agents, and especially those young athletes who were born in the poor countries of Latin America.[7]

Second, a worldwide draft would discourage such large-market teams as the Boston Red Sox, New York Yankees and Los Angeles Dodgers from signing each year the most talented and experienced American-born and international players. That is, the rich clubs would be forced to rank the players with the greatest potential from their perspective and then, if available in any round from one to fifty, attempt to draft them. This, in turn, would ensure that the highly skilled ballplayers in a draft are more equitably distributed among the league's small- and large-market teams. Furthermore, an international draft increases the probability of realizing baseball's goal of competitive balance within and between the clubs in the East, Central and West divisions of the AL and NL.

Third, a global draft will establish a consistent, uniform and open process of selecting foreign players from a pool that includes the athletes from all nations. As such, this system impedes teams from colluding and making illegal deals with scouts, sports agents and other officials who may represent the best players in the draft. Fourth, a worldwide draft is beneficial for the sport's image in that it would spread bonus money more equitably between American and foreign-born players. As a result, the athletes from poverty-stricken countries who are picked by teams in the first round would receive substantial signing bonuses that generally are allocated only to the players selected from the U.S. and Canada.

Fifth, a worldwide draft provides an incentive for MLB teams to invest in baseball academies and also, to improve the effectiveness of their scouting efforts in Asia, Latin America, and in other regions of the world. With these investments of resources and money in their operations, such small-market teams as the Cincinnati Reds, Kansas City Royals, Milwaukee Brewers, Pittsburgh Pirates and Tampa Bay Devil Rays have a better opportunity to recruit, train and sign the players at field positions that balance and improve their rosters.

Similarly, for years there have been a number of individuals, specific groups and organizations that have expressed their reasons why they oppose the concept, development and implementation of an international player draft in MLB. From one to five, these opponents and their disputes are listed as follows. One, a few but powerful team owners prefer the current draft since it provides them with advantages and benefits relative to the other proprietors of teams. That is, the owners of large- and mid-market franchises have substantial cash inflows and gross revenues. Therefore, they can afford the bonuses and salaries that the top players seek when drafted and then after these players had applied to become free agents. As a result, it will be difficult for MLB to reach a consensus about, and adopt a global draft system that satisfies the 30 team owners as a group.

Two, the MLBPA has philosophically opposed an international draft because of restraint-of-trade issues involving its membership. Furthermore, the union is not thrilled about the possibility that players' bonuses will be depressed, which may occur because of the increase in market supply that results when international athletes are included in a draft. Moreover, the small-market teams would be likely to offer less in bonuses and salaries as a result of obtaining the rights to sign new players in the draft. Thus, during the early 2000s the MLBPA proposed that two drafts be implemented. The first would be eight rounds for amateur players from the U.S., and the second should consist of eight rounds for foreign amateur players. If not selected in these rounds, then the non-drafted athletes became free to negotiate with any of the 30 clubs.

Three, those individuals and groups in opposition are concerned that the proponents of an international draft have not addressed or reached an agreement about the most contentious issues to be resolved. These problems include what number or series of rounds that a draft should entail, and which U.S. and foreign players are eligible to be drafted and at what age? During its negotiations with the MLBPA in 2002, the league proposed one 40-round draft that included amateur players from every nation except Cuba. Furthermore, those athletes who played on teams in the professional baseball leagues of other countries would be eligible for the draft after they had applied and received approval through a posting system, which is what Ichiro Suzuki did in Japan. Indeed, the Seattle Mariners purchased the rights to Suzuki from the Orix Blue Wave for $13.125 million in the early 2000s and then signed him to a three-year $14 million contract.

Four, some of the sports agents who have successfully represented international baseball players are adamantly against a worldwide draft. Their concerns were expressed, in part, by agents Joe Cubas and Alan Nero. Cubas made the following statement. "It is interesting that MLB never felt the need to regulate the draft in the decades in which star prospects signed for a pittance. This only became an issue when it hit them [team owners] in the wallet." Likewise, Nero said, "It's just another infiltration of communism, like revenue-sharing and the luxury tax. It's anti-competition, anti–American." The real concern of these agents, however, is that their influence and power would diminish when they had to negotiate with MLB team owners on behalf of their clients who are drafted.[8]

Five, the Chicago Cubs' Pacific Rim coordinator Leon Lee believes that MLB is underestimating the difficulties of getting players freed and out of some foreign countries. In Korea, for example, the players may have military commitments to complete and also be constrained by the territorial rights of their local professional team. "These are company-owned teams," Lee says. "If they [Korean companies] have a losing product, their stock goes down. The idea of losing their young players [to a MLB team] is a very serious thing."[9]

In short, before 2007 or 2008 MLB and the MLBPA will compromise their differences and agree to establish a quarterly, semiannual and/or annual worldwide draft. This policy, in part, is expected to include provisions that determine the total pool of U.S. and foreign players who have been declared eligible, and thus, are available for each session of the respective draft. Besides the issue of eligibility, the league and union need to also set the number of rounds and age requirements, and to settle on a policy regarding how and when to draft the foreign athletes on teams in the professional baseball leagues of other nations. However, for the policy to be administratively effective and universally applied, MLB should consult with the top baseball officials from the other countries so that these individuals comprehend the new draft procedures and will cooperate with the league. About the date for implementing such a plan, the former Boston Red Sox interim general manager Mike Port observed, "The devil will be in the details, but with the world in so many respects becoming a smaller place and with baseball growing and expanding and the search for talent expanding, somewhere, at some point, the worldwide draft is something we're going to see."[10]

Comprehensive Drug Prevention and Treatment Program

In a series of articles published during 2003, the *Washington Post* reported that a large proportion of baseball prospects and minor league players from the Dominican Republic had injected animal steroids and dietary supplements to boost their performances during games. When this report had emerged, a MLB official responded by declaring that a program to randomly test players from that nation and Venezuela must not be prohibitively expensive and impractical to operate. The official's statement was unacceptable to Indiana University professor of international law David P. Fidler. He remarked, "They [MLB] have set up this system to recruit Latin American talent. They depend on this talent as an institution. The players are part of the official minor-league system. In terms of the policy objectives, the integrity of the game and the health of the players, it seems like an obvious case."[11]

As a result of criticism from the sports media, and from a number of fans and the athletes' families, in May of 2004 the league announced that it would implement a program to test ballplayers in the Dominican summer league for consuming illegal drugs. That is, all of the players would be eligible to be tested when the 72-game schedule began on June 1. Then, later in 2004 some news reports surfaced that several major league players including Barry Bonds, Jason Giambi and Gary Sheffield had been supplied with steroids and perhaps other performance enhancing drugs during the early 2000s from an organization named the Bay Area [California] Laboratory Co-operative.

After the program and reports emerged, during the Spring of 2005 former big leaguers Jose Canseco and Mark McGwire testified to a committee of the U.S. Congress about the extent of drugs used by players in professional baseball. After the testimony of these and other athletes, which appeared on America's national television networks, the league became more vigilant and increased its frequency of randomly testing all players on teams in the major and minor leagues. Regarding the drug tests of Latino players, MLB's executive vice president of labor Rob Manfred declared in a press release that, "Commissioner Selig and Major League Baseball are committed to eradicating illegal performance-enhancing substances in the Major and Minor Leagues, the Dominican Republic and wherever Major League Baseball has jurisdiction." Manfred further added, "We [MLB] also are required to follow the laws of the Dominican Republic and every other nation in which we test and will continue to follow those laws. Unfortunately, the laws in the Dominican Republic forbid us from suspending steroid violators and make the operation of an optimal program more difficult."[12]

Before mid–May in 2005, a total of three major and 47 minor league players had been suspended because their tests were positive from using drugs. Two of the three big leaguers suspended were pitchers from Venezuela and the Dominican Republic, and the other was an outfielder from Cuba. This had occurred even though only 23.5 percent or 194 of the 829 players listed on opening day rosters and disabled lists had been born in Cuba, the Dominican Republic, Mexico or Venezuela. With respect to the 47 drug abusers in the minor leagues, 51 percent or 24 of them were foreign-born, that is, 11 from Venezuela, ten from the Dominican Republic, two from Mexico and one from Puerto Rico. Meanwhile, the 2,446 players from these four countries represented approximately 40 percent of the total 6,117 minor leaguers in organized baseball.[13]

If these incidents accurately reflect the presence of drugs in professional baseball, why have a disproportionate number of baseball players from the Spanish-speaking nations tested as positive? Is it because of the athletes' apathy, ignorance, irrational decision making or for other reasons? Some observers believe there is a problem because teams are not effectively communicating the league's drug policy to their players. As a result, the Latino players who do not understand or speak the English language are simply unaware of the rules and therefore, consume the banned substances including over the counter supplements and medicines issued by their trainers, and doctors and pharmacies. According to Boston Red Sox slugger David Ortiz, who is from the Dominican Republic, "My English isn't the best, but I read and write and understand what people say to me and I sometimes have trouble with this stuff, so you can imagine what it is like for the guys who don't understand English as well." To better inform the athletes, Ortiz recommended that officials from the MLBPA periodically meet with all foreigners who play on teams in the major and minor leagues, and clearly speak to them in their language about the league's rules, and especially about the consequences of possessing and consuming illegal drugs.[14]

However, other persons affiliated with the sport contend that a portion of these products are legal in many foreign countries and can be easily obtained over the counter at local pharmacies and in large quantities. Indeed, some players or their relatives and friends may walk into a food store in Caracas, Santo Domingo, Monterrey or San Juan during the off season, buy some pills and then take them until they travel to their baseball training camps that are held beginning each February in Arizona or Florida. With traces of the substances in their blood streams, these players are likely to test positive in March, April or May and then be suspended.

Even so, perhaps one or more international players are not threatened by or concerned about the league's policy regarding the use of banned substances. This view was expressed by the Washington National's outfielder Jose Guillen in a statement to the media when he said, "You can trust me on thisæthey all know what's going on and they're all aware. They've been watching the TV. It's been all over the place in Spanish and in English." Undoubtedly, a veteran big leaguer such as Guillen has some knowledge and perhaps evidence of drug use by players or he would not have spoken openly about it to newspapers' reporters.[15]

As it exists, MLB's drug policy will not be effective unless the league demands that team owners, trainers and physicians also be held accountable for the players' actions. This means franchises, in part, must allocate more of the teams' resources and revenues to their communication systems, and to establish drug prevention, detection and treatment programs.

Baseball Security and Safety Issues

The actual terrorist attacks and threat of more in the U.S., and the dissension from the Iraq War have each affected America's international relations and the global operations and business of baseball. Because of these and such events as implementation of the U.S. Patriot Act, MLB has become increasingly concerned about the security of its franchises, and safety of fans at the ballparks in which the 30 teams play their home and away games. As a result, the league has reacted to threats and potential crimes by initiating actions to protect the individuals, organizations and facilities that are affiliated with the sport.

Four days after the tragedies in New York City, the Washington, D.C. area and western Pennsylvania, MLB's senior vice president for security and facility management Kevin Hallinan outlined the league's short- and long-run responses to these disasters in a question and answer interview with a sports writer from MLB.com. The basic changes that Hallinan mentioned as precautionary measures were the mandatory inspection of individual's small bags at the admission gates and not allowing people to carry coolers, backpacks or large bags into ballparks; assigning more police and to secure each stadium and close inspection of the facility before fans had arrived for a game; increased inspection of the teams' charter flights to and from cities for away games; and briefing ballplayers before games about how to be safe when they signed autographs for the spectators and posed for photographs. As a former New York City police officer and member of a terrorist task force for the Federal Bureau of Investigation, Hallinan has enough experience to better ensure the safety of teams' players and the fans that attend games at the MLB stadiums in Chicago, New York City, Los Angeles and elsewhere.[16]

To cite another precaution initiated by organized baseball, during March of 2003 Commissioner Bud Selig canceled a two-game, regular season opening series between the Seattle Mariners and Oakland Athletics that was scheduled at the 55,000-seat Tokyo Dome in Japan. In turn, this decision created a substantial financial loss for the league and two teams since both games had been sold out, while the Japanese companies that sponsored the series incurred a cost of more than $4 million in cancellation fees. Consequently, the impending U.S war with Iraq had caused Selig to consider the health and welfare of the teams' coaches and players, and the fans as the primary factors in terminating the series. Despite the setback, MLB International's vice president of marketing development Jim Small said, "I don't think any long-term harm has been done. The fans love the game so much. From what I've read and had translated in the Japanese newspapers, there's no animosity."[17]

Besides the league's responsibilities, commitments and actions to deter terrorism at baseball activities, the following are three security issues that involve global aspects of the sport. First, it may be necessary and beneficial for an U.S. government agency to partially subsidize and provide adequate safety coverage for the American amateur baseball teams that travel to foreign countries to play games and series, and participate in tournaments. The latter include such events as the Intercontinental Cup, Olympic Games and Pan American Games, and competition in the World Cup, World Junior AAA and World Youth AA. For the U.S. to continue as an international power in amateur baseball, this nation's teams need to visit and compete against the elite clubs that may exist in Cuba and Japan, and in other countries.

Second, international teams must be safe and protected from terrorist activities while they perform in ballparks and travel across the U.S. This security applies to foreign teams when they play in the previously named tournaments that are held in U.S. cities, and when they qualify for the World Series rounds in the Little League, Junior League, Senior League and Big League. Third, there should be some effective and reasonable security measures established by local baseball officials at games that are played among teams in America's amateur and semiprofessional leagues, and especially those performing at ballparks in metropolitan areas of Arizona, California, Florida, New Mexico and Texas. Since these States have relatively large ethnic populations and host huge inflows of foreign tourists during a year, their cities are vulnerable to attacks by a terrorist and/or small radical groups.

Summary

This chapter identified, highlighted and discussed a number of issues that influence and/or are affected by the globalization and worldwide activities, events and markets of a sport. Relative to professional baseball, the chapter first focused on the private and publicly owned academies that exist for baseball players in various cities of the Dominican Republic, Mexico, Puerto Rico and Venezuela. These facilities have become increasingly important to the success of the AL and NL teams because they are places to recruit, educate and train their foreign athletes, and to prepare them for the big leagues. To effectively accomplish these tasks, MLB must ensure that the living conditions at and structures within the academies are adequate so that they meet the housing standards and real estate laws set by the local governments. Furthermore, the league must oversee the ethics and actions of independent sports agents and players' advisors who have investments in, or are affiliated with the academies.

After that issue was presented, the next topic exposed how MLB and the MLBPA are jointly involved in developing plans to organize and schedule a quarterly, semiannual and/or annual international draft that includes all eligible players from the U.S. and those athletes from foreign nations. The efforts to design this system will be more inclusive if the league and union coordinate the proposed draft with officials from various amateur and professional baseball organizations in places where the sport is popular as in some countries of Asia and Latin America.

The third issue in this chapter concerned the testing and punishment of U.S. and international baseball players who use banned substances such as steroids and other illegal drugs to enhance their performances on the baseball field. Eventually, MLB will adopt a pragmatic but comprehensive and enforceable drug policy that includes all players who are listed on the rosters and disabled lists of the numerous teams in the major and minor leagues. Furthermore, it is recommended that the policy also extend to MLB teams' players who have been signed to contracts and live in baseball academies, especially those located in any of the Latin American countries.

When the third section concluded, some security and safety issues in baseball were examined with respect to the leagues and teams in America and foreign nations. In sum, these and other baseball organizations must inform their coaches and players about hostile acts and provide the resources to protect them from terrorists during international games and tournaments that are played at major and minor league ballparks in cities of the U.S. and at the facilities in other countries.

PART IV. MANAGEMENT AND LEADERSHIP

16. *How Commissioners Govern Baseball*

Between 1901 and 1903, a decentralized system of governance existed in Major League Baseball (MLB). That is, instead of unifying their administrative functions and consolidating into one office, the American League (AL) and National League (NL) each had a president who had the power and authority to establish and enforce rules for their respective baseball organization. This governance system, however, was reformed in 1903 when a three-person supervisory group, named the National Commission was created to jointly control professional baseball by interpreting and implementing the terms and provisions of the National Agreement, which was endorsed that year by the leagues, and by enacting and enforcing fines and suspensions. Meanwhile, B. Bancroft Johnson and Harry C. Pulliam served, respectively, as presidents of the AL and NL.[1]

As to the Commission's innovations, in 1904 it had adopted a set of rules for the World Series that included a seven-game format, the assignment of two umpires from each league, and a formula for the two teams in the Series to share revenues. Furthermore, the Commission's rules committee banned the use of foreign substances by the teams' pitchers. However, because of the self-interests and biased decisions of various team owners including chairman August Herrman of the Cincinnati Reds, the Commission failed to effectively carry out its mission regarding matters related to the governance of MLB's affairs.

In the end, the Commission collapsed because its members hesitated about investigating a scandal in which eight Chicago White Sox players had allegedly accepted bribes from gamblers to intentionally lose the World Series in 1919. After White Sox owner Charles Comiskey had suspended these players, in 1921 the AL and NL agreed to dissolve the National Commission and create an administrative executive position titled Baseball Commissioner. According to a statement issued by the NL, this leader is to be a person "of unquestionable reputation and standing in fields other than baseball" whose "mere presence would assure that public interests would first be served, and that therefore, as a natural sequence, all existing evils would disappear." Consequently, the office of Baseball Commissioner was established with the ratification of the Major League Agreement.

Given the events that had damaged the sport's reputation during the latter years of the 1910s, it became evident then that professional baseball required a strong and perhaps autocratic commissioner who was a fan of the game and knowledgeable about the history of the sport, and who was independent of MLB's power structure, and a visionary. In other words, the best person for the position should be a mature, experienced and determined individual with integrity and ethics, and not be a weak-minded accomplice, figurehead or a mouthpiece of the owners, teams or players.

From the early 1920s to the mid–1940s, baseball's first commissioner was Judge Kenesaw Mountain Landis. To most sports historians, he possessed the will power, moral courage and confidence to be baseball's savior and administrative leader. Thus, to evaluate Judge Landis and the eight other commissioners who have followed him, the next section of this chapter discusses different aspects of interest about this unique group of individuals. In the research, one objective is to infer how effective and successful they each were at governing MLB during their reign as commissioner.

MLB Commissioners

There have been numerous facts and historical evidence published in articles and books about the characteristics, experiences and leadership qualities, and the managerial decisions and performances of the various commissioners who have regulated MLB. Rather than restate verbatim the information contained in these publications, this section highlights and summarizes the commissioners' primary actions within and contributions to the sport. To that end, Table 16.1 lists the nine men who have served as a commissioner of MLB. Given their terms in office, the table contains the total number of AL and NL baseball teams that existed during each of the commissioner's tenure and the teams' average attendance at a regular season game. As such, these numbers show how the composition and popularity of professional baseball had changed when the nine men began and concluded their respective term as the top administrative executive in the sport. The following is a brief analysis of each commissioner's role.[2]

TABLE 16.1. MLB COMMISSIONERS, 1920–PRESENT

Name	Terms		Teams		Att/Game	
	From	To	From	To	From	To
Kenesaw M. Landis	11/1920	11/1944	16	16	7,391	7,063
Albert B. Chandler	4/1945	7/1951	16	16	8,814	13,016
Ford C. Frick	9/1951	11/1965	16	20	13,016	13,827
William D. Eckert	11/1965	12/1968	20	20	13,827	14,217
Bowie K. Kuhn	2/1969	9/1984	20	26	14,217	21,256
Peter V. Ueberroth	10/1984	9/1988	26	26	21,256	25,238
A. Bartlett Giamatti	4/1989	9/1989	26	26	26,198	26,198
Francis T. Vincent, Jr.	9/1989	9/1992	26	26	26,198	26,529
Allan H. Selig	9/1992	Present	26	30	26,529	30,261

Note: Commissioners Landis and Giamatti died while in office. Selig was the acting baseball commissioner from September 1992 to July 1998. That is, in the latter month he was permanently appointed to the position. Term consists of the beginning or From month/year, and the ending or To month/year that the individual had served as commissioner. Teams are the number of clubs that existed in MLB at the Term From and To month/year dates. Att/Game is the average attendance per regular season game at the Term From and To month/year.

Source: "Sports Commissioners," at http://www.kenn.com cited 19 February 2005; "Ballparks of Baseball," at http://www.ballparksofbaseball.com cited 19 February 2005; "Commissioners," at http://www.mlb.com cited 19 February 2005.

Kenesaw M. Landis

Judge Landis became baseball's first commissioner when the MLB owners agreed to reduce his $50,000 salary by $7,500 for also serving as a United States Judge for the Northern District of Illinois. Since he had presided over the Federal League's unsuccessful injunction against baseball for its reserve clause, and because he was an ardent fan that studied the sport's history, Landis seemed to be the perfect choice for the position. Indeed, the league hired and granted him the authority and power to rid the game of its criminal elements, illegal activities and unethical players. To a great extent, that was the overriding objective he pursued and attempted to accomplish.

To illustrate, between 1921 and 1943 the judge proceeded to ban eight Chicago White Sox players involved in the World Series scandal that had occurred in the Fall of 1919, and also banned other players for their theft and receipt of stolen property, for a suggestion to leave their clubs in order to lose the NL pennant, and for bribing opposing players. Furthermore, he had barred one team's president for betting on regular season games, and suspended the New York Yankees' Babe Ruth and Bob Muesel for barnstorming after the 1921 World Series without the permission of the league. Landis' other noteworthy accomplishments included establishing the first non-waiver trade deadline, creating a 40-man major league roster, volunteering to cut his salary by $25,000 in 1933 because of the Great Depression, and authorizing the redistribution of votes for the all-star teams from fans to the team's managers.

Despite the baseball owners' regrets and suspicions subsequent to appointing him as the commissioner, Judge Landis was the type of independent leader that the sport needed from 1920 to 1944, when he died at St. Luke's hospital in Chicago from a heart attack at the age of 78. In fact, after Landis' death the Major League Agreement was amended by the owners to give teams the right to challenge the commissioner's decisions in court, and to make sure that the commissioner could deem no conduct that conformed to the league's regulations as detrimental to baseball's best interests. Described by sports writers as colorful, flinty and often arbitrary, Landis is likely the sport's greatest commissioner.

Albert B. Chandler

In April 1945, the former governor and presidential candidate but then the current senator from Kentucky, "Happy" Chandler, was unanimously selected by the clubs to succeed Judge Landis and be MLB's second commissioner. During his six-year term, some revolutionary changes had occurred that impacted the sport. For example, Organized Baseball became integrated when African American Jackie Robinson broke the race barrier by playing for the International League's Montreal Royals in the Spring of 1946 and the Brooklyn Dodgers in 1947. Two years later, the commissioner was persuaded by the owners to eliminate the five-year suspensions of 18 players who, for more money, had enthusiastically joined the outlaw Mexican League in 1946.

Furthermore, between 1947 and 1951 Chandler negotiated a seven-year $4.37 million contract with the Gillette Razor Company and Mutual Broadcasting System to provide radio rights to the 1949 World Series, and then a $6 million deal with the two companies for the television rights to the 1950 World Series and All-Star Game; in 1947, he suspended the former Los Angeles Dodgers coach Leo Durocher the entire season for associating with gamblers and the Dodgers Chuck Dressen for conduct detrimental to baseball; also, Chandler fined the New York Yankees' president Larry McPhail $2,000 for his relationship with Dressen and another Dodgers coach John Corriden; authorized that six umpires would be used in the World Series games; assisted in establishing a three-year $475,000 player pension fund using the proceeds from the radio rights to the World Series; and encouraged one or more of the AL and NL east coast teams to consider the large cities on the U.S.' west coast as viable locations.

Given these actions, Chandler was a MLB commissioner who participated in and witnessed some of the most significant developments in the game's history. However, when he resigned in July 1951, his accomplishments as a baseball commissioner were not especially prominent. According to Jules Tygiel, who authored *Baseball's Great Experiment: Jackie Robinson and His Legacy*, "At best, one can describe Chandler's role as endorsement by abstinence. Chandler's own claims to posterity notwithstanding, he appears as no more than a bit player in these historic events."[3]

Ford C. Frick

After his employment as an English teacher, sports writer and broadcaster, and publicity director, in 1934 Frick succeeded John A. Heydler and became president of the NL. While in that position, he endorsed proposals to establish a National Baseball Museum and Baseball Hall of Fame, helped Chandler to integrate baseball, and worked hard to save baseball franchises in Boston, Brooklyn, Cincinnati, Philadelphia and Pittsburgh from financial weakness and bankruptcy. As a result of that exposure, interest and success, Frick was named baseball's third commissioner in September of 1951.

Because of Frick's leadership as the league's commissioner, baseball experienced a period of expansion, reconstruction and transition to reach a higher level of stability. This reformation included the following elements. First, the Major League Agreement was modified by the team owners to restore the provision waiving any right of recourse in the courts to challenge a commissioner's decision. Also, the Agreement was amended to change the language from "detrimental to the best interests of baseball" to "not in the best interests of baseball." Second, the league adopted new programs such as the free agent draft and college scholarship plan, and revised and clarified the trade deadline and waiver rules. Third, MLB expanded by 25 percent or from 16 to 20 teams with the addition of the Houston Astros, Montreal Expos, New York Mets and San Diego Padres, and existing clubs relocated from Boston to Milwaukee, Brooklyn to Los Angeles, New York to San Francisco and Milwaukee to Atlanta.

Fourth, a Cy Young award was established to honor the league's outstanding pitcher, while the players, coaches and managers, rather than the fans received the right to select the outstanding players for the all-star teams. Fifth, the international scope of the game broadened because Frick actively consulted with sports groups in Japan, Latin and Central America, Holland, Italy and Africa, and introduced baseball to them. In fact, Masanori Murakami became the first Japanese player in the big leagues. In retrospect, because of these five achievements, the owners had made a smart decision in 1951 to choose Ford Frick and not Cincinnati Reds president Warren Giles to be the commissioner. At the age of 71, Frick retired after serving two seven-year terms in office.[4]

William D. Eckert

After earning his master's degree at the Harvard Graduate School of Business, and then retiring from the military as a lieutenant general, working as a management consultant to the aviation industry and serving on the boards of directors of several corporations, William D. Eckert became the fourth commissioner of baseball in November of 1965. Hired because of his advanced education, and his impressive business experiences and management abilities, Eckert clearly improved MLB's decision-making efforts, internal operations and the profitability of various teams. That is, he made the baseball organization more efficient by streamlining its business methods, developing more effective committee actions and stabilizing some franchises whose teams played in larger stadiums with long-term lease agreements.

Similar to Frick, Eckert also promoted the game of American baseball abroad. For example, friendly relations were established with Asian officials, which resulted in the Los Angeles Dodgers' visit to Japan after the 1966 season, and during later years, in an opportunity for other major league teams to travel overseas on goodwill and promotional campaigns. Nevertheless, when the attendances at baseball games had only marginally increased from 1965 to 1968, a majority of franchise owners became dissatisfied with that progress. Thus, they did not approve of Eckert's effort and leadership style, and gradually lost confidence in him. As a result, he was forced to resign as commissioner in December of 1968.

Bowie K. Kuhn

After Eckert's departure from the position, the team owners then decided to recruit for commissioner a person that was more familiar with the game of baseball, its type of business and the people involved in the sport. After vigorously disagreeing whether to elect New York Yankees president Mike Burke or NL president Chub Feeney, the owners compromised and choose Bowie K. Kuhn as MLB's fifth commissioner. As a New York lawyer, Kuhn had spent 19 years working in baseball's legal affairs and also had represented the NL in a lawsuit brought against it by the City of Milwaukee when the Braves moved to Atlanta, Georgia after the 1965 season. Consequently, he knew the legal problems of baseball and the sport's internal affairs.

During Kuhn's term in office, several major events occurred that involved new challenges with respect to professional baseball. First, the number of teams increased from 20 to 26 or by 30 percent, and the attendance per game in the regular season rose from 14,217 to 21,256 or approximately 50 percent. Second, the commissioner decided to suspend former New York Giants superstar Willie Mays and the Yankees Mickey Mantle for their association with casinos, New York Yankees owner George Steinbrenner for his contributions to the campaign of politician Richard Nixon, Atlanta Braves owner Ted Turner for tampering with potential free agent Gary Matthews and for other activities considered detrimental to the best interests of baseball, and players such as pitchers Denny McClain and Vida Blue for drug use. Third, after at least 40 tedious and stressful bargaining sessions, Kuhn helped baseball avoid a strike in 1969 by negotiating a new three-year contract between team owners and the Major League Baseball Players Association (MLBPA). In 1972 and 1981, however, the league had to endure, respectively, a 13-day and 57-day player strikes. Fourth, after being treated separately for many years, the Negro League players who were inducted into Baseball's Hall of Fame were granted full membership when Kuhn became commissioner.

Fifth, in Curt Flood's challenge of baseball's reserve clause in 1970, the U.S. Supreme Court upheld the lower courts' decisions by ruling that the federal antitrust laws did not apply to the sport. Then, in 1975 arbitrator Peter Seitz ruled, in the Messersmith-McNally case, that players were free to negotiate with any club after the option year of their contracts had expired. As a result, after six years in the big leagues players could become free agents. Sixth, Kuhn won a court decision in a lawsuit filed against baseball by the Oakland Athletics owner Charles O. Finley in 1976, when he had attempted to sell for $3.5 million his best pitcher to the large-market New York Yankees and two other star players to the wealthy Boston Red Sox. Seventh, MLB finally allowed female reporters access to the players' locker rooms and postseason games to be played at night. Given the publicity and significance of these and other events, in September of 1984 Bowie Kuhn left office after 16 years as baseball's fifth commissioner.

Peter V. Ueberroth

By a unanimous vote in late 1984, the 26 baseball owners hired businessman Peter V. Ueberroth to be baseball's sixth commissioner. During his career, Ueberroth had founded and sold First Travel Corporation, and for five years served as the president and chief executive officer of a private, non-profit Los Angeles Olympic Organizing Committee, which had staged and operated the 1984 Olympic Games in southern California. Undoubtedly, these responsibilities and experiences helped Ueberroth to be an accomplished and popular commissioner of baseball. For example, he successfully arbitrated a dispute by the Major League Umpires Union who had struck MLB because of their problems with compensation during the 1984 postseason. Indeed, with a settlement the umpires had returned to work for the final game of the NL Championship Series. Furthermore, Ueberroth negotiated two lucrative four-year television deals, that is, a $1.1 billion contract with the Columbia Broadcasting System and a $400 million national cable agreement with the Entertainment Sports Program Network. Moreover, the commissioner financially improved the baseball industry by establishing corporate sponsorships and arranging licensing contracts with vendors such that the majority of teams were profitable before 1988.

Besides these actions, Ueberroth also lifted the ban that had been levied against Willie Mays and Mickey Mantle, initiated an investigation by baseball to determine whether superstar Pete Rose had gambled on games, and assigned one-year suspensions to seven players for drug-related activities. Finally, after labor arbitrators ruled that two or more team owners had acted in collusion against free agent players in 1985 and 1986, Ueberroth decided not to seek a second term and resigned in 1988. Before leaving office, however, he campaigned for A. Bartlett Giamatti to succeed him as baseball's top administrative official.

A. Bartlett Giamatti

After serving eight years as president of Yale University and then two as the NL's president, Giamatti was elected by the team owners to a five-year term as the seventh commissioner of MLB. While leading the NL, he had earned a reputation for emphasizing and promoting the ethics, traditions and values of baseball, and for improving the experiences of fans that attended games at the ballparks. Therefore, after studying a report from attorney John Dowd that Pete Rose had associated with bookies and possibly bet large sums of money on baseball games, Giamatti convinced Rose to sign an agreement. Although it stipulated Rose's permanent suspension from Organized Baseball, the agreement included the clause, "Nothing in this agreement shall be deemed either an admission or a denial by Peter Edward Rose...."

In short, the commissioner's actions came after Rose was thoroughly investigated by baseball and a rigorous and lengthy court battle. Unfortunately, after five months in office Giamatti died suddenly from a heart attack at his summer home in Martha's Vineyard, Massachusetts. Within two weeks after Giamatti's death, the team owners met and voted deputy commissioner Francis T. Vincent, Jr. to be MLB's eighth commissioner.

Francis T. Vincent, Jr.

Before being appointed as the first deputy commissioner of baseball by Giamatti, and then elected as the organization's commissioner in September of 1989, Fay Vincent had specialized in corporate banking and the securities business as a lawyer, and in the 1980s, he served as president and chief executive officer of Columbia Pictures and executive vice president of the Coca-Cola Company. Unquestionably, these experiences contributed to Vincent's leadership to ensure that the World Series was completed after a massive earthquake had disabled the City of San Francisco in October of 1989. Regarding the growth of MLB during the early 1990s, Vincent decided in advance that the AL would receive $42 million of the NL's $190 million in fees that was generated from adding the Florida and Colorado franchises. In turn, the AL must provide players to these teams in the expansion draft. This exchange of money and players between clubs in the AL and NL had occurred for the first time in the expansion history of the sport.

During his term, Commissioner Vincent also influenced other important events that had affected baseball. After one month of spring training for teams to prepare for the 1990 season, he assumed command and negotiated a four-year contract between MLB and the MLBPA. Although the negotiation period delayed the opening day of the season by one week, it ensured that a full slate of 162 games would be played. Besides that event, in 1990 Vincent decided to ban New York Yankees owner George Steinbrenner for paying an individual $40,000 to spy on outfielder Dave Winfield, prohibited the use of smokeless tobacco by players and coaches in the Class A and Rookie Leagues, and banned pitcher Steve Howe from baseball for life after Howe's seventh suspension for drug infractions. However, after reinstating Steinbrenner and attempting to realign the NL, Vincent received a no confidence vote of 18–9 from the team owners. Consequently, in September of 1992 Fay Vincent decided to resign his position as the eighth commissioner of MLB. To fill the vacancy left by Vincent, Allan H. "Bud" Selig was immediately selected to be chairman of MLB's executive council and the acting or interim commissioner of baseball.

Allan H. Selig

While growing up in the State of Wisconsin, Bud Selig was an avid baseball fan of a Milwaukee Brewers minor league team and the Chicago Cubs, and then he rooted for the Milwaukee Braves during the 1950s and early 1960s. Before the Braves had officially moved to Atlanta in 1965, Selig founded an organization and named it Teams, Inc. This group was formed to lure a MLB team back to the Milwaukee area. After Selig and his group failed to acquire the Chicago White Sox, in 1970 a bankruptcy court awarded the Seattle Pilots to Selig and his investors. The team was renamed the Milwaukee Brewers and assigned to compete in the West Division of the AL.[5]

During Selig's tenure as president of the franchise, the Brewers appeared in but lost the 1982 World Series to the St. Louis Cardinals in seven games, and won seven awards for being the organization of the year and three consecutive Baseball America awards. For his active role in baseball and the Milwaukee community, Selig had received numerous honors. These included Executive of the Year, Sportsman of the Year, Baird Award for Management Excellence, Distinguished Citizen and the Ellis Island Medal of Honor. Because of these and other awards, and his involvement in the 1994 players strike and commitment to improve relations between the owners, players and fans, Selig was confirmed to be the ninth commissioner of the sport in July of 1998.

For various reasons, MLB was able to implement and withstand a number of impressive structural reforms and controversial policy initiatives since Selig had become acting commissioner in 1992. Listed in no specific order or priority, these matters included the scheduling of regular season games between various AL and NL teams and allowing games to be played in Japan, Mexico and Puerto Rico; furthermore, the redistribution of money from high to low revenue clubs, expansion of divisions in each league, restructure of the playoff system and adoption of the wild card, construction of new multimillion dollar baseball stadiums in several cities that host teams, and the consolidation of administrative functions of the AL and NL into the commissioner's office. Therefore, because of Selig's ability to rule by consensus and his aggressive leadership style and risk-taking, MLB has changed as a sport since the early 1990s.

Although many baseball experts consider the foregoing reforms and policies as generally benefiting the sports team owners, players, fans and communities, others have been critical about Selig's activities and decisions as a commissioner. They cite, for example, the cancellation of the 1994 World Series and the delayed start of the 1995 season because of a 234-day work stoppage, elimination of the AL and NL as legal entities, reinstatement and then suspension of player Darryl Strawberry, announcement of plans for MLB to contract the number of teams, decision to enforce the 60/40 equity/debt ratio rule in 2002 despite the Brewers' 100/97 violation of it in the late 1990s, allowing the 2002 All-Star Game to finish in a tie at 7–7, weak punishment of former Cincinnati Reds owner Marge Schott for her frequent prejudiced remarks about African American players, and the plan to have the All-Star game winner to determine the home field advantage for teams in the World Series. In short, because Selig has been exceedingly cooperative with and an accomplice of the team owners, the significant problems and troubles in baseball have not been satisfactorily resolved, especially for the sport's fans and the cities of MLB teams. For proof, during the 1990s the National Football League, National Basketball Association and perhaps college football and basketball have each surpassed professional baseball as the most popular sports in America.

According to a survey of baseball fans that was published on the web site rateitall.com, and which measured the performances of commissioners in the NFL, NBA NHL and MLB, Bud Selig rated average to below average and scored only two stars out of five. Those fans who supported Selig provided such comments as, "[He] managed to lead baseball into its greatest era; [The] first commish to establish labor peace with [the] union in history in '02; [He] led the way for minority hiring unlike the NFL's miserable record on coaches and QB's [quarterbacks]." Meanwhile, the fans' negative remarks included, "A nepotistic fool, more concerned with his pathetic image than of the game he is supposed to be guardian of; In the pocket of the owners. Talk about putting the fox in with the chickens; He is hell-bent on destroying ages-old traditions and amalgamating the NL and AL, yet [he] won't do anything about the stupid DH [designated hitter] rule." Based on these and other quotes, apparently Selig has been a radical but controversial commissioner of MLB.[6]

Governance Reforms in MLB

Given the observations of sports fans and what the research indicates about the role and power of a commissioner in MLB, Bud Selig and his executive staff should be committed to restoring baseball as America's national pastime. Some recommendations to achieve that goal consist of one or more of the following actions. First and foremost, there should be a change in the league's governing structure such that the commissioner's office is explicitly independent of the owners and players so that he or she will strive to make baseball's best interest as the top priority; second, adopt a policy that allows the AL and NL to be autonomous organizations and reestablish the offices of the presidents; third, minimize interleague games during the regular season so that the best teams from the AL and NL compete against each other in the World Series.[7]

Fourth, the league should restrict expansion in order to maintain the competitiveness of the existing teams and the quality of regular season and postseason games; fifth, reduce the revenue gap between small- and large-market teams in each division but do not advocate or seek complete parity of these clubs; sixth, in a multi-year experiment, establish and enforce a salary cap so that all teams have a reasonable opportunity to win enough games to qualify for the playoffs; seventh, outlaw the designated hitter rule in the AL and permit pitchers to hit; eighth, slow the escalation in ticket prices at ballparks as an incentive to further penetrate and extend the local and regional baseball markets of teams; ninth, rid the sport of performance enhancing drugs including amphetamines and various steroids, and set strict rules and enact harsh penalties for any players who use marijuana, cocaine and other illegal substances. With respect to these nine reforms, if a MLB commissioner applies his or her authority in a fair, prudent and consistent manner, then baseball fans across America will show their respect by attending more games, purchasing additional baseball products, and rooting for their favorite teams and players.

Summary

Since the death of Kenesaw Mountain Landis in 1944, the majority of baseball commissioners have not been admired as role models or effective, efficient and equitable leaders of the sport. Although most of them had established and enforced new regulations, implemented league wide policies to improve teams' competitiveness and the entertainment value of the game, the results were not necessarily in the best interest of baseball.

As such, this chapter primarily discusses how the nine individuals governed and what they achieved as the commissioner of baseball. There is a table that lists each commissioner's term, and also the number of teams and attendances per game that existed from the year when the person entered and left the office. Interestingly, the commissioners' efforts and accomplishments have not returned baseball to the golden era when the sport was dominant in America and far more popular and beloved by sports fans than professional and collegiate football, basketball, hockey and soccer. In part, baseball's relative decline in prestige and entertainment occurred because of the dependence, ineptness and self-interest of particular commissioners who had considered themselves and the wealth of franchise owners to be more important than the integrity and ethics of the sport, and more of a priority than the needs of the fans and communities that have supported the leagues' teams.

In sum, because baseball's commissioners, franchise owners and players union have jointly and selfishly abused their economic powers, MLB has become a moderately damaged brand and thus, has lost market share to professional football and other types of sports entertainment in North America. To be successful and prosper in the twenty-first century, big league baseball and the game would be optimally governed by a noble, forthright and dedicated commissioner, who has the spirit, morality and vision of the great Judge Kenesaw Mountain Landis.

17. The Strategy and Prosperity of Franchise Owners

From a business perspective, the owners of American League (AL) and National League (NL) franchises in Major League Baseball (MLB) are a unique and wealthy group of sports entrepreneurs and proprietors. Generally, the group includes private corporations, family entities, and one or more investors who have organized to form a syndicate, trust or limited partnership, which is the most common structure of ownership in professional baseball. To be sure, an investment in an elite and valuable sports enterprise such as a MLB franchise requires a substantial amount of capital and some knowledge of business principles, and involves a combination of short- and long-term economic risks and financial liabilities.[1]

Given an opportunity in the sport, there have always been a sufficient number of ambitious individuals with various experiences and/or organizations of investors, who are dedicated to purchasing a new or relocated franchise in order to control and operate a baseball team in the big leagues. It was reported, for example, that nearly 30 groups had indicated an interest in bidding for the Expos when the club was approved by MLB to relocate from Montreal, Canada to the Washington, D.C. area in early 2005. Therefore, in some respects a professional baseball franchise is perceived by risk-taking investors to be an economically attractive and potentially profitable business to own despite the fierce competitiveness, inflated costs and other uncertainties, relationships and problems associated with sports markets.

As to its essential themes, this chapter will focus on and discuss a few primary and secondary topics and relevant issues concerning owners and the personal and business implications, responsibilities and decisions of operating a team in MLB. Specifically, there is one table that presents some basic information and performance data with respect to the owners of 14 AL and 16 NL franchises. These individuals and groups had their baseball teams competing in regular season games to win their divisions, and then in the postseason to achieve a victory in the playoffs and World Series in ballparks, which are located in small, mid-sized or large U.S. cities and metropolitan areas and in Montreal and Toronto, Canada. Subsequently, another table depicts 26 franchises that, for several reasons, had experienced a change in owners, and lists in two columns, the respective teams' performances based on the year in which the franchises were sold. The contents of these tables are each analyzed from an ownership viewpoint.

Because of how this chapter is organized, the teams' owners are identified and a portion of them evaluated relative to their managerial strategies and successes in the AL or NL and in MLB, especially during the early 2000s. In part, this analysis will highlight the most opportunistic and productive team owners based on their clubs' most recent seasons, and will explain why these businesspersons or corporations had out competed their peers. After that discussion, the chapter concludes with a summary and a sequence of notes.

Barons of Baseball

A national media corporation or a large global company in the consumer goods or entertainment business, or a person who attained success with, or was the leader of, a firm in a non-sports industry and had earned a significant amount of money, and/or two or more private investors with high net worth's, each meet the sport's requirements to be the proprietor of an AL or NL franchise. Other desirable attributes, but not absolute requirements of current and prospective owners include prior decision-making experiences with the operation and marketing of baseball teams in the major or minor leagues; an ability to recognize, recruit and hire general managers and baseball coaches; the skills to negotiate and conclude contracts with U.S. and foreign players and to acquire loans from banks; and if necessary, the patience and professionalism to compromise and establish long-term deals with local politicians in order to use taxpayers subsidies for the construction of a new and modern baseball stadium. Collectively, these are the behaviors, characteristics and qualities that MLB considers important for admission to and membership in the league.[2]

Based on economic theory, the short- and long-term goal of each franchise owner is to maximize profits from operating a baseball enterprise in the AL or NL. Consequently, as an investor and leader, an owner should be familiar with a number of the organization's business activities. These are, one, the team's dollar amounts and percentage growths of its revenues, cash flows, expenses and asset valuations; two, the liquidity, equity, debt, turnover and earnings ratios; three, the legal obligations and benefits of any tax write-offs; and four, the marketing functions of the club, which includes such activities as establishing corporate partnerships and sponsorships, selling venue advertising, leasing suites and setting prices for game tickets and merchandise at the ballpark, and being aware of the market exposure and penetration from broadcasting games.

Besides these core activities, owners should also be cognizant of the performances by the team's coaches and key players, of important problems and decisions involving the general manager, of current and future community events and public relations campaigns, and of any legal issues and rule changes that may affect the operations of the franchise. Indeed, to be well-informed about the team's productivity in its AL or NL division and about the staff's effectiveness in completing their tasks, an owner must allocate enough resources upgrading the technology and software, and training employees to establish an efficient communication network and management information system that provides timely feedback to support the organization.

To identify and study the individuals and groups that are the financiers and leaders of professional baseball franchises, Table 17.1 was developed. Accordingly, it reveals some interesting facts about the distribution of owners in the AL and NL, and how their teams had performed in various seasons. Before analyzing the table's contents, however, a few observations must be specified and remembered about its format, data and quality.

First, because there are different types of owners listed in column two, and there are variations in the ownership years in column three and structures in column four, any comparison or evaluation of the teams' performances in columns five and six do not entirely reflect the managerial capabilities and decisions of these set of owners. In other words, there were no adjustments made in the data for the differences and deviations in ownership years and structures. Second, in the AL and NL there are divisions such that each consists of four or more competitive teams. Therefore, some large-market, high payroll and successful clubs like the New York Yankees and Boston Red Sox are rivals who compete in the same division. This distribution, in turn, might distort or skew the number of regular season victories per team, which means that winning percentage (WIN%) and postseason appearances (PSEAS) may not be the best measurements of the teams' performances and thus, the relative effectiveness of the respective owners.

Third, although 2000–2004 represents five consecutive baseball seasons, there may have been other circumstances, factors and events such as the opening of a new stadium, or a drastic change in the local economy, or the death of a limited partner that positively or negatively influenced a team's performances and the owner's decisions during one or more of the five seasons. Fourth, in the table winning percentages were calculated as averages or arithmetic means and not as geometric means, medians or modes. In other words, one or two very successful seasons played at or above .500 would have disproportionately inflated the WIN% of the most inferior clubs and thus misrepresented their owners' effectiveness during the five-year period.

Fifth, since the table was prepared during early-to-mid–2005, some changes have occurred in one or more of the columns. For example, to compete in the 2005 regular season the Expos had relocated its operations from Montreal, Canada to Washington, D.C. and were renamed the Washington Nationals; in January 2005 Los Angeles investor Matt Attanasio was approved by MLB to assume ownership of the Milwaukee Brewers, which ultimately affects the team's ownership years (OYRS) in column three and possibly its ownership structure (OSTR) in column four as presented in the table; besides the OYRS and OSTR, for business and other reasons some teams may have changed their names; finally, after the 2005 regular season most teams had new averages for WIN% and a portion of them increased their PSEAS when they qualified for and performed in the playoffs for being division winners or wild cards.

Sixth, the information in each column was determined primarily by researching relatively current journal and magazine articles, and by accessing various sources on the Internet. These web sites, however, are credible research sources such as cnnsi.com, mlb.com, sportsbusinessnews.com and usatoday.com. Therefore, the columns of teams, names, years, structures, percentages and number of seasons were assumed to be authentic and accurate, which eliminated the requirement to ever cross-reference the sources or double-check the data. Given these six observations, it is necessary for the reader of this chapter to study Table 17.1.

Analysis of Owners

According to the table, during early 2005 the 30 baseball franchises had primary owners who were listed in number and identified in gender as 25 males and one female, and

TABLE 17.1. MLB TEAM OWNERSHIP DATA AND
PERFORMANCES, BY LEAGUE, SELECTED YEARS

Team*	Name	OYRS	OSTR	2000–2004 WIN%	PSEAS
AL					
Angels	Arturo Moreno	2	LP	.521	1
Athletics	Steve Schott	10	IG	.597	4
Blue Jays	Rogers Communications	5	Corp	.486	0
Devil Rays	Vincent Naimoli	7	LP	.395	0
Indians	Lawrence Dolan	5	LP	.497	1
Mariners	Hiroshi Yamauchi	13	LP	.563	2
Orioles	Peter Angelos	12	LP	.436	0
Rangers	Thomas Hicks	7	GP	.464	0
Red Sox	John Henry	3	IG	.588	2
Royals	David Glass	5	Corp	.425	0
Tigers	Michael Ilitch	13	Hold	.399	0
Twins	Carl Pohlad	21	LP	.531	3
White Sox	Jerry Reinsdorf	24	LP	.528	1
Yankees	George Steinbrenner	32	LLC	.604	5
NL					
Astros	Drayton McLane	13	Corp	.528	2
Braves	AOL Time Warner	9	Corp	.595	5
Brewers	Wendy Selig Preib	35	FT	.410	0
Cardinals	William DeWitt, Jr.	10	LP	.586	4
Cubs	Tribune Company	24	Corp	.490	1
Diamondbacks	Jerry Colangelo	10	LP	.506	2
Dodgers	Frank McCourt	1	Corp	.594	1
Expos	Major League Baseball	3	FO	.479	0
Giants	Peter Magowan	12	LP	.585	3
Marlins	Jeffrey Loria	3	LP	.520	1
Mets	Fred Wilpon	19	LP	.480	1
Padres	John Moores	11	LP	.459	0
Phillies	Bill Giles	24	LP	.498	0
Pirates	Kevin McClatchy	9	IG	.433	0
Reds	Carl Lindner	6	LP	.461	0
Rockies	Jerry McMorris	13	LP	.457	0

* Team excludes its first name, which is a U.S. or Canadian city, or a State in America. Name is the franchises' major investor, managing director or primary owner/partner. OYRS is the longevity of the current ownership in years, and OSTR is the type of ownership structure. Based on the results of the 2000–2004 seasons, WIN% is the teams' average winning percentages, and PSEAS is the number of post-season appearances. LP is a limited partnership, IG an investment group, while Corp means Corporation and GP is a general partnership. Hold means holdings, LLC is a limited liability company, FT indicates a family trust and FO is franchise ownership by the other MLB team proprietors.

Source: "MLB Owners (Current)," at http://www.forbes.com cited 9 January 2005; "Teams," at http://www.mlb.com cited 9 January 2005; "The Owners: Who Are These Guys?" at http://www.resonator.com cited 20 November 2001; "2000 Inside the Ownership of Professional Sports Teams," at http://www.teammarketing.com cited 20 November 2001.

complemented by three corporations and one owner titled as the league, that is, Major League Baseball. Particularly intriguing about these teams and names, for example, was the Brewers' Wendy Selig Preib who is the daughter of baseball's Commissioner, Bud Selig. He turned the club over to her when he became MLB's full-time commissioner in 1998.

Five years later, the club had no president because Ulice Payne Jr. resigned. Interestingly, for many years the Alan Selig Trust had been in control of the franchise. During late 2004, however, Trust Company of the West managing director Mark Attanasio had signed a letter of intent to purchase the team from the Trust for approximately $200–225 million and become its new owner. Because of debts exceeding $100 million, and a debt/equity ratio above the league average, Attanasio stated his preference to recruit and add Milwaukee investors as minority owners. Recently he said, "I am looking to bring in partners. I'd like to see the partners have a passion for baseball … and the community. So I'm collecting all the facts I can about potential local and national owners, and about friends of mine who are interested in owning a piece of the team." With the lowest payroll in baseball at $27 million, Attanasio must decide soon whether significantly reducing the Brewers' debt, or increasing its payroll to acquire free agents and win games is the team's first priority.[3]

Regarding the distribution of ownership years or OYRS in column three of Table 17.1, the AL owners' average tenure was more than 11 years, which ranged from the Angels' two years to the Yankees' 32. Sequenced by decade, in the AL one ownership change occurred in the 1970s, two in the 1980s, five in the 1990s and five in the 2000s. This list excludes the Tampa Bay Devil Rays because the franchise's ownership proportions have remained essentially constant since 1998 with Vincent Naimoli at 15 percent, the limited partners at 37 percent and minority investors at 48 percent. Furthermore, between the four franchises' first year in the AL and 2004, there were 16 total ownership changes for the Indians, ten for the Red Sox and Tigers, and nine for the White Sox.

Meanwhile, in Table 17.1 the NL proprietors had averaged more than 12 years, which varied from the Dodgers' one to the Cubs' and Phillies' 24 years, and not to the Brewers' 35 years since the club had switched from the AL to NL in 1998. Arranged by decade, the number of NL ownership changes that took place were zero in the 1970s, three in the 1980s, seven in the 1990s and three in the 2000s. Alternatively, there have been no ownership changes for the NL's Brewers, Diamondbacks and Rockies. With respect to turnover, the Cubs, Dodgers, Pirates, Padres and Giants have each been controlled by at least four different groups. Eventually, each leagues' distributions will change after the sale of the Brewers was completed in early 2005, after the purchase of the former Expos franchise occurs, and according to speculation, the potential sale of the Athletics by Steve Schott and his partner Ken Hoffman, and the likely sale of the Braves by AOL Time Warner and the Reds by Carl Lindner. Indeed, billionaire and philanthropist Ted Turner has reportedly expressed an interest in re-owning the Braves after he had sold the club in 1995.

According to column four in Table 17.1, 16 or 53 percent of the teams are structured as an LP, or limited partnership, and six or 20 percent are established as a Corp, or corporation. Relative to these structures, any investors who are not actively engaged in an LP have limited liabilities with respect to team operations, yet they will receive the tax benefits that are passed through to them from the team. The investors in LPs, however, are subject to capital calls. For example, if an individual purchases 10 percent of a team with losses of $10 million, an additional commitment of $1 million in cash may be required from that investor. In contrast, as owners the shareholders in corporations are protected from legal liabilities and also, are not subject to capital calls. Unfortunately, some or all shareholders may not earn back their original invested amounts if a corporation's share price or value had significantly declined because of such problems as inferior team and player performances, or the failure to accurately budget the revenues, expenses and cash flows of the franchise, or below average attendances at home games and contraction of the fan base, or executive mismanagement and indecision. Besides LPs and corporations, the other ownership structures listed in Table 17.1 also have legal advantages and disadvantages for investors. These relate to various types of exposure to risks and to bankruptcy, debt obligations, creditor claims, tax write-offs and deductions, lawsuits and contractual disputes, allocation of profits, and the deaths of one or more principal or minority owners.[4]

In Table 17.1, columns five and six are two measurements of team performances, that is, the winning percentage or WIN% and the number of postseason appearances or PSEAS for the baseball seasons during 2000–2004 in which the respective owners controlled the franchise. To illustrate, Mexico's Arturo Moreno owned the Angels in 2003–2004 and Vincent Naimoli the Devil Rays in 2000–2004. As a result, in each league the performance measures per team may represent from one to five seasons because of differences in years of the designated ownership. Furthermore, for clarification, by restricting the time period to 2000–2004 or five regular baseball seasons, avoids extreme relationships. For example, the effort to compare and analyze how the Dodgers performed in 2004 when Frank McCourt owned the franchise in Los Angeles to how the Phillies performed from 1981 to 2004 when Bill Giles owned his franchise in Philadelphia.

Anyway, the most productive proprietors in the AL and NL were, respectively, George Steinbrenner who owned the Yankees and Steve Schott the Athletics, and AOL Time Warner, which owned the Braves and William DeWitt, Jr. who controlled the Cardinals. To average between a 58 and 61 WIN% during regular season games, and qualify for at least four PSEAS, the annual payrolls of the Yankees had increased on average by 24 percent, Athletics by 25 percent and Cardinals by 8 percent. In other words, the three clubs' owners had spent more money to hire better players in an effort to excel. The Braves, meanwhile, won nearly 60 percent of its games and appeared in five division playoffs in the NL despite an average payroll decrease of 3 percent. Perhaps owner AOL Time Warner had decided to cut the Braves' payroll because of the company's declining stock price and accounting losses during the early 2000s. Alternatively, the less effective owners were the Devil Rays' Vincent Naimoli and Tigers' Michael Ilitch in the AL, and the Brewers' Wendy Selig Preib and Pirates' Kevin McClatchy in the NL. Except for Ilitch's Tigers, these poor team performances had occurred, in part, because of average payroll cuts implemented by Naimoli at 15 percent, Preib at 5 percent and McClatchy at 1 percent.[5]

There were other interesting facts about the owners and team performances. With respect to the AL group, Arturo Moreno increased the Angels' payroll in 2004 by 44 percent but failed to win the division series; Carl Pohlad expanded the payroll of his small-market Twins approximately 56 percent per year and the club appeared in three postseasons; besides Naimoli's Devil Rays, payrolls also declined on average for Angelos' Orioles, Dolan's Indians and Roger Communications' Blue Jays, which partially explains the sub-.500 winning percentages of these clubs; finally, in his three seasons as the Red Sox owner, John Henry had modestly increased the team's average payroll by 6 percent yet the club won two East division titles and the 2004 World Series.

In the NL, the owners who had generously increased their teams' payrolls per year were the Phillies' Bill Giles at 28 percent and Cubs' Tribune Company at 17 percent, while the largest cuts in average payrolls per season were 5 percent by the Brewers' Wendy Selig Preib and 3 percent by the Diamondbacks' Jerry Colangelo and the Braves' AOL Time

Warner; even though Major League Baseball, which controlled the Expos from 2002 to 2004, and the Rockies' Jerry McMorris and Reds' Carl Lindner had each expanded their club's payroll by 2 percent per year, that strategy unfortunately resulted in below average winning percentages and zero division titles and wild card spots for these franchises; lastly, with 15 percent payroll increases per year each from owners Peter Magowan and Drayton McLane, Jr., the Giants and Astros combined had succeeded to appear in five division series, two championship playoffs and one World Series. In short, during 2000–2004 there were 13 inferior MLB owners because their teams won less than 50 percent of regular season games and did not qualify for any of the playoff series. The other 17 owners, however, were either superior, above average or average since their teams had realized winning percentages that exceeded .500 and/or competed in at least one postseason.

Do Owners Matter?

Because of numerous commercial, economic and personal reasons, the current owner of a MLB franchise may decide to offer it for sale. After bids are submitted by prospective buyers and thoroughly evaluated by the league, a new owner is approved and the franchise is sold at a mutual price to another individual or group. Some sports literature, such as a data supplement in *Pay Dirt: The Business of Professional Team Sports* summarized the ownership histories of baseball teams in the Early National League (1876–1900), American Association (1882–1891), Union Association (1884), Players League (1890), Federal League (1914–1915), National League (1901–1991) and American League (1901–1991). Other publications have discussed personal information about a new owner including his or her assets, family wealth, current and former employment experiences, and the motivation and objective for purchasing a professional baseball team. Furthermore, in hundreds of magazine and journal articles many sports writers have analyzed the price paid for the franchise, described how the team had performed for the previous owner, and predicted the future performance of the team as a member of the AL or NL and as a business organization. Rather than restate the results of previous studies, the next section of this chapter explores how a number of MLB teams performed in seasons before and after a change in ownership had occurred. In part, the analysis will also identify who sold and purchased teams and indicate the consequences of selecting new owners by the league.[6]

After reviewing the facts about the sale of several professional baseball franchises, 26 MLB teams were selected to be the sample size. That is, 13 each from the AL and NL. After the previous and new owners were identified for the 26 sales, the average winning percentage or WIN% and the total number of postseason appearances or PSEAS were determined per team for three years prior to and immediately following the year of sale. To illustrate, if team A was sold to new owners in 1995, the average WIN% and number of PSEAS were derived for 1992–1994 reflecting the former owners, and for 1996–1998 representing the new owners. As a result of this process, the two sets of WIN% and PSEAS reveal how the 26 teams had performed before and after they were sold. For the analysis and discussion, Table 17.2 reports the results.

As an aside, the AL's Tampa Bay Devil Rays and the NL's Arizona Diamondbacks, Milwaukee Brewers and Colorado Rockies do not appear as entries in the table since

Table 17.2. Year of Sale, Franchise Ownership Changes and Team Performances, by League, Selected Seasons

Team	Owners From	To	WIN% From	To	PSEAS From	To
AL						
Angels (1999)*	Autry Family	Walt Disney Co.	.493	.526	0	1
Athletics (1995)	Charley Finley	Steve Schott	.486	.446	1	0
Blue Jays (2000)	John Labatt Ltd.	Rogers Comm.	.510	.502	0	0
Indians (2000)	Richard Jacobs	Larry Dolan	.560	.479	2	1
Mariners (1992)	Jeff Smulyan	Hiroshi Yamauchi	.479	.496	0	1
Orioles (1993)	Edward Williams	Peter Angelos	.478	.533	0	1
Rangers (1998)	George Bush	Thomas Hicks	.515	.491	1	1
Red Sox (2002)	Jean Yawkey	John Henry	.538	.588	1	2
Royals (2000)	Ewing Kauffman	David Glass	.420	.432	0	0
Tigers (1992)	Tom Monaghan	Michael Ilitch	.457	.467	0	0
Twins (1984)	Calvin Griffith	Carl Pohlad	.392	.479	0	1
White Sox (1981)	Bill Veech	Jerry Reinsdorf	.445	.535	0	1
Yankees (1973)	CBS	George Steinbrenner	.530	.559	0	1
NL						
Astros (1992)	John McMullen	Drayton McLane, Jr.	.465	.542	0	0
Braves (1996)	Ted Turner	AOL Time Warner	.621	.637	2	3
Cardinals (1995)	Anheuser Busch	William DeWitt, Jr.	.504	.502	0	1
Cubs (1981)	Wrigley Family	Tribune Company	.459	.495	0	1
Dodgers (1998)	Peter O'Malley	Fox Entertainment	.547	.512	2	0
Expos (1990)	John McHale	Charles Brochu	.520	.519	0	0
Giants (1993)	Robert Lurie	Peter McGowan	.477	.454	0	0
Marlins (1999)	Wayne Huizenga	John Henry	.465	.482	1	0
Mets (1980)	Lorinda de Roulet	Doubleday & Co.	.397	.406	0	0
Padres (1994)	Tom Werner	John Moores	.467	.505	0	1
Phillies (1981)	Rudy Carpenter	Bill Giles	.545	.535	2	1
Pirates (1996)	Pittsburgh Assoc.	Kevin McClatchy	.443	.466	0	0
Reds (1999)	Marge Schott	Carl Lindner	.481	.471	0	0

* The year of sale is in parenthesis after the team name. Owners From and To are self-explanatory. WIN% is a team's average winning percentage while PSEAS is its number of postseason appearances. The WIN% From column is a three-year average of the team prior to the year of sale, and the WIN% To column is a three-year average after the year of sale. The PSEAS From and To columns are, respectively, the total number of postseason appearances during three years prior to and after the year of sale. To represent John Henry as the club's new owner, the Red Sox' WIN% and PSEAS in the To columns include the year of sale, or 2002–2004 inclusive. The Pittsburgh Association sold the Pirates.

Source: "Teams," at http://www.mlb.com cited 9 January 2005.

these clubs' original ownership had not changed when this chapter was completed. Moreover, although MLB had approved Mark Attanasio and his investment group as the Brewers' new owner in January 2005, the team had obviously not participated in three seasons after its sale.

Given the ownership changes and sales relationships in Table 17.2, the average WIN% had increased for the 13 AL teams from .484 to .502, and for the 13 NL teams from .491 to .502. Specifically, nine or 69 percent AL and seven or 53 percent NL teams played more competitive baseball for their new owners. As to team performances per league, the best improvements in WIN% were the AL's White Sox and Twins and the

NL's Astros and Padres. Meanwhile, the AL's Indians and Athletics and NL's Dodgers and Giants experienced the largest declines in WIN%. In short, the majority of teams performed better during the three seasons after the year they were sold.

For the PSEAS column, the total number of playoff appearances increased from 12 to 17 when the teams' ownership changed. Interestingly, a few teams became World Series champions. These included the AL's Yankees in 1976, Angels in 2002 and Red Sox in 2004. World Series defeats, however, happened for the NL's Phillies in 1983 and Braves in 1998 and 1999. Consequently, based on the teams' seasons before and after the transfers that appear in columns two and three, which of the new MLB franchise owners had the most and least success?

When the teams in the AL and NL are grouped, the all-star owners who had succeeded included the AL Red Sox' John Henry in 2002–2004, Angels' Walt Disney Company in 2000–2002 and Yankees' George Steinbrenner in 1974–1976. In the NL, it was the Braves' AOL Time Warner in 1997–1999. When these four sports owners led their franchises, the average three-year WIN% increased on average from .545 to .577 and the clubs' PSEAS rose from three to seven. Alternatively, because their teams' WIN% and PSEAS had declined after they replaced Charley Finley in 1995, Richard Jacobs in 2000, Peter O'Malley in 1998 and Rudy Carpenter in 1981, the least competent new owners were, respectively, the AL Athletics' Steve Schott in 1996–1998 and Indians' Larry Dolan in 2001–2003, and in the NL, the Dodgers' Fox Entertainment in 1999–2001 and Phillies' Bill Giles in 1982–1984. Therefore, in contrast to the previous eight owners, 22 or approximately 73 percent of the individuals and organizations listed in column three of Table 17.2 had realized only marginal success or disappointment in the three seasons after the year they had assumed command of their baseball franchises.

Beside the investments in and economic returns from their sports teams, during the late 1990s and early 2000s some MLB barons owned various business interests that had experienced problems with successfully implementing plans, selling products and/or penetrating markets, which probably resulted in financial losses. As examples, there was Little Caesars pizza empire and Kmart holdings of the Tigers' Michael Ilitch and an international telecommunications and broadcasting subsidiary of the Rangers' Thomas Hicks; also, failures occurred for the American Financial Group and banana firm Chiquita of the Reds' Carl Lindner, and for the bankrupt trucking company NationsWay Transport of the Rockies' Jerry McMorris. There were declines in the stock prices of media company Cablevision owned by the Indians' Larry Dolan and of software business Peregrine Systems built by the Padres' John Moores. Finally, the Devil Rays' Vince Naimoli, who was the former chairman of Harvard Industries, which had filed for bankruptcy protection and then delisted from the NASDAQ stock exchange, incurred huge losses. In other words, success as an owner in the baseball business does not guarantee similar results when investing in other industries.[7]

Based on deals of the Angels' Arte Moreno, Dodgers' Frank McCourt and Brewers' Mark Attanasio, and the sale of the Athletics to Lewis Wolff, some baseball insiders speculate that individuals, families or small groups of local investors, and not multinational entertainment and media sports conglomerates will gradually become the dominate type of team ownership in MLB. Whether these experts' predictions become a permanent trend depends, in part, on the differences in the economic and social benefits and costs that will accrue to the league and its' teams and players, but most importantly, to the communities and fans.[8]

Summary

This chapter basically focused on first, identifying a sample of former and new owners of MLB franchises based on the year of sale and second, on measuring the performances of their teams during selected seasons, and to some extent, on these owners' strategies and prosperity as sports entrepreneurs, franchise leaders and businesspersons. With respect to the topics for analysis, there are two tables that contain the names of various franchise owners, and that list the average winning percentages and number of post-season appearances of their clubs.

Based on the tabled data, it is evident that teams improved in the seasons after they were sold. In sum, it is interesting and meaningful to research and reveal the unique group of individuals and corporations who have or have not succeeded by primarily investing in MLB baseball teams and not those in professional basketball, football, hockey and soccer.

18. The Performances of Managers in Coaching Professional Teams

In the organizational structure of a typical American League (AL) or National League (NL) franchise in Major League Baseball (MLB), the general manager (GM) reports to the owner, a senior executive or another high-ranking official, while the head coach or field manager of the team reports to the owner or GM. Although the key topic analyzed in this chapter is the head coach or field manager, the tasks and responsibilities of the GM are briefly outlined in the following two paragraphs.

Basically, the GM is assigned to conduct and control the majority of player transactions. These duties may consist of—but are not limited to—evaluating the team's current players as prospects for potential trades, monitoring which of these players may decide to retire after MLB's postseason concludes, and representing the club during contract negotiations with free agents, high school and college athletes who have been drafted, and with veteran players whose contracts are about to expire. Furthermore, the GM may be expected to offer advice and recommend to the owner that, based on the team's recent performances, the field manager should be retained or dismissed with respect to the next regular season or within a few seasons.

The present GMs of MLB teams have various personal backgrounds, interests and goals. To illustrate, the San Francisco Giants' Brian Sabean had scouted baseball players, the Boston Red Sox' Theo Epstein studied to earn an Ivy League education, the Arizona Diamondbacks' Joe Garagiola Jr.'s father was a sports announcer who played catcher for the St. Louis Cardinals, and the Oakland Athletics' Billy Bean had a unremarkable career in the big leagues. However, despite these and other differences, the GMs employed by MLB franchises are essentially decision makers who have similar attributes regarding organizational leadership qualities and interpersonal skills, the knowledge and ability to assemble and motivate a diverse staff, and a knack for identifying and hiring talented players. Furthermore, it is an advantage for individuals who want to become GMs to have performed business and/or sports work in baseball organizations. These positions include such departmental units as the director of player personnel, head of scouting and player development, assistant to an executive in the minor league farm system, vice president of baseball operations, assistant director of labor relations, director of office administration, consultant to the franchise's owner, the team's hitting coach and, of course, as an assistant to the current GM. Finally, there may be a number of former and current head coaches who are well qualified to become future GMs. Therefore, given that overview of the GM, which is an executive position, the following pages of this chapter discuss various aspects and historical facts about the experiences and performances of field managers who were and are head coaches of professional baseball teams, especially those in MLB.[1]

MLB Managers

In general, the manager is a professional baseball team's leader and primary decision maker. That is, before a game begins he implements a strategy by choosing the nine starting players and their respective field positions. Throughout the game, the manager may decide to replace one or more of the starters with other players in order for them to be a pinch hitter, and/or to pitch, catch, and play in the infield or outfield. To what extent he must control the team's players during a game depends on several factors. For example, some managers may select each kind of pitch, reposition the defense to prepare for the opposition's best batters, and provide the signals for his team's hitters to bunt a ball and for runners to steal a base. Alternatively, other managers are willing to allow certain players to judge when to make these types of decisions. It is most probable, however, that the majority of MLB managers strike a balance between the inclination to strictly control the team versus the need to rely on each player's intuition and ability to choose how to best play defense and hit against the pitcher of the opposing club.

With respect to the previous characteristics, roles and duties of a head coach in professional baseball, this chapter will explicitly identify the current individuals and some former outstanding field managers of MLB teams, and discuss these leaders' effectiveness and contributions to the sport. There are three tables that each highlight important facts about, and the historic achievements of, various managers including those who have been especially successful at coaching teams in the AL and NL during the regular seasons and postseasons from the early 1900s to the beginning years of the 2000s. Indeed, because the AL joined the NL to form MLB in 1901, that is the initial year of interest in this chapter rather than 1903 when the first World Series was played. Specifically, the final season is assigned to be 2004, when Lee Francona coached his Boston Red Sox team to a World Series championship in four games by defeating the St. Louis Cardinals, who were managed by the talented Tony LaRussa.[2]

For the benefit of learning some general and basic information about who and how many individuals have performed as head coaches of MLB teams for one or more seasons since 1901, five columns of information were organized to form Table 18.1. It shows the total number of former head coaches and the distribution of current managers of 14 AL and 16 NL franchises that existed in 2004. Thus, to analyze the topic of this chapter, what special insights does the table's columns reveal about the gentlemen who have either previously managed or presently coach the teams of these thirty franchises?

Table 18.1 denotes that during 104 seasons of baseball, there have been 358 managers of teams in each of the leagues. The total of 358 per league means that, on average each club has hired a new, or rehired a former coach approximately every four to five years. As expected, those teams which were organized to play in 1901 and that existed in such cities as Boston, Chicago, Cincinnati, Cleveland, Detroit, New York, Philadelphia and St. Louis have experienced the highest turnover of managers. In contrast, the expan-

TABLE 18.1. TOTAL AND CURRENT AL AND NL
MANAGERS, BY LEAGUE, 1901–2004

		Current Manager		
Team*	Total	Name	Year Hired	WPCT
AL				
Balt. Orioles/New York Yankees	33	Joe Torre	1996	.610
Boston Pilgrims/Red Sox	44	Lee Francona	2004	.605
Chicago White Sox	33	Ozzie Guillen	2004	.512
Cleveland Indians	39	Eric Wedge	2003	.456
Detroit Tigers	34	Alan Trammell	2003	.354
Kansas City Royals	16	Tony Pena	2002	.422
LA/California/Anaheim Angels	21	Mike Scioscia	2000	.522
Philadelphia/KC/Oakland Athletics	26	Ken Macha	2003	.577
Seattle Mariners	13	Mike Hargrove	2004	.389
St. Louis Browns/Balt. Orioles	36	Lee Mazzilli	2004	.481
Tampa Bay Devil Rays	3	Lou Piniella	2003	.412
Toronto Blue Jays	11	John Gibbons	2004	.416
Wash. Senators/Minnesota Twins	28	Ron Gardenhire	2002	.569
Wash. Senators/Texas Rangers	21	Buck Showalter	2003	.427
NL				
Arizona Diamondbacks	3	Bob Melvin	2004	.315
Boston/Milwaukee/Atlanta Braves	39	Bobby Cox	1991	.570
Brooklyn/Los Angeles Dodgers	18	Jim Tracy	2001	.549
Chicago Cubs	49	Dusty Baker	2003	.546
Cincinnati Reds	46	Dave Miley	2003	.447
Colorado Rockies	4	Clint Hurdle	2002	.450
Florida Marlins	7	Jack McKeon	2003	.552
Houston Colts/Astros	15	Phil Garner	2004	.568
Montreal Expos	11	Frank Robinson	2002	.465
New York Mets	18	Willie Randolph	2004	.438
New York/San Francisco Giants	21	Felipe Alou	2003	.591
Philadelphia Phillies	41	Charlie Manuel	2004	.531
Pittsburgh Pirates	25	Lloyd McClendon	2001	.435
San Diego Padres	15	Bruce Bochy	1995	.487
Seattle Pilots/Milwaukee Brewers	14	Ned Yost	2003	.418
St. Louis Cardinals	32	Tony LaRussa	1996	.545

* The teams appear in alphabetical order in the AL and then NL. Total is the total number of managers of each team during 1901–2004. WPCT is the current manager's regular season winning percentage. Although an AL club in the 1969–1997 seasons, the Brewers switched to the NL in 1998. The Montreal Expos relocated to Washington, D.C. in 2005 and became the Washington Nationals.

Source: *Official Major League Baseball Fact Book 2004 Edition* (St. Louis, MO: The Sporting News, 2004); *The World Almanac and Book of Facts* (New York, N.Y.: Newspaper Enterprise Association, Inc., 1950–2004); "Manager (Baseball)," at http://en.wikipedia.org cited 7 February 2005.

sion baseball franchises in Denver, Houston, Miami, Montreal, Phoenix, Seattle, Tampa Bay and Toronto had the fewest replacements of their head coaches.[3]

About the MLB teams in eight of these cities, the Cubs, Reds, Red Sox and Phillies have each employed at least 40 different coaches since the early 1900s while the Diamondbacks, Devil Rays, Rockies and Astros have each hired fewer than ten. Interestingly, the individuals with the longest tenure and total number of games as managers of the former four teams were, respectively, the Cubs' Charlie Grimm at 14 full and/or part seasons and 1,728 games; Reds' Sparky Anderson at nine and 1,449; Red Sox' Joe Cronin at 13 and 1,987; and the Phillies' Gene Mauch at eight and 1,330. In evaluating this group of leaders, the most successful was Anderson, whose Cincinnati teams won five division titles, four NL pennants and two World Series championships. For his 26 years of achievements in the sport, which included a total of 4,030 games and 2,194 victories, and the eighth highest winning percentage of all-time at .545, Sparky Anderson was inducted into baseball's Hall of Fame in 2000. As an aside, since Anderson's final season with the Reds in 1978, the franchise has won only two West Division titles and one NL pennant and World Series. The latter championship occurred in 1990 when Lou Piniella, who is the current head coach of the Tampa Bay Devil Rays, had managed the Reds to a four-game sweep of the powerful Oakland Athletics.

The third column of Table 18.1 lists the head coaches of the 14 AL and 16 NL were hired and their average winning percentages. Between 2001 and 2004, 25 or approximately 83 percent of these individuals had joined their current team to be the field leader. This high percentage reflects the frequent turnover of baseball managers who have replaced former coaches that simply quit for more job security or a better salary with another other franchise, or because their team played uninspired baseball, or they had decided to retire due to illness, age or for other reasons.

Since their teams won titles, pennants and World Series during the 1990s, the Yankees' Joe Torre and Braves' Bobby Cox have the most seniority within the group of 30 clubs. In fact, Torre's Yankee teams, which recently have the highest payroll in MLB, win between six and seven games out of ten. Undoubtedly, this performance pleases owner George Steinbrenner and especially the Yankee fans in the New York and New Jersey areas. Philanthropist Ted Turner and then Time Warner Inc., who owned the Braves in 2004, must realize that Cox is the best leader available for the team and thus, are very reluctant to replace him. Indeed, for their efforts as coaches Torre was the AL's Manager of the Year in 1996 and 1998, and Cox the NL's in 1991 and 2004.

For the two groups of coaches listed in Table 18.1, the average winning percentages based on the numbers in column five were .482 for the AL and .494 for the NL teams. In total, 15 or 50 percent of the individuals' teams had more losses than wins. Besides the Yankees' Torre and Braves' Cox, the other most successful coaches hired before 2004 included the Athletics' Ken Macha, Twins' Ron Gardenhire, Dodgers' Jim Tracy, Cubs' Dusty Baker, Marlins' Jack McKeon and Giants' Felipe Alou. Alternatively, the league's lowest winning percentages with respect to the managers who were hired before 2004 belonged to the Tigers' Alan Trammell and Devil Rays' Lou Piniella, and the Brewers' Ned Yost and Pirates' Lloyd McClendon.

Ranked somewhere between the NL's group of managers who had the highest and lowest average winning percentages, and had began coaching their respective teams before 2000 were the Cardinals' Tony LaRussa and Padres' Bruce Bochy. Because his Cardinals' teams won division titles in 1996, 2000, 2002 and 2004, and the NL pennant in 2004, LaRussa is popular and a hero in St. Louis, especially among Cardinals fans. As such, he will remain the team's manager for many years. Indeed, after being selected as the AL Manager of the Year while coaching the White Sox in 1983 and the Athletics in 1988 and 1992, LaRussa won the coveted NL award in 2002. Meanwhile, Bochy's Padres won the NL's West division title in 1996, and again two years later when the team defeated the highly talented Braves in six games to earn its second pennant in 30 years. If the Padres, however, fail to qualify for a postseason position before 2007 or 2008, then Bochy may be pressured by the Padres' owner to resign as the team's manager. Therefore, despite being successful and winning awards during the late 1990s and early 2000s, the majority of current head coaches of MLB teams have little if any job security beyond a term of three to five years.

In the next section of this chapter, the managers who had received a special award for their leadership of teams during one or more of 46 full or partial seasons and postseasons are identified with respect to their performances. As such, these individuals deserve to be recognized and congratulated.

Manager of the Year

Since 1959, a Manager of the Year has been selected from at least one team in each league. To earn this award, these AL and NL head coaches had to accomplish more than what was expected of them with the players that were hired by the team owner. In other words, to be chosen for this honor these managers' teams did not necessarily win a division title, league pennant or World Series championship. So, to discuss which individuals have been the most successful at winning this award and why, some data was collected and formatted to prepare the five columns in Table 18.2. It includes 19 individuals who were Manager of the Year for at least two MLB seasons. But, to be brief it excludes a list of the 39 men who had received the award for one baseball season. An analysis of the results appears following the note and source below the table.[4]

Columns one and two in Table 18.2 denote that between 1959 and 2004, these 19 head coaches had accumulated 54 or 58 percent of the awards that were issued. Based on their teams' postseason performances as reflected in the table's last column, the top five managers in the group were first, Walt Alston, second, a tie between Sparky Anderson and Tommy Lasorda, fourth, Tony LaRussa and fifth, Billy Martin. Even though each of them had received four Manager of the Year awards between 1959 and 2004, it was Alston's Los Angeles Dodgers that had won three NL championships and the World Series in 1959, 1963 and 1965. Although he did not receive an award in 1963, his team in Los Angeles claimed a World Series by defeating the New York Yankees in four games.

During the seasons they were voted Manager of the Year, the other four outstanding coaches achieved the following titles in the postseasons. That is, three pennants plus two World Series each for Anderson's Reds in 1975 and Tigers in 1984, and Lasorda's Dodgers in 1981 and 1988; one pennant in 1988 and no World Series victory that year for LaRussa's Athletics; and one pennant in 1976 and zero Series that year for Martin's Yankees. However, as Table 18.2 shows, LaRussa's teams were more successful because they had appeared in four postseasons and Martin's in two. Nevertheless, in other MLB seasons in which Martin coached, his Yankees' teams won the World Series such as in 1977, and again in 1978 when Martin was fired by owner George Steinbrenner and replaced by Bob Lemon. As an aside, Alston was elected to baseball's Hall of Fame in 1983, Lasorda in 1997 and Anderson in 2000.

If the performances of the six coaches who had each won three awards are evaluated based on postseason appearances and results, certainly Joe Torre ranks as the most successful and then Bobby Cox, Earl Weaver, Dusty Baker, Dick Williams and Gene Mauch. When he was voted Manager of the Year, Torre's Yankee clubs won the World Series in 1996 and 1998, and also during the other seasons of 1999 and 2000. The AL's Blue Jays

TABLE 18.2. MANAGER OF THE YEAR,
TWO TO FOUR AWARDS, 1959–2004

Name	Awards	League (Years)*	Teams	Postseasons
Billy Martin	4	AL (1974, 1976, 1980, 1981)	2	2
Sparky Anderson	4	AL (1984, 1987); NL (1972, 1975)	2	4
Tommy Lasorda	4	NL (1977, 1981, 1983, 1988)	1	4
Tony LaRussa	4	AL (1983, 1988, 1992); NL (2002)	3	4
Walt Alston	4	NL (1959, 1965, 1966, 1974)	1	4
Bobby Cox	3	AL (1985); NL (1991, 2004)	2	3
Dick Williams	3	AL (1967, 1971); NL (1979)	3	1
Dusty Baker	3	NL (1993, 1997, 2000)	1	2
Earl Weaver	3	AL (1973, 1977, 1979)	1	2
Gene Mauch	3	NL (1962, 1964, 1973)	2	0
Joe Torre	3	AL (1996, 1998); NL (1982)	2	3
Buck Showalter	2	AL (1994, 2004)	2	1
Danny Murtaugh	2	NL (1960, 1970)	1	2
Hank Bauer	2	AL (1964, 1966)	1	1
Jack McKeon	2	NL (1999, 2003)	2	0
Jim Leyland	2	NL (1990, 1992)	1	2
Lou Piniella	2	AL (1995, 2001)	2	2
Ralph Houk	2	AL (1963, 1970)	1	1
Red Schoendienst	2	NL (1967, 1968)	1	2

* (Years) is when the managers received their awards. Teams are the number of clubs that the manager had coached for his awards. Postseasons are the number of playoffs that each manager's teams had participated. In 1996, the Yankees' Joe Torre and Rangers' Johnny Oates shared the AL award. There were a total of twenty-two individuals in the AL and seventeen in the NL that had received this award for one year.

Source: "Manager of the Year," at http://www.baseball-almanac.com cited 16 November 2004; "MLB Awards," at http://www.baseball-reference.com cited 16 November 2004.

and NL's Braves, meanwhile, each qualified for the postseason when Cox, as head coach, was the recipient of a manager's award. That occurred for the Blue Jays in 1985 and the Braves in 1991 and 2004. Likewise, in other seasons Cox's Braves teams had successfully won several division titles and in 1995, became the World Series champions by defeating the Indians in six games. Because of their skill and leadership at motivating players beyond expectations, after they retire Torre and Cox will be excellent candidates for being inducted into baseball's Hall of Fame.

Regarding the other four managers with three awards each, the Orioles, led by Earl Weaver won an AL pennant in 1969–1971 and again in 1979. In the seasons when he was not voted as the Manager of the Year, the Orioles won the World Series in 1970 by defeating the Reds in five games and finished runner-up in 1969 to the Mets and in 1971 to the Pirates. For his leadership abilities as a head coach of the Orioles, in 1996 Weaver was elected into the Hall of Fame.

Because their teams had won fewer league titles and appeared in less postseasons than Weaver's did, it means that through 2004 the managerial accomplishments of Baker, Williams and Mauch are less impressive in rank. Since Baker has changed teams by moving from the Giants to coaching the Cubs, there is an opportunity for him to win more division titles and thus, be rewarded as Manager of the Year. Although the Cubs traded their home run hitter Sammy Sosa in early 2005, the club's pitching staff is excellent which is a necessary requirement to be competitive particularly in the postseason. It is likely, therefore, that Baker may manage one or more division-leading Cubs teams at Wrigley Field in Chicago. Since Williams and Mauch have retired, their performances as managers are completed.

With respect to the eight individuals who had each received two awards for being selected as Manager of the Year, the Pirates' Danny Murtaugh and Cardinals' Red Schoendienst had coached teams that appeared in at least two postseasons and won one World Series. Nevertheless, because his teams won NL East division titles in 1970–1971 and 1974–1975, and league championships in 1960 and 1971, Murtaugh was more productive as a manager than Schoendienst. Besides these two individuals, the Pirates' Jim Leyland coached three clubs that conquered contenders in the East division during 1990–1992. But, then his Pirates' teams failed to perform up to expectations against the Reds and Braves in the three NL championship series. Thus, Leyland was out coached by Lou Piniella since his Reds team won the World Series in 1990, as did his Mariners clubs with West division titles in 1995, 1997 and 2001. Meanwhile, Hank Bauer's Orioles triumphed in the 1966 World Series, and likewise did McKeon's Marlins in the 2003 World Series. However, Manager of the Year Bucky Showalter was denied the opportunity for his Yankees to compete in the Series when it was cancelled in 1994, and his 2004 Rangers' team played well but finished three games behind the Anaheim Angels and thus, not qualify for the postseason. In short, Murtaugh's performance ranked moderately to significantly ahead of those of the other seven coaches who were listed in Table 18.2 as two-time award winners.

Between 1937 and 2000, there were 17 managers elected into baseball's Hall of Fame, which is located in Cooperstown, Pennsylvania. For various reasons, these gentlemen are recognized by most observers of the game to be the greatest coaches of professional baseball teams of all time. To illustrate and compare their accomplishments as leaders, Table 18.3 contains some statistics about the managerial performances of this select group of individuals. Based on the sequencing of their induction dates, the managers are listed in the table and discussed according to the year when they entered into the Hall of Fame, that is, from Connie Mack and John McGraw in 1937 to Sparky Anderson in 2000.

Managers in the Hall of Fame

Given the performance information presented in Table 18.3, on average the managers had coached big league baseball teams for approximately 24 seasons. In turn, each manager earned about 1,919 victories in games when their teams played, which amounts to an average winning percentage of .546, and most of them coached championship teams in one or more World Series. As reported in columns three to six of the table, the number of seasons coached and games won ranged from, respectively, 16 and 1,284 for Frank Selee to 53 and 3,731 for Connie Mack; a low winning percentage of .486 for Connie Mack to a high of .615 for Joe McCarthy; and zero World Series championships for Al Lopez, Ned Hanlon and Frank Selee to five for Connie Mack. To further contrast and rank the performances of these outstanding baseball coaches, some specific details are provided about their experiences in the sport.[5]

Admitted into the Hall of Fame because of successfully coaching the Pittsburgh Pirates during the mid–1890s and Philadelphia Athletics between 1901 and 1950, Connie Mack's teams appeared in a total of 7,755 games. Despite finishing eighth in 17 seasons,

TABLE 18.3. MLB MANAGERS IN THE HALL
OF FAME, BY YEAR, 1937–2000

Name	Year*	Seasons	Wins	WPCT	World Series
Connie Mack	1937	53	3731	.486	5
John McGraw	1937	33	2763	.586	3
Wilbert Robinson	1945	19	1399	.500	0
Joe McCarthy	1957	24	2125	.615	7
Bill McKechnie	1962	25	1896	.524	2
Miller Huggins	1964	17	1413	.555	3
Casey Stengel	1966	25	1905	.508	7
Bucky Harris	1975	29	2157	.493	2
Al Lopez	1977	17	1410	.584	0
Rube Foster	1981	NA	NA	NA	NA
Walter Alston	1983	23	2040	.558	4
Leo Durocher	1994	24	2008	.540	1
Earl Weaver	1996	17	1480	.583	1
Ned Hanlon	1996	19	1313	.530	0
Tommy Lasorda	1997	21	1599	.526	2
Frank Selee	1999	16	1284	.598	0
Sparky Anderson	2000	26	2194	.545	3

* Year is the year that the individual was inducted into baseball's Hall of Fame. Seasons are the number of MLB regular seasons the manager served as head coach. Wins, WPCT and World Series are, respectively, the total number of wins, winning percentage and the number of World Series won by each manager's teams. NA means the column is not applicable to that manager. That is, Rube Foster coached in the Negro Baseball League and not in MLB.

Source: "Sports History," at http://www.hickoksports.com cited 7 February 2005; "World Series Championships," at http://www.baseball-almanac.com cited 7 February 2005; "Managerial Wins All-Time Leaders," at http://www.baseball-almanac.com cited 8 February 2005; "Managers," at http://www.baseball-almanac.com cited 7 February 2005.

his Athletics' clubs won nine AL pennants and the World Series in 1910–1911, 1913 and 1929–1930. Besides

Mack, John McGraw also became a coaching legend when he managed the Baltimore Orioles and New York Giants in 4,796 games. His teams proceeded to win nearly six out ten games played and especially those of the Giants, who had finished with ten NL titles and three World Series championships. For their great achievements in the sport, Mack and McGraw are among the most respected managers in baseball's Hall of Fame.

Wilbert Robinson, meanwhile, played seventeen years in the American Association and then managed the Baltimore Orioles in 1902 and the Brooklyn Dodgers for 18 seasons, that is, from 1914 to 1931. He coached in 2,819 games, and his teams won 50 percent of them including NL pennants in 1916 and 1920. After Robinson's contribution to the sport was recognized in 1945, 12 years later Joe McCarthy became the fourth manager to be inducted into the Hall of Fame. McCarthy was honored because in 3,487 games distributed over 24 seasons, his Cubs, Yankees and Red Sox teams on average won nearly 62 percent of their contests and that included nine league titles and seven World Series. Indeed, in 1936–1939, 1941 and 1943 McCarthy's Yankees were the world champions of baseball. For his illustrious record and career as a big league manager, McCarthy must be ranked about equal in leadership and professionalism with Connie Mack and John McGraw.

During the 1960s, Bill McKechnie and then Miller Huggins and Casey Stengel entered baseball's Hall of Fame. In 1915, McKechnie coached the Newark Pepper in the outlaw Federal League, which had disbanded that year, and in 1922–1946, he led various teams of the Pittsburgh Pirates, St. Louis Cardinals, Boston Braves and Cincinnati Reds. His clubs played 3,647 games and in total, won four NL pennants and also a World Series by the Pirates in 1925 and the Reds in 1940. Although Huggins had managed eight fewer seasons than McKechnie, his Yankees' clubs had relatively greater success. That is, they won consecutive NL championships in 1921–1923 and 1926–1928, and the World Series in 1923 and 1927–1928. Because of Yankee sluggers Babe Ruth, Lou Gehrig and Earle Combs, and such pitchers as Waite Hoyt, Herb Pennock and George Pipgras, Huggins' teams succeeded in their quest to be champions. Then, in 1949 Casey Stengel became the coach of the Yankees after three years leading the Brooklyn Dodgers and six years the Boston Braves without a postseason appearance. After 12 of Stengel's Yankees teams won a total of nine AL titles and seven World Series, he left the dynasty and managed the New York Mets from 1962 to 1965. Unfortunately, his Mets' teams finished the four seasons with a win-loss record of 175–404. However, despite that performance with the Mets, Casey Stengel was an outstanding manager who deserves to be a member of professional baseball's Hall of Fame.

For 29 seasons that consisted of 4,408 games, Bucky Harris had managed several MLB teams. These included the Boston Red Sox, Detroit Tigers, New York Yankees and Washington Senators. Although some of Harris' teams performed below average, in 1924 the Senators won a World Series and so did the Yankees in 1947. As a result of his long career in baseball, Harris was inducted in 1975 as the eighth coach into the Hall of Fame. Two years later, Al Lopez gained admission and joined Harris in the Hall of Fame even though his competitive teams never won a World Series. Nevertheless, Lopez had coached the Cleveland Indians for six seasons and White Sox for 11, which amounted to an average winning percentage of .584 in 2,425 games that his teams played. The Indians and White Sox each won an AL championship, that is, the Indians in 1954 with 111 regular season victories and the White Sox in 1959 with 94 wins. However, in the World Series that Cleveland team was defeated in four games by the New York Giants and in 1959, the White Sox lost the Series to the Dodgers in six games. Because he ranks twenty-first in total victories and his teams won nearly 60 percent of their games, Lopez was one of MLB's most productive managers for almost 20 years.

In the 1980s, big league baseball honored Rube Foster and then Walt Alston. Although Foster never coached a MLB team, some historians of the sport still consider him to be the best black pitcher that ever played the game. Indeed, he won more than 50 games in one season and even outperformed the Philadelphia Athletics' great strikeout leader Rube Waddell in a pitching duel. While his reputation as a player continued to improve, in 1910 Foster organized and coached a black team named the Chicago American Giants, which eventually won 11 championships. Ten years later, he founded the Negro National League and successfully managed the Giants until the mid–1920s. When Foster died in 1930, the Negro National League had lost a leader and was forced to terminate its operations. Meanwhile, Walt Alston had succeeded to manage the Brooklyn and Los Angeles Dodgers for a total of 3,658 games in 23 seasons. With an average winning percentage of .558 and 2,040 wins, his teams earned seven NL pennants and four World Series. Alston was a smart and tactical leader of the Dodgers, and well respected by his rivals and loved by baseball fans in southern California. In short, Foster and Alston will forever be recognized as all time great and distinguished managers of professional teams.

Between 1994 and 1999, there were five individuals who became the twelfth to six-teenth managers admitted into baseball's Hall of Fame. Besides the performance statistics cited in Table 18.3, there were other facts that represented their abilities as leaders of teams. To illustrate, Leo Durocher coached his various clubs for a total of 3,739 games, winning three NL pennants and in 1954, a World Series title; Earl Weaver's seventeen Orioles teams played 2,541games and won NL pennants in 1969–1971 and 1979, and a World Series championship in 1970; prior to 1908, Ned Hanlon had managed the Balti-more Orioles and Cincinnati Reds, and also such teams as the Pittsburgh Alleghenys, Pitts-burgh Burghers and Brooklyn Superbas. Because of his leadership, Hanlon's clubs had excelled by finishing first, second or third in the NL between 1894 and 1902; in 3,041 games, Tommy Lasorda's Dodgers achieved 1,599 victories and won eight division titles, four NL pennants and two World Series. For his efforts, Lasorda was voted baseball's Man-ager of the Year in 1983 and 1988; while coaching the Boston Beaneaters for 12 seasons and then the Chicago Cubs in 1902–1905, Frank Selee's teams were the American Asso-ciation champion in 1891 and the NL titlists in 1892–1893 and 1897–1898. Interestingly, the Beaneaters' Kid Nichols pitched his team to at least 30 wins in each of these five sea-sons. Consequently, during the 1990s the Hall of Fame welcomed the induction of tal-ented managers whose last names were Durocher, Weaver, Hanlon, Lasorda and Selee.

When he coached the Cincinnati Reds for nine seasons and Detroit Tigers for 17, which totaled 4,030 games, Sparky Anderson's teams won two AL East and five NL West division titles, one AL and five NL pennants, and three World Series. He was rewarded as the Manager of the Year in 1972, 1975 and 1984, and again in 1987 when the Minnesota Twins beat his Tigers team in the AL championship series. Thus, based on their coach-ing performances, the Atlanta Braves' Bobby Cox and New York Yankees' Joe Torre, and perhaps the St. Louis Cardinals' Tony LaRussa will eventually join Anderson and the other 16 individuals as managers in the Hall of Fame.

Summary

In sum, this chapter analyzed the managerial performances of numerous individu-als. They included three groups, that is, the 30 head coaches of MLB teams during 2004, the recipients of 39 Manager of the Year awards that were presented beginning in 1959, and the 17 coaches who have been inducted into baseball's Hall of Fame from 1937 to 2000. Some statistics and other facts that indicated how well these gentlemen had per-formed, and for what professional teams and in which baseball seasons were researched and incorporated in the columns of one or more tables.

Consequently, the data on performances that was provided in the tables and then discussed reveals the reasons why managing MLB teams is generally an intense, chal-lenging and short-term activity for most coaches, and to some extent, even for such great leaders as Connie Mack, John McGraw and Bucky Harris. Indeed, that information reflects the characteristics, experiences and successes that distinguish superior managers from those who are average and inferior based on their performances while coaching various teams and players in America's professional baseball leagues.

19. Team Dynasties and Leaders Since 1903

During the regular seasons of the American League (AL) and National League (NL) in Major League Baseball (MLB), normally there are a diverse group of superior, average and inferior professional baseball teams. That is, their performances vary each season based on such criteria as winning percentage, games behind the division leader and eligibility to appear in the postseason. The superior teams are very competitive since they usually win more than 60 percent of their regular season games, place first or second in the division and qualify for the playoffs. Generally, these baseball organizations are led by committed owners who are familiar with business activities and involved with team operations, by savvy general managers who initiate, implement and enforce administrative policies, and by coaches who successfully motivate the team's players to perform and excel as a unit throughout the 162-game schedule.

Meanwhile, the average and inferior teams perform at or less than .500 in winning percentage, finish third, fourth, fifth or sixth in their respective divisions, and do not play well enough to participate in the postseason. For one or more seasons, the owners, general managers and coaches of these clubs are less effective and not as efficient or smart as those of the superior teams. However, because of free agency, trades and the injuries to and retirement of players, the majority of AL and NL clubs are unable to consistently rank as superior, average or inferior relative to their peers for many seasons.

To analyze the performances of the superior teams in MLB and for purposes of this chapter, there are two distinct groups of years or eras to be evaluated. Since the 1904 World Series did not occur, the first set of years includes the regular MLB seasons in 1903 and 1905–1968. This period consisted of 65 regular seasons that had each concluded when the top team from the AL and NL ultimately competed to be the champion of baseball by winning a World Series. Indeed, the world and championship series that occurred between teams in the NL and American Association prior to 1903, such as in 1884–1890 and 1892, were considered to be exhibitions by baseball officials and therefore, are excluded herein-after as events.[1]

In 1969, MLB initiated a championship series whereby the two teams with the highest winning percentage played each other for their league's championship, and the AL and NL winners proceeded to meet in a World Series. Nonetheless, this postseason system was reorganized first in 1981 and after 1994 when the highest performing teams who won their divisions, and second after 1998 when those clubs who earned a wild card spot, had to compete in the divisional playoffs and then, in either the AL or NL championship series. The AL and NL champions, of course, finally met in the World Series. In any event, since the 1994 World Series was cancelled because of a players strike, the second era or group of years to evaluate consisted of 35 regular seasons, or 1969–1993 and 1995–2004. In total, 100 years of MLB games are incorporated in Eras I and II.

In previous studies of the sport, several baseball statistics have been used to measure a team's performance for a regular season. For example, there are the club's number of wins and losses, winning percentage, games behind the division's top team, and an index of the players' batting average, earned run average, runs scored, runs batted in and other statistics. For this chapter, however, the number of postseason wins was deemed to be the most relevant aspect of a team's performance. Consequently, the first era consisted of those teams that played in a World Series and won it or finished as the runner up. These results appear in Table 19.1.

Furthermore, the second era included the performances of teams that had qualified for one or more years of postseason appearances because they finished first in their respective division or were selected as a wild card and won a divisional playoff, and perhaps a postseason championship series and a World Series. The teams and their postseason achievements are listed in Table 19.2. So, to identify the best clubs in each of the groups, this chapter primarily focuses on which AL and NL baseball teams had outstanding performances in at least two or more consecutive years, or in an intermittent series of postseasons either during the first era, which was 1903 and 1905–1968 or in the second era, which was 1969–1993 and 1995–2004. In other words, the most successful teams in these eras were superior in performance since they excelled for more than one regular season in the sport.

Era I: 1903 and 1905–1968

Table 19.1 lists the MLB teams that had performed in 65 World Series during Era I. According to the table, the AL teams competed to win 39 or 60 percent of the World Series championships and finished as runner up in 26 or 40 percent. Unquestionably, the dominant MLB team was the Yankees who were champions or finished second in 29 or 44 percent of the 65 World Series.

Besides the Yankees, the AL's Tigers and Athletics appeared in eight Series and the Red Sox in seven. In the NL, the Cardinals performed the best in the world championship games by winning eight or 12 percent of them, while the Giants and then Dodgers and Cubs ended up in second place during 27 or 41 percent of the 65 Series. Given these performances, which of the clubs stood out as being the most successful in Era I? It was, undoubtedly, the New York Yankees.

To be specific, the Yankees played postseason games in three or more consecutive World Series during seven separate groups of years. That is, in 1921–1923, 1926–1928, 1936–1939, 1941–1943, 1950–1953, 1955–1958, and 1960–1964 the Yankee teams were crowned champions in 17 or 65 percent of the 26 Series. The Yankees' championship seasons with the highest and lowest winning percentages were, respectively, in 1936–1939 at .670 and 1955–1958 at .621. Relative to the teams' home attendances, the highest average was 1.79 million spectators per season during 1950–1953. Alternatively, as a result of the

TABLE **19.1.** MLB TEAM PERFORMANCES IN WORLD
SERIES, BY LEAGUE, **1903** AND **1905–1968***

	World Series	
Team	Champion	Second Place
AL		
Boston Pilgrims/Red Sox	5	2
Chicago White Sox	2	2
Cleveland Indians	2	1
Detroit Tigers	3	5
New York Yankees	20	9
Philadelphia/Kansas City/Oakland Athletics	5	3
St. Louis Browns/Baltimore Orioles	1	1
Washington Senators/Minnesota Twins	1	3
NL		
Boston/Milwaukee Braves	2	2
Brooklyn Robins/Dodgers/Los Angeles Dodgers	4	9
Cincinnati Reds	2	2
Chicago Cubs	2	8
New York/San Francisco Giants	5	10
Philadelphia Phillies	0	2
Pittsburgh Pirates	3	2
St. Louis Cardinals	8	4

* There was no World Series in 1904. The previous name changes of teams included the AL Red Sox in 1907, Athletics in 1954 and 1967, Orioles in 1953 and Twins in 1961, and the NL Braves in 1953, Dodgers in 1932 and 1958, and Giants in 1958.
Source: "Postseasons," at http://www.baseball-reference.com cited 1 January 2005.

Great Depression and World War II, the teams' attendances fell to 834,000 per season in 1941–1943. However, despite the large decline in attendances during the late 1930s and early 1940s, the Yankees had excelled as baseball champions. Even so, in 1945 Jacob Ruppert's nieces and friends, who principally owned the franchise, decided to sell their share of the club and Yankee Stadium to a syndicate led by Dan Topping.[2]

Based on the consensus of baseball experts, the Yankee teams that ranked as the greatest of all time, prior to 1969, included those who performed in 1927, 1932, 1936–1939, 1942, 1953 and 1961. These clubs had many players who are considered legends and thus, elected to baseball's Hall of Fame. Indeed, they were famous and charismatic athletes who led their teams to postseason championships, which attracted big crowds to home games played at Yankee Stadium. The 1927 team, for example, demoralized competitors by winning 71 percent of its games before more than 1.1 million spectators in New York City because that club featured such home run hitters as Babe Ruth, Lou Gehrig and Tony Lazzeri in "Murderers' Row"; in 1939, the Yankees overcame early-season obstacles to win 106 games and defeat the NL's Cincinnati Reds 4–0 to win their fourth consecutive World Series; and in 1961, the Yankee team had a stellar defense consisting of shortstop Tony Kubek, infielder Bobby Richardson and catcher Yogi Berra, clever pitchers such as Whitey Ford and Don Larsen, and of course, the home run duo and superstar sluggers Mickey Mantle and Roger Maris. Besides winning the 1958, 1961 and 1962 World Series, that team had also finished second in 1960, 1963 and 1964.

During Era I, the other formidable AL teams that appeared in consecutive, or nearly consecutive World Series, and had formed dynasties were the four-time champion Boston Red Sox in 1912, 1915–1916 and 1918, and the Philadelphia Athletics in 1910–1911 and 1913–1914, and 1929–1931. These Athletics' teams won five World Series and in 1931, the club contained six players, including Al Simmons, Jimmy Foxx and Mickey Cochrane who were inducted in the Hall of Fame and featured three pitchers, that is, Lefty Grove, George Earnshaw and Rube Walberg who had each won 20 or more games. Finally, there were the Detroit Tigers who finished in second place during the 1907–1909 World Series, and finished again as the runner up in 1934 but defeated the Chicago Cubs to be champion in 1935, and the Washington Senators of 1924 and 1925. The Senators defeated the NL's New York Giants 4–3 in the 1924 World Series, but the following season lost the Series to the Pittsburgh Pirates in seven games. Thus, besides the Yankees, these were the leading and most successful AL teams in Era I.[3]

With respect to a sequence or nearly consecutive appearances and victories in the World Series during Era I, the outstanding NL clubs included the Giants in 1911–1913 and 1921–1924, Cardinals in 1942–1944 and 1946, Cubs in 1906–1908, and Dodgers in 1952–1953, 1955–1956, 1963 and 1965–1966. That is, the Giants, Cardinals and Cubs each won two World Series and the Dodgers three. If ranked by performances, the all time great NL teams in the group were the Giants in 1912, Cubs in 1906 and Cardinals in 1942–1944. Each team won at least 68 percent of their games and played competitively in the World Series.

Regarding their best players in those seasons, the Giants' stars included three great pitchers. They were Christy Mathewson, Rube Marquard and Jeff Tesreau. In 1912, Matthewson earned his three-hundredth victory, Marquard recorded 19 consecutive wins and Tesreau led the NL with an earned run average of 1.96. For the Cubs, infielder Frank Chance led the NL in runs and stolen bases and pitchers Mordecal Brown, Jack Pfiester and Jack Taylor each won at least 20 games. While World War II raged throughout Europe during the early 1940s, the Cardinals won two of three World Series because of such hitters Stan Musial, Enos Slaughter and Marty Marion, and pitchers Howie Pollet, Mort Cooper and Johnny Beazley. Interestingly, the Cardinals had become the first team in MLB to win three consecutive pennants with unproven players who had developed their skills in the team's minor league farm system.

Besides these great teams and players, the Dodgers' Sandy Koufax, Don Drysdale and Claude Osteen performed brilliantly as pitchers in a seven-game World Series triumph against the Minnesota Twins in 1965, but less effective in a 4–0 game defeat to the Baltimore Orioles in 1966. Generally, the Dodgers had lost that Series due to weak hitting except for all-stars Ron Fairly and Maury Wills, and former Rookie of the Year Jim Lefebvre. In total, during Era I the Giants, Cubs, Cardinals and Dodgers won 19 or 29 percent of the World Series that were played and finished as runner ups in 31 or 47 percent of those seasons. Lastly, as denoted in Table 19.1, the Braves, Reds, Phillies and Pirates had limited success in the postseasons because, in part, they each lacked the leadership qualities and cohesion that inspired their coaches and/or players to be consistent winners.

There were, however, other memorable AL and NL teams that did not appear in consecutive World Series prior to 1969. For example, the AL's Boston Pilgrims captured the first modern World Series in 1903 by defeating the Pittsburgh Pirates in eight games. During the regular season, the team's pitcher, Cy Young, hurled over three hundred innings and won 28 of the 34 games that he completed. Furthermore, in 1903 Pilgrims' players lead the AL in runs, hits, total bases, home runs and runs batted in. Although the team also finished first in 1904 when Cy Young pitched the century's first perfect game by retiring all 27 Athletics hitters, the postseason was cancelled because New York Giants' owner John T. Brush and manager John McGraw refused to meet the Pilgrims in a World Series. Another renowned AL team was the Cleveland Indians, who lost the World Series in four games to the Giants in 1954. That year, the Indians won 111 games because of its outstanding players. Besides the AL's first black athlete, Larry Doby, Cleveland's players included the league's top hitter Bobby Avila, pitchers Bob Lemon, Early Wynn and Mike Garcia, and sluggers Al Rosen and Vic Wertz.

In the NL, the 1909 Pittsburgh Pirates had a combined 152-game regular season and seven-game postseason winning percentage of .717. That win-loss percentage is the highest of any modern World Series champion. The Pirates pitchers Howie Camnitz and Vic Willis won 47 games and Babe Adams completed three in the World Series against the Detroit Tigers. Moreover, the Pirates best player and Hall of Famer Honus Wagner had led the NL in batting average at .339, total bases at 242 and runs batted in at 100. During the postseason against Detroit, he hit .333, drove in seven runs and stole six bases. Because of Camnitz, Willis, Adams and Wagner, the Tigers lost their third consecutive World Series.

Ten years after the Pirates victory, the Cincinnati Reds triumphed to win its first World Series by beating the Chicago White Sox in eight games. Unfortunately, incriminating evidence was revealed that some Sox players had accepted bribes from gamblers to deliberately lose the Series. As a result, in 1920 eight Chicago players were indicted by a grand jury including star center fielder "Shoeless" Joe Jackson and 20-game winner Ed Cicotte, who had hit the Reds' leadoff batter Morrie Rath with the first pitch during the first game of the 1919 Series. That pitch signaled to bettors that the game would be fixed. One year after being suspended by White Sox owner Charles Comiskey, MLB Commissioner Kenesaw Mountain Landis banned the eight players from baseball for life even though a Chicago jury had cleared them of conspiracy charges. Consequently, that scandal had tainted the Reds' victory and claim to be the world champion of baseball in 1919.

The previous section concludes the discussion of analyzing the superior AL and NL team performances that occurred in Era I, or 1903 and 1905–1968. To indicate, therefore, which clubs won division titles, and those that succeeded in the championship series and/or World Series in Era II, Table 19.2 was developed. It shows the distribution of AL and NL team performances, by league for 35 seasons. As such, the table contains the results to evaluate baseball's dynasties since 1969.

Era II: 1969–1993 and 1995–2004

Table 19.2 is composed of the number of postseason wins for 15 AL and 16 NL clubs. As indicated in column two, there were 14 various AL and 13 different NL teams that appear as division titlists. Also, 11 different AL and NL teams won the championship series, while nine each triumphed in the World Series. Grouped, the AL teams had defeated their opponents in the NL in 20 or 57 percent of the World Series. Less dominate as a team than in Era I, the Yankees played well enough to win 13 of 80 or 16 percent of the AL division titles, ten of 35 or 28 percent of the AL championship series, and six of 35 or 17 percent of the World Series. Relative to the total of 29 titles and series for the Yankees, the Athletics had succeeded to earn 23 postseason wins, the Orioles 15, Twins 11 and the Red Sox, Royals and Blue Jays each nine. In contrast, the Devil Rays failed to win a division title. Meanwhile, the White Sox, Mariners, Devil Rays and Rangers finished their various seasons without an AL championship series, and those four teams plus the

TABLE 19.2. MLB TEAM POSTSEASON PERFORMANCES, BY LEAGUE, 1969–1993, 1995–2004

Team	Postseason Wins		
	Division Title	Championship Series	World Series
AL			
Anaheim Angels	4	1	1
Baltimore Orioles	8	5	2
Boston Red Sox	5	3	1
Chicago White Sox	3	0	0
Cleveland Indians	6	2	0
Detroit Tigers	3	1	1
Kansas City Royals	6	2	1
Milwaukee Brewers	1	1	0
Minnesota Twins	7	2	2
New York Yankees	13	10	6
Oakland Athletics	13	6	4
Seattle Mariners	3	0	0
Tampa Bay Devil Rays	0	0	0
Texas Rangers	3	0	0
Toronto Blue Jays	5	2	2
NL			
Arizona Diamondbacks	3	1	1
Atlanta Braves	15	5	1
Chicago Cubs	3	0	0
Cincinnati Reds	8	5	3
Colorado Rockies	0	0	0
Florida Marlins	0	2	2
Houston Astros	6	0	0
Los Angeles Dodgers	9	5	2
Milwaukee Brewers	0	0	0
Montreal Expos	1	0	0
New York Mets	4	4	2
Philadelphia Phillies	6	3	1
Pittsburgh Pirates	9	2	2
San Diego Padres	3	2	0
San Francisco Giants	6	2	0
St. Louis Cardinals	7	4	1

Note: There was no postseason in 1994. The Milwaukee Brewers was in the AL from 1970 to 1997 and then the NL since 1998. The Championship Series and World Series columns include teams that qualified for the postseason as a wild card. The AL wild cards that appeared in the division playoffs included the Red Sox in 1999, 2003 and 2004, Mariners in 2000 and Angels in 2002. In the NL, theses clubs were the Marlins in 1997 and 2003, Mets in 1999 and 2000, Giants in 2002 and Astros in 2004.

Source: "Postseasons," at http://www.baseball-reference.com cited 1 January 2005.

Indians and Brewers did not achieve a final victory in a World Series during Era II. Although the large-market White Sox won the 1906 and 1917 World Series, the club lost the championship in 1959 to the Dodgers in six games. Then, the Sox were defeated in the AL series by the Orioles in 1983 and Blue Jays in 1993, and in the divisional playoffs by the Mariners in 2000. Consequently, the Yankees and Athletics each had the most, and Devil Rays and Brewers the fewest, postseason wins during Era II.

In the NL, a variety of teams excelled to achieve impressive postseason wins. The Braves won the largest number of division titles at 15 of 80 or 18 percent of them, and the Braves, Reds and Dodgers combined to win 15 of 35 or 42 percent of the championship series. Relative to the total ten victories by the Yankees and Athletics in the World Series during Era II, the Reds finished first in three or 8 percent of the Series and four other NL teams each won two or 22 percent of them. Unfortunately, during Era II the Rockies, Marlins and Brewers did win a division title since joining the NL. However, the Denver-based Rockies appeared as a wild card in 1995, as did the Miami-based Marlins in 1997 and 2003, which resulted in two World Series championships.

Furthermore, after their only postseason appearance for winning a division in the 1981 regular season, the Expos lost to the Dodgers in five games for the NL championship. Based on the results of NL teams during the postseasons of Era II, the most successful clubs and their number of wins included the Braves at twenty-one, Reds and Dodgers at 16 and Pirates 13. Besides the Rockies and Brewers, who each won zero division titles, the other disappointing clubs were the Expos at one and Cubs at three. Therefore, given the numbers in Table 19.2, the six highest-performing MLB teams since 1969 have been the Yankees, Athletics, Braves, Reds and Dodgers, and Orioles.

To identify the groups of teams that played in postseasons and appeared in the World Series during at least two, or approximately two consecutive seasons in Era II, there were four clubs in the AL and three in the NL. Listed next in no specific order, the former four teams consisted of the Orioles in 1969–1971, Athletics in 1972–1974 and 1988–1990, Yankees in 1976–1978 and 1998–2001, and the Blue Jays in 1992–1993. The latter three included the Reds in 1970, 1972 and 1975–1976, Braves in 1991–1992 and 1995–1996, and Dodgers in 1977–1978. Unexpectedly, during the 35 years of Era II there were only two more teams, and significantly, less concentration of them that had played in the World Series than in the 65 years of Era I. This occurred, in part, because of free agency, expansion of the AL and NL, and the recruitment and inflow of an increasing number of foreign baseball players into the big leagues from several Central and Latin American countries.

Since 1969, the two most successful groups of AL teams were the Yankees in 1998–2001 and Athletics in 1972–1974. Because the average winning percentage and home attendance of these four Yankee teams were respectively, .610 and 3.17 million, they performed each season in a World Series and won three of them. The club's star players included sluggers Bernie Williams, Derek Jeter and Paul O'Neill, and pitchers Mariano Rivera, Roger Clemens and Andy Pettitte. In fact, without a superstar in 1998, the Yankees' entire roster played consistent and excellent baseball, which helped them establish an AL record by winning 114 regular season games. Alternatively, in 1972–1974 the Athletics' teams won about 58 percent of their games and three consecutive World Series. Besides home run hitter Reggie Jackson, these teams featured such great pitchers as Catfish Hunter, Vida Blue and Rollie Fingers. In short, these were the best of the team groups in Era II.

In the AL, the Orioles and Blue Jays also had teams that appeared in consecutive

World Series. The Orioles, in 1969–1971, defeated their opponents in approximately 66 percent of their regular season games primarily because of the teams' great pitchers. As such, they had the skills to win 20 or more games in nearly each of the three seasons. With a mixture of fastballs, curveballs and changeups, these Oriole pitchers were Jim Palmer, Mike Cuellar, Dave McNally and Pat Dobson. As a result, the three teams finished consecutive seasons with 109, 108 and 101 victories. Indeed, the Orioles had combined outstanding pitching with an alert defense to win each of their AL championship series by an identical 3–0 advantage.

The Blue Jays, meanwhile, became World Series winners in 1992 when they defeated the Braves in seven games, and in 1993 the Phillies in six games. At the SkyDome in Toronto, the Blue Jays had attracted more than four million spectators in each of the two regular seasons. As Joe Carter and Dave Winfield hit numerous home runs to discourage the opposing teams, Paul Molitor and Roberto Alomar hit for a high average and Jack Morris and Jimmy Key fooled hitters with off-speed pitches. Other than the successful championship series and World Series in 1992 and 1993, the Blue Jays did not win the AL playoffs in 1985, 1989 and 1991 even though the club had finished first in its division, which included the powerful Yankees and Red Sox. Apparently, during 1992 and 1993 the Canadian-based team performed beyond expectations and had its two best seasons ever. Nevertheless, after ten seasons of dismal performances, in early 2005 the Blue Jays owner Rogers Communications decided to revive his club by renaming the SkyDome to be the Rogers Centre, installing Field Turf in the ballpark, and committing to increase the club's payroll from $50 million to $70 million per year in 2005–2007.[4]

During Era II, there were a few AL teams that excelled for one season and then became a mediocre or inferior performer. In other words, these clubs were temporarily superior in performances because of winning a World Series, but failed to sustain that greatness to be identified forever as a dynasty. Three of the clubs included the Tigers in 1984, Royals in 1985 and Twins in 1987. Relative to each team's success, the Tigers refused to accept defeat in games against their opponents and thus, became the third club ever to spend an entire season leading the AL. After 104 wins in the regular season, the Tigers defeated the Royals 3–0 for the championship and then the NL Padres 4–1 in the World Series. The AL's Most Valuable Player and Cy Young Award recipient Willie Hernandez, pitcher Jack Morris and sluggers Alan Trammell and Kurt Gibson starred for the Tigers who were coached by Manager of the Year Sparky Anderson. Sparky also had won the award in 1972 and 1975 for his leadership of the Cincinnati Reds.

After the Royals lost the championship to the Tigers in 1984, one year later the team finished first in the West Division by one game, defeated the Blue Jays in a seven-game playoff, and then beat the Cardinals in seven games to claim the World Series title. Pitchers Bret Saberhagen and Dan Quisenberry, and batters George Brett and Willie Wilson excelled as the Royals' best players that season. Regarding the Twins, in 1986 the club finished 21 games behind the Angels in the West Division. Nonetheless, because of such key hitters as Kirby Puckett and Gary Gaetti, and strike out pitchers Frank Viola and Bert Blyleven, in 1987 the Twins defeated an excellent Cardinals team in seven games to win its first World Series.

During Era II in the NL, it was the Reds in the mid–1970s, Dodgers in the late 1970s, and Braves in the mid–1990s that appeared in consecutive World Series. With a combination of power and speed, in 1975 and 1976 Cincinnati's "Big Red Machine" won the West Division by at least ten games, and respectively, swept the Pirates and then Phillies in the

NL championship series, and outperformed the Red Sox and Yankees in the World Series. Indeed, the Reds had such superstars as George Foster, Pete Rose, Johnny Bench, Joe Morgan, Dave Concepcion and Tony Perez to hit for power, steal second and third base at every opportunity, and score runs.

When the Reds' performances declined in the 1977 and 1978 regular seasons, the Dodgers became the best team in the NL. Although the Yankees had played well enough to win consecutive World Series, the Dodgers' played competitively by fielding an outstanding defense and using an excellent pitching staff. In fact, the Yankees required six games to conquer the Dodgers in each World Series. The Dodgers' best players included pitchers Tommy John and Don Sutton, slugger Steve Garvey, and clutch hitter Dusty Baker, who had successfully coached the San Francisco Giants in the 1990s and early 2000s.

Following the Reds' and Dodgers' successful performances of the 1970s, the Braves unquestionably dominated the NL during the 1990s. That is, the team won five division titles and championships, and in 1995, the World Series. Pitchers Greg Maddux, Tom Glavine and John Smoltz had joined with power hitters Fred McGriff, Chipper Jones and Javy Lopez to keep the Braves competitive in about every regular season and postseason game the team had played. Maddux, for example, won the Cy Young Award in 1992–1995, Glavine in 1991 and 1998, and Smoltz in 1996, while McGriff or Jones usually batted in 100 runs per season. Likewise, the Braves' Bobby Cox earned Manager of the Year in 1991 and received nearly enough votes for the award in other years. Even so, because of the departure of Maddux, Glavine, McGriff and Lopez, the Braves will struggle to win another World Series. Furthermore, the Reds last won their division in 1995 and the Dodgers did not compete in a championship series between 1989 and 2004. In short, if the strong teams continue to diminish in performances, then the future dynasties in MLB may be other AL and NL teams such as, respectively, the Angels, Indians and Rangers, and the Astros, Giants and Padres.[5]

Summary

Since the early 1900s, there have been several successful AL and NL teams that appeared in and won two or more consecutive, or nearly consecutive World Series. This chapter identifies these teams and discusses their achievements during Era I, which was 1903 and 1905–1968, and Era II or 1969–1993 and 1995–2004. With respect to Era I, there is a table that lists the number of World Series that each team appeared in and the results. For Era II, another table depicts which teams had won division titles, championship series and the World Series.

Besides an analysis of the information displayed in the tables, this chapter contains some of the teams' average winning percentages and home attendances, and highlights the players who had excelled for these clubs on offense as batters and on defense as pitchers, catchers, infielders and outfielders. Indeed, the majority of outstanding teams in Eras I and II were comprised of at least one or two superstars. As a group, these athletes and their teammates played heads-up defense and produced a sufficient number of runs for their teams to win the majority of regular season games and qualify for the postseason competition.

Even though a number of AL and NL teams had the best performances during various years of the twentieth century and early 2000s, other clubs may dominate their divisions in the future because of free agency, expansion and the import of foreign players. Indeed, if the current and prospective owners of mid-level and inferior franchises provide leadership and an opportunity to be successful by spending more money for free agent players and outstanding general managers and coaches, and by committing the resources necessary to establish a fan base in their local communities, then their baseball teams may perform beyond expectations and compete in more than one season to win a title and championship, and the World Series.

20. Expansion Teams in the Major Leagues

For various demographic, economic and business reasons, the number of franchises in the National League of Professional Baseball Clubs (NL) fluctuated for 16 years, that is, from when the organization had formed at the Grand Central Hotel in New York City in 1876 to 1892. To illustrate, teams in Philadelphia and New York were expelled from the NL because they refused to make road trips to Chicago and St. Louis but decided, however, to play non-league games in their home cities; a Louisville team was banished from the league when four of its players cheated and threw the pennant to gamblers; the operator of the Cincinnati club sold beer at Sunday games and the team was then expelled; and, teams in Syracuse and Cleveland dropped out of the league while those in Brooklyn, Pittsburgh and St. Louis joined the NL. Finally, in 1900 the league eliminated weak franchises in Baltimore, Cleveland, Louisville and Washington, D.C. As a result, in 1901 the NL consisted of eight teams with one each located in Boston, Brooklyn, Chicago, Cincinnati, New York, Philadelphia, Pittsburgh and St. Louis that would remain intact until expansion occurred in the early 1960s.[1]

In 1901 Ban Johnson, who with Charles Comiskey operated the Western League, renamed it the American League (AL) and proclaimed that group to be a "major league" of professional baseball clubs. Similar to the NL, the AL also contained eight teams until expansion began during the early 1960s. Those AL competitors were located in Baltimore, Boston, Chicago, Cleveland, Detroit, Philadelphia, St. Louis and Washington, D.C. Thus, Major League Baseball (MLB) consisted of 16 franchises from 1901 to 1961.[2]

Business of Expansion

Other than attracting an existing team that is relocating, such as the NL's Montreal Expos, cities like Norfolk in Virginia, Las Vegas in Nevada and Portland in Oregon may each seek to become a home site of a professional baseball club when MLB owners vote as a group, and in the majority, decide to expand the league's members by adding one or more new franchises before the next regular season begins. Indeed, expansion is a legitimate but costly way for a city to obtain a MLB team.

For a prospective city to qualify for and bid on a new MLB franchise, the league's decision makers likely consider and evaluate several factors. Listed in no specific order or priority, these factors are reported as follows. First, the population, population density and growth of the host city and metropolitan area reflect the local market's fan base and its potential demand for professional baseball. Second, the city and municipality's per capita and disposable income levels represent the purchasing power and affordability of consumers to attend sports entertainment events and participate in other leisure activities. Third, the number and quality of professional and amateur sports teams in the host city denote alternative options for consumers as fans to spend their after-tax incomes. Fourth, a local owner with sufficient operating capital and wealth or an ownership group that has access to funds and capital loans is an important advantage for a city in applying to the league for an expansion franchise.[3]

Fifth, the city must be home to an existing or new stadium that has a location, capacity and amenities to support and sustain a major league baseball team. Sixth, the infrastructure of the area surrounding the stadium should be satisfactory with respect to accessibility to roads and traffic lanes particularly before and after regular season home games. Seventh, if the stadium is not domed, then the city's and area's climate and average temperature during April to October are also important for the league to evaluate. Eighth, cities with successful minor-league baseball teams or, are the former sites of major league baseball clubs, are other facts to be included in the decision process. In short, these are eight factors that, relatively and in total, determine which city or cities are the best places to be awarded an expansion franchise by MLB.

By the early 1960s, it had become apparent to MLB's franchise owners that there was excess demand for professional baseball from sports fans located in North America. As such, several U.S. and at least two major Canadian cities were attractive sites to host a MLB expansion team or to relocate an existing club. Besides that observation, some sports officials also viewed these cities as potential home sites for teams in other U.S. professional baseball leagues, and perhaps for relocating and expansion franchises in the National Football League, National Basketball Association and National Hockey League, which were each based in America. With respect to the economic effects between member franchises in MLB, the entry of an expansion team into a city requires that the new team owner or owners must pay millions of dollars in fees to the current baseball club owners. These cash flows, and the growth and development of local, national and international television and radio markets after the 1950s meant more revenues would be earned by the existing teams in the league. Consequently, this money provided an economic incentive for MLB to experiment by expanding its membership, beginning in the early 1960s, and introducing the sport to fans that resided in various cities and regions of North America.

Given the strong business reasons for MLB to expand in the early 1960s, it had nonetheless been a concern of baseball's commissioners and other league officials that as the number of clubs increased, the quality of teams, games and such tournaments as the division playoffs would decline since there was a limited supply of skilled baseball players to draft and sign contracts with from America's high schools, colleges and universities. This problem was alleviated after the 1960s, in part, because the MLB clubs increasingly scouted, recruited, trained and employed talented players from several Latin and South American countries like the Dominican Republic, Mexico, Panama, Puerto Rico and Venezuela, and then sought players from Japan, Korea and the Philippines. In fact, during the 2004 season international players comprised about 30 percent of the active rosters of MLB teams and 45 percent of minor league clubs.[4]

Besides issues about expansion diluting the quality of teams, games and the playoffs, after a few years current franchise owners must totally share the league's television revenues from national and international broadcasts, and a portion of league-wide merchandise and equipment sales with more teams including the expansion club. For some teams in such small markets as the NL Pirates in Pittsburgh and Brewers in Milwaukee, and the AL Athletics in Oakland and Devil Rays in Tampa Bay, the amounts shared total to millions of dollars that are not available to invest in their player development programs and other critical needs. Therefore, as a result of expansion the low payroll, small market team owners forego proportionately more of their revenues to the expansion team than do the owners of the high payroll, large market teams that have home ballparks in Chicago, Los Angles and New York.

Between the early 1960s and 2000s, there were other aspects of expansion that directly impacted or indirectly influenced the operations of MLB and its specific teams, and the Major League Baseball Players Association (MLBPA) and image of the sport. These include the revision of regular season schedules, number and date of interleague games, realignment of divisions, team rivalries, home and away attendances, antitrust laws, teams' tax policies and ticket prices, and the financial appreciation of franchises. Several of these topics have been thoroughly studied and analyzed in books and articles penned by sports economists like Roger G. Noll, James Quirk, Rodney D. Fort, Andrew Zimbalist, Benjamin A. Okner, Gerald W. Scully, Ira Horowitz, Lance E. Davis and Steven R. Rivkin. To learn more about these topics and their relationship to expansion in MLB, see the endnotes of this chapter and the book's Bibliography.[5]

In the next section of paragraphs, there are two tables of statistics that identify and present some characteristics and facts about, and measurements of, the post–1960 expansion teams in MLB. These tables, in turn, establish a basis for a discussion with respect to the demographics, performances, attendances and other matters that are related to the business operations of the teams. As such, the research reveals, in part, how visionary and effective the league's commissioners and other leaders have been in structuring, managing, controlling and operating various franchises in MLB that were established from the early 1960s to the late 1990s.

MLB Expansion Teams

Based on the expansion year, Table 20.1 lists the home markets of 14 MLB expansion teams as represented by three numerical characteristics of their Standard Metropolitan Statistical Areas (SMSAs). These measurements, as described in the table's note, are the SMSAs' total population, per capita personal income and percentage growth in population. With this demographic data, it is interesting to analyze why one or more of the markets in Table 20.1 were selected as sites with respect to these AL and NL expansion franchises.[6]

First, the data indicates that the 14 SMSA's hosting expansion teams were either medium-sized to large in population and/or experienced above average population growth. Second, except for the Dodgers in Los Angeles and Yankees in New York, there were no other MLB teams located in the remaining 12 SMSAs. Third, big league ballparks existed in the metropolitan areas or new stadiums were being constructed for expansion teams. Fourth, the respective individuals or groups that successfully bided for an expansion team convinced MLB that their sites had a strong fan base and commitments from local businesses to support a major league baseball club.

Table 20.1. AL and NL Expansion Franchises
and Area Demographic Data, by Year

Year	Franchise	Population*	Income	%Growth
AL				
1961	Los Angeles	6.8	3,050	16.6
1961	Washington	2.1	2,969	38.8
1969	Kansas City	1.2	4,133	14.9
1969	Seattle	1.4	4,339	28.7
1977	Seattle	2.0	9,172	12.8
1977	Toronto	2.7	—	14.0
1998	Tampa Bay	2.3	27,224	15.9
NL				
1962	Houston	1.4	2,411	39.8
1962	New York	10.9	3,424	4.5
1969	Montreal	2.1	—	30.0
1969	San Diego	1.3	3,884	31.4
1993	Colorado	2.1	23,363	30.4
1993	Florida	3.3	21,108	21.4
1998	Arizona	2.9	26,686	45.3

* Population is the total population in millions in the SMSA for the expansion year. Income and %Growth are, respectively, the per capita personal income in thousands of dollars in the expansion year, and the percentage growth of the SMSA population during the decade of expansion. The sources do not provide Income for Toronto and Montreal, Canada. Specifically, the Colorado Rockies are based in Denver, Florida Marlins in Miami and Arizona Diamondbacks in Phoenix.

Source: See various editions of *The World Almanac and Book of Facts, Statistical Abstract of the United States, Survey of Current Business* and *Census of the Population*; Frank P. Jozsa, Jr., and John J. Guthrie, Jr., *Relocating Teams and Expanding Leagues in Professional Sports: How the Major Leagues Respond to Market Conditions* (Westport, CT: Quorum Books, 1999), 46, 49.

Besides providing three characteristics of their SMSAs in Table 20.1, it is also useful to measure and highlight the success of each expansion franchise. To this end, Table 20.2 lists the average winning percentages and home attendances of the expansion teams for two groups of seasons. As a result of this data, the AL and NL teams' management and leadership efforts are exposed and contrasted relative to five and ten seasons effective the expansion year. The following is an analysis of Table 20.2.

First, the average win-loss percentages for the AL and NL teams in five and ten seasons were, respectively, .409 and .454, and .433 and .438. Based on these seasons and averages, the highest performing teams consisted of the AL Royals in Kansas City and NL Diamondbacks in Phoenix, Arizona and Rockies in Denver, Colorado. Alternatively, the AL Bluejays in Toronto and Mariners in Seattle, and NL Mets in New York and Padres in San Diego produced the lowest performances per league. Furthermore, some calculations of the numbers revealed that after five seasons the average performances of eight teams improved, two declined — NL Marlins in Miami, Florida and Rockies in Denver — and one remained at .470, that is, the Angels in Los Angeles, California who moved to Orange County in 1965 and was renamed the California Angels.

In short, these percentages indicate that the large majority of expansion teams had improved their performances between five and ten seasons, especially the Bluejays and Mets. As an aside, from five to seven seasons following expansion the average winning

TABLE 20.2 AL AND NL EXPANSION FRANCHISES
SELECTED DATA, BY SEASONS, BY YEAR

Year	Franchise	*Performance**		*Attendance*	
		Five Seasons	Ten Seasons	Five Seasons	Ten Seasons
AL					
1961	Los Angeles	.470	.470	779	947
1961	Washington	.380	.420	604	726
1969	Kansas City	.480	.520	911	1,267
1969	Seattle	.395	—	678	—
1977	Seattle	.390	.410	906	944
1977	Toronto	.360	.450	1,369	1,708
1998	Tampa Bay	.393	—	1,583	—
NL					
1962	Houston	.410	.440	1,278	1,301
1962	New York	.320	.410	1,487	1,792
1969	Montreal	.430	.440	1,263	1,147
1969	San Diego	.370	.410	594	983
1993	Colorado	.485	.475	3,786	3,539
1993	Florida	.473	.454	2,162	1,892
1998	Arizona	.543	—	3,097	—

* Performance and Attendance are, respectively, the five- and ten-year averages of win-loss percentages, and the regular season home attendances of the teams expressed in hundreds of thousands. The — indicates that the data is not applicable or available.

Source: See "Team Sites," at http://www.mlb.com cited 20 December 2004.

percentages of the Devil Rays in Tampa Bay moderately rose from .393 to .399 and the Diamondbacks in Phoenix fell from .543 to .506. These results occurred for these clubs because the Devil Rays replaced some unproductive players and coaching staff while the Diamondbacks' star pitcher Randy Johnson joined the New York Yankees and other key players experienced injuries.

Table 20.2 also presents the expansion teams' average home attendances for five and ten seasons. With respect to teams in the AL and then NL, it was the Devil Rays at Tropicana Field and Bluejays at the SkyDome, and the Rockies at Coors Field and Diamondbacks at Banc One Stadium that attracted the greatest number of spectators to their home games during the initial five seasons. When the AL and NL teams are grouped and evaluated, for ten seasons the average attendances were highest for the Rockies and then the Marlins, Mets and Bluejays, and lowest for the Senators in Washington, D.C. and then the Padres in San Diego, and Angels and Mariners in their respective ballparks. In other words, when the winning percentages of seven teams increased from five to ten seasons, so did their home attendances. However, when the win-loss percentage rose for the Expos in Montreal, their average attendance decreased. In contrast, the average performances and attendances of the Rockies and Marlins each fell from their fifth to tenth season. Finally, from the fifth through seventh seasons following expansion the Devil Rays and Diamondbacks each attracted fewer fans at their home ballparks. It appears that these clubs were victims of the honeymoon effect because of the drop in home attendances after five seasons.

In sum, the data in Table 20.2 denotes that the expansion teams' performances and home attendances are positive and highly correlated. Moreover, there was a small and direct association between a marginal decline in average performances and attendances as experienced by the Rockies, and a larger association by the Marlins. The Angels, meanwhile, drew more spectators to its home games from the fifth to tenth season despite no change in winning percentages, and the Expos played slightly better yet the team's attendances declined by 3 percent at Olympic Stadium in Montreal. Interestingly, significant improvements in winning percentages and attendances were realized especially by the small-market Royals in Kansas City, Kansas and Padres in San Diego, California.

In Chapter 5 of *Relocating Teams and Expanding Leagues*, authors Frank P. Jozsa, Jr. and John J. Guthrie, Jr. compared a total of ten MLB expansion franchises to each other and then ranked them as superior, average or inferior based on points awarded for best to worst on three criteria. These criteria were the teams' average winning percentage, which measured their performance, and also average home attendance and the estimated value of each franchise. Given the criteria and type of data collected, each team was assigned a rank of superior, average or inferior for the 1990–1997 seasons inclusive. Since the Tampa Bay Devil Rays and Arizona Diamondbacks initially entered MLB to compete during the 1998 season, they were not included in Table 5.2 of Chapter 5.[7]

After awarding points and totaling them for each criteria, the teams were ranked as follows: Colorado Rockies, Toronto Bluejays and Seattle Mariners as superior; New York Mets, Florida Marlins, Houston Astros and Anaheim (formerly Los Angeles and California) Angels as average; and the Montreal Expos, Kansas City Royals and San Diego Padres as inferior. If the clubs' performances, attendances and values were extended from the late 1990s through early 2000s, the listing of teams would include as superior in rank the Mariners, Astros and Angels, as average in rank the Rockies, Bluejays and Mets, and as inferior in rank the Marlins, Expos, Royals and Padres. These results are apparent because some teams such as the Astros and Angels have improved their performances and home attendances since the late 1990s, others like the Rockies and Bluejays have attendance problems and played poorly, while the Marlins, Royals and Padres struggle each season to maintain their competitiveness and estimated values as small-market teams. In 2004–2005, the Expos relocated from Montreal and was renamed the Nationals playing in Washington, D.C. It is anticipated that within three to six years the Nationals will likely increase in rank to average because of the revenues from a new ballpark, an increase in home attendances from the honeymoon effect, and appreciation in market value. It is indeterminate, however, whether the performances of the former expansion team from Montreal will improve at its new site in the nation's capital city.[8]

The final topic discussed in this chapter is the antithesis of expansion, that is, a reduction in the current number of franchises in America's elite professional baseball league.

Contraction of Teams by MLB

Rather than discuss the economic and social benefits, costs and risks of expansion, during the late 1990s to early 2000s there were numerous media reports that Commissioner Bud Selig and the league's franchise owners had seriously threatened to reduce the number of teams in MLB by elimination and/or merger. As it evolved, contraction became the term used by baseball officials, reporters and commentators to describe this strategy. To highlight the concept of contraction, in 1999 the San Diego Padres President Larry Lucchino called eliminating some franchises "a very appropriate subject of debate" and

Texas Rangers owner Thomas O. Hicks said that "over half, certainly of the 30 team owners are genuinely interested in downsizing." At that time, some prominent newspaper and magazine articles mentioned that if such teams as the Oakland Athletics, Montreal Expos, Kansas City Royals and Minnesota Twins were consolidated to form three or even two clubs, the remaining 27 or 28 franchises would benefit because of greater revenues and also, as a result of less subsidies to be shared with the poorest teams whose operations would be combined.[9]

During late 2001, MLB owners voted and overwhelmingly authorized commissioner Selig to eliminate two teams before the 2002 season. The vote particularly irritated the MLBPA's Executive Director Donald Fehr since the league's authorization to Selig was announced only hours before baseball's collective bargaining agreement had expired. Remarked Fehr, "We consider this action to be inconsistent with the law, our contract, and perhaps most important, the long term welfare of the sport." In response to Fehr's concerns, the commissioner said, "Is this a tacit admission that something is fundamentally wrong with baseball? Absolutely not, it shows we're willing to address our problems. It shows a willingness to do what we have to do." Based on these statements, it seemed likely that Fehr and Selig were establishing bargaining positions for their respective constituencies with respect to the possibility of contraction by the team owners.[10]

In the early 2000s, some sports reporters suggested that some cities including Charlotte in North Carolina, Las Vegas in Nevada, Orlando in Florida, Portland in Oregon, and Monterrey, Mexico and Mexico City had a sizable local population and wealthy households, corporate financial support, and the political leadership to be attractive relocation sites for existing MLB teams that struggle for revenues in their small markets. The other option put forth by these reporters, therefore, was for MLB to eliminate at least two teams. In turn, this strategy would remove the 50 worst players on active rosters and avoid the constant whining of team owners about the unequal division of baseball's billions of dollars in revenues between the high- and low-payroll franchises. As Wall Street columnist Stefan Fatsis put it, "Major League Baseball's plan to eliminate two teams has less to do with general economic malaise than with that sport's business model and operations: no cost control, not enough revenue sharing. Regardless, the issue of killing off or moving weak teams will dominate the sports conversation for a long time to come."[11]

Based on the literature, there are a few but significant disadvantages to contraction. First, some baseball fans and sports experts may view that abandoning markets in Oakland, Miami, Minneapolis and of course, Montreal, as a negative attitude by and defeat for MLB from business and global perspectives; second, the league and/or current owners must pay the market price when they buyout the franchises to be eliminated and that transaction would possibly cost hundreds of millions of dollars; third, consolidation is not a long-term solution that will narrow the gap in the amounts teams collect in local revenues from broadcasting games and other baseball programs; fourth, eliminating teams is bad public relations and not an equitable or efficient solution for baseball fans who reside in the communities that lose their franchises; and fifth, in the cities and metropolitan areas that forego teams there may be lawsuits filed by the franchise owners, by local and regional government units that funded, built and owned baseball stadiums, and by those local businesses that are economically damaged when the team abandons the city and area.[12]

Consequently, MLB's decision to eliminate one or more weak clubs may trigger Congressional hearings and a furious and partisan political debate about deleting or restricting baseball's antitrust exemption. Indeed, the former and now deceased Senator Paul Wellstone of Minnesota introduced the Fairness in Antitrust in National Sports (FANS) Act of 2001 in Congress. Although not approved, the Act's purpose is to amend the Clayton Act and make the antitrust laws, which were created by a Supreme Court decision in 1922, applicable to the elimination or relocation of MLB franchises. After the Act was introduced, lawyers for players and owners agreed that the union's grievances to save two teams would be heard. Thus, because of the potential political and social risks and economic costs of contracting one or more teams, it appears that MLB will likely implement other strategies such as an increase in revenue sharing and/or the luxury tax to keep the small-market franchises in operation after 2004–2005.[13]

Summary

This chapter focused on and discussed the expansion of teams in MLB from the early 1960s to the late 1990s. After the business reasons and advantages for expansion were presented, two tables provided some demographic characteristics and performance statistics, respectively, about the fourteen new professional baseball franchises. Besides expansion, the league's strategy of eliminating teams or contraction was also analyzed. In sum, there is no doubt that expansion and contraction of teams in MLB will be an important topic to be evaluated between Commissioner Bud Selig, franchise owners and the MLBPA after 2004.

V. SPORTS MARKETING

21. The Business of Marketing a League

According to author and professor Matthew D. Shank, "sports marketing is the specific application of marketing principles and processes to sport products and to the marketing of nonsports products through association with sport." Shank's statement means, in part, that Major League Baseball (MLB) officials and the decision makers of the league's 14 American League (AL) and 16 National League (NL) teams are compelled to design, develop and implement a marketing strategy for their respective organizations. These strategies, in turn, are expected to include four specific and interdependent marketing mix variables. That is, the product and price, place or distribution, and promotion.[1]

Some examples of each variable are first, as baseball products are the scheduling of regular season home games and the performances of the clubs' players; second, as prices are the admission costs paid by spectators and groups to attend home games and the distributions of current players' salaries; third, as places are the expansion of the teams' television programming networks into foreign markets and the ballparks' cities and sites; and fourth, as promotions are the advertising and public relations efforts of MLB and the sponsorships of teams. In short, the league and each team must devise, establish and apply a mix of variables in order to attract, inform and entertain sports fans, to differentiate their brands, and to penetrate local, regional, national and international baseball markets.

Except for adults who follow more than one sport and have annual household incomes between $35,000 and $50,000, and excluding individuals aged 59 and over, since the mid–1980s baseball has been gradually declining as the favorite sport of Americans in the other income levels and age groups. Despite this evidence, in 2004 MLB adopted an ambitious branding campaign and the majority of the league's teams initiated numerous commercial and social programs and promotions that were moderately successful in communicating with and reaching their target markets. As a result of these efforts, that year the sport's short-term radio and television ratings stabilized, more box scores and feature stories about teams, coaches, players and games appeared in local newspapers, baseball interviews were frequently reported on the Entertainment Sports and Programming Network (ESPN), most teams' ballpark sales increased, and finally, there was a record number of sponsorships, partnerships and licensing deals concluded between the league and clubs, and small, medium and large nonsports businesses. Furthermore, the 2004 regular season games, playoffs and World Series of MLB were broadcasted on the Internet and satellite television to millions of fans in more than 170 nations across the world.[2]

Based on this exposure, since the early-to-mid-1990s the marketing concepts, mixes and strategies of the league as an organization, and the league's teams have become more culturally relevant and increasingly connected to U.S. and international sports fans. Indeed, this growth in the sport's potential is identified and discussed in the other chapters of Part V, and especially with respect to the league's and teams' innovations and activities regarding brands, pricing and programming, and sponsorships, partnerships and licensing.

There are numerous and controversial issues, and well-known and current topics in sports marketing. Obviously, each of them cannot be analyzed in this and the previous and following readings. However, to an extent some baseball products, prices, places and promotions were likely referenced, alluded to and/or briefly mentioned in Parts I–IV of this book. It is necessary and prudent, therefore, to reveal and focus in this chapter on a few significant marketing concepts, strategies and programs that MLB and/or the league's teams have incorporated in their plans and operations as for-profit organizations competing in the sports entertainment business. Consequently, the following pages represent what the research has revealed to be important for introducing the business of marketing baseball, MLB and the operations of one or more teams to current and potential fans and students of the sport.

Baseball Products

As defined, a sports product is a good, service, or any combination of these goods and services that provide tangible or intangible economic, financial and/or social benefits to consumers, spectators and sponsors. There are special marketing features and contents of products that involve their design, life cycle, line extension and pricing, mix and pricing strategy, and quality. Relative to professional baseball, a few examples of products are each team's 162-game regular season game schedule, interleague play, the AL and NL wild card and playoff systems, and MLB's World Series that in 1903 and since 1905 was played between the AL and NL pennant winners. Because they are preplanned and form the core structure of the sport, these events are arranged and performed at ballparks each year by clubs with different logos and brands, and unique names, uniforms and rosters.

Because of such factors as location, tradition and luck, during the regular season there are longstanding rivalries between some teams in a few but not all of the divisions of the AL and NL. This competition generates an interest in games, attracts spectators to the ballparks, and produces more exposure and revenue for the respective teams. For example, there are intense pressures for players to excel and expectations to win games in the AL when the Boston Red Sox play the New York Yankees and the Cleveland Indians host the Detroit Tigers, and in the NL when the Chicago Cubs and St. Louis Cardinals confront each other, and the Los Angeles Dodgers are at home against the San Diego Padres. Besides the marketing of these and other divisional rivalries, teams have also benefited from interleague play. To illustrate, some of the most exciting games exist between the New York Mets and Yankees, Chicago Cubs and White Sox, Los Angeles Angels of Anaheim and Dodgers, Oakland Athletics and San Francisco Giants, and Baltimore Orioles and Washington Nationals. Indeed, these events have resulted in more media coverage, and above average attendances and cash sales for the participating clubs.

After a regular season concludes during September, one team from each league will qualify as the wild card. Then, in the postseason the three division winners and wild card meet to determine which club will eventually emerge as the champion of the AL and NL. These five-game series are televised, and they generally attract the most enthusiastic and avid baseball fans who are passionate about and cheer for their favorite team. Because of greater television audiences, more advertising revenue from sponsors and larger fan bases, MLB prefers that big-city clubs win their respective pennants and appear in a World Series. That is, from a marketing and economic perspective, a World Series played between the large-market Red Sox or Yankees and Braves or Mets are far more productive for the sport than one between the small-market Devil Rays or Royals and Brewers or Pirates.

Besides the regular seasons and postseason series, an annual All-Star game between clubs from the AL and NL is another product in the marketing mix of organized baseball. The players in each league are selected at their positions for this game based on the number of votes each receive from fans in the U.S., and as of 2005, from the citizens of seven foreign nations and territories. In recent years, international athletes have increasingly appeared as starters and reserve players in All-Star games. This, in turn, has attracted a global audience, which is an improvement in the exposure of and publicity for the sport. In fact, players from Cuba and the Dominican Republic, Puerto Rico and Venezuela are gradually becoming more prevalent on all-star rosters at various infield and outfield positions, and as pitchers, catchers and designated hitters. After a World Baseball Classic is held during 2006 between such nations as Australia, Canada, Japan, Mexico, South Korea, the U.S. and a few Latin American countries, then the sport will become more international and thus marketable to sports fans living in Asia and Europe, and in North, Central and South America.

The players on the AL and NL teams, and on clubs in the U.S. and Canadian minor leagues are also baseball products. Besides providing sports entertainment, these athletes are celebrities, heroes and role models to many kids, teenagers and young adults that play on teams in Little League Baseball, in junior high and high school conferences, and in amateur leagues. Some outstanding and well-recognized players that are worshipped by younger athletes include American-born Alex Rodriguez, Derek Jeter and Randy Johnson of the Yankees, and foreign-born Alfonso Soriano of the Rangers, Pedro Martinez of the Mets and Miguel Tejada of the Orioles. Since 2000, international baseball fans have been particularly interested in the batting achievements and marketability of the Mariners' Ichiro Suzuki and Yankees' Hediki Matsui from Japan, and the Cardinals' Albert Pujois and Red Sox's David Ortiz from the Dominican Republic. That is, these highly skilled performers stimulate the sales of baseball cards, clothing, merchandise and equipment for their teams, licensees and sponsors.

Besides the athletes on the current 25-man rosters of teams, many former players have contributed to the marketing and business success of MLB and specific franchises. Such honorable Hall of Famers as Ernie Banks, Frank Robinson, Hank Aaron, Willie Mays, Cal Ripken, Jr. and Yogi Berra rearrange their personal schedules and make appearances to support community programs, various big league games and other baseball activities, and also they may star in television commercials, participate as broadcasters, team executives and managers, and invest their wealth in minor league clubs. Indeed, as products of the sport, MLB uses them for public relations to promote character, loyalty and goodwill, and to project images and leadership qualities that represent dedication, service and seniority. In fact, males aged 59 and older are attached to sports and very passionate fans of baseball because they remember when teams were populated with well-respected veterans like the great Bob Gibson, Stan Musial, Ted Williams, Reggie Jackson, Nolan Ryan, Tom Seaver and Don Sutton.

Product Prices

In the marketing mix, price is the numerical value of a baseball good or service, or a combination of them, expressed in dollars. It represents, in part, the monetary benefits earned and/or received in a transaction or exchange between two or more individuals and/or groups. As reflected in the sports marketing literature, some important demographic, economic and social concepts and factors that influence prices in baseball are the sports fans' emotion, passion and psychology, size and wealth of the local market area and fan base, competition from businesses in the same and other industries, elasticities of demand and supply, and the quality and scarcity of the product or service.

Relative to the accounting, marketing and operation of a MLB club, price may be viewed as a cost or revenue. As an expense or cash outflow, a club's players earn salaries and perhaps receive other forms of compensation. As a receipt or inflow, teams establish prices for admission to games, and for food, merchandise and other products and services that are sold to spectators at ballparks before, during and after games. In short, professional baseball franchises treat price as a cost and revenue variable and thus, it is a strategic component of the marketing mix.

There are several ways that price affects the marketing of plans and programs of baseball organizations. For example, to sell additional tickets for their home games, the decision makers of teams create various types of sales discounts as incentives, and initiate other one-time and seasonal deals to lure more fans to their home ballparks. In June of 2005, the Atlanta Braves joined with two local amusement park businesses, Six Flags Over Georgia and Six Flags White Water, and offered a "Triple Play Ticket Pack." For a total of $49.99, which was 40 percent off the regular price, the Pack included a ticket to each of Atlanta's three pleasurable outdoor summer attractions. Interestingly, it was available for purchase only at the website atlantabraves.com and had to be acquired at least 10 days in advance of its use.[3]

Besides the cost of tickets to enter the ballparks, prices are also assigned by teams or vendors to other items purchased at games. With respect to the 1991–2005 MLB regular seasons, these values have appeared for each team in an annual Fan Cost Index (FCI), which is published by the Chicago-based Team Marketing Report Inc. For various reasons, generally such large-market clubs as the Red Sox in Boston, Cubs in Chicago and Yankees in New York City have high FCIs per year. That is, for a four-person family to attend a regular season game in 2005, these teams' FCIs were, respectively, $276, $210 and $193. Alternatively, the three clubs with the lowest FCIs in 2005 were the Royals in Kansas City at $119, Angels in Anaheim at $125 and Brewers in Milwaukee at $130. In short, this variation in prices partially explains why there are extreme gaps between the local revenues of superior and inferior teams in the AL and NL.

For the owner of a baseball franchise in MLB, another important aspect of prices is determining the annual payroll of his or her team. In 2005, the Yankees payroll exceeded $200 million while the Devil Rays had the lowest in the AL at less than $30 million. This difference of approximately $170 million indicates that the Yankees had a competitive advantage over the Devil Rays and 12 other AL clubs in marketing their brand and superstar players like Alex Rodriguez, Derek Jeter, Gary Sheffield and Randy Johnson. The data also explains how the Yankees, since 1990, had succeeded to win AL pennants in 1996, 1998–2001 and 2003, and World Series in 1996 and 1998–2000. Meanwhile, during 1998–2003 the Devil Rays finished last each season in the East Division. Thus, per division and league the distributions of payrolls roughly measure the productivity of professional baseball players and team performances. Consequently, for a baseball enterprise the prices in the marketing mix are related to business decisions, values and benefits, and to the organization's income, wealth and competitive environment.

Place or Distribution

The third marketing tool consists of the various activities and ways that MLB and specific teams jointly, and in cooperation with external businesses, make sports products available for sale to consumers and groups that exist in local, regional, national and international target markets. These places or distribution points include the sites of the teams' ballparks in metropolitan areas and cities, and radio and television networks that broadcast games, and retail outlets and the Internet. In other words, as an element in the marketing mix places are the institutions, systems, methods and routes that MLB and the league's teams use to distribute their products to groups and individual consumers in the U.S. and foreign markets.

In total, the regular season games and playoffs in the AL and NL, and the World Series are played in the ballparks of the 30 teams. As of 2005, the three oldest facilities in cities of clubs were Boston's Fenway Park at 93, Chicago's Wrigley Field at 91 and New York City's Yankee Stadium at 82. Conversely, the newest MLB stadiums included Philadelphia's Citizens Bank Park and San Diego's Petco Park each at one year old, and Milwaukee's Miller Park and Pittsburgh's PNC Park each at four years old. The latter ballparks, and those other big league stadiums that were constructed since the early1990s feature a number of sports and non-sports activities to entertain the spectators who decide to attend a baseball game. That is, within or adjacent to a modern ballpark there may be a sports museum and swimming pool, some retail shops, one or more video game arcades, a playground for children, designated areas for fans to throw and hit a baseball, and vendors selling team clothing, merchandise and equipment. These activities and a stadium's personal seat licenses, parking areas, club seats, luxury boxes and corporate suites not only generate more revenues for the league and franchises, they also ensure that participants and fans remember that home games are convenient and fun to attend and therefore, a memorable experience.

To expand their markets and consumer bases, an increasing number of the MLB teams' home and away games are being transmitted to sports fans in the U.S. and to households in other countries on radio, satellite and television networks and the Internet. To illustrate, since 2000 several clubs located in the U.S. southwest and west have signed multiyear agreements with media companies to have their games broadcasted into homes located throughout Central and South America and the Caribbean. This means that baseball addicts in the Dominican Republic, Mexico, Panama, Puerto Rico and Venezuela can listen and watch their favorite players compete for the AL's Angels, Athletics and Rangers, and NL's Astros, Diamondbacks, Dodgers, Giants and Padres. Moreover, in 2005 individuals in seven foreign nations and territories were allowed to vote for and help select the players on the AL and NL All-Star rosters. In turn, this opportunity resulted in a record number of international athletes being elected to these two teams.

According to one study, sports-related retail and licensed product sales exceeded $16 billion in 2003. One year later, MLB committed more than $500 million and endorsed a series of five-year agreements with Reebok, New Era Cap Company, Majestic Athletic and other prominent companies. Then, in 2005 MLB Properties (MLBP) created two new club retail promotions titled Celebrate Father's Day and Celebrate Fan Appreciation Month. The purposes of these campaigns were to drive traffic to and increase sales of officially licensed MLB products at ballpark concessionaires and club-owned retail outlets. To create awareness, the two promotions received exposure during regular season games from in-stadium signage, in-game scoreboard spots and public address announcements. Because of their ability to survey, contact and reach end users and final consumers, sports retailers are a growing and convenient way for MLB teams to make their goods and services available to them for distribution.[4]

Promotion Types

The fourth element in the marketing mix, promotion, consists of the activities, events and programs that the league and teams decide to schedule and undertake to communicate and promote baseball products, and also to penetrate one or more domestic and/or foreign targeted markets. In marketing, the promotional tools that are beneficial for baseball organizations include advertising, personal selling, public relations, sales campaigns and sponsorships. Each tool is differently implemented because of the sender's control of the communication, amount and speed of the feedback, direction of the message and its flow, speed in reaching small, medium-sized and large audiences, and the modes of communication. As applied to the marketing of a sport, the following are examples of three unique types of promotions that illustrate this element's role in the marketing mix of baseball teams.

First, during May of 2005 the Chicago White Sox launched the second round of an advertising campaign that took a humorous approach to the regular season's 'Win or Die Trying' tagline. Designed by an agency named Two x Four, this television, radio, print and outdoor campaign focused on "Grinder Rules," which were expressions supporting a public challenge made by the Sox's general manager Ken Williams to define the ways that the team played baseball. After research had revealed that fans preferred an aggressive, hard-working and team-oriented baseball club, three specific "Grinder Rules" eventually emerged. They were "Only one stat matters: W," "You're either counted on or counted out," and "A good outfielder doesn't see the wall. He tastes it." In television spots, some White Sox players are featured in a number of "Win or Die Trying" storylines such that each player must try hard or give everything to win. As a scene develops, each player finds himself in a train car faced with an angel or devil asking if he had played as hard as possible to win. According to Chicago White Sox vice president of marketing Brooks Boyer, "The Grinder Rules let our fans know how we want the game to be played and what the experience at U.S. Cellular Field is all about. The pride and the passion that is

White Sox baseball is our message, and our advertising communicates that message in a light-hearted tone that everyone will understand and enjoy."[5]

Second, in the Spring of 2005 there were approximately 12 baseball-themed museums in MLB cities and other places within the U.S. and Canada. To highlight one of these facilities, a Sports Legend museum opened in eastern Maryland at Camden Yards, which is the name of the home-field stadium of the Baltimore Orioles. Contained in a nineteenth century train depot that is adjacent to the ballpark, the museum celebrates many sports heroes including such Maryland legends as Babe Ruth and Cal Ripken, Jr. In Ruth's collection are his Louisville Slugger bat from 1927, and a scorecard from his first big-league game in 1914. Ripken's section includes four banners with the numerals 2131. These banners had hung from the Camden Yards warehouse in 1995 when he broke Lou Gehrig's consecutive game record of 2,130. Besides Ruth and Ripken in the Sports Legends, there are structures in other cities that honor former big league players. Three of these great athletes and their museum's locations are, respectively, the New York Yankees catcher Yogi Berra in Montclair, New Jersey, the Cleveland Indians pitcher Bob Feller in Van Meter, Iowa, and the Pittsburgh Pirates infielder Honus Wagner in Carnegie, Pennsylvania.[6]

Third, to reestablish the support of local and regional baseball fans after avoiding a strike by the Major League Baseball Players Association (MLBPA) in 2002, a majority of MLB team owners had decided to increase their expenditures on public relations programs and other promotional tools during the 2003–2005 regular seasons. For example, a number of Houston Astros players stood at turnstiles in their full uniforms to greet people that entered the ballpark to see a home game; the Detroit Tigers owner allowed 500 children to set up a camp in the outfield of Comerica Park and then showed the kids a movie on the ballpark's scoreboard; teams willingly donated a total of $40 million in promotional items such as $25 Wilson baseball gloves at a particular Chicago White Sox game; in Arlington, the Texas Rangers reduced soda prices to 10 cents each at a game, opened for free 4,500 parking spaces for automobiles at another game, and gave away 15,000 tickets to fans for a game in Houston with the Astros; and finally, some teams reconnected with their fans by providing more restrooms in, and offering better food and friendlier service at, their host ballparks. As a result of these and other actions, many teams' home attendances gradually increased after 2002, and so did their experiences at implementing new and effective promotions for their fans.

Alternative Marketing Campaigns

Because of the unfavorable publicity from the media and criticism from politicians about the drug scandals involving players, and the gradual loss of exposure, market share and sports fans to professional football and college basketball and football, since 2003 organized baseball and/or the MLBPA have allocated more resources and money to their marketing budgets. As a result, a number of league offices and union officials have invested increasing amounts of time, labor services and capital to organize, implement, host and participate in a variety of new programs. The following business deals are samples of these unique and interesting activities.

2004–2005

After the 2004 regular season concluded, current MLB players such as Nomar Garciaparra and Mark Prior of the Chicago Cubs, Hall of Fame managers Tommy Lasorda

and Frank Robinson, and others involved with professional baseball signed their autographs to cards in a fund raising campaign that was sponsored by USA Baseball and
Upper Deck. After the autographs were compiled, the result was a 204-card Box Set that
celebrated USA Baseball's 25 years as the National Governing Body for amateur baseball
in the U.S. At $49.99 each, the Box Set provided collectors with the opportunity to acquire
authentic signature and game-used jersey cards, and regular issue cards featuring USA
Baseball's 180 most distinguished alumni.[7]

During early 2005, the MLBP, MLBPA and MLB Advanced Media (MLBAM) had
established a series of long-term, third-party exclusive licensing agreements with Take-
Two Interactive Software, Inc., which is based in New York. These exclusives permitted
Take-Two to develop, publish and distribute a broad portfolio of interactive, officially
licensed video games on console, personal computer and handheld platforms. To take
effect in the Spring of 2006, the agreements provided this company with the rights to the
marks of the 30 MLB clubs, MLB players and teams' ballparks, minor league baseball clubs
and MLB.com online content. The multiple titles available from Take-Two are based on
traditional baseball simulations, and arcade and manager-style games including specially
timed releases during the baseball and holiday seasons. The development studios of Visual
Concepts and Kush Games were assigned the responsibility to create the baseball titles
under Take-Two's 2K sports publishing label. "The combination of Take-Two's position
as a leading video game publisher and distributor, and our experience with Visual Concepts in creating high quality games, makes this an ideal partnership with Major League
Baseball," said MLBP's senior vice president of licensing Howard Smith.[8]

In January of 2005, the MLBAM and MLBPA signed a five-year agreement to award
this baseball union nearly $50 million for the exclusive licensing of player's names, likenesses
and other related rights for use in online games, which includes the fantasy baseball leagues.
Potentially, this deal may result in developing new interactive baseball games and other
media that currently is unavailable to fans. Also, this agreement could enhance fantasy baseball in which the participants select actual players in a make-believe draft and then track
these players' statistics until the regular season ends. The fantasy team whose hitters and
pitchers perform the best is declared the winner of the league. As MLBAM's chief executive
officer Bob Bowman remarked, "This will greatly improve the fantasy experience, and more
generally improve the interactive experience for all of our fans, and we think we can grow
the business tremendously." Another aspect of the deal was that MLB.com served as the host
of the official MLBPA website, which was later re-launched as MLBPlayers.com. Indeed, to
portray this baseball union's view of its commitment with the MLBAM, the MLBPA's Director of Business Affairs and Licensing Judy Heeter said, "This agreement will leverage both
player and league rights to benefit MLB fans and business partners. We are especially pleased
by all the creative opportunities it provides to expand the reach and enhance the value of
the interactive experience with baseball fans everywhere."[9]

For nine days in June of 2005, MLB and Cerveza Presidente hosted a weeklong baseball festival in Santo Domingo, which is the capital of and largest city in the Dominican
Republic. Accordingly, the "Presidente Festival del Beisbol" provided fans with such MLB
experiences as swinging at pitched baseballs in batting cages, testing the speed and accuracy of baseballs thrown in pitching tunnels, and running the bases at a fast pace. For
each of the ten attractions at the festival, participants were allowed to challenge
friends and to compare their scores relative to those earned by MLB players. The telecommunications company Verizon sponsored events like the Strike Zone, Power Swing and

Interactive Zone, which featured broadband connections so that fans could access MLB.com. Furthermore, the festival included a newly designed mini-baseball field, photo studio and Sony Playstation2 consoles, and an 84-inch plasma television. The channel CDN, which is MLB's television partner in the Dominican Republic, each day provided live festival coverage during the evening news and sports shows, and also set up a broadcast booth at the festival with CDN commentators giving play-by-play commentary of MLB games presented on big screen televisions. About this special baseball event, MLB's senior vice president of international business operations Paul Archey stated, "There is a great passion for Major League Baseball in the Dominican Republic, and the 'Presidente Festival del Beisbol' provides us with a great opportunity to interact with a large number of fans and further strengthen their connection to the game." As an aside, the first stop of the festival was in early February of 2005 when approximately 4,000 people attended the activities per day in Mazatian, Mexico.[10]

Beginning in late May of 2005, the baseball fans in seven foreign countries and territories had the opportunity to vote for their favorite AL and NL players to start the seventy-sixth All-Star Game. That is, to be selected as starters were eight position players from each league and a designated hitter from an AL team. This All-Star Balloting Program represents the league's ongoing efforts to markets its products and brands to fans from the seven territories and foreign nations, which included Canada, Curacao, Dominican Republic, Japan, Panama, Puerto Rico and Venezuela. From these countries, the total international sponsors of the Balloting Program were, respectively, nine companies named Rogers Digital Cable, UTS, Presidente, Yomiuri, Grupo EGSA and TV Max, DirecTV, and Pepsi and Polar. Meanwhile, Ameriquest was authorized to be the title sponsor of in-stadium balloting at major and minor league ballparks and online balloting at MLB.com. As a result, this mortgage firm had to provide 25 million ballots to the 29 U.S. major league ballparks and 2.2 million ballots to 122 minor league baseball clubs. Furthermore, Pepsi and Frito Lay sponsored the 2005 MLB Retail All-Star Balloting and thus, had to distribute 20 million MLB All-Star ballots exclusively at more than 3,100 Wal-Mart stores during May and June of 2005. Since the MLB All-Star Balloting Program was the largest type of solicitation in professional sports, it could be accessed simply online in Spanish and Japanese at MLB.com.[11]

Despite the moderate to above average success of the previous campaigns and other promotional programs that involved professional baseball organizations, the marketability of several prominent MLB baseball players had plummeted because of their connections with illegal drugs and steroid controversies. For proof, in April of 2005 *SportsBusiness Daily* surveyed 81 marketing executives, sponsorship consultants and journalists. The results of the poll indicated that the marketability of San Francisco Giants' Barry Bonds, New York Yankees' Jason Giambi and Baltimore Orioles' Sammy Sosa ranked significantly lower after the reports while superstar athletes such as the New York Yankees' Derek Jeter and Alex Rodriguez ranked relatively higher because of their looks, integrity and leadership. Thus, the marketability of three popular MLB players had been damaged despite their achievements as sluggers and as athletes with multimillion-dollar annual salaries.[12]

Summary

To successfully operate in the sports entertainment business in the short- and long-term, the administrators of professional baseball organizations are compelled to con-

sider the marketing mix, which consists of the sport product, and price, place and promotion. This specific combination of variables determines, in part, the strategies that MLB
and the 14 AL and 16 NL teams each use to reach and expand their fan bases and markets, and to increase and sustain their cash inflows, revenue streams and profits.

Because of location, wealth and other demographic and economic factors, some
large-market teams such as the Atlanta Braves, Los Angeles Dodgers and New York Yankees have ample resources and money reserves to establish partnerships, sponsorships
and licensing contracts with private firms, and to initiate marketing programs that
improve the quality of their brands and images with baseball fans residing in targeted
regions and/or in local communities. Consequently, as a result of favorable win-loss
records in their divisions during several regular seasons, these and other clubs are usually competitive enough to challenge for a playoff spot, and frequently or occasionally
may win division titles and perhaps an AL or NL pennant.

Based on that information, this chapter discussed the relevance and application of
the four variables as necessary inputs in the marketing campaigns of professional sports
organizations. This is, for the league and one or more of the 30 MLB teams. Each variable was defined and then used to explain its role as a component of the league's and/or
teams' marketing mixes, plans and strategies. With respect to each variable, first, there
are marketing features and decisions about the concepts, characteristics and designs of
products, which are the goods and services or a combination of them that sports orga-
nizationsæleagues and teamsæcommunicate and provide to their audiences in the marketplace; second, prices are represented in a mix and included to measure the values,
costs, revenues and profits incurred from the operations of MLB and the 30 teams during each regular season and postseason; third, places refer to the distributions of the
league's and teams' products in ballparks and retail stores, and on television and radio
networks and the Internet, and as a result of partnership and licensing agreements; and
fourth, MLB and the teams adopt and implement promotions in the form of advertisements, personal selling, public relations, sales campaigns and sponsorships.

After these topics were identified and explored, the final portion of this chapter contained selected marketing activities, programs and/or agreements that involved the
MLBPA and MLB, and their various business partners. These were highlighted and discussed to further expose the union's and league's interests, promotional tools and strategies from a marketing perspective. In sum, this reading essentially complements the other
chapters contained in this Part of the book. It also provides additional examples and facts
about the marketing of sports brands, and how baseball organizations mix products,
prices, places and promotions with partnerships, sponsorships and licensing, and broadcast programming.

22. Evaluating Big League Team Brands

As an enterprise in the sports entertainment business, a Major League Baseball (MLB) franchise and its respective American League (AL) or National League (NL) team has a marketing staff assigned within the organization's structure. The responsibilities and sizes of the staffs will vary between franchises because of many factors. These include economic and financial conditions and differences in the qualifications, productivities and experiences of the marketing managers and employees and their knowledge of and interest in sports markets. It is likely, therefore, that some teams will decide to outsource a portion of their marketing events, programs, studies and tasks to licensees, partners and vendors, and to companies and/or individuals who specialize in an activity or function. For example, such work as analyzing a club's macroenvironment, forecasting market demand, identifying market segments, and designing pricing strategies may be performed more effectively by outsiders. In any event, in a professional sports organization there is a director or vice president that is the supervisor or manager who is accountable to the franchise owner or a top executive for the marketing operations of a team.

As to the literature, some academics and practitioners disagree about whether all of the teams in a professional sports league should be considered a brand, which is defined as "a name, term, sign, symbol, or design, or a combination of them, intended to identify the goods or services of one seller or group of sellers and to differentiate them from those of competitors." Based on that definition, if a particular baseball team has lost its appeal, identity and passion to a national audience of fans, and if those fans cannot articulate why it is important to them anymore, then the team remains in existence merely because it is a monopoly. As such, the sports enterprise is no longer a brand. Alternatively, others state that all professional teams must be considered brands because of their heritage, history, personality and reputation, and the fact that fans, to some extent care about them. Rather than elaborate about and justify which of these views are most realistic, it is assumed that the 30 teams in MLB are each brands even though a portion of them may have an extremely small national fan base, and recognizing they operate as local monopolies and exist in a league that is an economic cartel.[1]

For insights about sports marketing, in a study completed during 2002 the values of brands in dollars were estimated for a group of 15 teams that performed in organized baseball. The factors included in this analysis were each club's revenue streams and profits, size of its fan base and the local media market, the club's win-loss record on the field, stadium operations and a measure of its local, regional and national popularity. The results of the analysis indicated that in 2002 the values of these MLB teams as brands ranged from $39 million for the Arizona Diamondbacks to $334 million for the New York Yankees. For some reason, the company that performed the study did not estimate the values of the other 15 teams. As a result, the researchers concluded that MLB teams on average had comparably less value as brands than clubs in the National Basketball Association (NBA) and National Football League (NFL) but higher than the National Hockey League (NHL) teams. Consequently, the professional baseball teams that are weak brands would likely experience severe financial losses and perhaps bankruptcy if, for example, a lengthy players strike or owners lockout had occurred in the early 2000s.[2]

As individual brands, each of the MLB teams conveys a number of different meanings to their fans and other consumers in the sports markets. The most significant of these meanings are values, and culture and personality, and to a lesser extent attributes and benefits are conveyed. Given the various meanings, relevant facts and other data as revealed in the research, this chapter next lists and ranks, by division, the 14 AL and then 15 NL clubs and discusses their relative marketability as business brands owned and operated by baseball entrepreneurs and investors.

American League

East Division

Ranked from first to fifth place, the most powerful and valuable brands in this Division are the New York Yankees and Boston Red Sox, and then the Baltimore Orioles, Toronto Blue Jays and Tampa Bay Devil Rays. From a marketing perspective, the two leading brands reflect such qualities as competitiveness and intensity, and each team features great players, enthusiastic support and loyalty from their fans in local and regional areas and nationwide, and the potential to earn huge amounts of revenues and profits from their broadcasts and stadium operations. Because of longstanding traditions, previous performances and current locations, the large-market Yankees and Red Sox are regarded as superior sports organizations and thus, represent excellent brands to market. If the Yankees ultimately play their home games in a new, modern and lucrative ballpark somewhere in the New York City area, and when Fenway Park is renovated to generate more cash for the Red Sox in Boston, these clubs as brands will tend to increase in value for many years. As an aside, during early 2005 the Yankees named Deborah Tymon to be the club's senior vice president of marketing. Hired by the Yankees in 1985 as the director of group and season ticket sales, Tymon and her department is responsible for marketing, advertising, promotions and special events.[3]

Relative to the Yankees and Red Sox, the Orioles are average and Blue Jays below average in marketing and in their attractiveness as brands. Although the Orioles play at 48,190-seat Camden Yards, which is an excellent ballpark that contains a variety of entertainment options for spectators, the club's regular season attendances appear to have peaked in the late 1990s. Since 1901, this franchise has won nine division titles, seven AL pennants and three World Series championships. During the majority of regular seasons, the Orioles' teams have been good but not great competition for the Yankees, and the franchise's revenues and profits earned from operations are mediocre because the team exists in Baltimore, which is a relatively small market. Besides, the club's market value and customer base may remain stagnate or even diminish after 2005 because the Nationals in Washington, D.C. will appeal to a number of the Orioles' fans that live in eastern Maryland's metropolitan areas.

For decades, the most popular sports team in Toronto has been the NHL Maple Leafs. This means that the Blue Jays, who have not won a division title or attracted huge attendances for games held at the 45,100-seat SkyDome since 1993, are a brand in name and reputation that is below the league's average in dollar value and marketability. To improve this franchise's image, culture and personality for its fans, during early 2005 Blue Jays owner Rogers Communications increased the club's annual payroll by 40 percent or from $50 million to $70 million, changed the ballpark's name from the SkyDome to the Rogers Centre, installed FieldTurf on the diamond and replaced the JumboTron display with a new video board. As such, the payoffs from these actions will financially benefit this Canadian-based organization and Blue Jay performances in the AL's East Division.

Meanwhile, the Devil Rays rank as an inferior franchise with respect to the team's win-loss record, market size, fan base and the amounts of cash inflows generated from 44,445-seat Tropicana Field in Tampa Bay. Since the NFL Buccaneers and NHL Lightning primarily attract and entertain sports fans that live in areas of western Florida, since 1998 the Devil Rays have struggled to become a popular and deep brand in this territory. According to demographic trends, however, the high population growth and increasing real estate values of commercial and residential properties in the Tampa Bay area suggest that this baseball franchise needs to invest more resources and money in order to expand and exploit its fan base. Otherwise, by the mid–1910s MLB may be forced to contract this team or encourage its owner to relocate the organization to another city or urban area. In short, the marketing power of teams as brands in the AL's East Division ranges from superior for the Yankees and Red Sox to inferior for the Devil Rays.

Central Division

For the five franchises that compose this division, the Chicago White Sox, Cleveland Indians, Detroit Tigers and Minnesota Twins are average brands, and the Kansas City Royals are an inferior brand. In the Chicago metropolitan area, the White Sox competes for recognition and fans with the popular NL Cubs and with four other major professional sports teams. Because this large-market club has not won an AL pennant since 1959 and a World Series in nearly 90 years, the White Sox generally fails to draw capacity crowds to its home games at 44,000-seat U.S. Cellular Field, or formerly to New Comiskey Park. However, despite not winning championships the team improved its record during the early 2000s because of the performances of a group of young players and the leadership of manager Ozzie Guillen. If the club wins consecutive division titles and at least one AL pennant and a World Series in the next five seasons, this will make the brand more appealing to baseball fans that reside in the northeast counties of Illinois.[4]

In 1994, the Indians opened its regular season at 43,000-seat Jacobs Field in small-market Cleveland and then won five division championships and two AL pennants between 1995 and 1999. Because the city's manufacturing base and population have been declining for several years, and since sports fans in Cleveland are despondent about the performances of the NBA Cavaliers and NFL Browns during the early 2000s, the Indians are perceived as a moderately popular professional team in northern Ohio. Therefore, this franchise is an average brand and so are the brands of the Tigers in Detroit, Michigan and Twins in Minneapolis, Minnesota.

Although the mid-to-large-market Tigers play in 40,000-seat Comerica Park, which was built in 2000, the team is less popular in the Detroit area than the successful NBA Pistons and NHL Red Wings. Since 1935, the Tigers have won three division titles, five AL pennants and four World Series. However, the team's lackluster performances during the 1990s and early 2000s have prevented large increases in the franchise's value as a brand. Similar to the White Sox and Indians, the Tigers need to win a series of championships in order to receive publicity and become more popular to sports fans living in cities and rural areas of southeastern Michigan.

In contrast, the Twins are a relatively small-market, low-payroll franchise whose teams have usually been competitive during regular seasons in the Central Division. Yet, the club has not won an AL pennant and World Series since 1991. Consequently, if a modern, fan-friendly ballpark is constructed in the Minneapolis-St. Paul area to replace the 34-year-old 48,678-seat Metrodome, then the Twins will earn more revenues and profits from home game attendances and local radio and television broadcasts. In turn, this should have a positive affect on the club's culture, image and personality relative to those of the NBA Timberwolves, NFL Vikings and NHL Wild. Nevertheless, even with a new stadium it is doubtful that the Twins will become a superior brand in MLB.

The Kansas City Royals, meanwhile, are an inferior brand because of the team's poor performances in the Central Division, and its inadequate payroll and stadium operations, small media market and fan base, and below average revenue streams and annual net profits. Since the expansion year of 1969, the club has won six division titles, two AL pennants and in 1985, a World Series championship. In 2005, this franchise ranked twenty-seventh in market value and gross revenues among the 30 MLB teams, but also earned $3 million in operating income. Despite recent renovations to 33-year-old 40,793-seat Kauffman Stadium in Kansas City, the team's five highest regular season attendance totals occurred in the 1980s. As a result, the Royals' brand and the club's marketing values, culture and personality are unlikely to appreciate very much during the early 2000s. In fact, this baseball franchise and the NFL Chiefs have each threatened to relocate to another city when their stadium leases expire unless Missouri taxpayers wholly or partially fund the construction of new ballparks for them.

West Division

Based on their marketing strengths and programs, the Seattle Mariners is a superior brand, the Los Angeles Angels of Anaheim and Texas Rangers are average, and the Oakland Athletics is inferior. Although the club exists in small-market Seattle, as a MLB team during the early 2000s the Mariners on average placed first in operating profits at $17 million, third in home attendances at 3.3 million, fourth in total revenues at $163 million, fifth in media revenues at $53 million, and seventh in player payroll at $84 million. As of 2005, the franchise ranked fifth in market value at $415 million. Indeed, these are remarkable statistics for a baseball franchise that is twentieth in market size at 2.5 million and whose 2004 payroll of $85 million was approximately 50 percent of its revenues. This organization has successful operations, in part, because of Japanese player Ichiro Suzuki and a sweetheart deal at 47,772-seat Safeco Field. Furthermore, in recent seasons the NBA SuperSonics and NFL Seahawks improved their performances and that may have generated more interest in each of the professional sports teams located in the Seattle area. If Suzuki maintains his high batting average, the team will promote him in the media and that may make the organization's brand more valuable to local fans and other sports consumers throughout the U.S. and in Japan.[5]

In the West Division, following the Mariners in marketing power are the brands of the Angels and Rangers. These clubs have average fan bases in their respective local markets, but less popular images and reputations in their regional areas. The Angels must directly compete for its baseball fans with the Los Angeles Dodgers and to some extent, indirectly with the professional basketball, football, ice hockey and soccer teams that are located in the Greater Los Angeles Area. After winning a World Series in 2002, the club's attendances have exceeded three million per year at 45,000-seat Angel Stadium of Anaheim.

When Mexican Arturo Moreno purchased the franchise in 2003, his goal has been to promote the team's brand to Spanish-speaking people who live in southern California. Moreover, to obtain more revenues from advertising agencies and sponsors, and to negotiate a new television contract, Moreno decided to rename the team in early 2005. In order to block the change in names, the City of Anaheim then asked a judge in court to approve a restraining order. However, it appears that a judge or possibly a jury will settle this issue in late 2005 or early 2006. With the third highest payroll in MLB, the Angels is capable of winning the West Division again and further improving its value as a brand.[6]

Between 1994 and 1999, the Rangers won four division titles. As a result, the attendances at 49,000-seat Ameriquest Field in Arlington exceeded 2.8 million in 1996, 1997, 1998, 2000 and 2001. Franchise owner Thomas Hicks is a wealthy businessman who is trying to build the team's brand in areas of northeast Texas. To that end, he signed slugger Alex Rodriguez to a long-term contract valued at $25 million per year. Then, in 2003 Hicks sold Rodriguez to the New York Yankees. Surprisingly, in recent years the team's performances have improved but not its marketing power. In short, unless the Rangers can compete for a division title or wild card, the value of the club as a brand may soon decline.

For various reasons, the inferior brand in this division is the Oakland Athletics. After the great success of its teams during the late 1980s, the club won two division titles in the early 1990s and three between 2000 and 2003. However, this is a small-market low-payroll baseball organization whose teams play in 37-year-old Network Associates Coliseum, which seats 43,600. Furthermore, the Athletics brand is not well recognized or revered in its home market because of the publicity and attention given to the San Francisco Giants home run hitter and alleged steroid user Barry Bonds, and due to the Bay Area sports fans who prefer to support the Giants, NBA Warriors, NFL Raiders and 49ers, NHL Sharks and MLS Earthquakes. In 2005, the Athletics were sold to investor Lewis Wolff, which indicates that the future value and performance of the franchise is unpredictable. As such, from a marketing perspective the team as a brand will likely remain inferior at least for the next few years despite a wild card appearance and winning five West Division titles since 1989.

National League

East Division

With respect to their brands and marketing powers, the Atlanta Braves and New York Mets are ranked as superior, the Phillies and Marlins as average, and since the club's initial season began in April of 2005, the Washington Nationals are not rated in this chapter. First, between 1990 and 2004 the Braves won 13 division titles, five NL pennants and one World Series. As a result, the club's average attendances at 52,000-seat Fulton County Stadium and then at 50,000-seat Turner Field have exceeded 3 million per season. Undoubtedly, this large-market high-payroll team is more popular with the sports population and media in the Atlanta area than the NBA Hawks, NFL Falcons and NHL Flames. Each season, baseball fans expect the Braves to win the East Division so its brand represents dedication, efficiency and high performance. In fact, these were the attributes of former Braves pitchers Greg Maddux and Tom Glavine, and current pitcher John Smoltz and manager Bobby Cox. Even after AOL Time Warner had purchased the club from Ted Turner, the brand seemed to retain its attributes, benefits and values, and culture and personality. Because of a winning tradition, and a market value estimated at $382 million and annual revenues of $162 million in 2005, the Braves franchise is recognized as one of the highest quality organizations in MLB, which means it is a superior brand.

Although much less successful than the Braves in winning titles, pennants and championships, the Mets is a large-market high-payroll team that plays in America's most important city relative to the media, banking industry and international finance. This $500 million franchise shares a sports market with the Yankees and a total of eight other major professional teams that play within the New York City–New Jersey Area. Since 1969, the Mets have appeared in two playoffs as a wild card team, and succeeded to win four division titles and NL pennants, and two World Series. To establish a deeper relationship with baseball fans in New York City and the region, during 2005 the club invested in and implemented local programs and featured a full slate of Theme, Community and Heritage dates, and such social and marketing promotions and campaigns as Jackie Robinson Night, Travel Mug, Mets Alarm Clock, Build-a-Bear Workshop, Fireworks Night and Dynamets Dash. Furthermore, during the club's regular season the Mets players wore five different sets of uniforms. These consisted of white pinstripes, plain black, home black, road black and road gray. Before 2010, it is anticipated that the Mets will play their home games in a downtown complex that includes a new stadium. In 2002, FutureBrand ranked this MLB franchise as a brand second to the Yankees at $135 million.[7]

After evaluating the Braves and Mets in the East Division, the Philadelphia Phillies brand is ranked as average and Marlins as inferior, while the Washington Nationals is not rated because of the team's brief history of playing home games at 56,000-seat RFK Stadium in the nation's capital. With respect to the two teams' marketability, since 1903 the Phillies have won seven division titles, five NL pennants and one World Series championship. At 43,500-seat Citizens Bank Park, which was completed in 2004, the club set a regular season attendance record of 3.25 million spectators in 2004, and each year has earned more revenues at the Park than it did at 62,400-seat Veterans Stadium. In the Philadelphia metropolitan area, the most popular professional sports teams are the NFL Eagles and NHL Flyers, and then the NBA 76ers and Phillies. Nonetheless, because of the new ballpark and the club's average media market and fan base, the value of the Phillies as a brand has increased from $35 million in 2002 to approximately $40 million in 2005.

Between 1993 and 2003, the Florida Marlins qualified for and appeared in two wild card games and also won two each NL pennants and World Series. Even so, in the Greater Miami Area this 13-year-old baseball club is less popular among sports fans than the NBA Heat and NFL Dolphins. Since 1993, the Marlins have played their home games in 36,300-seat Joe Robbie Stadium, which was designed primarily as a football facility. During the Spring of 2005, the team's effort to have a modern baseball stadium built with taxpayer money was rejected by the Florida legislature. Meanwhile, Marlins' officials have spoken to the Mayor of Las Vegas about that city's interest in hosting a MLB franchise. Although the club is worth approximately $206 million, its revenue streams and profits are near the bottom among teams in MLB. As a result of these facts, the Marlins is an inferior brand that will likely decrease in value each year unless a new ballpark is constructed within or near the City of Miami.

Finally, the Washington Nationals are based in a high per capita income city where the NFL Redskins, NBA Wizards, NHL Caps and MLS United play their home games. After the relocation from Montreal, Canada to the D.C. area during early 2005, this franchise' market value appreciated by 114 percent to $310 million. Nevertheless, despite the team's contract with a cable company and the creation of a new revenue stream, the value of the Nationals' brand will ultimately depend, in part, on the entrepreneurial talent and leadership of the new owner, the volume of business and amount of money generated at a new baseball ballpark in the D.C. area, and the team's success in the East Division when competing against the Braves, Mets, Phillies and Marlins.

Central Division

To distinguish between the brand values and marketing strengths of baseball teams in this division, the St. Louis Cardinals and Chicago Cubs are ranked above average, the Houston Astros as average, the Pittsburgh Pirates and Cincinnati Reds as average to below average, and the Milwaukee Brewers as inferior. To be specific, the small-market Cardinals are very popular in the eastern Missouri and western Illinois regions because of the team's attributes, culture and personality, and also its history and tradition. That is, since 1903 this franchise has earned seven division titles, 16 NL pennants and nine World Series. In recent seasons, the Cardinals have further improved their performances while managed by Tony LaRussa and led by former hitting star Mark McGwire and current sluggers Albert Pujois, Jim Edmonds, Scott Rolen and Edgar Renteria. In fact, various Cardinals teams established annual attendance records from 1998 to 2001 at 50,354-seat Busch Memorial Stadium in St. Louis. When the club plays home games in a new ballpark in St. Louis, its fan base and revenues, profits and brand values will each increase from their respective totals.

The large-market Cubs, meanwhile, has a significant number of passionate fans that are waiting for the team to excel and play in a World Series. In Chicago, there are five other professional sports franchises and according to a study performed by the Future-Brand company, the brands of the NBA Bulls, NFL Bears and NHL Blackhawks are each more valuable than the brand of the Cubs. However, in 2005 this baseball franchise's estimated net worth at $398 million and annual revenues at $170 million ranked it in sixth place in MLB. Besides these values, the Cubs also benefit from a relatively large fan base and media market even though the franchise's teams have not won a NL pennant since 1945 and a World Series in nearly 100 years. When the team's high-salaried slugger Sammy Sosa was traded to the Baltimore Orioles after the 2004 season, the club changed its strategy to win games from hitting with power to defense and pitching. Therefore, in the early 2000s it is unlikely that the Cubs' brand will improve by an amount that equals or surpasses the value estimated for the Cardinals by FutureBrand.

The medium-sized to large-market Houston Astros is an average brand. This is because of the team's few playoff appearances, its mediocre attendances at 41,000-seat Minute Maid Park, and a small fan base relative to the NBA Rockets and NFL Texans.

To illustrate, since 1962 the club has qualified for one wild card game, and won six division titles but zero NL pennants and World Series championships. In 2003 and 2004, the Astros' regular season home attendances finally topped three million per season. However, this fact was less publicized in Houston than sports fans' support for the Rockets and player Yao Ming, and for the Texans at Reliant Stadium. Financially, the Astros are ranked eleventh in MLB with a market value at $357 million, and the team's annual revenues exceed $150 million per year. In 2002, FutureBrand estimated the Astros brand at $45 million, which was $5 million below the value of the Cubs.

The Pittsburgh Pirates and Cincinnati Reds are small-market teams that have struggled in the NL since the mid–1990s. After each franchise won two World Series during the 1970s, the great players from those championship clubs retired or were traded to another team in the 1980s. The Pirates, however, captured three division titles in the early 1990s and the Reds two in the mid–1990s. Because of the relatively new and modern 38,000-seat PNC Park in Pittsburgh and 42,000-seat Great American Ball Park in Cincinnati, the two franchises have established revenue streams, profit amounts and fan bases to score average to below average as brands. Interestingly, the Pirates share the Pittsburgh metropolitan area with the very popular NFL Steelers and less popular NHL Penguins, while the Reds and NFL Bengals co-exist in the southwest Ohio region. In short, the Pirates and Reds are brands that have little opportunity to become superior during the early 2000s unless their teams win a few division titles and NL pennants, and perhaps one or more World Series championships.

Since 1970, the small-market Milwaukee Brewers have won two division titles, one AL pennant and zero World Series. Although this club's brand is ranked as inferior, the attendances at games held in 41,900-seat Miller Park have increased during the early 2000s relative to those at 53,200-seat County Stadium prior to 2001. Moreover, in the 2004 regular season the Brewers' revenues exceeded $112 million and operating income $24 million, which were the fourth highest amounts in MLB. During early 2005, businessman Mark Attanasio purchased the franchise from the Selig Trust. Attanasio's long-run strategy is to gradually improve the team's performances by developing the scouting system, promoting young and talented players from teams in the minor leagues, and bargaining with other clubs to acquire better athletes who will excel as players in Milwaukee and at ballparks in away games.[8]

Interestingly, to attract and entertain fans in 2005 the Brewers organized and held numerous events at Miller Park and also sponsored and implemented other marketing activities and civic programs. Besides Bobble Head Days and such ticket specials as Badger Mutual Insurance Family Days, Daron & Bill's Buckethead Brigade and Spring Madness at the stadium, there was the 5K Run/Walk World Famous Sausage Race, Sawmill Slat Bat Factor and WDA Anti-Spit Tobacco Kids Comic Book. Nevertheless, based on demographics and other factors the team's brand is not likely to appreciate unless Attanasio invests more money and resources into the franchise such that the Brewers are able to qualify for the NL playoffs as a division winner or wild card team.

West Division

This is a five-team division that consists of two superior and two average brands, and one that is inferior. The two superior teams are the large-market Los Angeles Dodgers and San Francisco Giants, and the two average clubs are the small-market Arizona Diamondbacks and San Diego Padres. Between 1903 and 2004, the Dodgers claimed ten division titles, 18 NL pennants and six World Series. Estimated to be worth $424 million in market value, this franchise has been the most consistently successful and competitive in the NL. The team ranked fourth in baseball with annual revenues of $166 million in 2004, and more than three million spectators have attended the club's home games each season at 56,000-seat Dodger Stadium. Furthermore, the team is a leader in creating diverse and innovative marketing and safety programs and advertising campaigns that appeal to baseball fans in the Los Angeles area. In 2005, for example, rock music was played between innings at home games instead of traditional songs on an organ. Also, a free Women's Initiative and Network Program was launched by the franchise to offer women access to game experiences through such activities as baseball clinics, seminars and forums that involved Dodgers' players, coaches and staff. Then, the club established some strict and well-intentioned code of conduct guidelines and policies in order to minimize fan misbehavior and unruly conduct. These included the display of signs at the entrances to Dodger Stadium and throughout the facility's concourses, distribution of public address announcements and new safety brochures and the enforcement of penalties for any spectators who violate one or more of the 11 guidelines. These include immediate ejection from the ballpark, arrest and/or prosecution. Because of its strong leaders and long-run traditions as a baseball organization, the Dodgers will remain a superior brand throughout the early 2000s.[9]

According to FutureBrand's study, the Giants' value as a brand placed seventh in MLB at $78 million in 2002. Three years later, an article appeared in an issue of *Forbes* magazine. It listed the club's market value at $381 million and annual revenues at $159 million. Since 1903, the franchise's teams have won six division titles, 18 NL pennants and five World Series. At 41,300-seat Pacific Bell Park, which was built in 2000 and later renamed SBC Park, the club's attendances have exceeded 3.24 million in the regular seasons from 2000 to 2004. If 41-year-old Barry Bonds is forced to retire because of his injuries and/or suspended by the league for using steroids or other illegal substances, then the popularity and fan base of the Giants may decrease causing the club as a brand to decline in value. As of 2005, however, this elite baseball organization ranked as one of the most successful in the history of MLB.

For specific baseball and business reasons, the Arizona Diamondbacks and San Diego Padres are each average brands. In the Phoenix metropolitan area, the NBA Suns is more popular than the Diamondbacks, and the NFL Cardinals and NHL Coyotes. Even so, between 1998 and 2004 Diamondbacks teams won three division titles, one NL pennant and a World Series. At regular season games played in 49,000-seat Bank One Ballpark, the club has averaged approximately three million fans per year. Although that is an impressive number of spectators and fan support for this expansion team, in 2005 the franchise's stadium debt was estimated at 103 percent of its $286 million market value. The principal amount and annual interest payments on the debt are not only a financial obligation of the taxpayers in Phoenix, these liabilities also mean the Diamondbacks must be competitive and win so that the stadium is nearly sold out at home games and the club's revenues increase by million of dollars each season. After pitcher Curt Schilling was traded by the club to the Boston Red Sox and then Randy Johnson to the New York Yankees, it is doubtful that the team can compete throughout each season against its superior rivals in the West Division. In short, the Diamondbacks are a high-risk franchise and an average brand.

Besides the revenues from the Diamondbacks' games at Bank One Ballpark, the Padres have realized more cash inflows from ticket sales at 42,000-seat Petco Park, which was constructed for the team in 2004. In that season, the club established an attendance record of three million spectators at the ballpark. Regarding its performances, the team won division titles in 1984, 1996 and 1998, and NL pennants in 1984 and 1998. Six years later, the franchise was valued at $329 million as reported in *Forbes*. To expand the team's fan base in Mexico, during 2004 Padres officials held town hall meetings in Tijuana, established a bus service so that fans could make round trips for $2 on game days between Mexican border towns and San Diego, promoted baseball and the team on radio and television stations and in Mexican newspapers, and scheduled the broadcasts of games in Spanish on Uniradio Corporation's XEMO 860-AM to audiences in San Diego County and Tijuana, and in portions of Orange County. Because of these marketing innovations, activities at Petco Park and inferior performances of the NFL Chargers, the Padres is an average brand whose value will rise throughout the early 2000s.[10]

Two years after becoming an expansion team in 1993, the Rockies qualified for the postseason as a wild card in the NL but then was defeated by the Atlanta Braves in a division series. For the majority of its regular seasons, however, the team has lost more games than it won. Even so, at 50,449-seat Coors Field the Rockies attendances generally exceed three million per year. To expand its base in the Denver metropolitan area and surrounding counties, the club must compete for fans with the NBA Nuggets, NFL Broncos, NHL Avalanche and MLS Rapids. In 2004, the club ranked eighteenth in MLB with a market value of $290 million, an annual revenue stream of $132 million, and an operating loss of $7.8 million. If the Rockies' performances improve such that the team wins a few division titles and one or more NL pennants, then its value as a brand will increase from inferior to average.

Summary

In this chapter, the brands of 14 AL and 15 NL teams in MLB were identified, evaluated and ranked. The analysis was based on the financial values reported in a 2002 study completed by the FutureBrand Company, on baseball statistics from the *Official Major League Baseball Fact Book 2005 Edition*, on the contents of an article that appeared in *Forbes* magazine in April of 2005, and on information from the teams' websites as linked to MLB.com. These amounts and raw data included, for various MLB seasons, the teams' market values, debt to value ratios, annual and operating revenues, regular season home attendances, win-loss records, number of titles, pennants and championships, capacities of the ballparks, and the clubs' marketing and civic activities, events and programs.

As a result, in the AL three brands were ranked as superior, eight as average and three as inferior. Excluding the Expos, which had relocated from Montreal, Canada to Washington D.C. in early 2005, there were four superior brands, eight average and three inferior in the NL. Generally, the seven superior brands in MLB such as the AL New York Yankees and NL Los Angeles Dodgers have experienced success on the field, played their home games in stadiums located in large markets, and earned relatively high revenues from attendances at home games and local broadcasting operations.

Meanwhile, the 16 average brands such as the AL Minnesota Twins and NL St. Louis Cardinals have occasionally won division titles, NL pennants and a World Series, performed in stadiums placed in mid-sized or small markets, and received modest amounts of revenues from ticket sales at their club's games and from local radio and television broadcasts. Finally, the six inferior brands such as the AL Tampa Bay Devil Rays and NL Colorado Rockies have realized poor marketing opportunities in their local areas and regions, co-existed in a city with well-respected and popular teams from the NBA, NFL, NHL and/or MLS, and whose media markets and fan bases were relatively small in size.

In sum, from a marketing perspective MLB teams are brands that represent attributes and benefits, and convey values, culture and personality. Consequently, to be successful as brands, teams should invest in those assets, human resources and marketing programs that will provide the highest returns for the lowest risks.

23. Ticket Prices and Fan Costs

From a marketing perspective, there is a set of tools that firms typically use to pursue their objectives in a target market. A four-factor classification of these tools is called the marketing mix, which consists of place, product, promotion and price. For the American League (AL) and National League (NL) franchise owners and their respective teams in Major League Baseball (MLB), each tool has an identity and business application. To illustrate, there is the first factor, place, which represents the various activities that each team implements to make its games accessible and available or convenient for the baseball fans in its target market. These include the stadium location, the times and dates of the regular season schedule of games, and the different outlets to broadcast games on local, regional, national and international television and radio networks.[1]

The second factor, product, is the team's tangible offer to the market. It consists, in part, of the players' uniforms, the club's brand name and logo, and the roster of rookies and veteran players who perform at various positions such as pitcher, catcher, infielder and outfielder. The third factor is promotion, which are the activities a team uses to communicate and promote its product to targeted fans. For MLB franchises, this factor consists of advertising, direct marketing, sales campaigns and public relations programs in their home cities and metropolitan areas. The fourth and final factor is price. It is commensurate with the perceived value of the team's offer, or a cost that represents the amount of money paid by spectators for tickets, food, merchandise and equipment that are purchased at games and elsewhere by other consumers. Consequently, with respect to the fourth factor, the ticket prices and fan costs related to the regular season and postseason games of one or more MLB teams are the specific topics that were researched and discussed in this chapter.

Pricing Methods and Strategies

According to the majority of marketing experts, there are several types of pricing methods that firms may implement. These are markup, target-return, perceived value, value, going-rate and sealed-bid pricing. Indeed, it is likely that baseball team executives have developed a variety of organizational policies to determine which combinations of these methods are the most appropriate for their clubs. However, in the literature about professional sports leagues, there are few if any articles, reports and studies that explicitly reveal and analyze the policies adopted and types of methods used by MLB teams to price their tickets and other items at games, and to establish the costs of tangible products and intangible services offered to the public and especially to fans in the target market. Therefore, the actual and current decisions of team officials regarding the implementation of pricing policies are relatively unknown and generally not disclosed, except when the decisions and policies are reported in newspaper columns and sports magazine articles, and in online publications.

Based on economic theory, in a competitive baseball market there are forces such as population size, consumer income and wealth, amount and quality of advertising and fan expectations, which influence the demand, and factors as technology, input costs, taxes and seller expectations, which affect the supply. Graphically, the intersection of demand and supply determine the market's equilibrium price and quantity. However, because of antitrust exemptions, assignment of territorial rights by the league and other rules, each MLB team has market power and thus, operates in business as an imperfect competitor. Given that the economic goal of teams is to earn maximize profits, their pricing strategies may include a number of options. In part, these alternatives are block, peak-load, randomized, transfer and/or two-part pricing, and also commodity bundling, price matching and first-, second- and/or third-degree price discrimination. Again, it is somewhat uncertain whether MLB teams actually use one or more of these options in their pricing system. More than likely, it is the forces of demand that are quantified and evaluated by a team owner's marketing staff when setting, for example, the ticket price per seat at the ballpark. This activity, in turn, will affect a typical franchise's cash flows, revenues, costs and net earnings.[2]

Based on the sports literature and other documents, since the late 1990s to early 2000s such baseball teams as the AL's Indians and Yankees, and the NL's Braves and Rockies have imposed some form of variable pricing for tickets to games. To highlight these strategies, in one or more years the Indians had decided to lower the price of seats in the bleachers at Jacobs Field in Cleveland for spectators but charged an across-the-board premium of $5 per seat for home games against their most popular rivals. The Yankees, meanwhile, have offered discount promotions whereby customers pay less than $6 for a seat in the upper deck of Yankee Stadium in New York to watch games against low-drawing opponents. Furthermore, the Braves have charged an additional $4 for weekend games at Turner Field in Atlanta, as did the Rockies at Coors Field in Denver. To improve their attendances, the AL's Angels at Anaheim Stadium in southern California, and the NL's Mets at Shea Stadium in New York City and Giants at Pacific Bell Park in San Francisco have also implemented some types variable pricing strategies, that is, set seating prices contingent on when games are played, who is the opposing team and where the seat is located in the ballpark.[3]

Besides these AL and NL teams, the Twins, Mariners and Cubs have each adopted innovative pricing schemes to increase their clubs' revenues. Titled the Flex Plan by the Twins' ticket sales director Scott O'Connell, customers are authorized to buy vouchers for a given number of tickets, and then permitted to allocate those tickets to attend any combination of home games they or others prefer and sit in any seat at the ballpark, which is the Metrodome in Minneapolis. For example, if one voucher equals one ticket, a fan who chooses to buy 40 vouchers may watch 40 games, or ten games with three family members, or five games with seven employees, or one game with 39 friends. According to David Carter, a consultant for the Los Angeles-based Sports Business Group, "If I'm the Twins, I bend over backwards for these ticket purchasers. They represent the best potential source of incremental turnstile revenue." Meanwhile, in 2001 the Mariners in Seattle launched an online service to auction tickets for games on its web site. For each ticket sold, the team collected 15 percent from the seller and 10 percent from the buyer. The Mariners shared the remaining cash with MLB's media company and LiquidSeats, which provided the technology to support the service. Although some tickets had sold at a premium price relative to face value, which is an illegal transaction in Seattle, the Mariner's attorneys concluded that knowing the addresses of ticket-holders would block fans in the area from selling their tickets at excess prices and therefore, the team's strategy avoids any conflicts with the law. Since 2001, other MLB teams have implemented similar plans as the Mariners and offered their home game tickets online. Interestingly, the numbers of tickets sold and revenues received from online services has not been disclosed by the AL and NL teams or reported in the media.[4]

Alternatively, in 2002 the Cubs initiated a multilevel ticket policy. That is, relative to its home season schedule of 81 games at Wrigley Field in Chicago, the franchise identified and then charged lower prices for eight value games and higher prices for 19 prime games. Since 2002, the numbers of regular and value games have each decreased while the proportion of prime games have increased. As a result of redefining its home games, the clubs' average ticket price is significantly higher. Furthermore, at Wrigley Field there are seats in the upper deck outfield reserve section, and in the terrace reserve outfield and terrace reserve infield sections. After the ticket prices in these sections were adjusted, the Cubs realized even more revenues from admissions to its home games. As DePaul University economics instructor Peter Bernstein stated, "Put together the increase in the number of prime games and the newly defined infield ticket prices and that terrace reserve seat well behind home plate will cost you 19 percent more this season [2005] than in 2004." Finally, despite not qualifying for the divisional playoffs in 2004 the Cubs also raised Wrigley Field's club box seats by 28 percent. In short, this multi-faceted pricing strategy suggests that the team's owner, players and coaches will become richer.[5]

With respect to the pricing structure of a team that recently relocated, the Baseball Expos, L.P. announced in November 2004 that average ticket prices for the Washington Nationals' 2005 home games are expected to range from $24 to $26, with reserve seats starting at $7. As Baseball Expos, L.P. president Tony Tavares put it, "We are committed to offering tickets at a wide range of price points so that baseball is affordable and fun for fans throughout the Washington [D.C.] area. This is part of our overall commitment to making RFK Stadium a family-friendly ballpark." To successfully sell its inventory of home season tickets, the team has established a partnership with Ticketmaster, which is a well-known business firm that serves the ticketing needs of five professional clubs in the D.C. region. About the relationship with the Nationals, Ticketmaster Group president and chief executive officer Patrick R. Darr declared, "We are bringing all of Ticketmaster's resources and technology to the table to provide a smooth and effortless ticket-buying experience for fans during the inaugural season at RFK Stadium."[6]

Distribution of Ticket Prices

To examine the ticket prices of MLB teams for selected seasons, Table 23.1 was prepared. It shows the average ticket prices per season for each club in the AL and NL. To be consistent, the tabled prices of the American teams are reported in U.S. dollars, while those of the Toronto Blue Jays and Montreal Expos were converted to U.S. dollars by using the currencies' exchange rates in those years. Based on the distribution of values in the table and other baseball-related information, the following paragraphs contain an analysis of the amounts and percentage changes in ticket prices relative to 1995–2004, and also to selected years for various franchises in the AL and NL.

During the ten-year period, the average admission price per team increased 84 percent or by $9.09. Relative to each league, between 1995 and 2004 the AL teams' average price rose by 76 percent and the NL clubs by 97 percent. In general, this percentage difference meant that the NL teams had relatively more market power than AL clubs to raise their ticket prices at home even when the U.S. economy was sluggish during the early 2000s. To compare seasons, the largest and smallest average percentage increases were, respectively, 12.1 percent in 2000 and 3.7 percent in 2002. Despite moderate to high percentages, however, the dollar price of baseball tickets per game appeals to sports fans and remains a bargain for admission when compared to those in the National Football League, National Basketball Association and National Hockey League.[7]

For the AL teams, the ten-year average high and low percentage increases in ticket prices ranged from 201 percent for the Red Sox to 33 percent each for the Blue Jays, Rangers and Royals, and in the NL, the spread was 167 percent for the Phillies to 21 percent for the Expos. For the dollar amounts per ticket, in 2004 the AL Red Sox had the most expensive price at $40.77 and the Royals established the cheapest at $13.42, while the NL Cubs' tickets at $28.45 cost the most and Marlins at $12.78 was priced the least. Consequently, the teams located in large markets such as the Boston and Chicago metropolitan areas tended to charge higher prices for their tickets than clubs that performed in small- or medium-sized markets as Kansas City and Miami.

After analyzing Table 23.1, there are other interesting facts, values and trends about one or more of the AL and NL teams' ticket price amounts and percentage changes. First, when new ballparks were constructed and opened, during those seasons the average ticket prices of the teams generally increased by substantial amounts and percentages. This occurred, for instance, in 1997 for the Braves at Turner Field in Atlanta, in 2000 for the Mariners at Safeco Field in Seattle, in 2001 for the Brewers at Miller Park in Milwaukee, in 2003 for the Reds at the Great American Ball Park in Cincinnati, and in 2004 for the Padres at Petco Park in San Diego. Yet, even though their ticket prices had inflated, these teams' home attendances also rose because of baseball fans' interest to visit the new facilities and observe their teams play in the new stadiums. After measuring the boost in home attendances, it was 19 percent for the Braves, 7 percent for the Mariners, 78 percent for the Brewers, 27 percent for the Reds, and 48 percent for the Padres. The direct and positive relationship between playing in new stadiums and higher attendances is called the honeymoon effect, which means that home attendances will increase and peak within a few years, and then gradually decline unless the club wins more regular season games and competes for its division title. Therefore, in the short-run a large increase in ticket prices when new ballparks are opened results in greater attendances and cash inflows for the home and visiting teams and thus, benefits the respective franchise owners and players. If home attendances are sustained at the higher level, then the team may earn more revenues to bid for talented free agents and to attract veteran players who are released by their clubs.

Second, the average ticket prices of 26 teams were higher in 2004 than in 1995. However, relative to 1995 the home attendances of six had declined in 2004. That is, for the

TABLE 23.1. MLB TEAM TICKET
PRICES*, BY LEAGUE, 1995–2004

Team	1995	1996	1997	1998	1999	2000	2001	2002	2003	2004
AL										
Angels	8.06	8.44	9.68	11.83	13.19	13.19	11.42	11.79	15.97	16.60
Athletics	10.62	11.34	10.53	10.58	10.10	11.35	14.07	14.94	15.65	16.49
Blue Jays	13.35	13.93	15.73	16.38	16.62	16.26	15.47	15.54	18.82	17.87
Brewers	9.51	9.37	9.58	—	—	—	—	—	—	—
Devil Rays	—	—	—	15.56	15.08	12.91	16.14	15.83	14.43	16.82
Indians	12.06	14.52	15.29	17.35	18.43	20.58	22.33	22.33	22.33	20.29
Mariners	9.73	11.59	13.40	14.94	19.01	23.43	22.98	24.60	24.60	24.01
Orioles	13.14	13.14	17.02	19.77	19.82	19.78	18.23	18.23	20.15	22.56
Rangers	12.07	11.96	13.92	16.49	19.93	19.67	18.03	18.03	18.19	16.08
Red Sox	13.51	15.43	17.93	20.63	24.05	28.33	34.86	39.68	38.59	40.77
Royals	10.05	9.74	9.65	10.69	11.76	11.76	12.98	12.30	12.13	13.42
Tigers	10.60	10.60	10.40	10.40	12.23	24.83	20.95	20.44	19.86	17.90
Twins	9.40	10.16	8.22	8.22	8.46	9.33	10.83	11.78	13.00	14.42
White Sox	12.93	14.11	13.33	14.48	15.04	14.30	18.73	18.73	22.51	21.56
Yankees	15.01	14.58	18.36	20.51	23.33	25.94	24.26	24.26	24.86	24.86
NL										
Astros	8.91	10.65	11.40	11.88	13.30	20.03	17.72	18.87	20.78	22.88
Braves	12.00	13.06	17.18	17.18	19.21	19.78	20.77	20.59	17.51	17.51
Brewers	—	—	—	10.28	11.02	11.72	16.32	17.63	16.86	16.86
Cardinals	9.80	9.91	12.72	15.47	16.53	17.60	21.43	21.43	23.76	23.76
Cubs	13.17	13.12	14.63	14.42	17.46	17.55	21.17	24.05	24.21	28.45
Diamondbacks	—	—	—	14.70	16.58	16.58	13.11	13.80	15.46	17.73
Dodgers	9.68	9.94	11.16	12.21	13.67	15.43	15.51	16.38	16.38	16.92
Expos	8.92	9.07	8.37	9.98	9.38	10.29	9.19	9.00	10.08	10.82
Giants	10.16	10.61	11.55	11.47	12.12	21.24	19.10	20.59	21.64	21.60
Marlins	9.65	10.37	10.89	12.15	12.17	12.53	12.72	12.72	12.78	12.78
Mets	10.89	11.83	13.06	16.11	19.89	24.29	22.53	22.53	23.61	23.92
Padres	9.12	9.88	10.79	11.34	11.92	13.02	13.74	15.20	16.23	21.41
Phillies	9.75	11.01	11.18	11.22	13.60	13.60	14.33	15.26	17.24	26.08
Pirates	9.73	10.09	9.86	9.33	10.71	11.80	19.51	20.52	19.53	17.08
Reds	7.95	7.95	8.37	8.37	9.71	10.74	15.41	16.66	18.12	18.17
Rockies	10.61	10.61	12.76	15.79	15.79	16.50	15.21	15.21	15.21	15.10
Average	10.73	11.32	12.39	13.66	15.00	16.81	17.64	18.30	19.01	19.82

* The average ticket price is a weighted average of season ticket prices for seating categories. It is determined by factoring the tickets in each price range as a percentage of the total number of seats in each ballpark. The table excludes luxury seats but includes season ticket pricing. The average ticket price for children was reported in the Team Marketing Report beginning in 1999. The Brewers moved from the AL to NL in 1998 and that year, the Devil Rays joined the AL and Diamondbacks the NL. In 1997, the Angels' first name changed from California to Anaheim. Canadian prices are converted to U.S. dollars for the Blue Jays and Expos. A — denotes that a club did not exist in the league.

Source: The teams' prices were reported in "Major League Baseball," at http://www.teammarketing.com cited 18 January 2005.

Blue Jays, Indians and Orioles in the AL, and for the Braves, Expos and Rockies in the NL. As such, did the rise in ticket prices that had generally occurred throughout the ten seasons ultimately result in lower home attendances for each of these six teams? Undoubtedly, the higher admission prices were one reason for the drop in spectators at the ballparks. Nonetheless, another factor causing a fall in the attendances may have been their fans' disappointment with the poor performances of the Blue Jays at the SkyDome in Toronto, Orioles at Camden Yards in Baltimore, Expos at Olympic Stadium in Montreal and Rockies at Coors Field in Denver. Furthermore, apparently the honeymoon effect on attendances had peaked during the late 1990s or early 2000s for the Indians who had opened the 1994 season at Jacobs Field in small-market Cleveland. Finally, perhaps some of the Braves fans had shifted their loyalty and season-ticket expenditures to the NFL's Atlanta Falcons who appeared in Super Bowl XXXIII in 1999, and because of quarterback Michael Vick and the excitement he created on the gridiron as the team's superstar player. As a marketing strategy, in 2004 the Blue Jays, Indians and Rockies decided to each cut their average price while the Braves price remained at $17.51 per ticket. In 2003, the Orioles increased their admission charge to $22.56 from $20.15 and for the former Expos, the average price of $10.82 in 2004 was raised to approximately $25 for the Nationals in 2005 at RFK Stadium in the nation's capital city. In short, the majority of MLB teams had experienced greater attendances and likely earned more revenues from their new ballparks despite charging significantly higher ticket prices.

Third, based on the average ticket prices and home attendances in the 1995 and 2004 regular seasons, the differences in gate receipts between the small- and large-market teams had become more unequal. To illustrate these differences for a sample of six teams in each league, in 1995 the receipts for the large-market AL Red Sox, White Sox and Yankees totaled $75.2 million versus $34.5 million for the small-market Athletics, Royals and Twins. In 2004, the total receipts were, respectively, $250.6 million and $86 million. As a result, in nine seasons the gap in paid attendances between the two groups of teams had expanded from $40.7 million to $164.6 million, or approximately $124 million. Likewise, in 1995 the gate receipts for the large-market NL Cubs, Dodgers and Mets equaled $65.6 million and $32.8 million for the small-market Padres, Pirates and Reds. Then in 2004, these amounts totaled, respectively, $204.1 million and $132.9 million. Thus, the gap in gate revenues between the small- and large-market NL teams widened from $32.8 million to $71.2 million, or by nearly $39 million.

Consequently, there were disparities in paid attendances of about $124 million between the small- and large-market teams in the AL, and $39 million in the NL. This had occurred even though ticket price inflation, in the 1995 to 2004 seasons, averaged close 76 percent for the AL clubs and 97 percent for those in the NL. Therefore, based on the sample of three small- and large-market teams in each league, it appears that the smaller average ticket price increase of 76 percent had expanded attendances and the revenue inequalities relatively more for franchises in the AL.

Following the previous analysis of teams' ticket prices, the discussion will next focus on the total dollar cost for a family of four to attend a typical MLB game. The Chicago-based Team Marketing Report Inc. (TMRI) appropriately named this amount as the Fan Cost Index of a team.

Distribution of Fan Costs

Since 1993, TMRI has derived a Fan Cost Index (FCI). It represents the total expenditure for a four-person family to attend a regular season game of each team in the AL and NL. Besides average-priced tickets for two adults and two children, the FCI includes the amounts spent for four small soft drinks and regular-sized hot dogs, two small draft beers, game programs and least expensive adult-sized caps, and for parking one automobile. To determine these costs each year, TMRI calls, interviews and obtains the data from representatives of the teams, venues and concessionaires. After the data is collected and organized, it is published annually in a report. One column of the report lists the FCI in dollars for each team and another column presents the team's index as a percentage change based on the amount in the previous season.

To analyze the FCIs of AL and NL clubs and MLB's average index each year from 1995 to 2004, the eleven columns in Table 23.2 were developed. Since the forthcoming analysis relies on the table, it emphasizes important aspects of various reports. As an aside, for the specific annual percentage changes of the teams' FCIs see the Resources portion of Major League Baseball at TMRI's web site, teammarketing.com.[8]

Based on the FCI's listed in columns two to ten of Table 23.2, in 2004 it cost families 60 percent more than in 1995 to attend a MLB game played at a team's ballpark. The FCI's largest annual percentage increases on average had occurred in the 2000 season at 9.1 percent and 1998 season at 7.5 percent. Alternatively, the smallest annual average percentage changes in MLB's FCIs were in 2004 at 2.7 percent and 2002 at 3.6 percent. In other words, as a group the baseball teams' admission prices at their stadiums and the costs for families to attend games increased at an above average rate during the late 1990s when the U.S. economy prospered and security markets had generated high returns for investors and more cash inflows for growth. With respect to each league, the average expense for families to watch AL and NL games rose, respectively, from an FCI of 101 in 1995 to 157 in 2004, and from an FCI of 93 in 1995 to 153 in 2004. Thus, during the ten seasons it costs adults with children proportionately more money to attend the games of NL teams relative to those in the AL.

Excluding the Brewers, who moved from the AL to NL after the 1997 season, and exempting the expansion Devil Rays and Diamondbacks, who had each played their inaugural seasons in 1998, it was from 1995 to 2004 that the cost indexes had increased for each of the 27 remaining teams. In the AL, the indexes inflated the most for the Red Sox at 134 percent and Mariners at 82 percent, and least for the Royals at 22 percent and Rangers at 30 percent. Meanwhile, in the NL FCIs were the most expansionary for the Phillies at 106 percent and Mets at 104 percent, and least in growth for the Expos at 26 percent and Braves at 27 percent. Evidently, the owners of the Red Sox, Mariners, Phillies and Mets must have decided that their teams' entertainment value at regular season games was relatively under priced for families, while the proprietors of the Royals, Rangers, Expos and Braves concluded to increase families' costs to their home games at approximately the rate of inflation.

As reported in Table 23.2, there are some interesting facts and unique relationships to consider about the FCIs of some teams. First, it cost families more dollars in each successive season to watch the Red Sox play their home games in Fenway Park, and the Dodgers in Dodger Stadium and Padres in Qualcomm Stadium and then Petco Park. Yet, the FCIs never declined up to 2002 but remained constant during 2002–2003 for the Indians at Jacobs Field in Cleveland, and up to 2000 and during 2000–2001 for the Mets at Shea Stadium in New York City. With respect to the other teams, the indexes of family costs were inconsistent and fluctuated, that is, during two or more consecutive seasons they increased and then decreased, or decreased and then increased, and/or remained flat after an increase or decrease.

Second, there were large percentage boosts in FCIs during the initial season when

TABLE 23.2. FCIs* OF MLB TEAMS,
BY LEAGUE, 1995–2004

Team	1995	1996	1997	1998	1999	2000	2001	2002	2003	2004
AL										
Angels	90	92	101	113	121	117	110	113	130	133
Athletics	101	104	94	98	92	94	120	124	139	145
Blue Jays	101	95	106	107	112	112	114	121	155	145
Brewers	86	85	94	—	—	—	—	—	—	—
Devil Rays	—	—	—	131	120	120	132	138	149	156
Indians	99	115	116	126	133	142	150	161	161	152
Mariners	95	106	118	125	136	179	180	173	175	173
Orioles	113	113	124	135	139	138	131	141	148	158
Rangers	100	101	113	127	139	156	150	150	139	130
Red Sox	112	117	129	144	160	168	209	228	238	263
Royals	98	96	85	96	110	100	119	113	112	120
Tigers	96	109	108	102	108	165	160	160	157	149
Twins	97	100	97	97	97	102	130	121	127	131
White Sox	110	118	115	120	123	122	138	159	159	160
Yankees	118	117	134	148	166	174	178	178	182	183
NL										
Astros	87	94	105	108	120	161	143	157	165	177
Braves	113	121	135	134	144	160	156	155	154	144
Brewers	—	—	—	97	95	100	124	130	128	124
Cardinals	91	91	105	129	127	133	151	151	168	170
Cubs	112	116	121	120	134	135	166	181	172	194
Diamondbacks	—	—	—	119	124	120	112	115	119	132
Dodgers	90	96	104	111	123	140	142	145	147	153
Expos	86	90	86	93	87	88	76	84	100	108
Giants	102	121	110	108	110	161	163	169	178	184
Marlins	86	92	93	102	100	104	110	110	112	114
Mets	91	104	114	132	154	175	175	177	182	186
Padres	82	86	101	102	114	124	127	133	146	154
Phillies	91	111	100	94	121	126	131	137	149	188
Pirates	93	96	86	94	99	107	150	151	147	143
Reds	81	81	82	89	96	104	129	127	140	140
Rockies	99	103	116	132	135	130	138	141	141	140
Average	97	103	107	115	121	132	140	145	151	155

* The team's FCIs, which are rounded to dollars, include the prices of adult and child tickets, beers, sodas, hot dogs, parking, game programs and baseball caps. The FCIs that changed from one year to the next by $1 likely occurred because of rounding totals and not prices. For more specific details about the prices, see the note below Table 23.1. A — indicates the club did not exist in the league.
Source: "Major League Baseball," at http://www.teammarketing.com cited 18 January 2005.

teams had competed in a new ballpark at home. These include, for example, 12 percent for the Braves in 1997 at Turner Field, 31 percent for the Mariners in 2000 at Safeco Field, 24 percent for the Brewers in 2001 at Miller Park, 10 percent for the Reds in 2003 at the Great American Ball Park, and 26 percent for the Phillies in 2004 at Citizens Bank Park. Apparently, it was necessary for the owners of at least these five franchises to raise their ticket and other prices in order to generate more cash flows to spend on team operating expenses including taxes, on lease payments for the home ballpark if it was publicly owned, and on the salaries and benefits due to coaches, players and staff personnel. Furthermore, since local baseball fans demanded to see games in the teams' new ballparks, they were willing and able to pay for higher ticket prices and spend more money for food, beverages, parking, programs and caps. As discussed before in this chapter, the teams' home attendances significantly increased at their new ballparks when they were opened. In short, it was a prudent business decision for the respective team owners to respond to an increase in demand for games from baseball fans by incrementally raising prices.

Third, the average differences in FCIs between a sample of three large- and three small-market teams in each league were the family costs of $15 per game in 1995 and $70 in 2004 for the AL, and $14 and $53 per game for the NL. This means that it cost $55 or 366 percent more in 2004 than in 1995 for a four-person family to attend the regular season games of a typical large-market AL team, and $39 or 278 percent more to attend games of a large-market NL team. Indeed, the average FCIs of the AL's Red Sox, White Sox and Yankees far exceeded those of the NL's Cubs, Dodgers and Mets, whereas the differences in the average FCIs of the small-market teams were moderately unequal, that is, between the AL's Athletics, Royals and Twins, and the NL's Expos, Marlins and Padres.

Given the previous statements, this concludes the analysis of ticket prices and FCIs for the clubs that existed in the AL and NL during some or all of the 1995 to 2004 seasons. With that effort completed, a summary of this chapter's contents appears next followed by the notes. In turn, the notes identify the publications that were researched and used to support the discussion of the topics.

Summary

As one of four components of the marketing mix, pricing is a tool applicable to the ownership and operation of franchises in MLB. That is, there are business objectives when teams establish the ticket prices for spectators to be admitted into a ballpark to attend games. Also, the expenditures by adults and their children for beverages, food, parking, programs and caps are other aspects of costs with respect to families who watch games at the local ballpark. As such, this chapter presented an array of teams' ticket prices in a table and then analyzed the absolute and relative dollar amounts and percentage changes of these prices during one or more of the seasons. The distribution of ticket prices between small- and large-market teams were also highlighted and discussed, especially with respect to how attendances had changed from the previous season.

Then, a table was constructed that contained the dispersion of FCIs among 30 MLB teams during ten consecutive years. The tabled FCIs and three interesting facts about the indexes of one or more teams emerged as the focus of the analysis. In sum, this chapter denotes why ticket prices charged by teams and game costs incurred by families were each essential factors in the business success or failure of professional baseball franchises during the late 1990s and early 2000s.

24. Marketing: Partnerships, Sponsorships and Licensing

To initiate and effectively perform production and marketing tasks in the U.S. and other nations, Major League Baseball (MLB) and its franchises in the American League (AL) and National League (NL) have formed various types of strategic alliances and other relationships with American and foreign small, medium and large companies. The business interactions are necessary because these latter organizations have the experience, capability and professionalism, and also the specialists and other resources to support this professional baseball league, and assist one or more of the 30 teams to increase their worldwide fan bases and thereby, generate more revenues and profits for them. In other words, it is pragmatic and more efficient for local, regional, national and international sports entertainment businesses to outsource their activities, events, programs, products and/or services to other firms and entities when that decision results in a decrease in operating and/or financial risks and an increase in economic returns.

When MLB and baseball franchises establish short- and long-run marketing relationships with one or a group of contractors, manufacturers, wholesalers and retailers, and with companies that provide specialized or a variety of services, there are relevant facts, data and other information to consider and evaluate. That is, the league will create value as the parent organization of a sport, and the teams will be rewarded as enterprises by auditing the performances and tangible and intangible assets and ownership structures of their existing and future partners, sponsors and licensees. After those matters have been verified, then business relationships can be established with confidence, support and trust between the parties.

Because MLB and the league's AL and NL teams provide sports entertainment, they contract with and outsource their requirements for baseball equipment, clothing and merchandise, and other products and services to American and non–U.S. organizations. That is, the professional league and member franchises simply do not have the resources or investment capital to profitably complete this type of work. Consequently, partnerships and licensing agreements are used as alternative ways to perform these functions. Furthermore, besides the cash inflows from admissions, broadcasting and the sales of products and services, MLB and the 30 clubs generate millions of dollars in advertising revenues from their sponsors. Indeed, there is very little risk of losses and good potential returns for the league and/or teams when they contract with sponsors.

As such, this chapter highlights and describes some of organized baseball's—which includes units of MLB, and Minor League Baseball (MLBB) and the Major League Baseball Players Association (MLBPA)—participation in a sample of unique partnerships, sponsorships and licensing agreements. For various economic and financial reasons, these business relationships are becoming more important especially in the marketing of the sport, MLB and the 30 big league teams. Generally, the contracts and other deals listed in the following three sections of this chapter are relatively current since they became effective during 2004 or between January and June of 2005.

Partnerships

League

During April of 2005, MLB Properties (MLBP) celebrated the opening of the regular season in a partnership with Toys 'R' Us. That is, this retail company's stores displayed MLB merchandise in special feature shops and hosted a number of events including personal appearances by the teams' players. The shops showcased a broad assortment of licensed merchandise including apparel, video games, baseball cards, sporting goods and collectibles. Furthermore, the shops offered exclusive items from McFarlane Toys such as a three-inch figure of former New York Yankees' star Don Mattingly and a boxed set of six-inch statues of slugger Barry Bonds and Hall of Famer Willie Mays. The customers that purchased $20 or more of merchandise from a shop received a commemorative MLB opening day pin. At the various ballparks, on opening day fans were given a mini-catalogue of MLB products that were available in Toys 'R' Us stores nationwide. Meanwhile, some popular players appeared at stores in the cities that hosted a big league team. "This partnership with Major League allows us to expand our team specific offerings to our customers across the country and provides kids with the opportunity to personally meet their favorite players," said Toys 'R' Us merchandising president Jim Feldt.[1]

Alternatively, Home Depot and MLB formed an integrated marketing partnership in April of 2005. This commitment included exclusive category rights, advertising, special events, community relation's activities and in-store promotions. For example, at its stores the company distributed the 2005 Major League Baseball Official Fan Guide. It featured regular season game schedules for the 30 teams and useful consumer information about garden and yard care. Home Depot also co-branded a television spot with a key vendor, The Scotts Company. The spot featured Atlanta Braves pitcher John Smoltz. Besides Home Depot, MLB also joined with LBi Software Engineering to develop an electronic baseball information system named the eBIS. This web-based program facilitates many functions of baseball operations ranging from the inputting of information about player's contract terms, trades, waivers and scouting, to the drafts. According to MLB's vice president of information technology Julio Carbonell, "Our business users, technical team and LBi exhibited utmost dedication and perseverance in ensuring the successful delivery of a complicated set of applications."[2]

In another partnership, MLBP and the MLBPA teamed with the Cartoon Network to jointly produce a program designed to promote youth interest in baseball and in collecting baseball cards. The program is a series of spots in which MLB players such as the Yankees' Derek Jeter, Angels' Vladimir Guerrero and Orioles' Miguel Tejada are a part of a story line that involved characters from *Codename: Kids Next Door*. These characters spoke about the excitement of opening packs of baseball cards and seeing which players were being added to their collection. In turn, each spot included visuals of card companies like Donruss, Fleer, Topps and Upper Deck and the tagging of information about retailers Target, Toys 'R' Us and the Shop at MLB.com. "This program is all about fun," said MLBPA director of licensing and business affairs Judy Heeter. "Action shots of Major League stars will bring the excitement of baseball cards to life for kids— and show them an important way to get closer to their favorite players."[3]

As MLB's interactive media and Internet company, MLB Advanced Media (MLBAM) announced in early 2005 the completion of a ten-year agreement with the National Association of Professional Baseball Leagues (NAPBL), which is the official name of MLBB. Besides being the exclusive provider of Internet-related and interactive media services to the NAPBL, the agreement specified that MLBAM is authorized to handle the online sale of merchandise, tickets, content, advertising and statistical syndication for the network, and to have the exclusive online use of NAPBL, league and team trademarks, names, logos, mascots, player names, likenesses, photos and game audio and video.[4]

Teams

To identify four partnerships between MLB teams and corporations, these are the Seattle Mariners and automobile manufacturer Dodge, Baltimore Orioles and CoverGirl, San Diego Padres and Cox Communications, and the Los Angeles Angels and General Motors (GM). The characteristics of each agreement may be summarized as follows. For three years at Safeco Field in Seattle, Dodge signs will be posted along the first-base line and above the Mariners' bullpen in left-center field. Furthermore, the company will be featured for one-half inning per game on the rotational sign behind home plate, give away a vehicle during one home game each season, and display an automobile or truck on the ballpark's Main Concourse near the left field gate.[5]

To promote the company's line of women cosmetics at five Orioles' games at Camden Yards during the 2005 season, CoverGirl distributed samples of Outlast All-Day Lipcolor to 10,000 female fans aged 13 years-old and over, and at makeover tents provided complimentary beauty consultants for fans during Mother's Day, Girl's Night Out, Miss USA Day, Latino Night and Student Night. Meanwhile, Cox Communications offered discounted monthly subscriptions to MLB.com All-Access and live in-market streaming of Padres games to its Internet customers with a High Speed connection in the San Diego area. For $14.95 per month, the All-Access service featured 300 out-of-market games, MLB.com GameDay audio, archived games, searchable video clips, customized highlight reels, ten-minute condensed recaps of all key plays of games, vintage radio and classic television broadcasts of MLB games, and pre-game text notes. According to MLBAM's vice president of marketing Art Reynolds, "This partnership is a win-win for our customers. By steaming live, in-market Padres games via Cox High Speed Internet, we are ensuring that our customers never have to miss another Padres game again, whether at home, at the office, or while on vacation."

In a three-year partnership agreement, a promotion titled "Saturday Night Drive Sweepstakes presentation by General Motors" was created. This program offers Angels' fans the opportunity to win one of 13 new GM vehicles throughout the 2005 season at 12 selected Saturday home games. At the team's Fan Appreciation Day on Sunday,

September 25, 2005, the final contestants who did not win an automobile on the previous Saturday home games will take part in "Second Chance Sunday" for the opportunity to win a 2006 Chevrolet Corvette. Anyway, to participate in the contest, fans may enter online through angelsbaseball.com or GM's findyourstyle.com, or fill out the entry stub on the back of any Angel's game ticket. All of the club's season ticket holders are automatically entered in the sweepstakes for each of the 12 contest periods.

Besides these four agreements, in April of 2005 the Seattle Mariners finalized deals with six Japanese companies. With respect to the terms of each partnership, Nintendo received two one-half innings of publicity at the Mariners home games on the rotational sign behind home plate while MasterCard Japan paid for one-half inning; Ajinomoto supplied amino acid-based drinks and supplements to the club in exchange for one-half inning per game on the home plate sign to promote the Amino Vital advanced sports performance supplement; Sanyo Electric's three-year agreement included one-half inning of signage per game and a display center on the Main Concourse of the ballpark to promote its products; Hitachi received one-half inning of advertisement on the home plate sign and Sato Pharmaceutical's two-year agreement included one-half inning of signage and the display of its logo on the padded railings in front of the home and visitors dugouts and on drinking cups and coolers provided for the players while inside their dugouts. To express his views about these agreements, Mariners executive vice president of business and sales Bob Aylward stated, "With tremendous interest in the Seattle Mariners in Japan, we are uniquely positioned to take advantage of these international opportunities. These companies are able to promote themselves to our fans at the ballpark and the many thousands of people who watch our games in Japan."[6]

Sponsorships

In a study performed by the world's leading provider of independent research, training and analysis on sponsorship, IEG, Inc. determined that the sponsorship of professional baseball leagues and teams increased approximately 6.7 percent per year or from $295 million in 2000 to $355 million in 2003, and then 9.3 percent to $388 million in 2004. The growth in 2004 occurred, in part, because of MLB's multi-million dollar deals with Ameriquest Mortgage, Bank of America and Taco Bell, and the growing ineffectiveness of traditional media and the subsequent rise of nontraditional marketing platforms. Then, in 2005, the league concluded annual or multiyear agreements with such companies as Home Depot, General Motors, General Mills and Deutsche Post's DHL, which is a delivery service company. Thus, despite the steroid scandals advertisers have continued to support MLB and its teams.[7]

For a sample of the sponsorships finalized by the league and teams with businesses during 2003 to 2005, the following information and facts about these deals are presented. First, U.S. commercial banks are one of the top sponsors of professional baseball since they operate at the local level and, to great extent, so do baseball teams. For example, in 2005 the Charlotte, North Carolina-based Bank of America (BOA) sponsored 10 or 33 percent of the MLB teams and served as the lead bank in a $1.4 billion league-wide credit line used by 20 of the clubs. After acquiring FleetBoston Financial Corporation in 2004, BOA increased its marketing efforts in Boston and New York City. Basically, BOA's total commitment to MLB is at least five years and includes broadcast and onsite branding and hospitality at the all-star game and playoffs, and sponsorship of AL and NL players of the week. Beside the league, the bank also has a four-year deal with Minor League Baseball that encompasses branding, promotional and hospitality opportunities, and a four-year agreement with Little League Baseball for branding at the Little League World Series and other promotions of youth baseball activities, events and programs.[8]

Meanwhile, another powerful financial institution that supports baseball is Citizens Bank, which has its headquarters in Providence, Rhode Island. In 2003, Citizens Bank signed an agreement to spend $95 million over 25 years to sponsor the Philadelphia Phillies. That total amount consisted of $57.5 million for the naming rights to the ballpark in Philadelphia and $37.5 million for the right to be the exclusive financial services advertiser on the Phillies television and radio broadcasts.

Second, in 2005 the Tampa Bay Devil Rays and BASF/Termidor Inc. agreed to a multiyear sponsorship affiliation. In part, Termidor received signage space on Center Field Street, print advertisement in the club's new Insider publication, radio exposure throughout the MLB season, and sponsorship of the "Termidor Defensive Play of the Game" feature on radio and on the Diamond Vision scoreboard in Tropicana Field. In evaluating this business relationship, BASF Professional Pest Control's senior marketing manager Karl J. Kisner remarked, "Our sponsorship guarantees Termidor's visibility at 81 home games in the Tampa–St. Pete area throughout peak termite season — not to mention over the airwaves through our full-season radio sponsorship. It's a combination of audience and frequency that has proven extremely effective for Termidor, one that we're excited to continue through the 2005 season."[9]

Third, in March of 2005 MLB signed a three-year sponsorship agreement with GM. This deal made Chevrolet the "Official Vehicle of Major League Baseball." For its commitment to baseball, Chevrolet was authorized to act as the presenting sponsor of the Most Valuable Player awards from the MLB All-Star Game and the World Series. As a result, the winners received the Chevrolet vehicle of their choice. Furthermore, the company sponsored the 2005 MLB All-Star Game Selection Show, which was broadcast in early July on the Entertainment Sports Program Network. Although Chevrolet has not been associated with MLB since 1996, the automobile division had marketing relationships with seven teams including the Chicago Cubs, New York Mets and Pittsburgh Pirates. Steve Tihanyi, who is GM's general director of marketing alliances and regional operations, believes that several more clubs will sign individual deals with Chevrolet in 2005. If that occurs, then Chevrolet is a sponsor for nearly one-half of MLB's franchises.[10]

In the sponsorship business, professional sports leagues experience various risks and potential financial losses. This occurred, for example, in 2004 when MLB and Columbia Pictures announced a $2.5 million plan to add Spider-Man 2 designs to bases during interleague games. After online poll results showed fans against the concept, the idea was axed. Consequently, was their research indicating those fans would or would not accept commercial logos on bases during regular season games? Could MLB have foreseen the backlash? Did the league underestimate its fans? Based on this and other incidents, it appears that the league occasionally fails to collect sufficient data before implementing its plans. Or, perhaps MLB is held to higher standards by baseball fans relative to those groups that support the National Basketball Association, National Football League, National Hockey League and Major League Soccer.[11]

Nevertheless, some sports business experts contend that organized baseball is simply less sophisticated in marketing than the other leagues and therefore, cannot generate huge amounts of money in sponsorship or television deals. Despite these viewpoints, it is expected that baseball's hierarchy will learn from their mistakes and gradually reduce the risks when implementing plans to reform the sponsorship business. In reaction to the Spider-Man 2 fiasco and the league's marketing successes, MLB's president and chief operating officer Bob DuPuy stated, "I would understand why people would think that historically we may not always have been ahead of the curve, but that's in part because of our reliance on the traditions of the game." Then he said, "The pull of tradition forces us to proceed slower than some marketing people would think."[12]

Licensing

With respect to professional sports organizations, the value of a team's logo, trademark and other distinctive features are derived, in part, because it is a member of a league. Even so, conflicts arise within a league because some small- and/or large-market teams insist on owning their logos, trademarks and other characteristics of value, and controlling the demand for and supply of them. Despite this problem, in MLB it is the league and not the individual teams that has gradually become the central office and administration for the licensing business.

During the late 1970s and early 1980s, MLB teams began to realize the value in protecting and registering their trademarks. As a result, a licensing program was implemented in baseball. However, while some teams wanted more money, others sought to have their own programs and a few wanted to grant national rights to the company or companies that retained local licensing rights. After successful negotiations occurred between franchise owners, these issues were resolved and the league's licensing program grew at a repaid rate for several years. For various economic and financial reasons, between the mid–1990s and early 2000s the licensing business of MLB experienced little growth. Since 1992, however, the league and/or teams have signed a number of agreements with licensees for millions of dollars in revenues. To illustrate, the following deals are presented.[13]

To earn more than $500 million, MLB signed five-year licensing agreements with several key partners during 2003. Accordingly, Majestic Athletic, Ltd. supplied an exclusive authentic collection of on-field game uniforms, batting practice jerseys and other clothing to the league's 30 teams and to stores in the domestic and international retail markets; New Era Cap Company, Inc. remained the exclusive authentic collection supplier of headwear to the MLB teams and domestic and international retail markets; Nike USA, Inc. furnished performance apparel and casual wear to the 30 clubs and retail markets; Twin Enterprises, Inc. provided non-authentic headwear to the domestic market, and maintained rights to produce authentic collection celebratory headwear for the wild card and division winning teams; VF Imagewear Inc. supplied non-authentic fleece and tee shirts for markets in the U.S., Canada and Latin America, and had the global rights to produce the official celebratory clothes worn by teams that participated in the postseason; Dynasty Apparel Industries Inc. provided non-authentic jerseys for the U.S. mass market and Latin America; and Drew Pearson International Inc. maintained rights to produce and distribute non-authentic headwear throughout Europe. In addition to royalties, the deals included marketing commitments, media expenditures and product supply with MLB and/or the 30 clubs. As expressed by MLB's executive vice president of business Tim Brosnan, "These agreements represent an expansion of our existing licensing model, which has successfully combined the service, dedication and marketing prowess of 'baseball centric' companies and major global brands."[14]

In 2005, the league or one of its divisions made several business deals with licensees. First, MLB.com announced the providers for the 2005 season fantasy game would be 18 companies such as Sportsline, STATS Inc., Fanstar Sports, iTV Entertainment, Sports Buff and Electronic Ballpark. Thus, as of February 2005 MLB.com and its official fantasy game licensees began to offer their fantasy game lineups and a selection of innovative, fun, exciting and challenging new games.[15]

Second, MLBAM and THQ Wireless Inc. agreed to develop and distribute a unique offering of officially licensed baseball-themed applications for mobile phones. These included strategy and trivia games, and player wallpapers and ringtones that were titled, respectively, MLB.com Trivia Challenge, MLB Player Wallpapers and Authentic MLB Player Ringtones. Furthermore, THQ Wireless offered fans other authentic baseball games officially licensed through the MLBPA. Three games were named as Big League Baseball 2005, Big League Home Run Challenge 2005 and Baseball Fantasy Five. Regarding this agreement, the company's president Tim Walsh said, "These fun and engaging products are an example of how THQ Wireless and MLBAM are combining efforts to bring America's favorite pastime to a broad mobile audience. These are applications that everyone, not just gamers, can enjoy."

Third, during April of 2005 Major League Baseball International (MLBI) and United Media K.K. launched a limited and exclusive co-branded licensing program in Japan. Entitled "Snoopy and Major League Baseball," the program features the popular beagle Snoopy, who appears in a cartoon strip. In fact, approximately 20 companies that have existing individual licenses in Japan with either MLBI or United Media will be selected to produce merchandise as part of the program. "We are very excited about this partnership with United Media," said MLBI's vice president of international licensing. "The popularity of both Major League Baseball and Snoopy in Japan will ensure a successful marriage between these two highly-regarded brands." In short, there has been a growth of MLBI's licensing business in that country because of the Japanese players on MLB teams, along with other factors such as conducting special events, executing localized advertising programs, and increasing the distribution of MLB licensed products.

Fourth, MLBP and Sportbox endorsed a five-year licensing agreement in May of 2005. As such, this company became the exclusive manufacturer of MLB branded terrestrial AM/FM radios. The radios receive live broadcasts from the teams' stadiums so that fans can hear the play-by-play of a game in their respective broadcast territories. Because they are designed for ballpark safety, the radios have rounded corners, no sharp edges, and are small in size and weight. Besides communication equipment, Sportbox also received the non-exclusive rights to produce MLB and club-branded MP3, CD, DVD and audio cassette players, VCR's, camcorders, and hand and power tools. Furthermore, Sportbox received authorization to produce an extensive line of MLB branded accessories for some of its MLB licensed products, along with a complete line of cellular accessories. About the agreement with MLBP, chief executive officer and founder of Sportbox Bill Frabizio remarked, "The true inspiration for this company is for everyone in the stadium to know everything that is gong on in the game while you are at the game. Sportbox, through its products, provides the live play-by-play to the 70+ millions yearly in attendance at games."

Finally, during March of 2005 the Minnesota Twins signed a licensing deal with Nielson Sports for the rights to use Sponsorship Scorecard^TM. This service provides a currency for advertisers to work from and verifies the value of all sponsored placed media in televised sporting events. Regarding its history, the service was developed in collaboration with Nielson Ventures and then launched in July of 2004. As an aside, Nielson Sports and Ventures are each subsidiaries of VNU Media Measurement and Information, which is a global information and media company with leading market positions and recognized brands in marketing information, media measurement and information, and business information.

Summary

Based on the signing of agreements for renewing old and initiating new partnerships, sponsorships and licensing relationships during the early 2000s, MLB and its units are applying different marketing methods and adopting advanced technology to entertain the teams' baseball fans at their homes and in the ballparks. In part, the chapter provides facts about and highlights the league's and/or its units' partnerships with such companies as Toys "R" Us, Home Depot and the Cartoon Network, sponsorships with Bank of America, Chevrolet and Columbia Pictures, and licensing deals with Nielson Sports, Sportbox and United Media K.K.

Some MLB teams have also established multiyear marketing deals with business firms. As samples, during 2004 and/or 2005 partnerships existed between the Los Angeles Angels and General Motors, and the Seattle Mariners and Dodge, sponsorships between the Philadelphia Phillies and Citizens Financial Group, and the Tampa Bay Devil Rays and BASF/Termidor, and a licensing agreement between the Minnesota Twins and Nielson Sports.

In sum, it is important to the future of the professional sport, baseball fans and sports marketing that these relationships be financially successful for MLB or MLBAM, MLBI and MLBP, and for the respective companies. To realize that condition, the league and its entities along with their partners, sponsors and licensees must monitor and enforce the terms of the agreements, and each fulfill their commitments and tasks from a business perspective. Otherwise, baseball entertainment will be inferior relative to the products and services provided by domestic and international leagues and teams in basketball, football, ice hockey and outdoor soccer.

25. *The Programming and Broadcasting Business*

To penetrate markets and provide its sports entertainment brands, Major League Baseball (MLB) competes for consumers and market share primarily against the products and services offered by other professional leagues and their basketball, football, ice hockey and outdoor soccer teams. That is, because of a regular season that extends each year from April to September and a postseason from early to late October, MLB must engage its domestic and global audiences by using a variety of marketing channels, concepts, mixes and processes. Consequently, the league has established operating units as components of its organizational structure and exploited technological advancements in order to focus on and expand the sport's appeal and demand to customers in North America and in other regions of the world.

Besides attracting spectators who attend the teams' regular season home and away games, which are in total played at the 29 local ballparks in the U.S. and the SkyDome in Canada, it is also necessary for the American League (AL) and National League (NL) clubs to frequently communicate and interact with, and be exposed to, sports fans in other ways. Furthermore, the league's types of activities, merchandise, programs and services need to be continuously improved, attractively displayed and effectively marketed for it to earn the cash flows to operate as a dynamic, elite and international sports organization. In short, MLB is a business that is generating income and profit by doing an array of things to increase the demand for and supply of its products, and to target, locate and expand its fan bases and markets.

At the league's Internet website MLB.com, for example, there are convenient links that connect the user to several revenue producing activities and events. The activities for a sample of these links have the following titles. There is MLB.TV, Gameday Audio and MLB Radio for the Multimedia link; Events, History and Press Pass for the News link; Beat the Streak, Ultimate Salary Cap and Bush League Baseball for the Fantasy link; and Message Boards, Free E-mail Newsletters and Chat Archives for the Fan Forum link. To complete the website's list, other links at MLB.com consist of International, MLBProductions.com, MLBlogs.com, MinorLeagueBaseball.com and MLBPlayers.com. Finally, at the league's homepage there is a window titled Team Sites. It provides, in part, specific information about the history and present status of the 30 baseball clubs, statistics regarding their former and current coaches and players, and the franchises' community service activities and championship titles.

Based on the foregoing facts, this chapter identifies and highlights some of the ways that the league, as a parent, and a portion of its teams have allocated their resources and invested capital to organize, market and distribute their brands and businesses from programming and broadcasting perspectives. Although the discussion, in part, will relate to other chapters in Marketing and perhaps to those in other sections, there are baseball-specific, league-wide and teams' marketing activities, events, methods and programs that have not been previously disclosed and analyzed in this book.

Achievements of MLB Productions

From the mid–1980s to 1997 inclusive, the league outsourced its television and video production requirements. Then, in 1998 the MLB Productions division was reinstated as an in-house organizational unit and thus assigned to develop baseball network specials, exclusive home videos, commercials and other specialty programming for a worldwide audience. Since its reinstatement, the division has been nominated for several New York Emmy awards in sports categories that pertain specifically to Camera, Editor, Writer of Short Forms, Historical/Cultural Programming, programming for a Single Program, and to a Special, Series and Segments. Five of these nominations were for producing volumes of the Yankeeography series, which was developed as a three-disc DVD set that features biographies of selected New York Yankees players. When released in April of 2004, Volume One contained episodes about such Yankee superstars as Babe Ruth, Thurman Munson and Don Mattingly, while in September of 2004 Volume Two provided profiles, in part, of Lou Gehrig, Mickey Mantle and Phil Rizzuto. As produced in April of 2005, Volume Three highlighted several other Yankee players like Hall of Famers Joe DiMaggio, Catfish Hunter and Reggie Jackson. The third volume, which was released in a partnership with Hart Sharpe Video at a retail price of $24.99, also included three hours of rare footage that incorporated exclusive interviews and milestone events such as Hunter's last appearance in a World Series and Jackson's Hall of Fame speech. Established in 2003 by Joe Amodei, Hart Sharpe Video possesses the know-how to develop, acquire, market and distribute a number of unique home video and DVD products in the feature film, special interest and sports categories.[1]

Besides the popular Yankeeography, MLB Productions decided to launch the twenty-seventh season of "This Week in Baseball" in 2004, and one year later announced the completion of a new half-hour series entitled "Maximum MLB." The former program, which is a 30-minute show that allows viewers to be closely connected to the game through the eyes of its best players, has succeeded to be the longest running sports anthology series in American broadcast history. Furthermore, "This Week in Baseball" has four regular segments that are titled Beyond the Fence, How 'Bout That, From the Vaults and Pitch, Hit & Run starring Olympic softball pitcher Jennie Finch. According to MLB Productions' vice president and executive producer David Gavant, "The show combines Major League Baseball with a variety of off-field elements and non-sport components such as musical guests and celebrity appearances, which is why we believe 'This Week in Baseball' has the rare ability to appeal to avid and casual fans alike."[2]

Arranged in cooperation with Spike TV, which is the first network for men and a division of MTV networks, "Maximum MLB" is a program that showcases a sensational series from the previous week of MLB games in a fun and humorous way. As the program was broadcasted during the 2005 regular season and postseason, each episode featured exclusive interviews with several popular players and managers, and provided amusing sound bites from players who had been wired for sound. The premier telecast, for example, included an in-depth look at the opening series of games between the defending World Series champion Boston Red Sox and the New York Yankees, and highlighted the debut of new Yankees pitcher Randy Johnson. To interest viewers, MLB Productions' vice president of programming and business affairs Elizabeth Scott said, "We are thrilled to build this new relationship with Spike TV. Maximum MLB will be a cutting-edge original series offering a fresh and original look at the game of baseball to the Spike TV audience, which is an important demographic for Major League Baseball."[3]

During 2005, MLB Productions also signed separate, multiyear DVD distribution agreements with a broad-based audio and home video entertainment company named Shout! Factory and with A&E Home Video, which is a business specializing in TV DVD non-theatrical programming and that acquires classic television, music and sports libraries. The three-year agreement with Shout! Factory, whose other DVD projects include television programming, concerts, animation and sports collections, and special interest documentaries, gives this company the right to be the official DVD distributor of new MLB Productions content such as the film of the World Series. About its business agreement with big league baseball, the company's chief operations officer Bob Emmer remarked, "Everyone at Shout! Factory is thrilled about our new partnership with Major League Baseball and the opportunity to offer baseball fans a variety of high-quality entertainment DVDs."[4]

With respect to the league's other three-year deal, A&E Home Video has the exclusive rights to MLB Productions' DVD and Home Video archive in order to create collector's edition box sets. Moreover, the video firm receives exclusive rights to the complete contents of MLB' library, which includes footage that dates from the early 1900s and also contains World Series films since 1943, games from 90 World Series and 41 All-Star Game exhibitions, and 57 no-hitters that were completed in nine innings by big league pitchers. As a result, this agreement provides for the first-ever release of sets on DVD of MLB games. Subsequently, the company's vice president of sales and marketing Kate Winn made this observation. "A&E Home Video is a leader in creating beautifully packaged, comprehensive collective DVD sets, and we look forward to developing sets from the rich library MLB Productions has to offer."[5]

MLB Programming Business

Besides the previously mentioned agreements that had been settled by MLB Productions, during 2004 and 2005 the league continued to adapt its business to technological advancements and thereby expanded its operations to generate an increase in revenues. That is, MLB created more online programming options, opportunities and innovations for users by marketing baseball activities, events and programs that appeal to its worldwide fan base and other sports consumers.

To illustrate, in early 2004 the league signed a multiyear contract with the Microsoft Inc. According to this business deal, subscribers to the MSN Premium service were permitted to watch live video broadcasts of baseball games on their personal computers at no additional cost, and the free MSN.com website contained some baseball content that included exclusive video highlights. While Microsoft agree to pay MLB an estimated $40 million over two years, in turn MSN had the right to manage and sell all advertising on MLB.TV, which is the league's live-game video service. Relative to the value of the MSN Premium service, a MLB Advanced Media spokesperson said that contract with Microsoft was a very efficient way of getting baseball games dispersed to the largest number of people in the marketplace.[6]

Before the playoff games that were scheduled in October of 2004, the website MLB.com provided four programming options for listeners on the league's Interactive Baseball Network. First, baseball fans in the U.S. who could not watch the live broadcasts of playoff games had an opportunity to listen and hear home or visiting team announcers on MLB.com Gameday Audio. Furthermore, international subscribers were invited to watch the postseason games live as broadcasted on MLB.TV. Finally, during every ballgame all baseball fans had an option of clicking on Gameday to receive pitch-by-pitch accounts, graphic depictions and real-time statistics. Second, for free on Cooperstown. TV, fans could watch classic games and player interviews similar to those shown in DVD supplemental features. These games included previous division series matchups and pitching duals between such athletes as the Houston Astros' Nolan Ryan and Los Angeles Dodgers' Fernando Valenzuela.[7]

Third, for free on BaseballChannel.TV, baseball addicts had the choice of viewing analysis, entertainment and/or news, which complemented the exclusive shows that were presented throughout the regular season on MLB.com Radio. Generally, the sportscasters analyzed the game's opponents, took telephone calls and e-mails from people, chatted with reporters at the ballpark before the event, and held press conferences when the game had concluded. And fourth, BaseballChannel.TV delivered original interviews and features such as previous segments of "The Show to Be Named Later," which drew prestigious celebrities and guests to the MLB.com Studios in New York City during the regular season.

Between March and April of 2005, MLB and its affiliates provided professional baseball fans with some interesting programming options. These are described as follows. In early March, there were three free games played by AL and NL teams that were broadcasted on MLB.TV. With a high-speed connection attached to a computer, viewers could even toggle back and forth and simultaneously watch for no fee two of the three games. Then, during the same month BellSouth allowed any of its customers who had subscribed to MLB Extra Innings from DIRECT TV to score up to 60 out-of-market AL and NL games per week. In effect, this service permitted subscribers to monitor and measure the progress of their favorite teams and players throughout the 2005 regular season.

With respect to the "I Live for This" advertising campaigns on the ESPN, FOX and TBS television networks, it was from mid–March to late April of 2005 that MLB showed six new 30-second commercials. These featured the winners in a search for America's most passionate baseball fans. As conceived by MLB's Advertising and Marketing Department, the commercials included the fans of six teams that had participated in the 2004 postseason. At the open casting calls that took place in each of the six markets, the people selected for the spots had to tell personal, unique and inspiring stories about their endless devotion to MLB and to their preferred AL and/or NL teams. As MLB's executive vice president of business Tim Brosnan put it, "The excitement generated by the fan casting call project and the new 'I Live for This' spots illustrates the intense dedication and enthusiasm our fans have for their favorite teams and players."[8]

Then, in May of 2005 a significant programming event occurred that pleased baseball fans who resided in a country of Asia. That is, to broadcast one to two games per week to audiences in the Far East, MLB signed a one-year agreement with Taiwan's Public Television Service, which is that nation's only non-commercial and over-the-air network. This deal was concluded, in part, because Taiwanese player Chien-Ming Wang made his debut as a pitcher for the New York Yankees. As of May 2005, Wang and Colorado Rockies relief pitcher Chin-hui Tsao were the only players from Taiwan on the 25-man major league rosters, while nine of the country's athletes appeared on the rosters of teams in the U.S. minor leagues. About the agreement to broadcast in Taiwan, MLB's senior vice president of international business operations Paul Archey stated, "Broadcasting games on a national network like Public Television Service will help satisfy the growing demand that exists among Taiwanese fans."[9]

Broadcast Business of Teams

During the late 1990s and early 2000s, the majority of MLB teams extended the television and/or radio coverage of their games and programs to millions of baseball fans of Spanish descent. This ethnic group, whose population growth rate is above the national average, adores the game of baseball and willingly spends significant dollar amounts on various sports activities, events and programs. Because of their relatively strong work ethic, some Latino individuals and families have earned more income from their employers even though they have tended to work in low- and medium-wage jobs in America. Thus, MLB teams have periodically sampled and surveyed their markets to discover that Spanish-speaking people are fans who demand baseball merchandise and equipment, enjoy attending games at ballparks and observing the clubs' events and programs on television and online, and enthusiastically listen to games on the radio. To illustrate that fact, the following are examples of how four AL and NL franchises have each marketed their brands, products and programs by broadcasting to Latino audiences in specific local, regional, national and international geographic areas.

American League

After a half-hearted attempt to attract Hispanic fans to their home and away games in 1999 with a Spanish-language broadcast team and special promotions scheduled for Mexican Independence Day, in 2003 the Texas Rangers decided to initiate a second campaign that included a variety of special promotions and a number of Spanish-language broadcasts of games on local and area radio and television stations. The Rangers must realize that Hispanic fans represent a potentially large, and mostly untapped market for professional baseball and the club's brand. That is, Latinos are approximately 35 percent of Texas' population and nearly one million of them live in Dallas and Tarrant Counties, which comprise the Rangers' regional market. Consequently, to attract that population a consulting group developed a series of radio and television spots in Spanish, and the team hired a media company to translate and distribute a Spanish-language version of the franchise's pocket schedule and a fans guide in its market area. Furthermore, the Hispanic Broadcasting Corporation signed a three-year contract with the club's officials to carry all of the Rangers' home and away games during the regular season.[10]

The Boston Red Sox and radio station NESN concluded an agreement with the local Spanish Beisbol Network (SBN) to provide the station's feed as the second audio program (SAP) on broadcasts. Since 2000, the SBN has progressed from being a startup venture that primarily broadcasted Red Sox home games to becoming a six-state distribution network of the team's full 162-game schedule through NESN. For SBN, the agreement moved it a step closer to financial viability because 100 percent of its live reads during the broadcast would be distributed throughout New England on the SAP. According to SBN's executive producer Bill Kulik, "As that [Latino] fan base grows, it's bound to get more passionate. That involvement figures to have spillover benefits in ratings, merchandising, advertising, and community awareness of the team."

After a seven-year absence of programming to Latino baseball fans, in 2003 the Oakland Athletics' home games were announced locally on Spanish radio. Then, in 2005 the club reported that it had reached an agreement with Spanish radio network Team Cinco Sports for 48 of its home games to be broadcast in Spanish. Although the Athletics' audiences are primarily located in the San Francisco Bay Area and San Joaquin Valley, and in Sacramento and on the Monterey Peninsula, other affiliate stations transmitted the team's games to Bakersfield, Fresno/Visalia, Modesto/Stockton and Salinas/Monterey.

The Tampa Bay Devil Rays' complete game schedule for the 2005 regular season was broadcast in Spanish on channel 1400 of radio station WZHR-AM. The SBN and franchise agreed to sign a four-year contract with a mutual option for the fifth year. Devil Rays senior vice president of business operations David J. Auker was especially enthused about the agreement. He said, "We have learned that an important component to our success in the marketplace is reading the Hispanic community with a Spanish language broadcast. We couldn't be more pleased than to partner with the experienced professionals at Spanish Beisbol Network to do just that for all 162 of our games."

National League

During March of 2005, San Diego Padres executive vice president of business affairs Steve Violetta announced that the team had finalized a one-year Spanish television-broadcasting contract with Telemundo Network's local affiliate XHAS TV-33. Based on the agreement, the Spanish-speaking baseball fans that reside in the Greater San Diego, California and Tijuana, Mexico region would have an opportunity to view 109 Padres games in their preferred language during MLB's 2005 regular season. As an aside, in 2005 XHAS TV-33 was the second largest Spanish Television network in the U.S., and made its debut in San Diego by broadcasting baseball games on a local level. Indeed, for 15 years the affiliate has been one of the leading Spanish language television stations in southern California because of its strong signal and popular on-air personalities, and its outstanding news, sports and in-depth public service and community involvement programs. XHAS' vice president and general manager Carlos Sanchez seemed delighted about the agreement with the Padres when he stated, "Our goal is to deliver programming to local Hispanics who enjoy watching sports, and sources indicate Pares Baseball to be at the top of the list. Whether or not you subscribe to cable, our partnership with the Padres will result in greater access to the games."[11]

Besides the NL's Arizona Diamondbacks and San Diego Padres, during 2003 the Milwaukee Brewers became the third franchise to offer original Spanish-language television productions. As such, the Brewers announced a 13-game television package with Telemundo. This deal featured a Fox Sports Net feed with Spanish language announcers and graphics. According to the team's executive vice president of business operations Rick Schlesinger, the club had responded to census figures that identified the Hispanic community to be the fastest-growing segment of the population in Milwaukee. That is, the number of Latino people had increased by 82 percent during the 1990s. In 2005, the team's agreement with Telemundo provided 12 broadcasts in Milwaukee and for the first time, programming in the Madison and Green Bay areas of Wisconsin. This means that the broadcast audiences in these places will grow because of the television affiliates in these two emerging markets.

For the programming activities of another NL team, an official of the San Francisco Giants announced that beginning on opening day, which was April 5, 2005, Cumbia 1170 AM would be the new host of the club's Spanish radio broadcasts. This 50,000-watt, all–Spanish station agreed to carry 50 of the Giants' regular season home games. With respect to its broadcasting capabilities, Cumbia 1170 AM is the Bay Area's first Spanish station devoted to playing the contemporary rhythmic sounds, known as Cumbia music, from Mexico and Central and South America. The Giants' senior vice president of corporate marketing Mario Alioto was thrilled about the team's partnership with Cumbia when he said, "The Giants have a rich Hispanic history with both former and current players including Juan Marichal, Orlando Cepeda, Felipe Alou, Pedro Feliz and Edgardo Alfonso, that we want to do all that we can to make it possible for our Hispanic fans to listen to our games on the radio."

The New York Mets, meanwhile, had implemented two innovations for the broadcasts of its 2005 regular season. First, MSG Networks agreed to simulcast the team's initial game and its home opener with a full Spanish productionælanguage and graphicsæon Fox Sports Net-New York in order to serve the Mets' growing fan base in New York City's Hispanic community. Furthermore, where feasible, televised games that were not simulcast in Spanish had the Spanish audio available as the SAP option. Second, at the Mets' 82 home games in Shea Stadium a series of 20 large high-definition flat-panel displays ran exciting, eye-catching advertisements and other contents. Located in high-visibility places within the Stadium, the displays ran full-motion video programming with CD-quality sound. These provided spectators with advertising, sports and team information that included live sports scores and more during games and other events. Basically, the network allowed advertisers and marketers to deliver advertising to a captive audience with unprecedented targeting and incredible flexibility, control and efficiency. In turn, the national sports and entertainment media company Arena Media Networks had created and managed the displays at the ballpark.[12]

Broadcasting Games in the Baltimore– Washington, D.C., Region

When MLB announced to the media that the Expos would relocate from Montreal, Canada to the Washington, D.C., area in time for the start of the 2005 regular season, the Baltimore Orioles owner Peter Angelos insisted that moving the Expos to the East Coast could have a "profound adverse impact" on his team. To avoid that end, after the announcement Angelos had to negotiate for months with baseball's president and chief operating officer Bob DuPuy to develop a compensation package that would address the television markets and franchise rights of the Orioles and Washington Nationals, which was assigned to be the new name of the team. However, baseball officials determined that MLB's sale of the Nationals to an individual owner or group had to be postponed until a settlement between Angelos and the league was finalized.[13]

During late March of 2005, an agreement was finally consummated between Angelos and DuPuy. Specifically, the negotiators decided to carve up the Baltimore-Washington, D.C. television market and also to create a regional sports network, which is a joint venture owned and controlled by the two teams. Operating as the Mid-Atlantic Sports Network (MASN), the new venture expected to pay the Nationals a fee estimated at $20–30 million for the right to televise the club's games in the first year, and also to distribute more than 75 of the Nationals' games to over-the-air television channels in the city of Washington, D.C. The team's remaining games would appear on cable and/or satellite stations if these broadcasters agree to carry the new network.

In fact, MASN reached a deal in May of 2005 with cable provider RCN. This company agreed to televise about 60 Nationals' games on channel eight and make the team's other games available on over-the-air channel WDCA or as national telecasts on ESPN or Fox. In the area, therefore, about 185,000 homes with cable received broadcasts of the games. Anyway, the Nationals' ownership interest in MASN will be transferred with the franchise when MLB ultimately sells it. Consequently, as a result of the agreement regarding the Orioles and Nationals television markets, the typical baseball fan that currently lives in the Baltimore-Washington region had an opportunity to view regular season games played by the AL and NL teams.

Interestingly, the Orioles have about two years left on its contract with Comcast SportsNet. Because of that deal, however, in late April of 2005 Comcast filed a lawsuit in the Montgomery County Circuit Court located in Rockville, Maryland, and asked that the Orioles, MASN and MLB be prevented from negotiating or licensing the local pay television rights to Orioles games given that Comcast owned these rights through the 2006 season. Furthermore, in the lawsuit Comcast claimed it had the exclusive right to negotiate an extension of the contract with the Orioles and the right to match any agreement reached with a third party. In short, the lawsuit stipulated that the Orioles had breached their contract with Comcast, who also seeks unspecified compensatory damages.

Since filing the lawsuit, the participants have responded as follows. MASN blames Comcast for refusing to distribute the Nationals' games and because of that claim, has purposely inflamed sports fans in the Washington, D.C. area. Obviously, MLB is disappointed by the lawsuit. Nevertheless, the league believes that the litigation will have no impact on the Nationals' 2005 television schedule or the rights fees paid to the club. Although the Orioles have not comment about the lawsuit, Comcast said it would not televise the Nationals' games on its cable channels in the cities' region while the suit is being litigated.

The various issues mentioned in this chapter, in part, relate to the 1961 Sports Broadcasting Act (SBA). That legislation permitted the packaging of league games to national broadcasters for over-the-air television, and involved individually owned teams coming together to form a television cartel that sells national broadcasting rights. Although the SBA made the latter activity legal for free television, it did not legalize the services of companies that charge a fee such as cable or satellite television. Moreover, an aspect of concern to economists is MLB's granting of exclusive broadcast territories to its teams.

The league has maintained this policy, although in 1953 it was declared illegal in a lawsuit. According to some sports economists, eliminating baseball's presumed antitrust exemption and exclusive territories would result in more competition and lower prices because of the increase in the number of broadcasting sellers who exist in each local and regional area. If so, the advantages of teams located in large markets would be diminished and these franchises would then be compelled to share their profits from local programming with teams that have relatively less revenues.[14]

Summary

Based on the research performed for this reading, it is apparent that the programming and broadcasting operations of MLB and the league's various teams have generated increasing amounts of cash flows for their respective organizations, especially since the mid-to-late 1990s. Organized baseball's commercial success has occurred, in part, because of the creative alliances and innovative programs established by MLB Productions, and due to the demand for technology-based activities, events and services as originated by MLB.com, MLB.TV, BaseballChannel.TV, MLBlogs.com and other interactive websites. In other words, the league has derived, structured and implemented a number of different programming options to entertain its hardcore fans and also to attract and retain new customers.

To expand the core audiences in their local markets and regional areas, the AL and NL teams have joined with several networks and media companies to broadcast more regular season and postseason games, and to provide baseball programs in the Spanish language. Since Hispanics are a growing segment of the populations in many cities and urban areas, this demographic group is a lucrative target for MLB clubs to focus on since these people enjoy watching baseball games and therefore, will spend their money for tickets and food products at the ballparks, and their dollars for baseball equipment, merchandise and memorabilia. For the Hispanics who have below average or low disposable incomes and little or no wealth, they prefer to remain at home with their families and friends and view baseball games on television or listen to teams compete on a local Spanish-language radio station.

In the last section of this reading, the issue discussed was the dispute that took place during 2004 and 2005 between MLB, a team owner and a cable company about the television rights and regional market areas of the AL Baltimore Orioles and NL Washington Nationals. Before and after the former Expos franchise had moved from Montreal, Canada to Washington, D.C. in early 2005, Orioles owner Peter Angelos was extremely upset but very determined to be compensated by the league for the invasion by the Nationals into his club's territory. After Angelos and MLB agreed to a method about the allocation of the Baltimore-Washington television and radio markets, and the organization, structure and ownership of a regional sports network, Comcast SportsNet then filed a lawsuit against the Orioles, MASN and organized baseball in a Rockville, Maryland circuit court for breach of contract and to collect compensatory damages. Indeed, the decision of the court in settling this lawsuit will have significant and long-run implications for the commissioner's office, the 30 member teams, and the local, regional and national television and radio broadcasters and networks that sign contracts with sports franchises.

To achieve competitive balance between AL and NL teams in, respectively, the East,

Central and West divisions, it may be necessary for Commissioner Bud Selig or his successor to redistribute a larger portion of the local and/or regional broadcasting revenues from teams located in large and mid-sized cities to those that play in small markets. If this occurs, then perhaps the Washington Nationals and such teams as the Cincinnati Reds, Cleveland Indians, Colorado Rockies, Kansas City Royals, Milwaukee Brewers, Oakland Athletics, Pittsburgh Pirates, San Diego Padres and Tampa Bay Devil Rays will have an opportunity win a World Series within a few years.

Chapter Notes

Introduction

1. For the history, facts and other information about team movements and league expansions in MLB and the NFL, NBA and NHL, see Frank P. Jozsa Jr. and John J. Guthrie, Jr., *Relocating Teams and Expanding Leagues in Professional Sports: How the Major Leagues Respond to Market Conditions* (Westport, CT: Quorum Books, 1999), and Frank P. Jozsa, Jr., *American Sports Empire: How the Leagues Breed Success* (Westport, CT: Praeger Publishers, 2003). Another book that discusses the relocation of a team in MLB is Neil J. Sullivan, *The Dodgers Move West: The Transfer of the Brooklyn Baseball Franchise to Los Angeles* (New York, N.Y.: Oxford University Press, 1987).

2. Since the 1960s, MLB has restructured and adopted strategies to become an international business organization. In part, these strategies are reflected by the league's member teams that employ foreign players and manage baseball academies in Latin American countries, and by the league's interest to host and sponsor a World Baseball Classic and to schedule exhibition games in various nations of Asia, Europe, and Central and South America. A recent title about this topic is Frank P. Jozsa, Jr., *Sports Capitalism: The Foreign Business of American Professional Leagues* (Aldershot, England: Ashgate Publishing Limited, 2004).

3. Author Harold Seymour was a high school baseball player, college professor, batboy for the Brooklyn Dodgers, organizer and field manager of amateur and semipro teams, and a major league bird dog. Seymour's second volume was praised by a *New York Times* reporter who said: "His book will grip every American who has invested part of his youth and dreams in the sport, and it will inform everyone else who is interested in an American phenomenon as native as apple pie." See Harold Seymour, *Baseball: The Early Years* (New York, N.Y.: Oxford University Press, 1960), and *Baseball: The Golden Age* (New York, N.Y.: Oxford University Press, 1971).

4. For a profound book about the economics of the sports business and public policy, which was edited by a former Brookings senior fellow and professor of economics at the California Institute of Technology, see Roger G. Noll, ed., *Government and the Sports Business* (Washington, D.C.: The Brookings Institution, 1974).

5. Gerald W. Scully, *The Business of Major League Baseball* (Chicago, IL: University of Chicago Press, 1989). According to some sports scholars, Scully's article "Discrimination: The Case of Baseball" that appeared as Chapter Seven in *Government and the Sports Business* is an excellent analysis of practices in the sport a generation after the color line was broken in 1947 when Brooklyn Dodgers owner Branch Rickey promoted Jackie Robinson from a minor league team to the Dodgers.

6. As stated in its Preface, this book "focuses on confrontations and relationships between players and management from the perspective of several hundred collective bargaining participants—those union and management officials who negotiate the labor agreement, and the union members who must approve and live with the labor agreement." These and other topics are discussed in Kenneth M. Jennings, *Balls and Strikes: The Money Game in Professional Baseball* (Westport, CT: Praeger Publishers, 1990).

7. See Paul M. Sommers, ed., *Diamonds Are Forever: The Business of Baseball* (Washington, D.C.: The Brookings Institution, 1992), and Daniel R. Marburger, *Stee-Rike Four! What's Wrong With the Business of Baseball?* (Westport, CT: Praeger Publishers, 1997).

8. The two books are authored by, respectively, Albert Theodore Powers, *The Business of Baseball* (Jefferson, N.C.: McFarland & Company, Inc., Publishers, 2003), and Andrew Zimbalist, *May the Best Team Win: Baseball Economics and Public Policy* (Washington, D.C.: Brookings Institution Press, 2003). As an aside, Powers is an international tax and finance lawyer and a member of the Society for American Baseball Research, while Zimbalist is the Robert A. Woods professor of economics at Smith College in Massachusetts and the author of *Baseball and Billions: A Probing Look Inside the Big Business of Our National Pastime* (New York, N.Y.: Basic Books, 1994). Specifically, in *The Business of Baseball* Powers provides sections for Baseball Inc.'s management and ownership structures, marketing and promoting baseball, internationalization, realignment of divisions, expansions, scheduling and playoffs, player drafts and legislation.

9. Listed in no specific order, other reputable books published about the sports business that include professional baseball are Phil Schaaf, *Sports, Inc.: 100 Years of Sports Business* (Amherst, N.Y.: Prometheus Books, 2004); Paul D. Staudohar and James A. Magnum, eds., *The Business of Professional Sports* (Champaign, IL: University of Illinois Press, 1991); Marvin Miller, *A Whole*

Different Ballgame: The Sport and Business of Baseball (New York, N.Y.: Birch Lane Press, 1991); James Quirk and Rodney D. Fort, *Pay Dirt: The Business of Professional Team Sports* (Princeton, N.J.: Princeton University Press, 1992); Hans Westerbeek and Aaron Smith, *Sport Business in the Global Marketplace* (New York, N.Y.: Palgrave Macmillan, 2003); Robert C. Berry and Glenn M. Wong, *Law and Business of the Sports Industry* (Westport, CT: Praeger Publishers, 1993); James Edward Miller, *The Baseball Business: Pursuing Pennants and Profits in Baltimore*, 2nd ed. (Chapel Hill, N.C.: University of North Carolina Press, 1991); and Ann E. Weiss, *Money Games: The Business of Sports* (Boston, MA: Houghton Mifflin Company, 1993).

Chapter 1

1. For some facts that reflect why baseball is successful, see Ken Rosenthal, "Can Money Really Buy Happiness in Baseball?" at http://www.sportsbusinessnews.com cited 15 October 2004; George Will, "Baseball Thrives Despite Intense, Unjust Criticism," *The Charlotte Observer* (3 April 2005), 3P.

2. According to one sports writer, the two business issues in MLB are adequate revenue sharing and guaranteed contracts. These are discussed in Rick Harrow, "Business of Baseball Pretty Good Right Now," at http://www.sportsbusinessnews.com cited 17 April 2005.

3. The ticket prices and FCIs of teams for various seasons were reported in "Major League Baseball," at http://www.teammarketing.com cited 18 January 2005.

4. See Hal Bodley, "Baseball Facing Big-League Debt," at http://www.usatoday.com cited 24 March 2005.

5. The topics in the CBA of 2002 and aspects of revenue sharing and luxury taxes are discussed in Doug Pappas, "Analysis— Summary of the [2002] Collective Bargaining Agreement," at http://www.businessofbaseball.com cited 5 January 2005; "Price of Glory: Yankees Will Pay More Than $30 Million in Luxury Taxes," at http://www.cnnsi.com cited 21 April 2005; Hal Bodley, "Revenue Sharing Paying Off," at http://www.usatoday.com cited 12 April 2005.

6. These views are in "You're Being Robbed!" at http://www.cnnsi.com cited 11 May 2005; Ian O'Connor, "Baseball Fuels Disparity," at http://www.usatoday.com cited 5 January 2005; Johnette Howard, "Well Worth Nothing— Small Market MLB Owners Are Angry," at http://www.sportsbusinessnews.com cited 4 February 2005.

7. For comments about parity in baseball, see Mike Bauman, "Is Economic Parity Possible?" at http://www.mlb.com cited 11 February 2005, and John Porretto, "Baseball Commissioner Sees More Parity," at http://www.cnnsi.netscape.com cited 12 April 2005.

8. The results of the poll are mentioned in "Enough About Steroids," at http://www.cnnsi.com cited 5 April 2005.

9. Information about Congress and the steroid problem in baseball is discussed, for example, in Gintautas Dumcius, "Lawmakers Push Bill Imposing Steroid Sanctions," *Wall Street Journal* (24 May 2005), D4; "The Clean Sports Act of 2005," at http://www.sportsbusinessnews.com cited 25 May 2005; "Lawmaker: Congress Won't Back Off," at http://www.cnnsi.com cited 8 July 2005.

10. This data is presented and described in Ronald

Blum, "MLB Sees Fewer Home Runs Amid Steroid Crackdown," at http://www.usatoday.com cited 11 May 2005.

11. For an overview of the article, see "The Boys of Summer Come Back," *Wall Street Journal* (1 July 2005), W11.

12. See Allan Barra, "And Very Sweet For the Yankees," *Wall Street Journal* (22 June 2005), D12; "Yankees to Announce New Ballpark," at http://www.cnnsi.com cited 18 June 2005; Ronald Blum, "Bombers to Stay in Bronx," at http://www.cnnsi.netscape.com cited 18 June 2005.

13. This topic is covered in "Ninth Season of Interleague Play Begins Friday," at http://www.sportsbusinessnews.com cited 20 June 2005, and Mike Bauman, "I'm Sorry' Has Never Been so Easy," at http://www.mlb.com cited 6 July 2005.

14. A brief discussion of these six special changes is contained in John Kuenster, "Fans Offer Six Ways to Improve Game at the Major League Level," *Baseball Digest* (December 2004), 17–19.

Chapter 2

1. For various financial statistics about MLB teams, see Kurt Badenhausen, et al., "Double Play," *Forbes* (15 April 2002), 92–94; "Is Major League Baseball Profitable?" at http://www.bauer.uh.edu cited 9 November 2004; Michael Ozanian and Kurt Badenhausen, "The Boys of Summer," at http://www.forbes.com cited 9 November 2004; Duff Wilson, "Sports Team Owners Just Got Richer," at http://www.sportsbusinessnews.com cited 15 October 2004; "Forbes Financial 2004 Valuation For MLB Franchise," at http://www.sportsbusinessnews.com cited 5 October 2004; "2001 Team-by-Team Revenues and Expenses Forecast," at http://www.usatoday.com cited 9 November 2004; Michael Ozanian and Kurt Badenhausen, "Baseball Going Broke? Don't Believe It," *Wall Street Journal* (27 July 2000), A22; Ronald Blum, "Cash Flow: Baseball Wants Some," *The Daily News* (15 July 2000), 1C, 3C.

2. The estimated values and revenues listed in Tables 1–3 were obtained from the *Sources* that appear below each table.

3. Andrew Zimbalist, *May the Best Team Win: Baseball Economics and Public Policy* (Washington, D.C.: Brookings Institution Press, 2003). Besides baseball franchise sales prices, other tables in the book include interesting information that involve MLB team payrolls, local revenues, work stoppages, revenue sharing schemes, marginal tax rates, luxury taxes, national media income and accounting statements.

4. The Society For American Baseball Research (SABR) is an international organization that is based in Cleveland, Ohio. As stated on its web site http://www.sabr.org as of November 26, 2004, SABR's mission "is to foster the study of baseball, to assist in developing and maintaining the history of the game, to facilitate the dissemination of baseball research and to stimulate interest in baseball." At SABR, author Doug Pappas served as pro bono legal counsel, parliamentarian at annual business meetings and chaired the Business of Baseball Committee. While vacationing at Big Bend National Park in Texas during the Spring of 2004, Pappas passed away.

5. For detailed information about the past, present and future ballparks of MLB teams, see "Ballparks," at http://www.ballparks.com cited 26 November

2004; "Major League Baseball," at http://www.mlb.com cited 26 November 2004.

6. Doug Pappas, "The Numbers: Local Media Revenues," at http://www.baseballprospectus.com cited 9 November 2004. Besides each team's local media money, the article reports the adjusted metro area population, media dollars per person and number of television/cable games of each franchise for a specific year.

7. Other sports books that include business, economic and financial matters about MLB and the league's teams are Frank P. Jozsa, Jr. and John J. Guthrie, Jr., *Relocating Teams and Expanding Leagues in Professional Sports How the Major Leagues Respond to Market Conditions* (Westport, CT: Quorum, 1999); Frank P. Jozsa, Jr., *American Sports Empire: How the Leagues Breed Success* (Westport, CT: Praeger, 2003); Idem., *Sports Capitalism: The Foreign Business of American Professional Leagues* (Aldershot, England: Ashgate Publishing Limited, 2004); Gerald W. Scully, *The Business of Major League Baseball* (Chicago, IL: University of Chicago Press, 1989); Albert Theodore Powers, *The Business of Baseball* (Jefferson, N.C.: McFarland & Company, Inc., Publishers, 2003).

Chapter 3

1. Various facts and other information about the past, present and future ballparks in MLB are available from several sources. There are, for example, the team's media guides and such online websites as http://www.ballparks.com, http://www.mlb.com, http://www.baseball-almanac.com, and http://www.ballparkwatch.com as suggested sources. Furthermore, a business-oriented commentary on stadium finance was written by Jay Weiner, "Thinking Out of the Batter's Box, *Business Week* (24 April 2000), 175, 178. For how stadiums constructed between 1992 and 2001 had influenced the home attendances of specific teams, read Allen St. John, "If You Build It ...," *Wall Street Journal* (22 July 2005), W6.

2. Dean Bonham, who has negotiated several naming rights deals, believes only a few ballparks are untouchable. That is, most notably Fenway Park in Boston and Yankee Stadium in New York City. To the horror of many fans and baseball tradititonalists, during late 2004 the Los Angeles Dodger's new owner Frank McCourt evaluated whether to sell the naming rights to Dodger Stadium. For Bonham's views and other naming rights issues in sports, see Lee Romney, "The Candlestick Name Game," at http://www.sportsbusinessnews.com cited 10 October 2004.

3. Four books contain a discussion of the business and economics of professional baseball and why baseball ballparks are an important topic to research. In no specific order, these include Albert Theodore Powers, *The Business of Baseball* (Jefferson, N.C.: McFarland & Company, 2003), Daniel R. Marburger, ed., *Stee-Rike Four!: What's Wrong With the Business of Baseball* (Westport, CN: Praeger, 1997), Gerald W. Scully, *The Business of Major League Baseball* (Chicago, IL: The University of Chicago Press, 1989), and Andrew Zimbalist, *Baseball and Billions: A Probing Look Inside the Big Business of Our National Pastime* (New York, N.Y.: Basic Books, 1994). Another contribution to the literature on stadium issues is Andrew Zimbalist, *May the Best Team Win: Baseball Economics and Public Policy* (Washington, D.C.: Brookings Institution Press, 2003).

4. When the Montreal Expos relocated to Washington, D.C. for the 2005 MLB season, the team will play in RFK Stadium for three seasons. According to reports, a new 41,000-seat, $450 million ballpark with 74 luxury boxes and 2,000 club-level seats will be built on the Anacostia waterfront. For more information about this facility, see S.A. Miller and Eric Fisher, "Baseball Back in D.C., Interesting Parties Against Proposed MLB Stadium," at http://www.sportsbusinessnews.com cited 8 October 2004; Jeff Barker, "Baseball in D.C., Ballpark Would Follow Camden Yards Trend," at http://www.sportsbusinessnews.com cited 8 October 2004; Eric Fisher, "Baseball in D.C., RFK Action Plan Ready," at http://www.sportsbusinessnews.com cited 8 October 2004; Peter Whoriskey, "Baseball in D.C., Stadium Deal Won Over Bud," at http://www.sportsbusinessnews.com cited 5 October 2004.

Chapter 4

1. For specific years about the formation of teams in the National League (1876–present) and American League (1901–present), see "MLB Franchise Chronology," at http://www.mlb.com cited 9 November 2004.

2. Frank P. Jozsa, Jr. and John J. Guthrie, Jr., *Relocating Teams and Expanding Leagues in Professional Sports: How the Major Leagues Respond to Market Conditions* (Westport, CT: Quorum Books, 1999). Other books that discuss the relocation of baseball teams include Charles C. Euchner, *Playing the Field: Why Sports Teams Move and Cities Fight to Keep Them* (Baltimore, MD: Johns Hopkins University Press, 1993); James Quirk and Rodney D. Fort, *Pay Dirt: The Business of Professional Team Sports* (Princeton, N.J.: Princeton University Press, 1992); Kenneth L. Shropshire, *The Sports Franchise Game: Cities in Pursuit of Sports Franchises, Events, Stadiums, and Arenas* (Philadelphia, PA: University of Pennsylvania Press, 1995).

3. See Roger G. Noll, ed., *Government and the Sports Business* (Washington, D.C.: The Brookings Institution, 1974). Besides that title, sports economist Noll teamed with Andrew Zimbalist to edit *Sports, Jobs and Taxes: The Economic Impact of Sports Teams and Stadiums* (Washington, D.C.: The Brookings Institution, 1997).

4. For information about the financial problems of the franchise, see Stefan Fatsis, "Montreal Expos: No Place to Call Home Plate," *Wall Street Journal* (7 August 2003), B1, B3; Mark Hyman, "So Long, Montreal. Hello, Washington?" *Business Week* (30 September 2002), 105; Idem., "Play Ball — Even If No One Loves You," *Business Week* (25 March 2002), 84; Stefan Fatsis, "Save Our Expos!" *Wall Street Journal* (29 March 2002), W6; "Millions of Dollars at Stake For Montreal," at http://www.montrealexpos.com cited 6 October 1998.

5. The contraction and/or relocation of teams in MLB is discussed in Philip Connors, "Baseball: Agony and Ecstasy in Minnesota," *Wall Street Journal* (23 July 2001), A13; Stefan Fatsis, "Twin Killing?" *Wall Street Journal* (4 May 2001), W8; Justin Catansos, "Baseball Should Go Where the Money Is," *Business Week* (29 June 1998), 131.

6. Besides *Relocating Teams and Expanding League in Professional Sports*, the other books that analyze U.S. and foreign cities as potential sites for professional baseball teams are Frank P. Jozsa, Jr., *American Sports Empire: How the Leagues Breed Success* (Westport, CT: Praeger Publishers, 2003); Idem., *Sports Capitalism: The Foreign Business of American Professional League* (Aldershot, England: Ashgate Publishing Limited, 2004).

7. A sample of articles and sources that provide

specific information about the Expos' relocation to Washington, D.C. include Barry M. Bloom, "MLB Selects D.C. For Expos," at http://www.mlb.com cited 9 November 2004; Mark Newman, "Baseball's Back in D.C., Next Step(s)," at http://www.sportsbusinessnews.com cited 30 September 2004; Barry M. Bloom, "Baseball Back in D.C., Bud Signals the End of the Jour-ney," at http://www.sportsbusinessnews.com cited 30 September 2004; David Steele, "Baseball in D.C., the Chaos Theory," at http://www.sportsbusinessnews.com cited 9 December 2004.

8. See Bloom, "MLB Selects D.C. For Expos."

9. Regarding the lawsuit, Jeffrey Loria's attorney Bradley I. Ruskin remarked, "We're thrilled with a complete and total victory for the Marlins. The arbitrators rejected every allegation and every claim made by the limited partners as having no merit." For more details, see Andrew Dunn, "Former Expos Limited Partners Finally Strike Out," at http://www.sportsbusinessnews.com cited 16 November 2004.

10. A few individuals and several groups were interested in bidding for the baseball franchise in Washington, D.C. These groups are discussed in Mark Hyman, "It's a Horse Race in Right Field," *Business Week* (18 October 2004), 48; Thom Loverro, "Baseball in D.C., Plethora of Prospective Owners," at http://www.sportsbusinessnews.com cited 1 October 2004; Eric Fisher, "Even Losing Can't Keep the Virginia Baseball Group Down," at http://www.sportsbusinessnews.com cited 15 October 2004; "Baseball in D.C., Has Kasten Casts His Eyes on Washington's New MLB Franchise," at http://www.sportsbusinessnews.com cited 30 September 2004; Matthew Barakat, "Virginia Baseball Agency Remains Open," at http://www.channels.netscape.com cited 20 January 2005.

11. The negotiation and agreement between Commissioner Bud Selig and Baltimore Orioles owner Peter Angelos with respect to the Expos' relocation to Washington, D.C. area was discussed in Ed Waldman, "Baseball in D.C., Mr. Angelos Goes to Visit Mr. Selig," at http://www.sportsbusinessnews.com cited 8 October 2004, and Jon Morgan, "Baseball in D.C., Camden Yards May Cost More," at http://www.sportsbusinessnews.com cited 29 September 2004.

12. For various facts and interesting information such as dates, meetings and debates about the proposed baseball stadium, D.C. City Council and MLB, see Eric Fisher, "Baseball in D.C., However There is Interest in a Privately Funded Stadium," at http://www.sportsbusinessnews.com cited 3 November 2004; Murray Chass, "Baseball in D.C., They Have a Name But No Money," at http://www.sportsbusinessnews.com cited 30 November 2004; Jeff Seidel, "Baseball in D.C., Stadium Vote Set," at http://www.sportsbusinessnews.com cited 30 November 2004; Eric Fisher, "Baseball in D.C., Yet Another Delay in Stadium Vote," at http://www.sportsbusinessnews.com cited 16 November 2004; Jeff Seidel, "There May be Peace and a Baseball Stadium in D.C. Yet," at http://www.sportsbusinessnews.com cited 16 November 2004.

13. For the amendment that required private financing, see Eric Fisher, "Baseball in D.C., D.C Council Tosses Egg at MLB," at http://www.sportsbusinessnews.com cited 15 December 2004; Jeff Seidel, "DC Council Passes Amended Bill," at http://www.mlb.com 15 December 2004; Idem., "Baseball in D.C., Operation Shuts Down (at Least For Now)," at http://www.sportsbusinessnews.com cited 16 December 2004.

14. The implications of MLB's decision on other teams and markets is presented, for example, in Barry Witt, "San Jose Still Interested in A's," at http://www.sportsbusinessnews.com cited 5 October 2004, and "San Jose Seeking Major League Team," http://www.cnnsi.com cited 22 March 2005.

15. Because of the move by the Expos, other MLB team owners are evaluating sites and cities. For more on this topic, see Mike Berardino, "Who's Next on MLB's Hit List?" at http://www.sportsbusinessnews.com cited 5 October 2004, and the articles in Note 14.

16. See Joe Frisaro, "Marlins Meet With Las Vegas Mayor," at http://www.mlb.com cited 10 December 2004; Jimmy Golen, "Goodman Tries to Lure Baseball to Vegas," at http://channels.netscape.com cited 15 December 2004.

Chapter 5

1. For further details about the history of the NAPBL/MLBB, see "Minor League Baseball History," at http://www.minorleaguebaseball.com cited 25 June 2005; "Minor League Baseball History: Timeline," at http://www.minorleaguebaseball.com cited 25 June 2005; "How Minor League Baseball Teams Work," at http://www.howstuffworks.com cited 25 June 2005.

2. *Ibid.*

3. The answers to such questions as "What do Minor League players earn?" and "How much is a Minor League team worth?" are available at "Official Info: FAQ," at http://www.minorleaguebaseball.com cited 25 June 2005.

4. The classification and composition of these MLLB organizations and their website links are contained in "Leagues," at http://www.minorleaguebaseball.com 24 December 2004. For a brief description of Triple-A, Double-A and Single-A, see "Top 3 Minor League Baseball Levels," at http://www.baseball.about.com cited 25 June 2005.

5. Two articles provide some information about the ownership of a MLBB team. See Jerome Cramer, "So, You Want to Own a Minor League Baseball Team," *Forbes* (Fall 2003), 82, 84–86, and Roy Rowan, "Play Ball!" *Fortune* (4 September 2000), 311–326.

6. Fans, families and investors have been eager to watch minor league teams since the early 2000s. These spectator's demand is discussed in Tom Lowry, et al., "For the Love of the Game—And Cheap Seats," *Business Week* (28 May 2001), 46–47.

7. A business model of MLBB's operations was briefly outlined in David M. Carter, "There's Nothing Minor About These Prospects," *2000 Charlotte Knights Souvenir Program* (Fort Mill, S.C.: Charlotte Knights Media Relations Office, 2000), 18.

8. For minor league team's stadiums and activities in them before, during and after games, see Charles Gerena and Betty Joyce Nash, "Playing to Win: Minor League Sports Score," *Region Focus* (Spring 2000), 13–19; Alex Wong, "Moving in on the Majors," *Newsweek* (23 August 2004), 13–15; Landon Hall, "Building Boom Brings Millions of Fans Back to Minor Leagues," at http://www.sports.yahoo.com cited 16 June 2001; Matt Bai, "A League of Their Own," *Newsweek* (11 May 1998), 68.

9. The events at ballparks are also described in Alan Schwarz, "Not Just Peanuts: Minor-League Baseball is More than Quaint Stadiums and Dancing Umpires," *Newsweek* (9 May 2005), 36, and "Put Me in, Coach: River City Rascals Auctioning One-Day Pro Contract," at http://www.cnnsi.com cited 11 May 2005.

10. See "Official Info: Licensing," at http://www. minorleaguebaseball.com cited 25 June 2005, and "Official Info: Sponsorship," at http://www.minor-leaguebaseball.com> cited 25 June 2005.

11. The baseball history and attendances of the Charlotte Knights at its stadium in Fort Mill is contained in several publications. For example, see Ted Reed, "Diamond Dreams," *The Charlotte Observer* (26 March 2001), 10D, and the *2005 Charlotte Knights Media Guide* (Fort Mill, S.C.: Charlotte Knights Media Relations Office, 2005). The Fan Cost Index of the Knights is reported in "Major League Baseball: 2004," at http://www.teammarketing.com cited 14 May 2005. For the team's interest in the design of Victory Field, the article is Mac Banks, "Knights Look to Indy as Model For Stadium Ideas," *Fort Mill Times* (3 August 2000), 11A.

Chapter 6

1. For a brief history of the MLBPA and other unions, and the court cases, see "The Major League Baseball Players Association," at http://www.bigleaguers.yahoo.com cited 5 January 2005; "Baseball Labor History," at http://www.xroads.virginia.edu cited 18 June 2005; Doug Pappas, "A Contentious History: Baseball's Labor Fights," at http://www.espn.go.com cited 18 June 2005.

2. Three books that provide specific information about various aspects of the CBAs in MLB are Albert Theodore Powers, *The Business of Baseball* (Jefferson, N.C.: McFarland & Company, Inc., Publishers, 2003); Roger G. Noll, ed. *Government and the Sports Business* (Washington, D.C.: The Brookings Institution, 1974); Marvin Miller, *A Whole Different Ballgame: The Sport and Business of Baseball* (New York, N.Y.: Birch Lane Press, 1991).

3. See Doug Pappas, "Analysis— Summary of the [2002] Collective Bargaining Agreement," at http://www.businessofbaseball.com cited 5 January 2005.

4. The labor disputes between the MLBPA and team owners are discussed in "Sports Work Stoppages," *The Charlotte Observer* (25 October 1998), 6H; Dan Lewis, "Look For the Union Label," at http://www.nationalreview.com cited 18 June 2005; "Contentious Labor Situation Casts Cloud Over Season, Sport," *The Charlotte Observer* (29 March 2002), 7C; Mike Lopresti, "Has MLB Recovered From Its 1994 Strike," at http://www.sportsbusinessnews.com cited 5 October 2004. For one owner's views about Commissioner Bud Selig's authority to discipline players such as the Texas Rangers' Kenny Rogers, read John Moores, "When Push Comes to Shove: Union Hurts Baseball," *Wall Street Journal* (12 July 2005), D8.

5. This quote was stated in Bruce Weber, "Fehr and Loathing," *Scholastic Coach & Athletic Director* (May/ June 2004), 16. The views of other sports journalists include Tony Kornheiser, "Baseball's Union Wields a Big Bat," *The Washington Post* (3 March 2004), D1, and Thomas Boswell, "Fehr Gets a Dose of His Own Medicine." *The Washington Post* (19 May 2005), D1.

6. As Tom Glavine further stated, "In Barry's case, the cloud remains as to whether he knew he was doing it or didn't. It kind of puts it back on the front page, and it becomes a hot-button issue that everyone is talking about." See Rich Draper, "Union Board to Discuss Steroids," at http://www.mlb.com cited 7 December 2004.

7. These reasons were discussed in "Statement of Donald M. Fehr, Executive Director, Major League Baseball Players Association, Before the Committee on Energy and Commerce, United States House of Representatives," at http://www.mlb.com cited 18 May 2005.

8. The MLBPA and its members donate money and resources to social programs, and also are involved in marketing partnerships with MLB and sponsors. For example, see "MLB, MLBPA Contribute $1 Million to Tsunami Relief," at http://www.mlb.com cited 14 March 2005, and "MLB, MLBPA Partnership With Cartoon Network Begins Second Season," at http://www.mlb. com cited 11 May 2005;

Chapter 7

1. The on-field and off-field pressures and problems experienced by MLB players to perform and excel are, in part, discussed in Chapter 6 of Kenneth M. Jennings, *Balls and Strikes: The Money Game in Professional Baseball* (Westport, CT: Praeger Publishers, 1990). As Jennings had predicted about drugs on page 153 of his book, "The future of drug testing in baseball will likely be influenced by two considerations: (1) the extent to which the player's role model responsibilities are agreed to exceed their individual rights; and (2) whether any other method comes along that is effective in identifying a drug problem."

2. For a brief overview of the drug violations by and indictments of selected MLB players, and their penalties during the 1970s, 1980s and 1990s, see Andrew Conte, "The Specter of Drugs Once Again Rears Its Ugly Head With MLB," at http://www.sportsbusinessnews. com cited 20 December 2004.

3. Barry Bonds' involvement with drugs, and his statements and other aspects about the issue are reported in various articles. See, for example, Rich Draper, "Bonds' Lawyer Blasts Report," at http://www.mlb.com cited 7 December 2004; John Shea, Henry Schulman and Susan Slusser, "Integrity For Baseball in Question," at http://www.sportsbusinessnews. com cited 19 October 2004; Barry M. Bloom, "MLB.com Reacts to Barry Bonds Steroid Report," at http://www. sportsbusinessnews.com cited 19 October 2004; Bridget Wentworth, "$7,500 For Five Minutes With Barry Bonds— Think They Cared About Roids," at http://www.sportsbusinessnews.com cited 13 December 2004.

4. Jason Giambi's $120 million multiyear contract with the New York Yankees is in jeopardy. The facts about the contract and the consequences of Giambi's drug use habits are reported in Ian O'Connor, "Yanks Urged to Dump Giambi Now," at http://usatoday.printthis.clickability.com cited 7 December 2004; Mark Feinsand, "Giambi Quiet Amid Speculation," at http://newyork.yankees.mlb.com cited 7 December 2004; "Report: Giambi Used Steroids," at http://www.mlb.com cited 7 December 2004.

5. When he testified before a grand jury in December of 2003, New York Yankees outfielder Gary Sheffield said he used the "the cream" before and during the 2002 season and the drug came from BALCO. This information appeared in Ken Davidoff, "BALCO— Sheffield Tells SI He Took Steroids," at http://www.sportsbusinessnews.com cited 8 October 2004. Other facts about Sheffield's relationship with Barry Bonds are reported in articles previously cited in Notes 2–4.

6. For more details about Commissioner Selig's goals regarding the drug testing of players in MLB, see Bill Ladson, "Selig: Tougher Drug Policy Needed," at http://www.

mlb.com cited 7 December 2004; "Commissioner's Statement," at http://www.mlb.com cited 7 December 2004;
Tim Brown, "Selig Calls For Tougher Drug Testing," at
http://www.sportsbusinessnews.com cited 19 October
2004; Barry M. Bloom, "Drug Talks to Continue Monday," at http://www.mlb.com cited 20 December 2004;
Hal Bodley, "Steroid Testing Negotiations Under Way," at
http://usatoday.printthis.clickability.com cited 15 December 2004.

7. The drug policies in the majors and minors are
listed in Hal Bodley, "Selig Should Show Leadership
Now," at http://usatoday.printthis.clickability.com cited
7 December 2004.

8. See Mark Hyman, "Steroid Scandal? Pass the
Peanuts," *Business Week* (20 December 2004), 44, and
"Gallup Poll Results," at http://usatoday.printthis.click-
ability.com cited 15 December 2004. For the result of
the first question in the Poll, 25 percent of the baseball
fans surveyed believe that MLB players have used
steroids or other performance enhancing drugs during
the past five seasons.

9. "Fans have short memories," says John Mansell,
a sports business analyst at Kegan Research. "They're
willing to forgive and forget." Consequently, the drug
scandals in baseball will soon be forgotten. These and
other views are expressed in Edward Iwata, "Marketers
Gun-Shy Amid Controversies," at http://usatoday.
printthis.clickability.com cited 15 December 2004.

10. Kenneth M. Jennings, *Balls and Strikes: The
Money Game in Professional Baseball*, 148–150 for "Drugs
and the Kuhn Administration" and 150–154 for "Drugs
and the Ueberroth Administration."

11. According to Arizona Republican Senator John
McCain, "I know that the president [George W. Bush]
would like to see it [stronger rules against steroid use
by MLB players] done through collective bargaining and
decision made by owners and labor." See "McCain Optimistic About Testing," at http://www.mlb.com cited 15
December 2004, and "McCain: Tighten Drug-Testing
Policy," at http://www.mlb.com cited 7 December 2004.

12. For the views of three sports writers about drug
testing in MLB, see Hal Bodley, "Selig Should Show
Leadership Now"; Mike Bauman, "Help Wanted: Solving Steroids," at http://www.mlb.com cited 15 December 2004; Mike Lopresti, "Baseball in Dire Need of a
Rescue Plan," at http://usatoday.printthis.clickability.
com cited 7 December 2004.

13. See Mark Starr, "Play Hardball," at http://
doris.pfeiffer.edu cited 25 December 2004. Essentially,
Starr believes that MLB's drug policies are a disgrace
that threaten the integrity of the game. So, to make
amends for its grievous failings on this issue, MLB must
go father than mimicking the policies of the minor
leagues.

14. The three sports writers are, respectively, Bob
Nightengale of the *USA Saturday Baseball Weekly*, Evan
Grant of the *Dallas Morning News*, and Paul Hagen of
the *Philadelphia Daily News*. Their comments and those
of other sports journalists are mentioned in Don Walker
and Drew Olson, "Roids in MLB — Bud 'Shout-Out' to
MLBPA," at http://www.sportsbusinessnews.com cited
9 December 2004.

Chapter 8

1. For an overview of MLB's history and relationship with players associations, see Sean Lahman, "A
Brief History of Baseball: Part II: Professional Baseball's

First Hundred Years," at http://www.baseball1.com cited
30 December 2004, and Lahman's "A Brief History of
Baseball: Part III: Labor Battles in the Modern Era," at
http://www.baseball1.com cited 30 December 2004.

2. There are several sports books that discuss player
strikes, management lockouts and other labor market
issues in MLB. For more about these topics, see Ken-
neth M. Jennings, *Balls and Strikes: The Money Game in
Professional Baseball* (Westport, CT: Praeger Publishers,
1990); Daniel R. Marburger, ed. *Stee-Rike Four! What's
Wrong With the Business of Baseball?* (Westport, CT:
Praeger Publishers, 1997); Andrew Zimbalist, *May the
Best Team Win: Baseball Economics and Public Policy*
(Washington, D.C.: Brookings Institution Press, 2003).

3. Various facts and forms of data about players
salaries for selected years and seasons are reported in
"Average Baseball Salary," at http://search.epnet.
com cited 5 January 2005; "Who Wants to be a Millionaire?" at http://www.cnnsi.com cited 5 April 2001; "Mo'
Money," at http://www.cnnsi.com cited 7 May 2000;
"Big Money," at http://www.cnnsi.com cited 6 April
2000; Sean Lahman, "Minimum & Average Player
Salaries 1967–1997," at http://www.baseball1.com cited
30 December 2004; "MLB Salary Database," at http://
www.sportsfansofamerica.com cited 30 December 2004;
"The Baseball Archive," at http://www.baseball1.com
cited 30 December 2004; Hal Bodley, "Annual Salary
Survey: MLB Teams Armed and Ready," http://www.
usatoday.com cited 7 April 2005; "2005 Salary Arbitration Figures," at http://www.mlb.com cited 20 January
2005; "Highest Baseball Salaries," at http://www.cnnsi.
com cited 25 January 2005.

4. Rather than a "market correction" as predicted
by teams' general managers, during 2004 and 2005 the
league's franchise owners spent hundreds of millions of
dollars on players who became free agents. This spending spree is described in Sean McAdam, "MLB Free
Agency — It Really Has Been Back to the Future," at
http://www.sportsbusinessnews.com cited 30 December 2004.

5. *Ibid.* According to McAdam, such newly hired
general managers as the New York Mets' Omar Minaya
"was charged with making is team relevant again, so he
nabbed Pedro Martinez and has bid for Sexson, Carlos
Delgado and others."

6. For information about the contracts of free agents
in 2004 and 2005, and Scott Boras' role as the player's
sports agent, see Anthony McCarron, "Scott Boras
Remains the King of Baseball Agents," at http://www.
sportsbusinessnews.com cited 9 November 2004; Evan
Grant, "When the Baseball Winter Meetings Begin — Scott
Boras Will be the Master of the Domain," at http://
www.sportsbusinessnews.com cited 9 December 2004;
"Indians Take Gamble on Millwood," *The Charlotte
Observer* (9 January 2005), 5C; Ronald Blum, "Beltran,
Mets Agree to Deal," *The Charlotte Observer* (10 January
2005), 8C. Other sports agents are identified in Mark
Hyman, "Sparks Fly at SFX," *Business Week* (18 June 2001),
86, 88.

7. These and other baseball officials are quoted in
Rich Hammond, "Scott Boras, as Baseball Free Agency
Begins, He is the King of His Domain," at http://www.
sportsbusinessnews.com cited 16 November 2004.

8. "Actually, economics can easily explain why baseball salaries are high. One simply has to look at supply
and demand." This statement appeared in Michael L.
Walden, "Has Baseball Struck Out? Money, Markets, and
Competition," *Carolina Journal* (September 2002), 23.

9. See Gary Lambrecht, "Age Benefits and Athletes,"

at http://www.sportsbusinessnews.com cited 16 November 2004.

10. "Payroll Comparison," at http://si.printthis.clickability.com cited 2 January 2005; "Final 2000 Payroll Figures," at http://www.cnnsi.com cited 21 March 2001; Ronald Blum, "Low Payrolls Represented in Postseason," *The Charlotte Observer* (3 October 2000), 5C.

11. In 2004, the average salary of players in MLB dropped and so did some payrolls as indicated in Table 8.3. The reasons are discussed in "Decline is First Since 1995," at http://sports.espn.go.com cited 5 January 2005. Meanwhile, the payroll of the New York Yankees rose in 2004 and 2005 as described in "Yankees 2005 Projected Payroll," at http://www.cnnsi.com cited 5 January 2005, and Hal Bodley, "Yanks' Payroll Soars as MLB Average Falls," at http://usatoday.printthis.clickability.com cited 5 January 2005.

Chapter 9

1. To learn how the U.S. professional sports leagues ranked in diversity in 1998 and 2003, see Ross Atkin, "High and Low Marks on a Sports Racial Report Card," *Christian Science Monitor* (26 February 1998), 14, and Rob Fernas, "NBA Leads Men's Leagues in Diversity Hiring: Major League Baseball and NHL Have Made Some Progress," *Los Angeles Times* (5 June 2003), 10.

2. There are books that describe the histories and experiences of various African American baseball players and teams, and the Negro Leagues. Three such books are Neil Lanctot, *Negro League Baseball: The Rise and Ruin of a Black Institution* (Philadelphia, PA: University of Press, 2004); Brad Snyder, *Beyond the Shadow of the Senators: The Untold Story of the Homestead Grays and the Integration of Baseball* (New York, N.Y.: McGraw-Hill, 2004); Michael E. Lomax, *Black Baseball Entrepreneurs, 1860–1901: Operating by Any Means Necessary* (Syracuse, N.Y.: Syracuse University Press, 2003).

3. The average ticket prices of MLB teams and Fan Cost Indexes for the 1995–2004 regular seasons are reported in "Major League Baseball," at http://www.teammarketing.com cited 18 January 2005.

4. For some statistics about and reasons for the decline in African Americans as fans and players in baseball, see Terry Armour, "What Happened to the Black Baseball Fans?" *Chicago Tribune* (30 August 2002), 1; Roger Thurow, "Thrown For a Curve: On the Field, Baseball is Integrated, For Fans It's a Different Story," *Wall Street Journal* (28 August 1998), A1; Tom Verducci, "Blackout: The African-American Baseball Player is Vanishing. Does he Have a Future?" at http://www.cnnsi.com cited 17 July 2003; Greg Baum, "Minorities Often Strike Out," at http://www.theage.com 1 March 2005.

5. Some information about the athletes in the book is discussed in Tom Singer, "12 Black Aces Span Generations," at http://www.mlb.com cited 1 March 2005.

6. Besides the Source below Table 9.1, see "Blacks Hold Powerful Posts in Major League Baseball," at http://www.findarticles.com cited 1 March 2005; Eric Gold, "Minorities Playing a Larger Role in Front Office," at http://www.sportsnetwork.com cited 28 February 2005; Ricardo Zuniga, "Minaya Brings Latin Touch to 'Los Mets,'" at http://www.channels.netscape.com cited 20 January 2005; Murray Chass, "Selig Gives New Push to Hiring Minorities," *New York Times* (25 April 1999), 8.

7. For more details about the payments by MLB, there is "Negro Leaguers to Receive $1 Million," at http://www.sportsbusinessnews.com cited 5 October 2004; "New Major League Baseball Program to Help Former Negro League Players," at http://www.mlb.com cited 24 February 2005; "Former Negro League Players Receive Benefits From Major League Baseball Via the Baseball Assistance Team (B.A.T.)," at http://www.mlb.com cited 24 February 2005.

8. See "Major League Baseball Celebrates Black History Month," at http://www.mlb.com cited 26 February 2005, and Mark Newman, "Reflecting on Black History Month," at http://www.mlb.com cited 24 February 2005.

9. The structure and goal of MLB's RBI program is discussed in "Baseball Wants Blacks Back," *Toronto Star* (14 July 2004), C4, and "Integrating Baseball-Chapter 2," at http://www.library2.cqpress.com cited 28 February 2005.

10. Some facts about this program are presented in "Baseball's Pitch For Diversity: 'America's Game' is Scoring With Minority Vendors," *Ebony* (July 2004), 118–120, and Alan Hughes, "Leveling the Field," *Black Enterprise* (February 2002), 26.

11. See "Baseball's Pitch For Diversity: America's Game' is Scoring With Minority Vendors."

Chapter 10

1. Besides Tom Brasuell, MLB's president and chief operating officer Bob DuPuy and executive vice president of business Tim Brosnan also support initiatives in the communities. For a brief overview of a few programs, see Mark Newman, "MLB Thankful For Chances to Give, " at http://www.mlb.com 12 March 2005.

2. To read about the social activities and investments of the league, click on Community at baseball's web site http://www.mlb.com. Some samples of activities sponsored include "Baseball Tomorrow Fund, MLB Clubs Host Equipment Collection Drives," at http://www.mlb.com cited 28 April 2005; Kerry Sheridan, "Baseball Program a Haven in Harlem," at http://www.mlb.com cited 11 April 2005; Tom Singer, "Boys & Girls Clubs Honor MLB," at http://www.mlb.com cited 9 June 2005. With respect to mlb.com, the programs of each team and the teams' players are reported on their respective web sites.

3. For the comments of Jim Martin and Randy Winn and other information about BAT, see Tom Singer, "Baseball Assistance Team," at http://www.mlb.com cited 3 March 2005, and "Baseball Tomorrow Fund Awards More Than $550,000 in Grants During Q4 2004," at http://www.mlb.com cited 12 March 2005.

4. See "MLB, MLBPA Contribute $1 Million to Tsunami Relief," at http://www.mlb.com cited 14 March 2005, and Christie Cowles, "MLB Takes Part in Citywide Clean Up," at http://www.mlb.com cited 14 March 2005.

5. The foundations of the three New York Yankees' players and one manager are discussed in Mark Feinsand, "Yankees Take Pride in Giving Back," at http://www.newyork.yankees.mlb.com cited 14 March 2005.

6. During early 2005, the Texas Rangers announced several local events and the sale of new retail items whose proceeds will be allocated to various causes and the team's Baseball Foundation. To be specific, the events were Baseball 101, Welcome Home Luncheon, 2005 Dr Pepper Texas Rangers Luncheon Series and In-Game Auctions, and the items were Go Rangers Wrist-

bands, Rudy Jaramillo Hitting Video and Texas Rangers Wives Cookbook. For these and other facts about the clubs' activities, see "Texas Rangers Baseball Foundation Upcoming Community Events," at http://www.texas.rangers.mlb.com cited 22 March 2005; "Ameriquest Mortgage Company Launches Baseball Ticket Giveaway in Texas," *Business Wire* (14 February 2005), 1; Jesse Sanchez, "Always Giving Season For Rangers," at http://www.texas.rangers.mlb.com cited 14 March 2005.

Chapter 11

1. For the central office staff and at the regional offices of MLBI, see "MLB International Directory," at http://www.mlb.com cited 15 April 2005. At MLB's website, click on a link titled International. As a result, there is information that discusses MLBI's operations in broadcasting, licensing, market development, sponsorships and events.

2. During 2004, the Envoy program's coaches conducted baseball clinics for children of U.S. Army, Navy and Air Force personnel living on military bases in Europe and Japan. This event is discussed in "Major League Baseball International Envoy Program Visits 27 Countries in 2004," at http://www.mlb.com cited 24 February 2005.

3. See "MLB International to Conduct Elite Baseball Camp in Europe," at http://www.mlb.com cited 28 April 2005. As an aside, since 1998 the Elite Camps have produced more than 70 participants that have been drafted by MLB clubs. That occurred, in part, because national and junior-national coaches from each nation's baseball federation accompany the players and benefit from many of the Camp's activities.

4. This event is discussed in "MLB, China Baseball League Bring MLB Road Show to Five Cities in China," at http://www.mlb.com cited 3 March 2005. Because of the 2008 Summer Olympics in Beijing, similar baseball events as the Road Show will be scheduled and held in China during 2006–2008. That is, more grassroots initiatives and baseball development programs for prospective Chinese players of all ages.

5. A brief description of how MLBAM is promoting the U.S. major and minor baseball leagues' experiences to various sports fans in foreign markets, see Mark Newman, "Baseball's International Movement," at http://www.mlb.com cited 8 February 2005, and "Sport and Technology," at http://www.empics.com cited 5 May 2005.

6. According to ELTA's vice president Peter Chang, "The fifteen to eighteen year old consumer downloads an average of 2.3 wallpapers per month, and there are over 1 million of these teenagers with advanced handsets, just the branding effect of MLB will open a whole new door of opportunities for sports fans." This stated in "MLB Advanced Media signs First Wireless Distribution Agreement in China and Taiwan," at http://www.mlb.com cited 26 April 2005.

7. During early 2005, MLBAM partnered with Six Apart to introduce MLBlogs. There, bloggers found tools that allowed them to create a page featuring their favorite MLB team's logo and colors. As a result, for a fee of $4.95 per month or $49.95 per year the blog allows text and multimedia to be shared and the development of a personal subdomain. See Mark Newman, "MLB.com Introduces MLBlogs," at http://www.mlb.com cited 3 May 2005.

8. These and other international cities were also evaluated as future sites for MLB teams in Chapter 1 of Frank P. Jozsa, Jr., *Sports Capitalism: The Foreign Business of American Professional Leagues* (Aldershot, England: Ashgate Publishing Limited, 2004).

Chapter 12

1. The history, development and growth of the game of baseball, and the presence of amateur and professional baseball leagues in nations besides the U.S. are analyzed in Frank P. Jozsa, Jr., *Sports Capitalism: The Foreign Business of American Professional Leagues* (Aldershot, England: Ashgate Publishing Limited, 2004), 29–68. Some countries' baseball programs were presented in "Globalization of Baseball," *The Boston Globe* (27 March 1998), F3–F8; Kevin Glew, "Book Details Canada's Baseball Impact," at http://www.mlb.com cited 26 July 2005; Barry M. Bloom, "A New Pastime in Cambodia," at http://www.mlb.com cited 26 July 2005.

2. See Gary Engel, "A History of Japanese Baseball," at http://www.mlb.com cited 22 March 2005; "SABR Asian Baseball Committee Japanese Baseball History," at http://www.robsjapanesecards.com cited 22 March 2005; "SABR Asian Baseball Committee Japanese Baseball Timeline," at http://www.robsjapanesecards.com cited 22 March 2005; Bruce Wallace, "Growth of Japanese Baseball Players in the Major Leagues Hurting Japan's Leagues," at http://www.sportsbusinessnews.com cited 5 October 2004.

3. For the section on baseball in South Korea, see "SABR Asian Baseball Committee Korean Baseball History," at http://www.robsjapanesecards.com cited 22 March 2005, and "SABR Asian Baseball Committee Korean Baseball Timeline," at http://www.robsjapanesecards.com cited 22 March 2005.

4. Other than the SABR web sites in endnotes 2 and 3, information about baseball and Taiwan is available in Joe Connor, "Teams Investing in Taiwan," at http://www.mlb.com cited 29 June 2004, and Thomas Harding, "Tsao First of Many, Rockies Hope," at http://www.mlb.com cited 25 July 2003.

5. See "MLB, China Baseball League Bring MLB Road Show to Five Cities in China," at http://www.mlb.com cited 3 March 2005; Howard W. French, "Bringing Baseball to China," at http://www.sportsbusinessnews.com cited 26 May 2004; Michael A. Lev, "Baseball in the People's Republic," at http://www.sportsbusinessnews.com cited 21 August 2003.

6. Three readings that discuss baseball in this nation are Bill Bathe, "Dominican Republic Baseball," at http://www.ezinearticles.com cited 24 March 2005; "Dominican Baseball," at http://www.cubanball.com cited 23 March 2005; Steve Fainaru, "MLB May be Looking to Regulate Dominican Agents," at http://www.sportsbusinessnews.com cited 18 September 2003.

7. For articles about Mexico and the sport, there is Jesse Sanchez, "History of Baseball in Mexico," at http://www.mlb.com cited 22 March 2005; Justin Martin, "Can Baseball Make it in Mexico?" *Fortune* (30 September 1996), 32–33; Jose De Jesus Ortiz, "Mexicans Far From Believers in MLB Dream," at http://www.sportsbusinessnews.com cited 16 March 2004; Jonathan Clark, "Baseball in Caribbean," *San Francisco Chronicle* (11 July 2004), 1–2.

8. The status of baseball on the island is discussed in E.J. Crawford, "Baseball's Marked Decline in Puerto Rico," at http://www.sportsbusinessnews.com cited 28

December 2004; Kevin Baxter, "Los Expos in Puerto Rico," at http://www.sportsbusinessnews.com cited 6 March 2003; John-Thor Dahlburg, "Looking Beyond Ball and Bat to See What Baseball Really Stands For in Puerto Rico," at http://www.sportsbusinessnews.com cited 19 August 2003.

9. See "Venezuelan Baseball League," at http://www.geocities.com cited 2 October 2003, and Peter Wilson and Nick Benequista, "Not a Great Season For the Venezuela's Professional Baseball League," at http://www.sportsbusinessnews.com cited 20 January 2003.

10. For European baseball, see "Major League Baseball in the UK," at http://www.baseballsoftballuk.com cited 29 March 2005; John Vinocur, "Baseball in Europe," at http://www.sportsbusinessnews.com cited 19 August 2003; Rafael Hermoso, "With Los Expos a Success, MLB Looking at Further Expanded Horizons," at http://www.sportsbusinessnews.com cited 22 August 2003; Gordon Edes, "MLB in Europe in 2005?" at http://www.sportsbusinessnews.com cited 22 September 2003.

11. The sport in Cuba is described in "History of Baseball in Cuba," at http://www.cubanball.com cited 23 March 2005; Steve Cummings, "Baseball and Cuba," at http://www.sportsbusinessnews.com cited 19 August 2003; Mark Hyman, "Where Beisbol is the Stuff of Revolution," *Business Week* (15 May 2000), 28, 30.

Chapter 13

1. For the numbers and countries of foreign athletes in MLB as of the late 1990s, see "Globalization of Baseball," *The Boston Globe* (27 March 1998), F3–F8. This article reports the percentages of international players on major league rosters at the start of spring training from the late 1950s to 1990s.

2. The history of baseball in Cuba, Canada, Japan, the Dominican Republic, Venezuela, Puerto Rico and Mexico, and detailed statistics and other information about tournaments and the leagues, teams and players of these nations is available in Peter C. Bjarkman, *Diamonds Around the Globe: The Encyclopedia of International Baseball* (Westport, CT: Greenwood Press, 2005).

3. See "Team Capsules and Lineups," *The Charlotte Observer* (3 April 2005), 12C–13C; "27.3 Percent of Major League Baseball Players Born Outside the United States," at http://www.mlb.com cited 29 March 2005; "29.2 Percent of Major League Baseball Players Born Outside the U.S.," at http://www.mlb.com cited 12 April 2005; "The Wide World of Baseball: Foreign-Born Players Are Filling Major League Rosters," *Baseball Digest* (February 2003), 30–39.

4. *Ibid.*

5. The publication that was researched for the career statistics of MLB players was the *Official Major League Baseball Fact Book 2005 Edition* (St. Louis, MO: The Sporting News, 2005).

6. In late April of 2005, MLB Commissioner Bud Selig presented the Historic Achievement Award to the Seattle Mariners right fielder Ichiro Suzuki for hitting more singles in a regular season than any player in the history of the big leagues. For comments from Selig and Suzuki about the award, see Jim Street, "Ichiro Honored at Safeco," at http://www.mlb.com cited 26 April 2005.

7. For interesting facts about previous and current foreign players in MLB, see Jim Caple, "America's Games Takes on World Flavor With Growth of Inter-

national Talent," *Baseball Digest* (September 2001), 48; John Donovan, "Globalization of the Grand Old Game Hits All-Time High," at http://www.cnnsi.com cited 17 July 2003; "Famous First Foreign Players," at http://www.baseball-almanac.com cited 16 April 2005; *The World Almanac and Book of Facts 2004* (New York, N.Y.: Newspaper Enterprise Association, Inc., 1950–2004).

Chapter 14

1. For an analysis of the international strategies of MLB and of global baseball markets and events, see Frank P. Jozsa, Jr., *Sports Capitalism: The Foreign Business of American Professional Leagues* (Aldershot, England: Ashgate Publishing Limited, 2004).

2. The histories, organizations and tournaments of the Little League, Junior League Baseball Division, Senior League Baseball Division and Big League Baseball Division are reported in "Little League Organization," at http://www.littleleague.org cited 4 April 2005. The years, winning and losing teams and championship game scores of the Little League World Series appear in the baseball section of *The World Almanac and Book of Facts*.

3. The facts about the individual baseball tournaments of the IBAF, including the Olympic Games were derived from "The International Baseball Federation," at http://www.baseball.ch cited 4 April 2005.

4. See, for example, Jonathan Mayo, "Winter Leagues Important to Many," at http://www.mlb.com 5 January 2005; "MLB, Caribbean Confederation Extend Winter League Agreement," at http://www.mlb.com cited 26 May 2005; Jesse Sanchez, "Mexico Captures Series Title," at http://www.mlb.com cited 8 February 2005; Jonathan Mayo, Caribbean Series Gets Under Way," at http://www.mlb.com cited 2 February 2005. For the culture and status of baseball in such nations as Cuba, The Dominican Republic, Venezuela, Puerto Rico and Mexico, and in Africa, Europe and the Pacific Rim, a recent publication is Peter C. Bjarkman, *Diamonds Around the Globe: The Encyclopedia of International Baseball* (Westport, CT: Greenwood Press, 2005).

5. To precede MLB's World Baseball Classic, *The Korea Times* reported that the winners of the professional baseball leagues in Japan, South Korea, Taiwan and China would compete in an Asia Series. Scheduled in November of 2005 at the Tokyo Dome, the tournament's teams will compete in a round-robin playoff, and the two top clubs advance to the final game. According to Korean Baseball Organization commissioner Park Young-oh, "Our first and foremost aim is to make the event a success, so more Asian countries will take part in the tournament in the future. For the article, see Kim Hyun-cheol, "Series to Test Asian Baseball's Elite," at http://www.times.hankooki.com cited 11 April 2005.

6. Some insightful articles about aspects of MLB's World Baseball Classic in 2006 are Barry M. Bloom, "World Cup Given Owners' Blessing," at http://www.sportsbusinessnews.com cited 1 October 2004; "Japan's Baseball Owners Reject World Cup Plan," at http://www.cnnsi.com cited 15 July 2004; "MLB Drug World Cup Testing Agreement in Place," at http://www.sportsbusinessnews.com cited 27 April 2004; Ronald Blum, "Players Approve World Cup Drug Testing," at http://www.cnnsi.com cited 24 February 2005; Amy Shipley, "Baseball Looking to Internationalize," at http://www.sportsbusinessnews.com cited 19 August

2003; "First World Baseball Classic Set For March," at http://www.mlb.com cited 15 July 2005; and "WBC Groups Revealed," at http://www.cnnsi.com cited 15 July 2005.

Chapter 15

1. For more about the team's facility, see "Cardinals to Open Latin American Academy," at http://www.stlouis.cardinals.mlb.com cited 3 May 2005.

2. The most important book that critiques baseball academies in Latin American countries is Arturo J. Marcano and David P. Fidler, *Stealing Lives: The Globalization of Baseball and the Tragic Story of Alexis Quiroz* (Bloomington, IN: Indiana University Press, 2003). The document submitted to MLB is summarized in Arturo J. Marcano and David P. Fidler, "Preliminary Analysis of MLB Academy Standards and Compliance Inspection Procedure," at http://www.sportinsociety.org cited 2 October 2003.

3. After Angel Macias quit playing baseball in 1974, he spent 30 years in human resources at steel and petrochemical exporter Grupo Alfa in Mexico. For Macias' views about the conditions of baseball academies and their role in developing players, see Jesse Sanchez, "Academy Schools Future Stars," at http://www.mlb.com cited 22 March 2005.

4. Young athletes in Puerto Rico train and play hard while living in a baseball academy. Their schedules are described in Bob Edwards, "Profile: Baseball Academy Hopes to Rekindle Puerto Rican Baseball Glory," at http://www.search.epnet.com 3 May 2005.

5. See Jim Souhan, "Latin American Academies Becoming the Norm," at http://www.sportsbusinessnews.com cited 14 January 2003, and Gary Marx, "An Expose on Baseball Training Facilities in Latin America," at http://www.sportsbusinessnews.com cited 19 August 2003.

6. A brief history of the draft and its relationship with international players and countries is discussed in Gary Rausch, "Evolution of the Draft," at http://www.mlb.com cited 3 May 2005, and Paul Hoynes, "Draft Should Span the Globe," *The Plain Dealer* (8 September 2002), C5.

7. Several articles review the various economic, social and political aspects of adopting a worldwide draft by MLB. For example, there is Josh Robbins, "Baseball Weighs Expanding Draft Worldwide," *Orlando Sentinel* (3 June 2001), 1; Gary Klein, "Global Draft," *Los Angeles Times* (3 June 2003), 6; Thomas Harding, "MLB and MLBPA Still Working on World-Wide Draft Plan," at http://www.sportsbusinessnews.com cited 25 November 2002.

8. Wayne Coffey, "Global Warming: Baseball Works to Implement Worldwide Draft," *New York Daily News* (30 May 2002), 6–8.

9. *Ibid.*

10. Some specific problems and other concerns of an international draft are expressed in Tom Singen, "MLB.com Looks at the Concept of a World-Wide Baseball Draft," at http://www.sportsbusinessnews.com cited 3 December 2002; Dave Shenin, "A World-Wide Baseball Draft Could be a Logistical Nightmare," http://www.sportsbusinessnews.com cited 19 August 2003; Kevin Kelly, "Worldwide Draft Caps Wealthy Teams' Monopoly," at http://www.sportsbusinessnews.com cited 19 August 2003; Arturo J. Marcano, "Worldwide Draft," at http://www.baseballguru.com cited 17 March 2005.

11. For professor Fidler's comments, see Steve Fainaru, "MLB to Consider Drug Testing For Foreign Players," at http://www.sportsbusinessnews.com cited 19 September 2003.

12. Rob Manfred has presented MLB's views about a drug-testing program for international players in "Major League Baseball Statement," at http://www.mlb.com cited 3 May 2005, and in Steve Fainaru, "Baseball Ponders Drug Testing of Foreign Prospects," *The Washington Post* (2 July 2003), D1.

13. These numbers were cited in "MLB Steroid Rules Trip Up Latin Americans," at http://www.cnnsi.netscape.com cited 6 May 2005, and Ronald Blum, "Suspended Players Are Largely Latino," *The Charlotte Observer* (5 May 2005), 5C.

14. Boston Red Sox slugger David Ortiz's concerns are stated in "Miscommunication? Language Problems Complicate Drug Policy For Latins," at http://www.cnnsi.com cited 11 May 2005, and in Gordon Edes, "A Slow Death to Baseball in the Dominican," at http://www.sportsbusinessnews.com cited 5 October 2004.

15. Blum, "Suspended Players Are Largely Latino."

16. See "A Q&A With MLB's Head of Security," at http://www.mlb.com cited 9 May 2005.

17. To read about the circumstances regarding this decision and how extraordinary it was for MLB officials, see Larry Stone, "Selig Discusses Cancellation of Overseas Opener," at http://www.sportsbusinessnews.com cited 27 March 2003.

Chapter 16

1. This essay's introduction was developed primarily from four sources. These were "The Commissionership: A Historical Perspective," at http://www.mlb.com cited 15 February 2005; "Commissioners of Major League Baseball," at http://www.baseball-almanac.com cited 17 February 2005; "The Baseball Archive," at http://www.baseball1.com cited 15 February 2005; *Official Major League Baseball Fact Book 2004 Edition* (St. Louis, MO: The Sporting News, 2004).

2. For a brief biography of each individual who has served as a MLB commissioner, see "Commissioners of Major League Baseball," at http://www.contractbud.com cited 19 February 2005; "History of the Game," at http://www.mlb.com 15 February 2005; Rob Neyer, "Landis Had Major Impact as First Commish," at http://www.espn.com cited 15 January 2005.

3. *Ibid.*

4. As an aside, a Ford C. Frick Award is presented annually for major contributions to baseball broadcasting. Some past recipients of the award include Ernie Harwell, Jack Brickhouse, Vin Scully, Harry Caray, Curt Gowdy and Jack Buck. The voice of the San Diego Padres, Jerry Coleman won the award in 2005. See Mike Scarr, "Coleman Honored With Frick Award," at http://www.mlb.com cited 24 February 2005.

5. The information about MLB's current commissioner was presented in "Bud Selig," at http://www.baseball-almanac.com cited 17 February 2005; Murray Chass, "What If We Had a Permanent Commissioner?" *New York Times* (12 February 1995), 86; "Baseball Needs a Firm Hand," *Business Week* (26 May 1997), 182; Mike Bauman, "Bud Selig Reflects Back on His Days as Owner of the Milwaukee Brewers," at http://www.sportsbusinessnews.com cited 30 January 2005; John Schlegal, "Selig Honored at RBI Dinner," at http://www.mlb.com cited 10 February 2005. For how the

commissioner communicates with baseball fans, see Barry M. Bloom, "Selig, Fans Share Dialogue at Town Hall," at http://www.mlb.com cited 15 July 2005.

6. The survey results and comments of baseball's commissioner are reported in "Bud Selig (MLB)," at http://www.rateitall.com cited 19 February 2005.

7. These recommendations were derived, in part, from the conclusion in Jacob F. Lamme, "The Twelve Year Rain Delay: Why a Change in Leadership Will Benefit the Game of Baseball," *Albany Law Review* (Fall 2004), 155–182. See, also, "How the Commish Calls It," *Business Week* (1 November 2004), 93, and "The Spoiled Boys of Summer," *Wall Street Journal* (9 September 2002), A8.

Chapter 17

1. For the ownership structures and historical information about teams in MLB, see "MLB Owners," at http://www.forbes.com cited 9 January 2005; "Teams," at http://www.mlb.com cited 9 January 2005; "The Owners: Who Are These Guys?" at http://www.resonator.com cited 20 November 2001; "2000 Inside the Ownership of Professional Sports Teams," at http://www.teammarketing.com cited 20 November 2001; John Steinbreder, "The Owners," *Sports Illustrated* (13 September 1993), 64–87; James Quirk and Rodney D. Fort, *Pay Dirt: The Business of Professional Team Sports* (Princeton, N.J.: Princeton University Press, 1992), 378–409.

2. The business of U.S.-based sport leagues, such as MLB, and their teams has been discussed in several books. There is Frank P. Jozsa, Jr. and John J. Guthrie, Jr., *Relocating Teams and Expanding Leagues in Professional Sports: How the Major Leagues Respond to Market Conditions* (Westport, CT: Quorum Books, 1999); Frank P. Jozsa, Jr., *American Sports Empire: How the Leagues Breed Success* (Westport, CT: Praeger Publishers, 2003); Harold Seymour, *Baseball: The Golden Age*, 2nd ed. (New York, N.Y.: Oxford University Press, 1989); Paul D. Staudohar and James A. Mangan, eds., *The Business of Professional Sports* (Champaign, IL: University of Illinois Press, 1991).

3. Mark Attanasio's purchase of the Brewers formally ended control of the franchise by Bud Selig and his investors, which was the longest-tenured ownership group in MLB. These and other facts are discussed in Adam McCalvy, "Attanasio Awaits Owners' Vote," at http://www.mlb.com cited 13 January 2005; Don Walker, "Sale of Brewers—Meet the Owners," at http://www.sportsbusinessnews.com cited 15 October 2004; Idem., "Sale of the Brew Crew—New Owner Looking For Local Investors," at http://www.sportsbusinessnews.com cited 15 October 2004; Tom Haudricourt, "Marking the 'End' of the Selig Ownership Era in Milwaukee," at http://www.sportsbusinessnews.com cited 15 October 2004; Bob Baum, "Owners Unanimously Approve Sale of Brewers," at http://sportsillustrated.netscape.cnn.com cited 18 January 2005.

4. In part, the financial issues confronting team owners are covered in Michael K. Ozanian, "How to Buy a Sports Team," *Financial World* (20 May 1996), 66–67; Alfred Edmond, Jr., "So You Want to Buy a Team?" *Black Enterprise* (September 1988), 84; Wayne M. Barrett, "Crying All the Way to the Bank," *USA Today Magazine* (January 1995), 59; Brian Garrity, "Sports Owners Look to Maximize Equity Value in Synergies," at http://www.proquest.umi.com cited 12 Sep-

tember 2004; Jay Greene and Ken Belson, "The Mariners Catch a Tsunami," *Business Week* (25 June 2001), 98, 100.

5. Team payroll data and some player's salaries for various seasons are reported in various articles. For example, see "Payroll Comparison," at http://si.printthis.clickability.com cited 2 January 2005; "Decline is First Since 1995," at http://sports.espn.go.com cited 5 January 2005; "Final 2000 Payroll Figures," at http://www.cnnsi.com cited 21 March 2001.

6. For an overview of the ownership histories of teams in former and current professional baseball leagues, see James Quirk and Rodney D. Fort, *Pay Dirt*, 378–409.

7. Sam Walker, "The Barons of Baseball," *Wall Street Journal* (2 August 2002), W4; Idem., "The Front-Office Blues," *Wall Street Journal* (9 August 2002), W4. For how some owners succeed, see "John Henry: Boston Red Sox," *Business Week* (10 January 2005), 61; Ian Browne, "Red Sox Nation—Owners Rejoice," at http://www.sportsbusinessnews.com cited 26 October 2004; Michael K. Ozanian, "All-Star Owners," at http://www.forbes.com cited 13 January 2005; Anthony Bianco, "The Money Machine," *Business Week* (28 September 1998), 105–108.

8. The sales of the Dodgers to Frank McCourt and the Athletics to Lewis Wolff are discussed, respectively, in John Schlegal, "Schlegal: All in the Family," at http://losangeles.dodgers.mlb.com cited 13 January 2005; Scott Van Voorhis, "Dodgers Make Playoffs, Owner Now a Popular Man," at http://www.sportsbusinessnews.com cited 8 October 2004; Jason Reid, "Dodgers Owner Wants More Success For Franchise," at http://www.sportsbusinessnews.com cited 15 October 2004; Mychael Urban, "A's Co-Owners Considering Sale," at http://www.mlb.com cited 13 January 2005; "L.A. Developer Could Target Athletics," at http://usatoday.printthis.clickability.com cited 7 January 2005; "It's Unanimous: Owners Approve A's Sale to Los Angeles Developer," at http://www.cnnsi.com cited 31 March 2005.

Chapter 18

1. A list of the current general managers in MLB, as of the 2004 regular season, and the top prospects for that position, as of early 2005, are reported in, respectively, "General Manager (Baseball)," at http://en.wikipedia.org cited 7 February 2005, and Josh Boyd, "Top 10 General Manager Prospects," at http://www.baseballamerica.com cited 7 February 2005. The role of Theo Epstein, who is the Boston Red Sox' general manager, is alluded to in Mike Drummond, "How Management Can Hit a Home Run," *The Charlotte Observer* (25 October 2004), 3D.

2. For an excellent book that discusses the talents and achievements of various former head coaches of MLB teams, see Bill James, *The Bill James Guide to Baseball Managers From 1870 to Today* (New York, N.Y.: Scribner, 1997). A review of the book is available at "The Bill James Guide to Baseball Managers From 1870 to Today," at http://www.amazon.com cited 8 February 2005.

3. The sources that were consulted to research information about the managers of teams are "Manager (Baseball)," at http://en.wikipedia.org cited 7 February 2005; *Official Major League Baseball Fact Book 2004 Edition* (St. Louis, MO: The Sporting News, 2004); *The World Almanac and Book of Facts* (New York,

N.Y.: Newspaper Enterprise Association, Inc., 1950–2004).

4. See the sources below Table 18.2. Furthermore, for a sample of articles about the performances of baseball's Manager of the Year, there is Doug Miller, "Scioscia Named Top Skipper," at http://www.mlb.com cited 16 November 2004; Matthew Leach, "LaRussa Receives NL Honor," at http://www.mlb.com cited 16 November 2004; Joe Frisaro, "McKeon Named NL's Best Manager," at http://www.mlb.com cited 16 November 2004; Mike Bauman, "NL Managers Excelled in 2004," at http://www.mlb.com cited 16 November 2004; Robert Falkoff, "Showater is AL Manager of Year," at http://www.mlb.com cited 16 November 2004.

5. See the sources below Table 18.3. Besides those readings, other references that provide the performances of baseball's greatest head coaches of all time include "Hall of Famers by Category: Manager," at http://www.baseball-almanac.com cited 16 November 2004, and Rob Neyer and Eddie Epstein, *Baseball Dynasties: The Greatest Teams of All Time* (New York, N.Y.: W.W. Norton & Company, 2000).

Chapter 19

1. The final results of each season are reported in various issues of *The World Almanac and Book of Facts* (New York, N.Y.: Newspaper Enterprise Association, Inc., 1950–2004), and in the *Official Major League Baseball Fact Book 2004 Edition* (St. Louis, MO: The Sporting News, 2004). For specific teams' performances during the regular seasons and postseasons, see "Teams," at http://www.mlb.com cited 9 January 2005, and "Postseasons," at http://www.baseballreference.com cited 1 January 2005.

2. For the ownership histories of professional baseball teams in the Early National League (1976–1900), American Association (1882–1891), Union Association (1884), Players League (1890), Federal League (1914–1915), National League (1901–1991) and American League (1901–1991), see James Quirk and Rodney D. Fort, *Pay Dirt: The Business of Professional Team Sports* (Princeton, N.J.: Princeton University Press, 1992), 378–409.

3. To determine the quality of teams based on their performances, and whether they rank as all-time great clubs relative to their competitors, three sources were consulted. These include "The Best and Worst Baseball Teams of All Time," at http://members.aol.com cited 31 January 2005; "Baseball's Greatest Teams," at http://www.baseballlibrary.com cited 31 January 2005; "The Greatest Baseball Teams Since 1901," at http://pages.prodigy.net cited 31 January 2005.

4. Since the early 1990s, the Toronto Blue Jays have struggled to defeat the Yankees, Red Sox and Orioles in the AL's East Division. Ted Rogers, who is the president of Rogers Communications and primary owner of the Blue Jays, has decided to invest more money into the franchise and its facilities. See "Extreme Makeover: Blue Jays Increase Payroll, Rename SkyDome," at http://www.cnnsi.com cited 3 February 2005.

5. In early 2005, lawyers Rick Climan and Eric Reifschneider teamed with mathematician Patrick Worfork to devise a Dynasty Index for professional sports clubs. The Index is a statistical measure that considers the number of championships won by a team over several seasons, and includes the number of teams in the league when the championship team excelled. To learn which three Yankees teams are in the top ten of all time, see

Allen St. John, "The Real Dynasties," *Wall Street Journal* (11 February 2005), W5. A book on this topic is Rob Neyer and Eddie Epstein, *Baseball Dynasties: The Greatest Teams of All Time* (New York, N.Y.: W.W. Norton & Company, 2000).

Chapter 20

1. For these and other facts and information about the early origins and activities of professional baseball in America and about expansion and relocation of teams, see Albert Theodore Powers, *The Business of Baseball* (Jefferson, N.C.: McFarland & Company, Inc., Publishers, 2003); Harold Seymour, *Baseball: The Early Years* (New York, N.Y.: Oxford University Press, 1960); David Q. Voight, *American Baseball: From Gentlemen's Sport to the Commissioner System* (Norman, OK: University of Oklahoma Press, 1966); "MLB Franchise Chronology," at http://www.mlb.com cited 9 November 2004; "Franchise Information: Expansion History," at http://www.mlb.com cited 1 December 2004.

2. Powers, *The Business of Baseball*, 15–22.

3. The internal and external business and economic factors that are involved with expanding teams are discussed in sports books. See, for example, Frank P. Jozsa, Jr. and John J. Guthrie, Jr., *Relocating Teams and Expanding Leagues in Professional Sports: How the Major Leagues Respond to Market Conditions* (Westport, CT: Quorum Books, 1999); Roger G. Noll and Andrew Zimbalist, eds., *Sports, Jobs and Taxes: The Economic Impact of Sports Teams and Stadiums* (Washington, D.C.: The Brookings Institution, 1997); Mark S. Rosentraub, *Major League Losers: The Real Costs of Sports and Who's Paying For It* (New York, N.Y.: Basic Books, 1997); Andrew Zimbalist, *Baseball and Billions: A Probing Look Inside the Big Business of Our National Pastime* (New York, N.Y.: Basic Books, 1992).

4. The growth of foreign players in professional baseball and how MLB teams established academies in Latin American countries is discussed in Frank P. Jozsa, Jr., *American Sports Empire: How the Leagues Breed Success* (Westport, CT: Praeger Publishers, 2003), and Arturo J. Marcano and David P. Fidler, *Stealing Lives: The Globalization of Baseball and the Tragic Story of Alexis Quiroz* (Bloomington, IN: Indiana University Press, 2003).

5. Several of these sports economists' studies and theories appear as articles in Roger G. Noll, ed., *Government and the Sports Business* (Washington, D.C.: The Brookings Institution, 1974).

6. Various perspectives about franchises and the expansion and relocation of MLB teams are presented in such sources as Kenneth L. Shropshire, *The Sports Franchise Game: Cities in Pursuit of Sports Franchises, Events, Stadiums, and Arenas* (Philadelphia, PA: University of Pennsylvania Press, 1995); Charles C. Euchner, *Playing the Field: Why Sports Teams Move and Cities Fight to Keep Them* (Baltimore, MD: John Hopkins Press, 1993); Simon Gonzalez, "Expansion Can't Explain All Big Numbers," *The Charlotte Observer* (14 July 1998), 4B; Justin Catanso, "Baseball Should Go Where the Money Is." *Business Week* (29 June 1998), 131.

7. For more details on the expansion teams, see pages 136–142 of Chapter 5, titled "Professional Teams Ranked by Sport," in *Relocating Teams and Expanding Leagues in Professional Sports*.

8. The deal between MLB and political officials, that concluded with the relocation of the Expos from Mon-

treal, Canada to Washington, D.C. in 2004–2005, is discussed in the essay of this book titled "Relocating Teams in Professional Baseball." Also, see Mark Hyman and Paula Dwyer, "What Does This Town Need? New Senators," *Business Week* (14 May 2001), 54, and the Washington Nationals' website at http://www.mlb.com.

9. To learn whether a smaller league is the answer to baseball's economic woes, see Mark Hyman, "And Then There Were 28 ...," *Business Week* (11 October 1999), 98, 100; Stefan Fatsis, "121 Teams? Not For Long," *Wall Street Journal* (16 November 2001), W10.

10. The possible contraction candidates are reported in Sean McAdam, "Baseball OKs Contraction," *The Charlotte Observer* (7 November 2001), 1C, 5C.

11. See Stefan Fatsis, "Twin Killing?" *Wall Street Journal* (4 May 2001), W8.

12. The Robert A. Woods Professor of Economics at Smith College Andrew Zimbalist discussed the downside to contraction of MLB teams in his article, "Why 'Yer Out!' is a Bad Call For Baseball," *Business Week* (12 November 2001), 120.

13. The Congressional legislation about teams folding and relocating is mentioned in "House Act Aimed at Contraction," *The Charlotte Observer* (15 November 2001), 5C. For the purpose, application and other matters of the law as it relates to contraction, see "Fairness in Antitrust in National Sports (FANS) Act in 2001," at http://www.theorator.com cited 22 December 2004.

Chapter 21

1. See Matthew D. Shank, *Sports Marketing: A Strategic Perspective*, 2nd ed. (Upper Saddle River, N.J.: Prentice Hall, 2002). A discussion of managing the marketing mix variables is contained in Philip Kotler, *Marketing Management: Analysis, Planning, Implementation, and Control*, 8th ed. (Upper Saddle River, N.J.: Prentice Hall, 1994).

2. For some marketing reasons why the business of MLB succeeded in 2004, there is "All in All Things Are Pretty Good For Those Selling MLB," at http://www.sportsbusinessnews.com cited 20 June 2005; "Record-Breaking Major League Baseball Remains Timeless," *MediaWeek* (18 October 2004), S3; "Inside the Marketing of Pro Sports," *MediaWeek* (18 October 2004), S1; David Haffenreffer, "The Business of Baseball: The World Series, CNNfn," *The America's Intelligence Wire* (2 October 2004), 1–2.

3. The information about this club's ticket deal was presented in "Atlanta Braves, Six Flags Over Georgia and Six Flags White Water Team Up to Offer 'Triple Play Ticket Pack,'" at http://www.atlanta.braves.mlb.com cited 7 June 2005.

4. The retail business of MLB and baseball promotions are described, respectively, in Rick Harrow, "Sports and the Retail Industry," at http://www.sportsbusinessnews.com cited 30 November 2004, and "Major League Baseball Properties Introduces 2005 Club Retail Promotions," at http://www.mlb.com cited 7 June 2005.

5. For the Sox's unique television advertising campaign, see "White Sox Launch Second Wave of 2005 Television Advertising," at http://www.chicago.whitesox.mlb.com cited 26 May 2005.

6. The National Baseball Hall of Fame in Cooperstown, Pennsylvania draws more than 300,000 visitors per year and the Negro Leagues Baseball Museum in Kansas City, Missouri focuses on baseball history. See Mark Hyman, "Take Me Out to the Museum," *Business Week* (11 April 2005), 103–104.

7. This commemorative set of baseball cards and other aspects of the release are discussed in "Baseball: USA Baseball & Upper Deck Launch Fundraiser," at http://www.sportsfeatures.com cited 16 November 2004.

8. See Nick Wingfield, "Take-Two, Baseball Union Sign Videogame Agreement," *Wall Street Journal* (24 January 2005), B4; "MLBPA Makes Bold Move to Grow Video Game Business," at http://www.sportsbusinessnews.com cited 25 January 2005; "Big Deal For MLB Video Games," at http://www.sportsbusinessnews.com cited 1 February 2005.

9. Online fantasy baseball games and interactive experiences featuring MLB players are flourishing as marketing tools. For information about this strategy, see Nick Wingfield, "Baseball Plans New Web Pitch For Fantasy Games," *Wall Street Journal* (20 January 2005), D3, and Mark Newman, "MLB.com, Players Forge Partnership," at http://www.mlb.com cited 20 January 2005.

10. Baseball festivals are popular events in Latin American nations. One of these is described in "Major League Baseball, Cerveza Presidente Bring Baseball Festival to the Dominican Republic," at http://www.mlb.com cited 7 June 2005.

11. The 76th MLB All-Star Game was televised in the U.S. by Fox Sports and abroad by MLB International. ESPN Radio provided national and MLB.com online coverage, and MLB.com Radio broadcasted the game on the Internet. See "MLB Launches 2005 International All-Star Balloting Program," at http://www.mlb.com cited 26 May 2005.

12. Based on many teams' 2005 attendances, robust advertising demand and strong national television ratings, the steroid scandal has not affected baseball fans' interest in the sport. For the impact on various players, see "Fading Images: Bonds, Giambi, Sosa Tumble in Marketability Survey," at http://www.cnnsi.com cited 5 April 2005.

Chapter 22

1. For an evaluation of MLB clubs as brands, see Martin Bihl, "Are Teams Brands?" at http://www.brandchannel.com cited 14 May 2005; Russell Redman, "More Baseball Ice Creams on Deck," *Supermarket News* (12 February 1996), 63; Rich Thomaselli, "Baseball Tries Makeover," *Advertising Age* (3 February 2003), 3–4; Vanessa O'Connell, "Baseball Strike Might Shut Out Teams With Soft Brand Status," *Wall Street Journal* (23 August 2002), A11; Betsy McKay, "Coke Taps Ripken For Home-Run Pitch," *Wall Street Journal* (7 September 2001), B6. The brand strategies of baseball teams include perceived quality and brand equity, loyalty, awareness, associations, positions, name and symbols. These components appear on pages 74–75 of Kelli D. Washington and Richard K. Miller, *The 2004 Entertainment, Media & Advertising Research Handbook*, Sixth Edition (Norcross, GA: Richard K. Miller & Associates, Inc., 2004).

2. This study included sections on the most valuable team sports brands, key trends, analysis by sport, ownership structures, media matters and why brands matter. See Sebastian Shapiro, *The Most Valuable Brands in Sports: The 2002 Report* (New York, N.Y.: FutureBrand, 2002).

3. The brands of two AL East Division teams are mentioned in "Yankees to Strengthen Marketing Department," at http://www.newyork.yankees.mlb.com cited 14 May 2005; Matthew Futterman, "Just What It

is Like to Market Evil Empire Memorabilia," http://
www.sportsbusinessnews.com cited 29 December 2004;
"Extreme Makeover: Blue Jays Increase Payroll, Rename
SkyDome," at http://www.cnnsi.com cited 3 February
2005.

4. Two AL Central Division teams and their brands
are discussed in "Twins Medallion Collectables Begin
Sunday," at http://www.minnesota.twins.mlb.com cited
28 April 2005, and "You Can Build Your Own 'Slider,'"
at http://www.cleveland.indians.mlb.com cited 24
March 2005.

5. Since 2000, the small-market Seattle Mariners
have been baseball's most profitable team. This view
was expressed in Victoria Murphy, "Seattle's Best-Kept
Secret," Forbes (25 April 2005), 86–88.

6. See "Anaheim Angels Adding Los Angeles to
Name," http://www.channels.netscape.com cited 5 January 2005; Greg Risling, "Angels Name Change May
Bring More Revenue," at http://www.cnnsi.netscape.
com cited 5 January 2005; "Anaheim Wants Judge to
Block 'Los Angeles' Angels," at http://www.usatoday.
com cited 7 January 2005; "November Trial For Angels'
Name Suit," at http://www.cnnsi.com cited 14 March
2005.

7. For more information about the Mets' brand,
there is "Bobblehead Dolls Featuring 'The New Mets'
Highlight 2005 Promotional Schedule," at http://
www.newyork.mets.mlb.com cited 14 March 2005, and
Ronald Blum, "Baseball Teams Expanding Their
Wardrobes," at http://www.cnnsi.netscape.com cited 19
April 2005.

8. Despite the team's lack of success in the NL Central Division, the Brewers provide numerous events at
Miller Park to build their brand in Mil-waukee. These
events were discussed in "Brewers Announce 2005 Promotional Lineup," at http://www.milwaukee.brewers.
com cited 22 March 2005.

9. See Tony Jackson, "Dodgers Trying to Mix Tradition Into Their 2005 Marketing," at http://
www.sportsbusinessnews.com cited 14 February 2005;
John Nadel, "Dodgers Launch WIN—a Program For
Women," at http://www.cnnsi.netscape.com cited 11
May 2005; "Dodger Blue and a Code of Conduct," at
http://www.sportsbusinessnews.com cited 11 May 2005.
As an aside, during late 2005 or early 2006 the Dodgers
planned to implement a new marketing program to its
fan base on www.dodgers.com. The program allows fans
to earn and record reward points on a loyalty card
whenever they buy tickets, merchandise and concessions
at Dodger Stadium or at other participating merchants.
In turn, fans can use the cards to redeem game
tickets and club merchandise. This campaign is
described in "Sports Loyalty Systems (SLS) Launches
an Interesting Sports Branding Program," at http://
www.sportsbusinessnews.com cited 29 July 2005.

10. For how this NL West Division team is improving its image and brand in the northwest region of Mexico, see Julie Poucher Harbin, "Padres Look South to
Help Market Team," San Diego Business Journal (29
March 2004), 14–16.

Chapter 23

1. The discussion of the marketing mix is contained
in Chapter 4 of Philip Kotler, Marketing Management:
Analysis, Planning, Implementation, and Control, 8th ed.
(Upper Saddle River, N.J.: Prentice Hall, 1994).

2. For the economic principles, laws and concepts,

and the types of pricing strategies that may or may not
apply to professional baseball teams, see Chapters 11 and
13 of Michael R. Baye, Managerial Economics and Business Strategy, Fourth Edition, (Boston, MA: McGraw
Hill, 2003). Baye's textbook also includes related economic topics such as Market Forces in Chapter 2 and
The Nature of Industry in Chapter 7.

3. There are several teams that have priced their
seats based on demand. For some examples and results,
see John Morell, "How Much For Tickets? You Need a
Scorecard," New York Times (8 June 2003), 3–4. According to president Daniel A. Rascher of Sports-Econom-
ics, which is a consulting firm based in Berkeley,
California, "Variable pricing is here to stay. Within five
years, it will be commonplace in most pro sports."

4. See Jay Weiner, "Twins Making Their Ticketing
Plans More Customer Friendly," at http://www.
sportsbusinessnews.com cited 30 November 2004;
Daniel B. Wood, "The Baseball Stat You Don't Want to
See," at http://www.csmonitor.com cited 18 January
2005; "Cyber-Scalping: Tickets Going For King's Ransom on Mariners' Web Site," at http://www.cnnsi.com
cited 18 January 2005. About the Twins' Flex Plan, the
University of Massachusetts sports management program professor Steve McKelvey said, "The consumer
rules now. This is benefits marketing. It helps consumers
who find it tough to be able to plan six months in
advance."

5. An analysis of the Chicago Cubs' 2005 ticket
prices indicates that the team has discovered three ways
to win from a business perspective. For more about the
club's strategy, see Peter Bernstein, "Cubs Have Fun
With Ticket Names, Pricing," at http://chicagosports
review.com cited 18 January 2005. Specific information
about regular season game tickets is available for the
Cubs at the league's worldwide web site mlb.com.

6. Baseball Expos, L.P. president Tony Tavares comments, "Establishing a ticketing system is an exciting
and important step in bringing baseball to fans in Washington, DC." See "Baseball in D.C., Season Tickets Set
to go on Sale," at http://www.sportsbusinessnews.com
cited 16 November 2004.

7. The average ticket prices in MLB and the NBA,
NFL and NHL are discussed in Chapter 6 of Frank P.
Jozsa, Jr., American Sports Empire: How the Leagues
Breed Success (Westport, CT: Praeger Publishers, 2003).

8. TMRI's Fan Cost Indexes for 1991–2004 contain
the prices established by each team in MLB. For more
details, see "Major League Baseball," at http://www.
teammarketing.com cited 18 January 2005.

Chapter 24

1. As of early 2005, Toys 'R' Us sold its merchandise in a total of 1,200 U.S. and foreign stores and
through three Internet sites. For the company's deal with
MLBP, see "Toys 'R' Us and Major League Baseball
Team Up to Celebrate 2005 Opening Day," at http://
www.mlb.com cited 7 April 2005.

2. With fiscal 2004 sales of $73.1 billion, The Home
Depot consists of approximately 1,900 stores and
employs 325,000 associates. Its agreement with baseball
is discussed in "Major League Baseball, The Home
Depot Build Integrated Marketing Partnership," at
http://www.mlb.com cited 5 April 2005.

3. Watched in 88 million U.S. homes and 170
nations, the 13 year-old Cartoon Network is Turner
Broadcasting System Inc.'s 24-hour, ad-supported cable

service that offers animated entertainment. See "MLB, MLBPA Partnership With Cartoon Network Begins Second Season," at http://www.mlb.com cited 11 May 2005.

4. Information about this marketing deal was reported in "MLB Advanced Media and National Association of Professional Baseball Leagues Announce Major Partnership Agreement," at http://www.mlb.com cited 18 January 2005.

5. For these four agreements, see "Dodge Signs Three-Year Deal With Seattle," at http://www.seattle.mariners.mlb.com cited 5 April 2005; "Orioles Joins CoverGirl For Unique Partnership," at http://www.baltimore.orioles.mlb.com cited 26 April 2005; "Cox Communications Partners With Padres, MLB Advanced Media For First-of-Its-Kind Offer Exclusive to Cox High Speed Internet Customers," at http://www.sandiego.padres.mlb.com cited 18 May 2005; "Angels and General Motors Reach Agreement on Three-Year Partnership," at http://www.angels.mlb.com cited 19 April 2005.

6. Because of player Ichiro Suzuki, Japanese products are popular in the Seattle area and Mariners' games receive national exposure in Japan. These relationships are highlighted in "Mariners Announce Partnership With Six Japanese Companies," at http://www.seattle.mariners.mlb.com cited 21 April 2005.

7. The *IEG Sponsorship Report* and MLB were mentioned in "Sponsorship of Professional Baseball Leagues and Teams to Total $388 Million in 2004," at http://www.sponsorship.com cited 20 May 2005.

8. How commercial banks support professional and amateur baseball is discussed in two articles. See David McPherson, "Banking on Baseball," *The Providence Journal* (8 May 2005), 1–2, and Rick Rothacker, "Bank of America Puts Brand on 3 Levels of Baseball," *Knight Ridder Tribune Business News Washington* (9 July 2004), 1–2.

9. The announcement of this affiliation is described in "Termidor Joins Rays' Growing List of Sponsor Partners," at http://www.tampabay.devilrays.mlb.com cited 26 April 2005.

10. See Jamie LaReau, "Chevrolet, Major League Baseball Sign Sponsorship Deal," *Automotive News* (4 April 2005), 28H, and Peter Zellen, "MLB Announces Three-Year Deal With GM," at http://www.mlb.com cited 24 March 2005.

11. For some insights about commercial logos on bases, read Richard Sandomir, "Sports and Sponsorship — is Baseball Being Held to a Higher Standard," at http://www.sportsbusinessnews.com cited 5 October 2004.

12. *Ibid.*

13. An overview of this marketing practice is discussed in Clark C. Griffith, "A Little History of Licensing in Major League Baseball," *The Licensing Journal* (January 2003), 31.

14. Michael Jacobsen, "Majestic Outpitches Russell For MLB Uniform Licensing," *Sporting Goods Business San Francisco* (September 2003), 12, and "MLB Announces New Licensing Agreements," at http://www.sportsbusinessnews.com cited 5 August 2003.

15. This section mentions five licensing deals. See "MLB.com Names Preliminary List of 2005 Fantasy Game Licensees," at http://www.mlb.com cited 15 March 2005; "MLB and the Wireless Universe," at http://www.sportsbusinessnews.com cited 7 April 2005; "Major League Baseball International, United Media Partner in Japan," at http://www.mlb.com cited 11 May 2005; "MLB Properties, Sportbox Reach Five-Year Licensing Agreement," at http://www.mlb.com cited 18 May 2005; "Twins Take Innovative Step in Sports Marketing," at http://www.minnesota.twins.mlb.com cited 14 May 2005.

Chapter 25

1. For the purposes and achievements of MLBP, see "About Us," at http://www.mlb.com cited 12 May 2005; "Major League Baseball Productions Nominated For Eight NY Emmy Awards," at http://www.mlb.com cited 3 March 2005; "MLB Productions, Hart Sharp Video Present Yankeeography Volume Three," at http://www.mlb.com cited 14 May 2005.

2. The features of this program are revealed in "MLB Productions Launches 27th Season of 'This Week in Baseball,'" at http://www.mlb.com cited 14 May 2005.

3. See "Major League Baseball Productions, Spike TV Step Up to the Plate for 'Maximum MLB,'" at http://www.mlb.com cited 14 May 2005.

4. When and why these companies have joined with MLB to develop and produce broadcasts of programs is discussed in "Major League Baseball Productions Reaches Distribution Agreements With Shout! Factory, A&E Home Video," at http://www.mlb.com cited 26 April 2005.

5. *Ibid.*

6. This agreement is a coup for Microsoft because RealNetworks has been MLB's primary partner for broadcasting games over the Internet. The deal is briefly explained in Kim Peterson, "MSN Scores Online Video For All Major League Baseball Games," *The Seattle Times* (23 March 2004), 1–2.

7. See more information about these programming options in "Interactive Baseball Network Debuts," at http://www.mlb.com cited 15 October 2004.

8. Two articles discuss this unique advertising campaign and the sports commercials. See "Major League Baseball Debuts Fan-Based 2005 'I Live For This' Commercials," at http://www.mlb.com cited 15 March 2005, and Mark Newman, "New MLB TV Ads Spotlight Fans' Passion," at http://www.sportsbusinessnews.com cited 15 March 2005.

9. The baseball fans in countries of Asia demand MLB games and programs. For how to entertain these fans, see "Major League Baseball Reaches National Broadcast Agreement in Taiwan," at http://www.mlb.com cited 11 May 2005.

10. Since 2003, four AL teams have made an effort to penetrate the Spanish audiences in their markets. These teams' programming campaigns are described in Sean Wood, "Rangers Target Hispanic Fans ... Again," at http://www.sportsbusinessnews.com cited 27 March 2003; Bill Griffith, "Red Sox Adding Spanish Broadcasts This Year," at http://www.sportsbusinessnews.com cited 27 March 2003; "A's Return to Spanish Radio," at http://www.sportsbusinessnews.com cited 19 August 2003; "Athletics to Launch Spanish Radio Network For 2005 Season," at http://www.oakland.athletics.mlb.com cited 17 March 2005; "Rays Sign 4-Year Deal to Broadcast Games in Spanish," at http://www.tampabay.devilrays.mlb.com cited 17 March 2005.

11. For the strategies of some NL teams that broadcast games to Hispanics in 2005, see "Padres and Telemundo Reach Broadcast Agreement," at http://www.sandiego.padres.mlb.com cited 29 March 2005; "Brewers to Join Telemundo For 12 Telecasts in 2005," at http://www.milwaukee.brewers.mlb.com cited 29

March 2005; "Giants Announce New Spanish Radio Partnership With Cumbia 1170 AM," at http://www.sanfrancisco.giants.mlb.com cited 5 April 2005; "Phillies Revive Hispanic Radio Broadcasts," at http://www.philadelphia.phillies.mlb.com cited 17 March 2005.

12. See "MSG to Provide Spanish Simulcasts," at http://www.newyork.mets.mlb.com cited 29 March 2005, and "Shea Stadium Goes Digital," at http://www.newyork.mets.mlb.com cited 22 March 2005.

13. For the difficulty in allocating a specific television territory between two MLB franchises, and information about the dispute between MLB, Baltimore Orioles owner Peter Angelos, Comcast and the MASN, read David Ginsburg, "Orioles Working on TV Agreement With Nats," at http://www.cnnsi.com cited 14 March 2005; Barry M. Bloom, "Path Cleared For Nationals on TV," at http://www.mlb.com cited 5 April 2005; Kasey Jones, "Comcast Sues Orioles Over TV Rights," at http://www.cnnsi.com cited 26 April 2005; Joseph White, "Washington Nationals Get First Cable Deal," at http://www.cnnsi.com cited 18 May 2005.

14. The economic and public policy issues related to the sale of broadcast rights in professional sports are presented in Ira Horowitz, "Sports Broadcasting," *Government and the Sports Business* (Washington, D.C.: The Brookings Institution, 1974), 275–323.

Bibliography

Articles

"Ameriquest Mortgage Company Launches Baseball Ticket Giveaway in Texas." *Business Wire* (14 February 2005): 1.

Armour, Terry. "What Happened to the Black Baseball Fans?" *Chicago Tribune* (30 August 2002): 1.

Atkin, Ross, "High and Low Marks on a Sports Racial Report Card." *Christian Science Monitor* (26 February 1998): 14.

Badenhausen, Kurt, et al. "Double Play." *Forbes* (15 April 2002): 92–94.

Bai, Matt. "A League of Their Own." *Newsweek* (11 May 1998): 68.

Banks, Mac. "Knights Look to Indy as Model for Stadium Ideas." *Fort Mill Times* (3 August 2000): 11A.

Barra, Alan. "And Very Sweet for the Yankees." *Wall Street Journal* (22 June 2005): D12.

Barrett, Wayne M. "Crying All the Way to the Bank." *USA Today Magazine* (January 1995): 59.

"Baseball Needs a Firm Hand." *Business Week* (26 May 1997): 182.

"Baseball Wants Blacks Back." *Toronto Star* (14 July 2004): C4.

"Baseball's Pitch for Diversity: "'America's Game' Is Scoring with Minority Vendors." *Ebony* (July 2004): 118–120.

"BellSouth Makes Pitch for 'MLB Extra Innings' from DirecTV." *Wireless News* (30 March 2005): 1.

Bianco, Anthony. "How to Build Your Dream Team." *Business Week* (31 March 2003): 104–105.

_____. "The Money Machine." *Business Week* (28 September 1998): 105–108.

Blum, Ronald. "Beltran, Mets Agree to Deal." *The Charlotte Observer* (10 January 2005): 8C.

_____. "Cash Flow: Baseball Wants Some." *The Daily News* (15 July 2000): 1C, 3C.

_____. "Low Payrolls Represented in Postseason." *The Charlotte Observer* (3 October 2000): 5C.

_____. "Suspended Players Are Largely Latino." *The Charlotte Observer* (5 May 2005): 5C.

Boswell, Thomas. "Fehr Gets a Dose of His Own Medicine." *The Washington Post* (19 March 2005): D1.

"The Boys of Summer Come Back." *Wall Street Journal* (1 July 2005): W11.

Caple, Jim. "America's Game Takes on World Flavor with Growth of International Talent." *Baseball Digest* (September 2001), 48.

Carter, David M. "There's Nothing Minor About These Prospects." *2000 Charlotte Knights Souvenir Program* (Fort Mill, S.C.: Charlotte Knights Media Relations Office, 2000): 18.

Catansos, Justin. "Baseball Should Go Where the Money Is." *Business Week* (29 June 1998): 131.

Chass, Murray. "Selig Gives New Push to Hiring Minorities." *New York Times* (25 April 1999): 8.

_____. "What If We Had a Permanent Commissioner?" *New York Times* (12 February 2005): 86.

Chen, Albert. "Inside Baseball." *Sports Illustrated* (28 April 2003): 66.

Clark, Jonathan. "Baseball in Caribbean." *San Francisco Chronicle* (11 July 2004): 1–2.

Coffey, Wayne. "Global Warming: Baseball Works to Implement Worldwide Draft." *New York Daily News* (30 May 2002): 6–8.

Connors, Philip. "Baseball: Agony and Ecstasy in Minnesota." *Wall Street Journal* (23 July 2001): A13.

"Contentious Labor Situation Casts Cloud Over Season, Sport." *The Charlotte Observer* (29 March 2002): 7C.

Cramer, Jerome. "So, You Want to Own a Minor League Baseball Team." *Forbes* (Fall 2003): 82, 84–86.

Drummond, Mike. "How Management Can Hit a Home Run." *The Charlotte Observer* (25 October 2004): 3D.

Dumcius, Gintautas. "Lawmakers Push Bill Imposing Steroid Sanctions." *Wall Street Journal* (24 May 2005): D4.

Edmond, Alfred Jr. "So You Want to Buy a Sports Team." *Black Enterprise* (September 1988): 84.

Fainaru, Steve. "Baseball Ponders Drug Testing of Foreign Prospects." *The Washington Post* (2 July 2003): D1.

Fatsis, Stefan. "Montreal Expos: No Place to Call Home." *Wall Street Journal* (7 August 2003): B1, B3.

_____. "121 Teams? Not for Long." *Wall Street Journal* (16 November 2001): W10.

_____. "Save Our Expos!" *Wall Street Journal* (29 March 2002): W6.

_____. "Twin Killing?" *Wall Street Journal* (4 May 2001): W8.

Fernas, Rob. "NBA Leads Men's Leagues in Diversity Hiring: Major League Baseball and NHL Have Made Some Progress." *Los Angeles Times* (5 June 2003): 10.

Fitzpatrick, Frank. "Citizens at Bat: Baseball's Community All-Stars." *Policy Review* (July–August, 1996): 22–28.

Gerena, Charles, and Betty Joyce Nash. "Playing to Win: Minor League Sports Score." *Region Focus* (Spring 2000): 13–19.

"Globalization of Baseball." *The Boston Globe* (27 March 1998): F3–F8.

Gonzalez, Simon. "Expansion Can't Explain All Big Numbers." *The Charlotte Observer* (14 July 1998): 4B.

Grant, Evan. "Dominican Academies Prepare Players for Life in Big Leagues." *The Dallas Morning News* (31 March 2000): 66.

Green, Ron Sr. "Drawing Crowds to Parks Now Major Fun for Minors." *The Charlotte Observer* (4 September 2001): 5C.

Greene, Jay, and Ken Belson. "The Mariners Catch a Tsunami." *Business Week* (25 June 2001): 98, 100.

Griffith, Clark C. "A Little History of Licensing in Major League Baseball." *The Licensing Journal* (January 2003): 31.

Haffenreffer, David. "The Business of Baseball: The World Series, CNNfn." *The America's Intelligence Wire* (2 October 2004): 1–2.

Hall, Kevin G. "Mexico's 'Little Giants' Flex Major Muscles." *The Charlotte Observer* (9 November 2003): 18A.

Harbin, Julie Poucher. "Padres Look South to Help Market Team." *San Diego Business Journal* (29 March 2004): 14–16.

Horowitz, Ira. "Sports Broadcasting." *Government and the Sports Business* (Washington, D.C.: The Brookings Institution, 1974): 275–323.

"House Act Aimed at Contraction." *The Charlotte Observer* (15 November 2001): 5C.

"How the Commish Calls It." *Business Week* (1 November 2004): 93.

Hoynes, Paul. "Draft Should Span the Globe." *The Plain Dealer* (8 September 2002): C5.

Hughes, Alan. "Leveling the Field." *Black Enterprise* (February 2002): 26.

Hyman, Mark. "And Then There Were 28 ..." *Business Week* (11 October 1999): 98, 100.

_____. "It's a Horse Race in Right Field." *Business Week* (18 October 2004): 48.

_____. "Play Ball — Even If No One Loves You." *Business Week* (25 March 2002): 84.

_____. "So Long, Montreal. Hello, Washington." *Business Week* (30 September 2002): 105.

_____. "Sparks Fly at SFX." *Business Week* (18 June 2001): 86, 88.

_____. "Steroid Scandal? Pass the Peanuts." *Business Week* (20 December 2004): 44.

_____. "Take Me Out to the Museum." *Business Week* (11 April 205): 103–104.

_____. "Where Beisbol Is the Stuff of Revolution." *Business Week* (15 May 2000): 28, 30.

Hyman, Mark, and Paula Dwyer. "What Does This Town Need? New Senators." *Business Week* (14 May 2001): 54.

"Indians Take Gamble on Millwood." *The Charlotte Observer* (9 January 2005): 5C.

"Inside the Marketing of Pro Sports." *MediaWeek* (18 October 2004): S1.

Jacobsen, Michael. "Majestic Outpitches Russell for MLB Uniform Licensing." *Sporting Goods Business San Francisco* (September 2003): 12.

"John Henry: Boston Red Sox." *Business Week* (10 January 2005): 61.

Klein, Gary. "Global Draft." *Los Angeles Times* (3 June 2003): 6.

Kornheiser, Tony. "Baseball's Union Wields a Big Bat." *The Washington Post* (3 March 2004): D1.

Kuenster, John. "Fans Offer Six Ways to Improve Game at the Major League Level." *Baseball Digest* (December 2004): 17–19.

Lamal, P.A. "A Gold Mine for Bar Bets and Stumpers." *The Charlotte Observer* (25 October 2004): 17A.

Lamme, Jacob F. "The Twelve Year Rain Delay: Why a Change in Leadership Will Benefit the Game of Baseball." *Albany Law Review* (Fall 2004): 155–182.

LaReau, Jamie. "Chevrolet, Major League Baseball Sign Sponsorship Deal." *Automotive News* (4 April 2005): 28H.

Lowry, Tom, et al. "For the Love of the Game — And Cheap Seats." *Business Week* (28 May 2001): 46–47.

Martin, Justin. "Can Baseball Make it in Mexico?" *Fortune* (30 September 1996): 32–33.

McAdam, Sean. "Baseball OKs Contraction." *The Charlotte Observer* (7 November 2001): 1C, 5C.

McKay, Betsy. "Coke Taps Ripken for Home-Run Pitch." *Wall Street Journal* (7 September 2001): B6.

McPherson, David. "Banking on Baseball." *The Providence Journal* (8 May 2005): 1–2.

Moores, John. "When Push Comes to Shove: Union Hurts Baseball." *Wall Street Journal* (12 July 2005): D8.

Morell, John. "How Much for Tickets? You Need a Scorecard." *New York Times* (8 June 2003): 3–4.

Murphy, Victoria. "Seattle's Best-Kept Secret." *Forbes* (25 April 2005): 86–88.

O'Connell, Vanessa. "Baseball Strike Might Shut Out Teams with Soft Brand Status." *Wall Street Journal* (23 August 2002): A11.

Ozanian, Michael, and Kurt Badenhausen. "Baseball Going Broke? Don't Believe It." *Wall Street Journal* (27 July 2000): A22.

Ozanian, Michael K. "How to Buy a Sports Team." *Financial World* (20 May 1996): 66–67.

Parsons, Tom. "Hotels in Major League Cities Pitching Special Baseball Packages." *The Charlotte Observer* (23 June 2005): 5E.

Peterson, Kim. "MSN Scores Online Video for All Major League Baseball Games." *The Seattle Times* (23 March 2004): 1–2.

"Players Consider Testing for Cup." *The Charlotte Observer* (29 March 2003): 9C.

"Record-Breaking Major League Baseball Remains Timeless." *MediaWeek* (18 October 2004): S3.

Redman, Russell. "More Baseball Ice Creams on Deck." *Supermarket News* (12 February 1996): 63.

Reed, Ted. "Diamond Dreams." *The Charlotte Observer* (26 March 2001): 10D.

Robbins, Josh. "Baseball Weighs Expanding Draft Worldwide." *Orlando Sentinel* (3 June 2001): 1.

Rothacker, Rick. "Bank of America Puts Brand on 3 Levels of Baseball." *Knight Ridder Tribune Business News Washington* (9 July 2004): 1–2.

Rowan, Roy. "Play Ball!" *Fortune* (4 September 2000): 311–326.

St. John, Allen. "If You Build It ..." *Wall Street Journal* (22 July 2005): W6.

_____. "The Real Dynasties." *Wall Street Journal* (11 February 2005): W5.

Schwarz, Alan. "Not Just Peanuts: Minor-League Baseball Is More Than Quaint Stadiums and Dancing Umpires." *Newsweek* (9 May 2005): 36.

Sommers, Paul M. "Ticket Prices and Player Salaries in Major League Baseball." *Journal of Recreational Mathematics* (Winter 1994): 274–276.

"Spitballing the Minors." *Wall Street Journal* (22 April 2004): A18.

"The Spoiled Boys of Summer." *Wall Street Journal* (9 September 2002): A8.

"Sports Work Stoppages." *The Charlotte Observer* (25 October 1998): 6H.

Steinberg, Brian, and Suzanne Vranica. "Sticking with the National Pastime." *Wall Street Journal* (30 March 2005): B3.

Steinbreder, John. "The Owners." *Sports Illustrated* (13 September 1993): 64–87.

"Team Capsules and Lineups." *The Charlotte Observer* (3 April 2005): 12C–13C.

Thomaselli, Rich. "Baseball Tries Makeover." *Advertising Age* (3 February 2003): 3–4.

Thurow, Roger. "Thrown for a Curve: On the Field, Baseball Is Integrated, for Fans It's a Different Story." *Wall Street Journal* (28 August 1998): A1.

Vardi, Nathan. "Hardball." *Forbes* (26 April 2004): 67, 70–71.

Walden, Michael L. "Has Baseball Struck Out? Money, Markets, and Competition." *Carolina Journal* (September 2002): 23.

Walker, Sam. "The Barons of Baseball." *Wall Street Journal* (2 August 2002): W4.

_____. "The Front-Office Blues." *Wall Street Journal* (9 August 2002): W4.

_____. "The Long-Distance Fan." *Wall Street Journal* (18 July 2003): W1, W4.

_____. "Strike Averted, Baseball Teams Try to Woo Fans." *Wall Street Journal* (3 September 2002): B1–B2.

Weber, Bruce. "Fehr and Loathing." *Scholastic Coach & Athletic Director* (May/June 2004): 16.

Weinbach, Jon. "When Players Don't Pay." *Wall Street Journal* (17 June 2005): W1, W8.

Weiner, Jay. "Thinking Out of the Batter's Box." *Business Week* (24 April 2000): 175, 178.

Whitmire, Tim. "Expensive Gamble But No Show." *The Charlotte Observer* (28 May 2001): 1B, 5B.

"The Wide World of Baseball: Foreign-Born Players Are Filling Major League Rosters." *Baseball Digest* (February 2003): 30–39.

Will, George. "Baseball Thrives Despite Intense, Unjust Criticism." *The Charlotte Observer* (3 April 2005): 3P.

Wingfield, Nick. "Baseball Plans New Web Pitch for Fantasy Games." *Wall Street Journal* (20 January 2005): D3.

_____. "Take-Two, Baseball Union Sign Videogame Agreement." *Wall Street Journal* (24 January 2005): B4.

Wong, Alex. "Moving in on the Majors." *Newsweek* (23 August 2004): 13–15.

"Yanqui Doodle Dandy." *Wall Street Journal* (20 February 2004): W11.

Zimbalist, Andrew. "Why 'Yer Out!' Is a Bad Call for Baseball." *Business Week* (12 November 2001): 120.

Books

Acton, Jay, and Nick Bakalar. *Green Diamonds: The Pleasures and Profits of Investing in Minor-League Baseball*. New York: Kensington, 1993.

Barzilla, Scott. *Checks and Imbalances: Competitive Disparity in Major League Baseball*. Jefferson, NC: McFarland, 2002.

_____. *The State of Baseball Management: Decision-Making in the Best and Worst Teams, 1993–2003*. Jefferson, NC: McFarland, 2004.

Baye, Michael R. *Managerial Economics and Business Strategy*. Fourth Edition. Boston: McGraw-Hill, 2003.

Berry, Robert C., and Glenn M. Wong. *Law and Business of the Sports Industry*. Westport, CT: Praeger, 1993.

Bjarkman, Peter C. *Diamonds Around the Globe: The Encyclopedia of International Baseball*. Westport, CT: Greenwood, 2005.

Burk, Robert F. *Much More Than a Game: Players, Owners, and American Baseball Since 1921*. Chapel Hill: University of North Carolina Press, 2001.

Carino, Peter, ed. *Baseball/Literature/Culture: Essays, 1995–2001*. Jefferson, NC: McFarland, 2003.

_____. *Baseball/Literature/Culture: Essays, 2002–2003*. Jefferson, NC: McFarland, 2004.

Echevarria, Roberto Gonzalez. *The Pride of Havana: A History of Cuban Baseball*. New York: Oxford University Press, 1999.

Ehrenberg, Ronald G., and Robert S. Smith. *Modern Labor Economics: Theory and Public Policy*. Sixth Edition. Reading, MA: Addison-Wesley, 1997.

Euchner, Charles C. *Playing the Field: Why Sports Teams Move and Cities Fight to Keep Them*. Baltimore, MD: Johns Hopkins University Press, 1993.

Helyar, John. *Lords of the Realm: The Real History of Baseball*. New York: Ballantine, 1994.

Holtzman, Jerome. *The Commissioners: Baseball's Midlife Crisis*. New York: Total Sports, 1998.

James, Bill. *The Bill James Guide to Baseball Managers from 1870 to Today*. New York: Scribner, 1997.

Jennings, Kenneth M. *Balls and Strikes: The Money Game in Professional Baseball*. Westport, CT: Praeger, 1990.

Jones, Michael E. *Sports Law*. Upper Saddle River, N.J.: Prentice Hall, 1999.

Jozsa, Frank P., Jr. *American Sports Empire: How the*

Leagues Breed Success. Westport, CT: Praeger, 2003.

_____. *Sports Capitalism: The Foreign Business of American Professional Leagues.* Aldershot, England: Ashgate, 2004.

Jozsa, Frank P., Jr., and John J. Guthrie, Jr. *Relocating Teams and Expanding Leagues in Professional Sports: How the Major Leagues Respond to Market Conditions.* Westport, CT: Quorum, 1999.

Kotler, Philip. *Marketing Management: Analysis, Planning, Implementation, and Control.* 8th ed. Upper Saddle River, N.J.: Prentice Hall, 1994.

Lanctot, Neil. *Negro League Baseball: The Rise and Ruin of a Black Institution.* Philadelphia: University of Pennsylvania Press, 2004.

Lewis, Michael. *Moneyball: The Art of Winning an Unfair Game.* New York: Random House, 2003.

Lomax, Michael E. *Black Baseball Entrepreneurs, 1860–1901: Operating by Any Means Necessary.* Syracuse, N.Y.: Syracuse University Press, 2003.

Marburger, Daniel R., ed. *Stee-Rike Four! What's Wrong with the Business of Baseball?* Westport, CT: Praeger, 1997.

Marcano, Arturo J., and David P. Fidler. *Stealing Lives: The Globalization of Baseball and the Tragic Story of Alexis Quiroz.* Bloomington: Indiana University Press, 2003.

McCarver, Tim, and Danny Peary. *Tim McCarver's Baseball for Brain Surgeons and Other Fans: Understanding and Interpreting the Game So You Can Watch It Like a Pro.* New York: Villard, 1999.

Miller, James Edward. *The Baseball Business: Pursuing Pennants and Profits in Baltimore.* 2nd ed. Chapel Hill: University of North Carolina Press, 1991.

Miller, Marvin. *A Whole Different Ballgame: The Sport and Business of Baseball.* New York: Birch Lane, 1991.

Neyer, Rob, and Eddie Epstein. *Baseball Dynasties: The Greatest Teams of All Time.* New York: W.W. Norton, 2000.

Noll, Roger G., ed. *Government and the Sports Business.* Washington, D.C.: The Brookings Institution, 1974.

Noll, Roger G., and Andrew Zimbalist, eds. *Sports, Jobs and Taxes: The Economic Impact of Sports Teams and Stadiums.* Washington, D.C.: The Brookings Institution, 1997.

Powers, Albert Theodore. *The Business of Baseball.* Jefferson, NC: McFarland, 2003.

Quirk, James, and Rodney D. Fort. *Pay Dirt: The Business of Professional Team Sports.* Princeton, N.J.: Princeton University Press, 1992.

Rosentraub, Mark S. *Major League Losers: The Real Costs of Sports and Who's Paying for It.* New York: Basic, 1997.

Schaaf, Phil. *Sports, Inc.: 100 Years of Sports Business.* Amherst, N.Y.: Prometheus, 2004.

Scully, Gerald W. *The Business of Major League Baseball.* Chicago: University of Chicago Press, 1989.

Seymour, Harold. *Baseball: The Early Years.* New York: Oxford University Press, 1960.

_____. *Baseball: The Golden Age.* 2nd ed. New York: Oxford University Press, 1989.

Shank, Matthew D. *Sports Marketing: A Strategic Perspective.* 2nd ed. Upper Saddle River, N.J.: Prentice Hall, 2002.

Shropshire, Kenneth L. *The Sports Franchise Game: Cities in Pursuit of Sports Franchises, Events, Stadiums, and Arenas.* Philadelphia, PA: University of Pennsylvania Press, 1995.

Snyder, Brad. *Beyond the Shadow of the Senators: The Untold Story of the Homestead Grays and the Integration of Baseball.* New York: McGraw-Hill, 2004.

Sommers, Paul M., ed. *Diamonds Are Forever: The Business of Baseball.* Washington, D.C.: The Brookings Institution, 1992.

Staudohar, Paul D., and James A. Mangan, eds. *The Business of Professional Sports.* Champaign: University of Illinois Press, 1991.

Sullivan, Neil J. *The Dodgers Move West: The Transfer of the Brooklyn Baseball Franchise to Los Angeles.* New York: Oxford University Press, 1987.

Szymanski, Stefan, and Andrew Zimbalist. *National Pastime.* Washington, D.C.: The Brookings Institution, 2005.

Tygiel, Jules. *Baseball's Great Experiment: Jackie Robinson and His Legacy.* New York: Oxford University Press, 1997.

Voight, David Q. *American Baseball: From Gentlemen's Sport to the Commissioner System.* Norman: University of Oklahoma Press, 1966.

Weiss, Ann E. *Money Games: The Business of Sports.* Boston: Houghton Mifflin, 1993.

Westerbeek, Hans, and Aaron Smith. *Sport Business in the Global Marketplace.* New York: Palgrave Macmillan, 2003.

Will, George F. *Bunts: Curt Flood, Camden Yards, Pete Rose and Other Reflections on Baseball.* New York: Scribner, 1999.

The World Almanac and Book of Facts. New York: Newspaper Enterprise Association, 1950–2004.

Zimbalist, Andrew. *Baseball and Billions: A Probing Look Inside the Big Business of Our National Pastime.* New York: Basic, 1992.

_____. *May the Best Team Win: Baseball Economics and Public Policy.* Washington, D.C.: The Brookings Institution, 2003.

Dissertations

Corzine, Nathan M. "American Game, American Mirror: Baseball, Beer, the Media and American Culture, 1933–1945." M.A. diss., University of Missouri-Columbia, 2004.

Ferguson, Raymond. "Organized Baseball, A Business." M.S. diss., Drexel Institute of Technology, 1960

Jozsa, Frank P., Jr. "An Economic Analysis of Franchise Relocation and League Expansion in Professional Team Sports, 1950–1975." Ph.D. diss., Georgia State University, 1977.

Kammer, David John. "Take Me Out to the Ballgame: American Cultural Values as Reflected in the Architectural Evolution and Criticism of the Modern Baseball Stadium." Ph.D. diss., University of New Mexico, 1982.

Miller, Janine Leigh. "Modeling Major League Baseball Wins." M.S. diss., University of California, 2003.

Smith, Robert W. "The Business Side of Major League Baseball." B.A. diss., Princeton University, 1948.

Snyder, Todd Keith. "The Unaccountability of Organized Baseball: A Sport Turned Business." B.A. diss., Tulane University, 1980.

Internet Sources

"About Us." http://www.mlb.com cited 12 May 2005.

"All in All Things Are Pretty Good for Those Selling MLB." http://www.sportsbusinessnews.com cited 20 June 2005.

"All-Star Ratings Bottom Out Again." http://www.cnnsi.com cited 15 July 2005.

"Anaheim Angels Adding Los Angeles to Name." http://www.channels.netscape.com cited 5 January 2005.

"Anaheim Wants Judge to Block 'Los Angeles' Angels." http://www.usatoday.com cited 7 January 2005.

"Angels and General Motors Reach Agreement on Three-Year Partnership." http://www.angels.mlb.com cited 19 April 2005.

"A's Return to Spanish Radio." http://www.sportsbusinessnews.com cited 19 August 2003.

"Athletics to Launch Spanish Radio Network for 2005 Season." http://www.oakland.athletics.mlb.com cited 17 March 2005.

"Atlanta Braves, Six Flags Over Georgia and Six Flags White Water Team Up to Offer 'Triple Play Ticket Pack.'" http://www.atlanta.braves.mlb.com cited 7 June 2005.

"Average Baseball Salary." http://search.epnet.com cited 5 January 2005.

"Ballparks." http://www.ballparks.com cited 26 November 2004.

"Ballparks of Baseball." http://www.ballparksofbaseball.com cited 19 February 2005.

Barakat, Matthew. "Virginia Baseball Agency Remains Open." http://www.channels.netscape.com cited 20 January 2005.

Barker, Jeff. "Baseball in D.C., Ballpark Would Follow Camden Yards Trend." http://www.sportsbusinessnews.com cited 8 October 2004.

"The Baseball Archive." http://www.baseball1.com cited 15 February 2005.

_____. http://www.cnnsi.com cited 30 December 2004.

"Baseball, DHL Team for Marketing Partnership." http://www.amusementbusiness.org cited 14 April 2005.

"Baseball in D.C., Has Kasten Casts His Eyes on Washington's New MLB Franchise." http://www.sportsbusinessnews.com cited 30 September 2004.

"Baseball in D.C., Season Tickets Set to go on Sale." http://www.sportsbusinessnews.com cited 16 November 2004.

"Baseball Labor History." http://www.xroads.virginia.edu cited 18 June 2005.

"Baseball to Start Testing Latin American Players." http://www.cnnsi.com cited 4 September 2003.

"Baseball Tomorrow Fund Awards More Than $550,000 in Grants During Q4 2004." http://www.mlb.com cited 12 March 2005.

"Baseball Tomorrow Fund, MLB Clubs Host Equipment Collection Drives." http://www.mlb.com cited 28 April 2005.

"Baseball: USA Baseball & Upper Deck Launch Fundraiser." http://www.sportsfeatures.com cited 16 November 2004.

"Baseball's Greatest Teams." http://www.baseballlibrary.com cited 31 January 2005.

Bathe, Bill. "Dominican Republic Baseball." http://www.ezinearticles.com cited 24 March 2005.

Baum, Bob. "Owners Unanimously Approve Sale of Brewers." http://sportsillustrated.netscape.cnn.com cited 18 January 2005.

Baum, Greg. "Minorities Often Strike Out." http://www.theage.com cited 1 March 2005.

Bauman, Mike. "Bud Selig Reflects Back on His Days as Owner of the Milwaukee Brewers." http://www.sportsbusinessnews.com cited 30 January 2005.

_____. "Help Wanted: Solving Steroids." http://www.mlb.com cited 15 December 2004.

_____. "I'm Sorry' Has Never Been so Easy." http://www.mlb.com cited 6 July 2005.

_____. "Is Economic Parity Possible?" http://www.mlb.com cited 11 February 2005.

_____. "NL Managers Excelled in 2004." http://www.mlb.com cited 16 November 2004.

Baxter, Kevin. "Los Expos in Puerto Rico." http://www.sportsbusinessnews.com cited 6 March 2003.

Berardino, Mike. "Who's Next on MLB's Hit List?" http://www.sportsbusinessnews.com cited 5 October 2004.

Bernstein, Peter. "Cubs Have Fun with Ticket Names, Pricing." http://chicagosportsreview.com cited 18 January 2005.

"The Best and Worst Baseball Teams of All Time." http://members.aol.com cited 31 January 2005.

"Big Deal for MLB Video Games." http://www.sportsbusinessnews.com cited 1 February 2005.

"Big Money." http://www.cnnsi.com cited 6 April 2000.

Bihi, Martin. "Are Teams Brands?" http://www.brandchannel.com cited 14 May 2005.

"The Bill James Guide to Baseball Managers from 1870 to Today." http://www.amazon.com cited 8 February 2005.

"Blacks Hold Powerful Posts in Major League Baseball." http://www.findarticles.com cited 1 March 2005.

Bloom, Barry M. "Baseball Back in D.C., Bud Signals the End of the Journal." http://www.sportsbusinessnews.com cited 30 September 2004

_____. "Drug Talks to Continue Monday." http://www.mlb.com cited 20 December 2004.

_____. "MLB.com Reacts to Barry Bonds Steroid Report." http://www.sportsbusinessnews.com cited 19 October 2004.

_____. "MLB Selects D.C. for Expos." http://www.mlb.com cited 9 November 2004.

_____. "A New Pastime in Cambodia." http://www.mlb.com cited 26 July 2005.

_____. "Path Cleared for Nationals on TV." http://www.mlb.com cited 5 April 2005.

_____. "Selig, Fans Share Dialogue at Town Hall." http://www.mlb.com cited 15 July 2005.

_____. "World Cup Given Owners' Blessing." http:// www.sportsbusinessnews.com cited 1 October 2004.

Blum, Ronald. "Baseball Teams Expanding Their Wardrobes." http://www.cnnsi.netscape.com cited 19 April 2005.

_____. "Bombers to Stay in Bronx." http://www. cnnsi.netscape.com cited 18 June 2005.

_____. "MLB Sees Fewer Home Runs Amid Steroid Crackdown." http://www.usatoday.com cited 11 May 2005.

_____. "Players Approve World Cup Drug Testing." http://www.cnnsi.com cited 24 February 2005.

"Bobblehead Dolls Featuring 'The New Mets' Highlight 2005 Promotional Schedule." http://www. newyork.mets.mlb.com cited 14 March 2005.

Bodley, Hal. "Annual Salary Survey: MLB Teams Armed and Ready." http://www.usatoday.com cited 7 April 2005.

_____. "Baseball Facing Big-League Debt." http://www.usatoday.com cited 24 March 2005.

_____. "Is MLB Armageddon Dead Ahead?" http:// www.sportsbusinessnews.com cited 5 October 2004.

_____. "Revenue Sharing Paying Off." http:// www.usatoday.com cited 12 April 2005.

_____. "Selig Should Show Leadership Now." http://usatoday.printthis.clickability.com cited 7 December 2004.

_____. "Steroid Testing Negotiations Under Way." http://usatoday.printthis.clickability.com cited 15 December 2004.

_____. "Yanks' Payroll Soars as MLB Average Falls."http://usatoday.printthis.clickability. com cited 5 January 2005.

Boyd, Josh. "Top 10 General Manager Prospects." http://www.baseballamerica.com cited 7 February 2005.

"Brewers Announce 2005 Promotional Lineup." http://www.milwaukee.brewers.mlb.com cited 22 March 2005.

"Brewers to Join Telemundo for 12 Telecasts in 2005." http://www.milwaukee.brewers.mlb.com cited 29 March 2005.

Brown, Tim. "Selig Calls for Tougher Drug Testing." http://www.sportsbusinessnews.com cited 19 October 2004.

Browne, Ian. "Red Sox Nation — Owners Rejoice." http://www.sportsbusinessnews.com cited 26 October 2004.

"Bud Selig." http://www.baseball-almanac.com cited 17 February 2005.

"Bud Selig (MLB)." http://www.rateitall.com cited 19 February 2005.

Capozzi, Joe. "MLB in Mexico, Is Italy Next?" http://www.sportsbusinessnews.com cited 5 October 2004.

"Cardinals to Open Latin American Academy." http://www.stlouis.cardinals.mlb.com cited 3 May 2005.

Chass, Murray. "Baseball in D.C., They Have a Name But No Money." http://www.sportsbusinessnews. com cited 30 November 2004.

"City and Area Population." http://www.world-gazetteer.com cited 28 April 2005.

"The Clean Sports Act of 2005." http://www. sportsbusinessnews.com cited 25 May 2005.

"Commissioners." http://www.mlb.com cited 19 February 2005.

"Commissioners of Major League Baseball." http://www.baseball-almanac.com cited 17 February 2005.

_____. http://www.contractbud.com cited 19 February 2005.

"Commissioner's Statement." http://www.mlb. com cited 7 December 2004.

"The Commissionership: A Historical Perspective." http://www.mlb.com cited 15 February 2005.

"Community." http://www.mlb.com cited 14 March 2005.

Connor, Joe. "Teams Investing in Taiwan." http:// www.mlb.com cited 29 June 2004.

Conte, Andrew. "The Specter of Drugs Once Again Rears Its Ugly Head with MLB." http://www. sportsbusinessnews.com cited 20 December 2004.

Cowles, Christie. "MLB Takes Part in Citywide Clean Up." http://www.mlb.com cited 14 March 2005.

"Cox Communications Partners with Padres, MLB Advanced Media for First-of-Its-Kind Offer Exclusive to Cox High Speed Internet Customers." http://www.sandiego.padres.mlb.com cited 18 May 2005.

Crawford, E.J. "Baseball's Marked Decline in Puerto Rico." http://www.sportsbusinessnews.com cited 28 December 2004.

Cummings, Steve. "Baseball and Cuba." http:// www.sportsbusinessnews.com cited 19 August 2003.

"Cyber-Scalping? Tickets Going for King's Ransom on Mariners' Web Site." http://www.cnnsi.com cited 18 January 2005.

Dahlburg, John-Thor. "Looking Beyond Ball and Bat to See What Baseball Really Stands for in Puerto Rico." http://www.sportsbusinessnews.com cited 19 August 2003.

Davidoff, Ken. "BALCO — Sheffield Tells SI He Took Steroids." http://www.sportsbusinessnews.com cited 8 October 2004.

"Decline Is First Since 1995." http://sports.espn. go.com cited 5 January 2005.

Dellios, Hugh. "Monterrey Wants the Expos." http://www.sportsbusinessnews.com cited 10 February 2004.

DiCarlo, Lisa. "The Business of Baseball: Minor-League Baseball Grows Up." http://www.forbes. com cited 13 January 2005.

"Dodge Signs Three-Year Deal with Seattle." http://www.seattle.mariners.mlb.com cited 5 April 2005.

"Dodger Blue and a Code of Conduct." http:// www.sportsbusinessnews.com cited 11 May 2005.

"Dominican Baseball." http://www.cubanball. com cited 23 March 2005.

Donovan, John. "Globalization of the Grand Old Game Hits All-Time High." http://www.cnnsi. com cited 17 July 2003.

Draper, Rich. "Bonds' Lawyer Blasts Report." http://www.mlb.com cited 7 December 2004.

_____. "Union Board to Discuss Steroids." http:// www.mlb.com cited 7 December 2004.

Dunn, Andrew. "Former Expos Limited Partners Finally Strike Out." http://www.sportsbusiness-news.com cited 16 November 2004.

"Economic Block: Baseball Panel Urges Increase in Revenue Sharing." http://www.cnnsi.com cited 1 December 2002.

Edes, Gordon. "MLB in Europe in 2005?" http://www.sportsbusinessnews.com cited 22 September 2003.

_____. "A Slow Death to Baseball in the Dominican." http://www.sportsbusinessnews.com cited 5 October 2004.

Edwards, Bob. "Profile: Baseball Academy Hopes to Rekindle Puerto Rican Baseball Glory." http://www.search.epnet.com cited 3 May 2005.

Engel, Gary. "A History of Japanese Baseball." http://www.mlb.com cited 22 March 2005.

"Enough About Steroids." http://www.cnnsi.com cited 5 April 2005.

"An Expose on Baseball Training Facilities in Latin America." http://www.sportsbusinessnews.com cited 19 August 2003.

"Extreme Makeover: Blue Jays Increase Payroll, Rename SkyDome." http://www.cnnsi.com cited 3 February 2005.

"Fading Images: Bonds, Giambi, Sosa Tumble in Marketability Survey." http://www.cnnsi.com cited 5 April 2005.

Fainaru, Steve. "MLB May be Looking to Regulate Dominican Agents." http://www.sportsbusinessnews.com cited 18 September 2003.

_____. "MLB to Consider Drug Testing for Foreign Players." http://www.sportsbusinessnews.com cited 19 September 2003.

"Fairness in Antitrust in National Sports (FANS) Act in 2001." http://www.theorator.com cited 22 December 2004.

Falkoff, Robert. "Showater Is AL Manager of Year." http://www.mlb.com cited 16 November 2004.

"Famous First Foreign Players." http://www.baseball-almanac.com cited 16 April 2005.

Feinsand, Mark. "Giambi Quiet Amid Speculation." http://newyork.yankees.mlb.com cited 7 December 2004.

_____. "Yankees Take Pride in Giving Back." http://www.newyork.yankees.mlb.com cited 14 March 2005.

"Final 2000 Payroll Figures." http://www.cnnsi.com cited 21 March 2001.

"First World Baseball Classic Set for March." http://www.mlb.com cited 15 July 2005.

Fisher, Eric. "Baseball in D.C., D.C. Council Tosses Eggs at MLB." http://www.sportsbusinessnews.com cited 15 December 2004.

_____. "Baseball in D.C., However There Is Interest in a Privately Funded Stadium." http://www.sportsbusinessnews.com cited 3 November 2004.

_____. "Baseball in D.C., RFK Action Plan Ready." http://www.sportsbusinessnews.com cited 8 October 2004.

_____. "Baseball in D.C., Yet Another Delay in Stadium Vote." http://www.sportsbusinessnews.com cited 16 November 2004.

_____. "Even Losing Can't Keep the Virginia Base-ball Group Down." http://www.sportsbusiness-news.com cited 15 October 2004.

"Forbes Financial 2004 Valuation for MLB Franchise." http://www.sportsbusinessnews.com cited 5 October 2004.

"Foreign Legions." http://www.sportsillustrated.com cited 4 April 2003.

"Former Negro League Players Receive Benefits from Major League Baseball Via the Baseball Assistance Team (B.A.T.)." http://www.mlb.com cited 24 February 2005.

"Franchise Information: Expansion History." http://www.mlb.com cited 1 December 2004.

French, Howard W. "Bringing Baseball to China." http://www.mlb.com cited 26 May 2004.

"Frequently Asked Questions." http://www.bigleaguers.yahoo.com cited 25 December 2004.

Frisaro, Joe. "Marlins Meet with Las Vegas Mayor." http://www.mlb.com cited 10 December 2004.

_____. "McKeon Named NL's Best Manager." http://www.mlb.com cited 16 November 2004.

Futterman, Matthew. "Just What It Is Like to Market Evil Empire Memorabilia." http://www.sportsbusinessnews.com cited 29 December 2004.

"Gallup Poll Results." http://usatoday.printthis.clickability.com cited 15 December 2004.

Garrity, Brian. "Sports Owners Look to Maximize Equity Value in Synergies." http://www.proquest.umi.com cited 12 September 2004.

"General Manager (Baseball)." http://en.wikipedia.org cited 7 February 2005.

"Giants Announce New Spanish Radio Partnership with Cumbia 1170 AM." http://www.sanfrancisco.giants.mlb.com cited 5 April 2005.

Ginsburg, David. "Orioles Working on TV Agreement with Nats." http://www.cnnsi.com cited 14 March 2005.

Glew, Kevin. "Book Details Canada's Baseball Impact." http://www.mlb.com cited 26 July 2005.

Gold, Eric. "Minorities Playing a Larger Role in Front Office." http://www.sportsnetwork.com cited 28 February 2005.

Golen, Jimmy. "Goodman Tries to Lure Baseball to Vegas." http://channels.netscape.com cited 15 December 2004.

Grant, Evan. "When the Baseball Winter Meetings Begin — Scott Boras Will be the Master of the Domain." http://www.sportsbusinessnews.com cited 9 December 2004.

"The Greatest Baseball Teams Since 1901." http://pages.prodigy.net cited 31 January 2005.

Griffith, Bill. "Red Sox Adding Spanish Broadcasts This Year." http://www.sportsbusinessnews.com cited 27 March 2003.

Gurnick, Ken. "Dodger Blue and a Code of Conduct." http://www.sportsbusinessnews.com cited 11 May 2005.

Hall, Landon. "Building Boom Brings Millions of Fans Back to Minor Leagues." http://www.sports.yahoo.com cited 16 June 2001.

"Hall of Famers by Category: Manager." http://www.baseball-almanac.com cited 16 November 2004.

Hammond, Rich. "Scott Boras, as Baseball Free Agency Begins, He Is the King of His Domain."

http://www.sportsbusinessnews.com cited 16 November 2004.

Harding, Thomas. "MLB and MLBPA Still Working on World-Wide Draft Plan." http://www.sportsbusinessnews.com cited 25 November 2002.

_____. "Tsao First of Many, Rockies Hope." http://www.mlb.com cited 25 July 2003.

Harrow, Rick. "Business of Baseball Pretty Good Right Now." http://www.sportsbusinessnews.com cited 17 April 2005.

_____. "Sports and the Retail Industry." http://www.sportsbusinessnews.com cited 30 November 2004.

Haudricourt, Tom. "Marking the 'End' of the Selig Ownership Era in Milwaukee." http://www.sportsbusinessnews.com cited 15 October 2004.

Hermoso, Rafael. "With Los Expos a Success, MLB Looking at Further Expanded Horizons." http://www.sportsbusinessnews.com cited 22 August 2003.

"Highest Baseball Salaries." http://www.cnnsi.com cited 25 January 2005.

"History of Baseball in Cuba." http://www.cubanball.com cited 23 March 2005.

"History of the Game." http://www.mlb.com cited 15 February 2005.

"How Minor League Baseball Teams Work." http://www.howstuffworks.com cited 25 June 2005.

Howard, Johnette. "Well Worth Nothing — Small Market MLB Owners Are Angry." http://www.sportsbusinessnews.com cited 4 February 2005.

Hyun-cheol, Kim. "Series to Test Asian Baseball's Elite." http://www.times.hankooki.com cited 11 April 2005.

"Integrating Baseball-Chapter 2."http://www.library2.cqpress.com cited 28 February 2005.

"Interactive Baseball Network Debuts." http://www.mlb.com cited 15 October 2004.

"The International Baseball Federation." http://www.baseball.ch cited 4 April 2005.

"Is Major League Baseball Profitable?" http://www.bauer.uh.edu cited 9 November 2004.

Isidore, Chris. "Angels Catching Hell." http://www.cnnsi.com cited 18 January 2005.

"It's Unanimous: Owners Approve A's Sale to Los Angeles Developer." http://www.cnnsi.com cited 31 March 2005.

Iwata, Edward. "Marketers Gun-Shy Amid Controversies." http://usatoday.printthis.clickability.com cited 15 December 2004.

Jackson, Tony. "Dodgers Trying to Mix Tradition into Their 2005 Marketing." http://www.sportsbusinessnews.com cited 14 February 2005.

"Japan's Baseball Owners Reject World Cup Plan." http://www.cnnsi.com cited 15 July 2004.

Jones, Kasey. "Comcast Sues Orioles over TV Rights." http://www.cnnsi.com cited 26 April 2005.

Kelly, Kevin. "Worldwide Draft Caps Wealthy Teams' Monopoly." http://www.sportsbusinessnews.com cited 19 August 2003.

Kubatko, Roch. "The Art of Selling Minor League Baseball — Winning Doesn't Matter." http://www.sportsbusinessnews.com cited 5 October 2004.

Kyle, Bobette. "Profitable Target Marketing: 6 Lessons from Major League Baseball." http://www.developers.evrsoft.com cited 14 May 2005.

"L.A. Developer Could Target Athletics." http://usatoday.printthis.clickability.com cited 7 January 2005.

Ladson, Bill. "Selig: Tougher Drug Policy Needed." http://www.mlb.com cited 7 December 2004.

Lahman, Sean. "A Brief History of Baseball: Part II: Professional Baseball's First Hundred Years." http://www.baseball1.com cited 30 December 2004.

_____. "A Brief History of Baseball: Part III: Labor Battles in the Modern Era." http://www.baseball1.com cited 30 December 2004.

_____. "Minimum & Average Player Salaries 1967–1997." http://www.baseball1.com cited 30 December 2004.

Lambrecht, Gary. "Age Benefits and Athletes." http://www.sportsbusinessnews.com cited 16 November 2004.

"Latin American Academies Becoming the Norm." http://www.sportsbusinessnews.com cited 14 January 2003.

"Lawmaker: Congress Won't Back Off." http://www.cnnsi.com cited 8 July 2005.

Leach, Matthew. "LaRussa Receives NL Honor." http://www.mlb.com cited 16 November 2004.

"Leagues." http://www.minorleaguebaseball.com cited 24 December 2004.

Lev, Michael A. "Baseball in the People's Republic." http://www.sportsbusinessnews.com cited 21 August 2003.

Lewis, Dan. "Look for the Union Label." http://www.nationalreview.com cited 18 June 2005.

"List of Metropolitan Areas by Population." http://www.en.wikipedia.org cited 28 April 2005.

"Little League Organization." http://www.littleleague.org cited 4 April 2005.

Lopresti, Mike. "Baseball in Dire Need of a Rescue Plan." http://usatoday.printthis.clickability.com cited 7 December 2004.

_____. "Has MLB Recovered from Its 1994 Strike?" http://www.sportsbusinessnews.com cited 5 October 2004.

Loverro, Thom. "Baseball in D.C., Plethora of Prospective Owners." http://www.sportsbusinessnews.com cited 1 October 2004.

"Major League Baseball." http://www.mlb.com cited 26 November 2004.

_____. http://www.teammarketing.com cited 18 January 2005.

"Major League Baseball Celebrates Black History Month." http://www.mlb.com cited 26 February 2005.

"Major League Baseball, Cerveza Presidente Bring Baseball Festival to the Dominican Republic." http://www.mlb.com cited 7 June 2005.

"Major League Baseball Debuts Fan-Based 2005 'I Live for This' Commercials." http://www.mlb.com cited 15 March 2005.

"Major League Baseball in the UK." http://www.baseballsoftballuk.com cited 29 March 2005.

"Major League Baseball International Envoy Program Visits 27 Countries in 2004." http://www.mlb.com cited 24 February 2005.

"Major League Baseball International, United Media Partner in Japan." http://www.mlb.com cited 11 May 2005.

"The Major League Baseball Players Association." http://www.bigleaguers.yahoo.com cited 5 January 2005.

"Major League Baseball Partners with XM Satellite Radio for 11-Year, $650 Million Broadcast and Marketing Agreement." http://www.sportsbusinessnews.com cited 26 October 2004.

"Major League Baseball Productions, Hart Sharp Video Present: Yankeeography Volume Four." http://www.mlb.com cited 22 July 2005.

"Major League Baseball Productions Nominated for Eight NY Emmy Awards." http://www.mlb.com cited 3 March 2005.

"Major League Baseball Productions Reaches Distribution Agreements with Shout! Factory, A&E Home Video." http://www.mlb.com cited 26 April 2005.

"Major League Baseball Productions, Spike TV Step Up to the Plate for 'Maximum MLB.'" http://www.mlb.com cited 14 May 2005.

"Major League Baseball Properties Introduces 2005 Club Retail Promotions." http://www.mlb.com cited 7 June 2005.

"Major League Baseball Reaches National Broadcast Agreement in Taiwan." http://www.mlb.com cited 11 May 2005.

"Major League Baseball Statement." http://www.mlb.com cited 3 May 2005.

"Major League Baseball, The Home Depot Build Integrated Marketing Partnership." http://www.mlb.com cited 5 April 2005.

"Manager (Baseball)." http://en.wikipedia.org cited 7 February 2005.

"Manager of the Year." http://www.baseball-almanac.com cited 16 November 2004.

"Managerial Wins All-Time Leaders." http://www.baseball-almanac.com cited 8 February 2005.

"Managers." http://www.baseball-almanac.com cited 7 February 2005.

Marcano, Arturo J. "Worldwide Draft." http://www.baseballguru.com cited 17 March 2005.

Marcano, Arturo J., and David P. Fidler. "Preliminary Analysis of MLB Academy Standards and Compliance Inspection Procedure." http://www.sportinsociety.org cited 2 October 2003.

"Mariners Announce Partnerships with Six Japanese Companies." http://www.seattle.mariners.mlb.com cited 21 April 2005.

"Marlins and WDLP-22 to Offer a Full Hour of Marlins Programming Every Sunday." http://www.florida.marlins.mlb.com cited 28 April 2005

Marx, Gary. "An Expose on Baseball Training Facilities in Latin America." http://www.sportsbusinessnews.com cited 19 August 2003.

Mayo, Jonathan. "Caribbean Series Gets Under Way." http://www.mlb.com cited 2 February 2005.

_____. "Winter Leagues Important to Many." http://www.mlb.com cited 5 January 2005.

McAdam, Sean. "MLB Free Agency — It Really Has Been Back to the Future." http://www.sportsbusinessnews.com cited 30 December 2004.

"McCain Optimistic About Testing." http://www.mlb.com cited 15 December 2004.

"McCain: Tighten Drug-Testing Policy." http://www.mlb.com cited 7 December 2004.

McCalvy, Adam. "Attanasio Awaits Owners' Vote." http://www.mlb.com cited 13 January 2005.

_____. "Select Brewers Games to be Broadcast in Spanish." http://www.sportsbusinessnews.com cited 13 February 2003.

McCarron, Anthony. "Scott Boras Remains the King of Baseball Agents." http://www.sportsbusinessnews.com cited 9 November 2004.

Miller, Doug. "Scioscia Named Top Skipper." http://www.mlb.com cited 16 November 2004.

Miller, S.A., and Eric Fisher. "Baseball Back in D.C., Interesting Parties Against Proposed MLB Stadium." http://www.sportsbusinessnews.com cited 8 October 2004.

"Millions of Dollars at Stake for Montreal." http://www.montrealexpos.com cited 6 October 1998.

"Minimum MLB Salary Rises to $316,000." http://www.msnbc.msn.com cited 5 January 2005.

"Minor League Baseball History." http://www.minorleaguebaseball.com cited 25 June 2005.

"Minor League Baseball: Timeline." http://www.minorleaguebaseball.com cited 25 June 2005.

"Minor League Baseball: 2004." http://www.teammarketing.com cited 14 May 2005.

"Miscommunication? Language Problems Complicate Drug Policy for Latins." http://www.cnnsi.com cited 11 May 2005.

"MLB Advanced Media and National Association of Professional Baseball Leagues Announce Major Partnership Agreement." http://www.mlb.com cited 18 January 2005.

"MLB Advanced Media Signs First Wireless Distribution Agreement in China and Tai-wan." http://www.mlb.com cited 26 April 2005.

"MLB Affiliation." http://www.minorleaguebaseball.com cited 25 June 2005.

"MLB and the Wireless Universe." http://www.sportsbusinessnews.com cited 7 April 2005.

"MLB Announces New Licensing Agreements." http://www.sportsbusinessnews.com cited 5 August 2003.

"MLB Awards." http://www.baseball-reference.com cited 16 November 2004.

"MLB, Caribbean Confederation Extend Winter League Agreement." http://www.mlb.com cited 26 April 2005.

"MLB, China Baseball League Bring MLB Road Show to Five Cities in China." http://www.mlb.com cited 3 March 2005.

"MLB Drug World Cup Testing Agreement in Place." http://www.sportsbusinessnews.com cited 27 April 2004.

"MLB Franchise Chronology." http://www.mlb.com cited 9 November 2004.

"MLB Happy with ESPN, ESPN2 Ratings Numbers." http://www.sportsbusinessnews.com cited 8 October 2004.

"MLB in the Community." http://www.mlb.com cited 21 March 2005.

"MLB International Directory." http://www.mlb.com cited 15 April 2005.

"MLB International to Conduct Elite Baseball Camp in Europe." http://www.mlb.com cited 28 April 2005.

"MLB Launches 2005 International All-Star Balloting Program." http://www.mlb.com cited 26 May 2005.

"MLB, LBi Software Engineering Launch 'eBIS.'" http://www.mlb.com cited 5 April 2005.

"MLB, MLBPA Contribute $1 Million to Tsunami Relief." http://www.mlb.com cited 14 March 2005.

"MLB, MLBPA Partnership with Cartoon Network Begins Second Season." http://www.mlb.com cited 11 May 2005.

"MLB Owners." http://www.forbes.com cited 9 January 2005.

"MLB Productions, Hart Sharp Video Present Yankeeography Volume Three." http://www.mlb.com cited 14 May 2005.

"MLB Productions Launches 27th Season of 'This Week in Baseball.'" http://www.mlb.com cited 14 May 2005.

"MLB Properties, Sportbox Reach Five-Year Licensing Agreement." http://www.mlb.com cited 18 May 2005.

"MLB Salary Database." http://www.sportsfansofamerica.com cited 30 December 2004.

"MLB Steroid Rules Trip Up Latin Americans." http://www.cnnsi.netscape.com cited 6 May 2005.

"MLB.com Names Preliminary List of 2005 Fantasy Game Licensees." http://www.mlb.com cited 15 March 2005.

"MLBPA Makes Bold Move to Grow Video Game Business." http://www.sportsbusinessnews.com cited 25 January 2005.

"Mo' Money." http://www.cnnsi.com cited 7 May 2000.

Morgan, Jon. "Baseball in D.C., Camden Yards May Cost More." http://www.sportsbusinessnews.com cited 29 September 2004.

"MSG to Provide Spanish Simulcasts." http://www.newyork.mets.mlb.com cited 29 March 2005.

Nadel, John. "Dodgers Launch WIN — a Program for Women." http://www.cnnsi.netscape.com cited 11 May 2005.

"Negro Leaguers to Receive $1 Million." http://www.sportsbusinessnews.com cited 5 October 2004.

"New Major League Baseball Program to Help Former Negro League Players." http://www.mlb.com cited 24 February 2005.

Newman, Mark. "Baseball's Back in D.C., Next Steps(s)." http://www.sportsbusinessnews.com cited 30 September 2004.

_____. "Baseball's International Movement." http://www.mlb.com cited 8 February 2005.

_____. "MLB Thankful for Chances to Give." http://www.mlb.com cited 12 March 2005.

_____. "MLB.com, Players Forge Partnership." http://www.mlb.com cited 20 January 2005.

_____. "New MLB TV Ads Spotlight Fans' Passion." http://www.sportsbusinessnews.com cited 15 March 2005.

_____. "Reflecting on Black History Month." http://www.mlb.com cited 24 February 2005.

_____. "Watch Carlos Run Free — for Free." http://www.mlb.com cited 3 March 2005.

Neyer, Rob. "Landis Had Major Impact as First Commish." http://www.espn.com cited 15 January 2005.

"Ninth Season of Interleague Play Begins Friday." http://www.sportsbusinessnews.com cited 20 June 2005.

"N. Va. Group Makes New Bid for Nats." http://www.cnnsi.com cited 1 February 2005.

"November Trial for Angels Name Suit." http://www.cnnsi.com cited 14 March 2005.

O'Connor, Ian. "Baseball Fuels Disparity." http://www.usatoday.com cited 5 January 2005.

_____. "Yanks Urged to Dump Giambi Now." http://usatoday.printthis.clickability.com cited 7 December 2004.

"Official Info: FAQ." http://www.minorleaguebaseball.com cited 25 June 2005.

"Official Info: Licensing." http://www.minorleaguebaseball.com cited 25 June 2005.

"Official Info: Sponsorship." http://www.minorleaguebaseball.com cited 25 June 2005.

Olney, Buster. "MLBPA 'Leadership' and the Steroid Issue." http://www.sportsbusinessnews.com cited 5 October 2004.

"Orioles Join CoverGirl for Unique Partnership." http://www.baltimore.orioles.mlb.com cited 26 April 2005.

Ortiz, Jose De Jesus. "Mexicans Far from Believers in MLB Dream." http://www.sportsbusinessnews.com cited 16 March 2004.

"The Owners: Who Are These Guys?" http://www.resonator.com cited 20 November 2001.

Ozanian, Michael, and Kurt Badenhausen. "The Boys of Summer." http://www.forbes.com cited 9 November 2004.

Ozanian, Michael K. "All-Star Owners." http://www.forbes.com cited 13 January 2005.

"Padres and Telemundo Reach Broadcast Agreement." http://www.sandiego.padres.mlb.com cited 29 March 2005.

Palchikoff, Kim. "Youth Baseball in Russia." http://www.sportsbusinessnews.com cited 19 August 2003.

Pappas, Doug. "Analysis— Summary of the [2002] Collective Bargaining Agreement." http://www.businessofbaseball.com cited 5 January 2005.

_____. "A Contentious History: Baseball's Labor Fights." http://www.espn.go.com cited 18 June 2005.

_____. "The Numbers: Local Media Revenues." http://www.baseballprospectus.com cited 9 November 2004.

"Payroll Comparison." http://si.printthis.clickability.com cited 2 January 2005.

"Phillies Revive Hispanic Radio Broadcasts." http://www.philadelphia.phillies.mlb.com cited 17 March 2005.

"The Players Choice Group Licensing Program." http://www.mlbplayers.mlb.com cited 12 May 2005.

Porretto, John. "Baseball Commissioner Sees More Parity." http://www.cnnsi.netscape.com cited 12 April 2005.

"Postseasons." http://www.baseball-reference.com cited 1 January 2005.

"Price of Glory: Yankees Will Pay More Than $30 Million in Luxury Taxes." http://www.cnnsi.com cited 21 April 2005.

"Professional Football Leads Baseball by 2-to-1 as Nation's Favorite Sport." http://www.sportsbusinessnews.com cited 15 October 2004.

"Put Me In, Coach: River City Rascals Auctioning One-Day Pro Contract." http://www.cnnsi.com cited 11 May 2005.

"A Q&A with MLB's Head of Security." http://www.mlb.com cited 9 May 2005.

Rausch, Gary. "Evolution of the Draft." http://www.mlb.com cited 3 May 2005.

"Rays Sign 4-Year Deal to Broadcast Games in Spanish." http://www.tampabay.devilrays.mlb.com cited 17 March 2005.

"Regular Season MLB Games Outside 50 United States and Canada." http://www.mlb.com cited 1 February 2005.

Reid, Jason. "Dodgers Owner Wants More Success for Franchise." http://www.sportsbusinessnews.com cited 15 October 2004.

"Report: Giambi Used Steroids." http://www.mlb.com cited 7 December 2004.

Risling, Greg. "Angels Name Change May Bring More Revenue." http://www.cnnsi.netscape.com cited 5 January 2005.

Romney, Lee. "The Candlestick Name Game." http://www.sportsbusinessnews.com cited 10 October 2004.

Rosenthal, Ken. "Can Money Really Buy Happiness in Baseball?" http://www.sportsbusinessnews.com cited 15 October 2004.

"SABR Asian Baseball Committee Chinese Baseball Timeline." http://www.robsjapanesecards.com cited 22 March 2005.

"SABR Asian Baseball Committee Japanese Baseball History." http://www.robsjapanesecards.com cited 22 March 2005.

"SABR Asian Baseball Committee Korean Baseball History." http://www.robsjapanesecards.com cited 22 March 2005.

"SABR Asian Baseball Committee Korean Baseball Timeline." http://www.robsjapanesecards.com cited 22 March 2005.

"SABR Asian Baseball Committee Taiwanese Baseball Timeline." http://www.robsjapanesecards.com cited 22 March 2005.

"San Jose Seeking Major League Team." http://www.cnnsi.com cited 22 March 2005.

Sanchez, Jesse. "Academy Schools Future Stars." http://www.mlb.com cited 22 March 2005.

_____. "Always Giving Season for Rangers." http://www.texas.rangers.mlb.com cited 14 March 2005.

_____. "History of Baseball in Mexico." http://www.mlb.com cited 22 March 2005.

_____. "Mexico Captures Series Title." http://www.mlb.com cited 8 February 2005.

Sandomir, Richard. "Baseball in D.C., by the Ratings." http://www.sportsbusinessnews.com cited 5 October 2004.

_____. "Sports and Sponsorship — is Baseball Being Held to a Higher Standard." http://www.sportsbusinessnews.com cited 5 October 2004.

Scarr, Mike. "Coleman Honored with Frick Award." http://www.mlb.com cited 24 February 2005.

_____. "Fehr Discusses New Drug Policy." http://www.mlb.com cited 1 March 2005.

Schlegal, John. "Schlegal: All in the Family." http://losangeles.dodgers.mlb.com cited 13 January 2005.

_____. "Selig Honored at RBI Dinner." http://www.mlb.com cited 10 February 2005.

Seidel, Jeff. "Baseball in D.C., Operation Shuts Down (at Least for Now)." http://www.sportsbusinessnews.com cited 16 December 2004.

_____. "Baseball in D.C., Stadium Vote Set." http://www.sportsbusinessnews.com cited 30 November 2004.

_____. "DC Council Passes Amended Bill." http://www.mlb.com cited 15 December 2004.

_____. "There May be Peace and a Baseball Stadium in D.C. Yet." http://www.sportsbusinessnews.com cited 16 November 2004.

Shea, John, Henry Schulman, and Susan Slusser. "Integrity for Baseball in Question." http://www.sportsbusinessnews.com cited 19 October 2004.

"Shea Stadium Goes Digital." http://www.newyork.mets.mlb.com cited 22 March 2005.

Shenin, Dave. "A World-Wide Baseball Draft Could be a Logistical Nightmare." http://www.sportsbusinessnews.com cited 19 August 2003.

Sheridan, Kerry. "Baseball Program a Haven in Harlem." http://www.mlb.com cited 11 April 2005.

Shipley, Amy. "Baseball Looking to Internationalize." http://www.sportsbusinessnews.com cited 19 August 2003.

Singen, Tom. "MLB.com Looks at the Concept of a World-Wide Baseball Draft." http://www.sportsbusinessnews.com cited 3 December 2002.

Singer, Tom. "Baseball Assistance Team." http://www.mlb.com cited 3 March 2005.

_____. "Boys & Girls Clubs Honors MLB." http://www.mlb.com cited 9 June 2005.

_____. "MLB.com Looks at the Concept of a World-Wide Baseball Draft." http://www.sportsbusinessnews.com cited 3 December 2002.

_____. "12 Black Aces Span Generations." http://www.mlb.com cited 3 March 2005.

Smith, Paul C. "A Q&A with MLB's Head of Security." http://www.mlb.com cited 9 May 2005.

"Souhan, Jim. "Latin American Academies Becoming the Norm." http://www.sportsbusinessnews.com cited 14 January 2003.

"Sponsorship of Professional Baseball Leagues and Teams to Total $388 Million in 2004." http://www.sponsorship.com cited 20 May 2005.

"Sports Commissioners." http://www.kenn.com cited 19 February 2005.

"Sports History." http://www.hickoksports.com cited 7 February 2005.

"Sports Loyalty Systems (SLS) Launches an Interesting Sports Branding Program." http://www.sportsbusinessnews.com cited 29 July 2005.

Starr, Mark. "Play Hardball." http://doris.pfeiffer.edu cited 25 December 2004.

"Statement of Donald M. Fehr, Executive Director, Major League Baseball Players Association, Before the Committee on Energy and Commerce, United States House of Representatives." http://www.mlb.com cited 18 May 2005.

Steele, David. "Baseball in D.C., the Chaos Theory." http://www.sportsbusinessnews.com cited 9 December 2004.

Stone, Larry. "Selig Discusses Cancellation of Overseas Opener." http://www.sportsbusinessnews.com cited 27 March 2003.

Street, Jim. "Ichiro Honored at Safeco." http://www.mlb.com cited 26 April 2005.

"Team Sites." http://www.mlb.com cited 10 December 2004.

"Teams." http://www.mlb.com cited 9 January 2005.

"Termidor Joins Rays' Growing List of Sponsor Partners." http://www.tampabay.devilrays.mlb.com cited 26 April 2005.

"Texas Rangers Baseball Foundation Upcoming Community Events." http://www.texas.rangers.mlb.com cited 22 March 2005.

"Top 3 Minor League Baseball Levels." http://www.baseball.about.com cited 25 June 2005.

"Toys 'R' Us and Major League Baseball Team Up to Celebrate 2005 Opening Day." http://www.mlb.com cited 7 April 2005.

"Twins Medallion Collectables Begin Sunday." http://www.minnesota.twins.mlb.com cited 28 April 2005.

"Twins Take Innovative Step in Sports Marketing." http://www.minnesota.twins.mlb.com cited 14 May 2005.

"2000 Inside the Ownership of Professional Sports Teams." http://www.teammarketing.com cited 20 November 2001.

"2001 Team-by-Team Revenues and Expenses Forecast." http://www.usatoday.com cited 9 November 2004.

"2005 Salary Arbitration Figures." http://www.mlb.com cited 20 January 2005.

"27.3 Percent of Major League Baseball Players Born Outside the United States," http://www.mlb.com cited 29 March 2005.

"29.2 Percent of Major League Baseball Players Born Outside of the U.S." http://www.mlb.com cited 12 April 2005.

Urban, Mychael. "A's Co-Owners Considering Sale." http://www.mlb.com cited 13 January 2005.

Verducci, Tom. "Blackout: The African-American Baseball Player Is Vanishing. Does He Have a Future?" http://www.cnnsi.com cited 17 July 2003.

Vertuno, Jim. "Nolan Ryan's Minor League Team Debuts $25 Million Stadium." http://www.sports.yahoo.com cited 19 April 2000.

Wallace, Bruce. "Growth of Japanese Baseball Players in the Major Leagues Hurting Japan's Leagues." http://www.sportsbusinessnews.com cited 5 October 2004.

"WBC Groups Revealed." http://www.cnnsi.com cited 15 July 2005.

"What Is Little League Baseball?" http://www.little-league.org cited 4 April 2005.

"White Sox Launch Second Wave of 2005 Television Advertising." http://www.chicago.whitesox.mlb.com cited 26 May 2005.

"World Series Championships." http://www.baseball-almanac.com cited 7 February 2005.

"Venezuelan Baseball League." http://www.geocities.com cited 2 October 2003.

Vinocur, John. "Baseball in Europe." http://www.sportsbusinessnews.com cited 19 August 2003.

Voorhis, Scott Van. "Dodgers Make Playoffs, Owner Now a Popular Man." http://www.sportsbusinessnews.com cited 8 October 2004.

Waldman, Ed. "Baseball in D.C., Mr. Angelos Goes to Visit Mr. Selig." http://www.sportsbusinessnews.com cited 8 October 2004.

Walker, Don. "Sale of Brewers— Meet the Owners." http://www.sportsbusinessnews.com cited 15 October 2004.

_____. "Sale of the Brew Crew — New Owner Looking for Local Investors." http://www.sportsbusinessnews.com cited 15 October 2004.

Walker, Don, and Drew Olson. "Roids in MLB — Bud 'Shout-Out' to MLBPA." http://www.sportsbusinessnews.com cited 9 December 2004.

Wallace, Bruce. "Growth of Japanese Baseball Players in Major Leagues Hurting Japan's Leagues." http://www.sportsbusinessnews.com cited 29 June 2004.

Weiner, Jay. "Twins Making Their Ticketing Plans More Customer Friendly." http://www.sportsbusinessnews.com cited 30 November 2004.

Wentworth, Bridget. "$7,500 for Five Minutes with Barry Bonds— Think They Cared About Roids." http://www.sportsbusinessnews.com cited 13 December 2004.

White, Joseph. "Washington Nationals Get First Cable Deal." http://www.cnnsi.com cited 18 May 2005.

"Who Wants to be a Millionaire?" http://www.cnnsi.com cited 5 April 2001.

Whoriskey, Peter. "Baseball in D.C., Stadium Deal Won Over Bud." http://www.sportsbusinessnews.com cited 5 October 2004.

Williams, Pete. "Out with the Old ... in with the New." http://www.webmail.pfeiffer.edu cited 16 November 2004.

Wilson, Duff. "Sports Team Owners Just Got Richer." http://www.sportsbusinessnews.com cited 15 October 2004.

Wilson, Peter, and Nick Benequista. "Not a Great Season for the Venezuela's Professional Baseball League." http://www.sportsbusinessnews.com cited 20 January 2003.

Witt, Barry. "San Jose Still Interested in A's." http://www.sportsbusinessnews.com cited 5 October 2004.

Wood, Daniel B. "The Baseball Stat You Don't Want to See." http://www.csmonitor.com cited 18 January 2005.

Wood, Sean. "Rangers Target Hispanic Fans ... Again." http://www.sportsbusinessnews.com cited 27 March 2003.

"The World Cup of Baseball." http://www.sportsbusinessnews.com cited 25 November 2002.

"Yankees to Announce New Ballpark." http://www.cnnsi.com cited 18 June 2005.

"Yankees to Strengthen Marketing Department."

http://www.newyork.yankees.mlb.com cited 14 May 2005.

"Yankees 2005 Projected Payroll." http://www.cnnsi.com cited 5 January 2005.

"You Can Build Your Own 'Slider.'" http://www.cleveland.indians.mlb.com cited 24 March 2005.

"You're Being Robbed!" http://www.cnnsi.com cited 11 May 2005.

Zellen, Peter. "MLB Announces Three-Year Deal with GM." http://www.mlb.com cited 24 March 2005.

Zuniga, Ricardo. "Minaya Brings Latin Touch to 'Los Mets.'" http://www.channels.netscape.com cited 20 January 2005.

Media Guides

Official Major League Baseball Fact Book 2004 Edition. St. Louis, MO: The SportingNews, 2004.

Official Major League Baseball Fact Book 2005 Edition. St. Louis, MO: The Sporting News, 2005.

2000 Charlotte Knights Souvenir Program. Fort Mill, S.C.: Charlotte Knights Media Relations Office, 2000.

2005 Charlotte Knights Media Guide. Fort Mill, S.C.: Charlotte Knights Media Relations Office, 2005.

Washington, Kelli D., and Richard K. Miller. *The 2004 Entertainment, Media & Advertising Market Research Handbook.* Sixth Edition. Norcross, GA: Richard K. Miller & Associates, Inc., 2004.

Reports

Shapiro, Sebastian. *The Most Valuable Brands in Sports: The 2002 Report.* New York, N.Y.: FutureBrand, 2002.

Index